STUDIES IN CHRISTIAN HI

Leadership in the Salvation Army

A Case Study in Clericalisation

STUDIES IN CHRISTIAN HISTORY AND THOUGHT

A full listing of all titles in this series appears at the close of this book.

STUDIES IN CHRISTIAN HISTORY AND THOUGHT

Leadership in the Salvation Army

A Case Study in Clericalisation

Harold Hill

Foreword by Ian Breward

Paternoster: thinking faith

MILTON KEYNES · COLORADO SPRINGS · HYDERABAD

First published 2007 by Paternoster
Paternoster is an imprint of Authentic Media
9 Holdom Avenue, Bletchley, Milton Keynes, Bucks, MK1 1QR
1820 Jet Stream Drive, Colorado Springs, CO 80921, USA
OM Authentic Media, Medchal Road, Jeedimetla Village,
Secunderabad 500 055, A.P., India
www.authenticmedia.co.uk
Authentic Media is a division of IBS-STL UK, a company limited by guarantee
(registered charity no. 270162)

12 11 10 09 08 07 06   7 6 5 4 3 2 1

British Library Cataloguing in Publication Data
A catalogue record for this book is available from the British Library.

ISBN 978-1-84227-429-3

Typeset by the Author

Printed and bound in Great Britain
by Nottingham Alphagraphics

Studies in Christian History and Thought

Series Preface

This series complements the specialist series of *Studies in Evangelical History and Thought* and *Studies in Baptist History and Thought* for which Paternoster is becoming increasingly well known by offering works that cover the wider field of Christian history and thought. It encompasses accounts of Christian witness at various periods, studies of individual Christians and movements, and works which concern the relations of church and society through history, and the history of Christian thought.

The series includes monographs, revised dissertations and theses, and collections of papers by individuals and groups. As well as 'free standing' volumes, works on particular running themes are being commissioned; authors will be engaged for these from around the world and from a variety of Christian traditions.

A high academic standard combined with lively writing will commend the volumes in this series both to scholars and to a wider readership.

Series Editors

In Memory of A. J. Gilliard
1899 - 1973

Contents

FOREWORD

The nature of Salvation Army leadership is puzzling to outsiders. It has military parallels, placed in the context of war declared against evil, happily uniformed and focussed on personal holiness. At first sight this does not look like a recipe for success in religious and pastoral matters, especially in our contemporary context.

The historic impact of the Salvation Army internationally underlines that their leadership has been greatly blessed, even if it does not have the same kind of education used in other Christian bodies to form their leaders. Their officers have a well-earthed faith and ability to make themselves heard beyond their membership. The Salvation Army does not claim to be a church in the classical sense of this term. Its leaders are not ordained and serve short terms before moving elsewhere. They lack security and status. The founders hoped this would prevent their proven lay leaders from becoming clericalised and departing from the scriptures' imperatives.

They have partly succeeded, but the value of this study by Major Hill is that it shows there have been constant pressures to professionalize the officership. In turn, that raises questions which would be dealt with theologically in bodies with ordained ministry, but have been dealt with pragmatically in the Salvation Army, because few of the officers have a theological education comparable with that of clergy in major churches. That has been advantageous; therefore the Army has not wasted time on theological disputes which do little to enhance the appeal of the Gospel, focussing instead on human needs.

Major Hill's historical survey explores these matters with insight and depth, with primary reference to the English-speaking world. Thoroughly documented, it should be pondered by those who think that future ministry ought to be predominantly lay. Heading further in that direction has costs which need to be carefully weighed – as this study makes clear. Again and again the Army has moved towards clericalization, especially during the heyday of the ecumenical movement, when a great deal of attention was paid to the origins and nature of ministry, without noticeably improving its quality or input in the major churches and their communities.

The Salvation Army has some of the features of a lay religious community within the Roman Catholic Church, focussing on a particular charism of leadership which has worn well and is widely respected in and beyond the Christian community. Major Hill's study deserves to be widely read within and outside the Army itself.

Ian Breward,
Senior Fellow, History Department
University of Melbourne.

PREFACE

For a century, it sufficed that Salvation Army officers were "commissioned"; since 1978 they have also been "ordained". Within the Army this addition sparked debate between those who identified officership in the Salvation Army with the historic clerical role in the church, involving some kind of "status", and those who maintained that roles in the Salvation Army differed only in their "function", without any distinction in status between "clergy" and "lay". This polarisation has been evident through much of the lifetime of the movement. Evangelists of the Christian Mission and then officers of the Salvation Army were "lay", but in time they came to regard themselves, and the organisation to regard them, as equivalent to clergy in every respect. Function eventually gave rise to status.

The same tension can be traced back to early Church history. As the Church institutionalised, a process of "clericalisation" took place as it began to ascribe some ontological distinction to its leadership. At intervals, revival movements reacted against these developments, holding that a separate order of ministry was not of the essence of the Christian faith, but was what Emil Brunner characterised as a "misunderstanding of the Church".[1] Nevertheless such movements have usually succumbed to the same fate. Even when a distinction between Christians was denied in theory, almost invariably they came to behave as if there were one.

The Salvation Army recapitulates in microcosm the history of the Church as a whole, illustrating the way in which pragmatic measures become entrenched dogma, while charismatic revivals and alternative communities are reabsorbed into structures of power and control. The Army continues to exhibit a tension between its theology, which supports equality of status, and its military structure, which works against equality. The major part of this book records the interplay of these views throughout its history.

I hope that by putting the Army's history in such a context, this work may assist other Salvationists in locating the Army at what General John Larsson has called "a watershed in its self-understanding... a period of transition towards a fuller understanding of ourselves as a church."[2] The suggestions offered in the conclusion relate particularly to the Salvation Army, but since the Church as a whole shares similar challenges, I hope this account may also be of some ecumenical interest.

This book derives from a PhD thesis submitted to the Victoria University of Wellington in 2004, so acknowledgements include Professor Jim Veitch of the Religious Studies Department for supporting my research proposal. I am

---

1 Emil Brunner, *The Misunderstanding of the Church* (London: Lutterworth Press, 1953).

2 John Larsson, Opening Address to the International Theology and Ethics Symposium, Winnepeg, Canada, May 2001.

grateful to Paternoster Press for publishing it and to Dr Robin Parry, Mr Jeremy Mudditt and Dr Anthony R. Cross for patient help given a novice author. The Salvation Army allowed me to spend a good deal of its time on this project including much of 2002 on part-time study leave, and provided a travel grant to carry out research in Washington and London that year. General John Larsson kindly gave me access to relevant records of the General's Advisory Council and of International Leaders' Conferences, with Colonel Laurence Hay acting as guide and gatekeeper therein.

My thanks also go to Mr Gordon Taylor, archivist in London, Mr Scott Bedio in Washington, and Mrs Beverley McKenzie, Librarian at the Booth College of Mission, Trentham, for their help, and to Mr Tom Aitken (London), General Shaw Clifton (then in Wellington) and Professor Norman Murdoch (then in Cincinnati) for useful suggestions and corrections. Dr George Hazell, Major Kingsley Sampson, Mr Trevor Brieseman, Commissioner Gudrun Lydholm, Professor Ed. McKinlay, Colonel Earl Robinson, Dr Brett Knowles, Major Peter Smith, Dr Alan Jamieson and Mr Russell Rook also responded patiently to my questions or correspondence or shared insights and information. (They are not of course responsible for the use to which I have put that information, my general argument or the nature of my conclusions.) Professor Ian Breward encouraged me to turn a prolix Master's thesis into a Doctoral thesis and suggested its publication, and I am indebted further to him for providing the Foreword. Mr Kieran Windsor of the Salvation Army's Computer Section and Mrs Mary Cresswell have rescued my text from various computer Black Holes. The dedication to Commissioner Alfred J. Gilliard acknowledges the debt many of my generation owe to him from his four brief years in New Zealand in the early 1960s. Finally, the encouragement and support of my wife, Pat, have made this book possible.

Harold Hill
Wellington, 2006.

Abbreviations in Footnotes

BEM 111:	*Baptism, Eucharist and Ministry: Faith and Order Paper 111* (Geneva, World Council of Churches, 1982).
BEM 117:	*The Churches Respond to BEM: Faith and Order Paper 117* (Geneva, World Council of Churches, 1986).
IHQ:	International Headquarters.
SA:	The Salvation Army.
WC:	*The War Cry*.
WCC:	World Council of Churches.

Note on Style

The Salvation Army's foundation Deed Poll, and style guides for its publications, stipulate the capitalisation of the initial 'T' in its legal name. Within the organisation's literature, references to the Founder tend to be similarly capitalised. This note acknowledges this idiosyncrasy but the usual conventions will be followed in the text except where quotations from sources require otherwise.

Disclaimer

Every effort has been made to ensure the accuracy of quotations and to trace copyright holders and to obtain their permission for the use of copyright material. The author apologizes for any errors or omissions and would be grateful if notified of any corrections that should be incorporated in future reprints or editions of this book.

Part One: Leadership in Church History

Part One provides a context for the account of Salvation Army development which follows. In Chapter One, an opening section introduces two differing views on the nature of Church leadership. A brief overview of Church history shows how, as the church institutionalised, the clergy assumed a status distinct from that of ordinary, "lay" Christians. Various reactions against this tendency are explored in Chapter Two, while Chapter Three offers some analyses and explanations for the pattern described.

Chapter One

Clericalisation

Church history, what is it to me?
Because only clerics do I see.
Of Christians' concerns and of congregations,
Nothing seems to be told to me.

Johann Wolfgang von Goethe
Zahme Xenien IX.

Every field throws up its specialists. The ordinary person cannot be expected to master the expanding body of knowledge and range of skills required and naturally defers to and depends upon those who have made a special study of the subject. Religion was long pre-eminent amongst such fields. From pre-history, the medicine-men and shamans, spirit mediums, tohunga and priests, have stood between the unknown, magical and dangerous spiritual realm and the people, speaking for the people to the gods, and speaking for the gods to the people.

The one speaking for the gods enjoys a position of some influence. Spiritual hierarchs came to exercise both spiritual and temporal power. While the charismatic founder may be kept honest by a closeness to the *mysterium tremens et fascinans* and a single-minded commitment to a vision, the second generation and those following tend to keep a closer eye on the political implications. A Moses could exclaim, "Would that all the Lord's people might prophesy!" A Joshua's instinct is to complain, "Eldad and Medad are also prophesying," and to urge, "Make them stop – they're not authorised".[1] Against that trend, there has also been, especially in the Judaeo-Christian tradition, a counter-cultural, prophetic tradition of protest against the institutions of power. Walter Brueggemann says that "The task of prophetic ministry is to nurture, nourish and evoke a consciousness and perception alternative to the consciousness and perception of the dominant culture around us."[2] At times the prophets, like Nathan, have constituted an official and loyal opposition within the power structure.[3] At other times they

---

1 Numbers 11:26-27.

2 Walter Brueggemann, *The Prophetic Imagination* (Minneapolis MN, Fortress Press, 2nd edn 2001) p. 3.

3 2 Samuel 12.

have stood outside, like Amos, and denounced the abuse of power in the name of the God assumed to legitimate the cult.[4]

Jesus of Nazareth stood in this prophetic tradition. He may not have begun by attacking the institutions of received religion – he attended the synagogue, went up to Jerusalem for the Great Feasts, and sent his cleansed lepers to priests to be formally declared healed, as required by the Law. However, by the time he had challenged those who locked the doors of the Kingdom against others without entering themselves, poured scorn on the blind leaders of the blind and evicted the profiteers from the Court of the Gentiles, he had caused such an uproar that the whole system was in danger. It was inevitable that temporal and spiritual powers should combine to eliminate him before it was too late. And as his followers eventually came to understand it, his teaching made the whole apparatus of the cult irrelevant and unnecessary. Jesus offered, in Crossan's phrase, "the brokerless Kingdom of God".[5]

Although his disciples argued about their order of precedence, Jesus and the community which grew up after his death appear to have valued equality in contrast to the priestly hierarchies of received religion. Jesus is reported as saying,

> You know that foreign rulers like to order their people around. And their leaders have full power over everyone they rule. But don't act like them. If you want to be great, you must be the servant of all the others. And if you want to be first, you must be the slave of the rest. The Son of Man did not come to be a slave master, but a slave who will give his life to ransom many people.[6]

> But you are not to be called "Rabbi", for you have only one Master and you are all brothers. And do not call anyone on earth "father", for you have only one Father, and he is in heaven. Nor are you to be called "teacher", for you have only one Teacher, the Christ.[7]

There were evidently varieties of function within the early Christian community, but not of formal status. Over the first few centuries, however, as it institutionalised and developed structures to order its polity and conserve its message, and as it accommodated to Roman society and to traditional religious expectations, the Church developed such distinctions, between clerics in orders and laity.

---

4 Amos 6:21-24.

5 J. D. Crossan, *The Historical Jesus: The Life of a Mediterranean Jewish Peasant* (North Blackburn Vic.: Collins Dove, 1991) p. 422.

6 Matthew 20:25-28.

7 Matthew 23:8-10.

Defining the Terms

A word for this tendency, where church is concerned, is "clericalism", for which one definition is, "A policy of maintaining or increasing the power of a religious hierarchy". The process by which this assumption of status and a widening gap between leaders and led take place might be described as "clericalisation".

In most Christian traditions people have a variety of roles within the church organisation. Leadership, as the New Testament shows, is not incompatible with an underlying equality. However, there is a division between those traditions which claim that ordination to leadership changes a person's essential, ontological character, and those traditions which do not. Those arguing for a special character would say with the Second Vatican Council that

> the common priesthood of the faithful and the ministerial priesthood..., differ essentially and not only in degree...[8]

Those denying the existence of a separate ministerial caste are content that

> all minister, and that nowhere is to be perceived a separation or even merely a distinction between those who do and those who do not minister... There exists in the Ecclesia a universal duty and right of service, a universal readiness to serve and at the same time the greatest possible differentiation of functions.[9]

But even that line of demarcation does not tell the whole story. The difficulty is that office itself inevitably confers some degree of power and power offers at least the possibility of those who exercise it "tyrannising over those allotted to [their] care".[10] Power, like steroids taken by an athlete, may enhance performance but exact a long-term cost. This is can happen whether or not office and officer have been sacralised. Office-bearers whose roles are theoretically simply functional may come to share the same assumptions of status and behave in the same way as some who are conceived to belong to a different order or class of Christian. Having clerics does not necessarily involve clericalism. Not having clerics does not necessarily mean clericalism can be avoided.

Yves Congar pointed out that "Protestant communions, starting from strict congregationalist premises and an associational and community basis,

---

8 "Dogmatic Constitution of the Church, Article 10", in Austin Flannery (Ed.) *Vatican Council II: The Conciliar and Post Conciliar Documents* (Collegeville Min.: Liturgical Press, 1975) p. 361.

9 Brunner, *Misunderstanding of the Church*, p. 50.

10 1 Peter 5:3.

are in practice as clericalised as the Catholic Church… No doubt there are sociological laws in virtue of which the most 'charismatic' religious communities, those most made 'from below', quite soon become organisations with authority, traditions, a 'church' sociological structure."[11] Even in the contemporary unstructured house-church movement, as Miroslav Volf notes, "…a strongly hierarchical, informal system of paternal relations often develops between the congregation and charismatic delegates from the ascended Christ."[12] So, whatever the theory, whether special character is claimed or not, or even when no separate ministry is established, assumptions of superiority pose a special danger to those holding church office. Those who dissent from such assumptions would agree with Lord Acton that "all power tends to corrupt…"

The church operates within the culture of its times, however counter-cultural its beliefs and ideals may be, and it adapted itself to changing circumstances. Looking back from the mid-fourth century, "Ambrosiaster" approved the change, saying that whereas "in the early church, anyone could teach and baptise…, when all do everything, that is irrational, vulgar and abhorrent."[13] Some have seen in this change an erosion of the influence of the Holy Spirit while others have discerned the guiding hand of the Lord. Is the clericalisation of the church the plan of God or a consequence of the Fall? Perhaps the most we can say is that the danger of clerical attitudes is heightened when clerical caste is claimed.

This introductory chapter now traces the steps by which the instrument was created which could serve attitudes far removed from the ideal of humble service. It does so by exploring the development of Leadership, the reversion to Priesthood and the accommodation of the Church to the wider society.

Leadership

The earliest Christian texts, the letters of Paul, show that there were leaders but not "clergy" in the sense that ministry is understood by the churches today. There were "Apostles, prophets and teachers",[14] "elders" were appointed (and sometimes described as having the role of "overseeing"),[15]

---

11 Yves Congar, *Lay People in the Church: A Study for a Theology of Laity* (London: Bloomsbury, 1957) p. 45.

12 Miroslav Volf, *After Our Likeness: The Church in the Image of the Trinity* (Grand Rapids: Eerdmans 1998) p. 237.

13 "Ambrosiaster", *Commentary on Ephesians* 4:11-12, cited in Edward Schillebeeckx, *The Church with a Human Face* (New York: Crossroads, 1985) p. 73.

14 1 Corinthians 12:28.

15 Acts 14:23, Acts 20:17, 28.

and Paul describes ministries of *charismata*,[16] which were functional roles within the community. There is little agreement on the exact shape of these arrangements. Probably the New Testament texts reveal a variety of responses to local situations in a variety of Mediterranean and Asian cultural contexts and a consequent diversity of organisation in the churches of the Apostolic and immediate post-apostolic period. It may be that the names adopted for offices in the church were deliberately functional and chosen to avoid any comparison with existing status-laden titles, such as "priest" or "ruler".

At first all believers, including any holders of office, were the *laos* (from which we get "laity"), the *people* of God; no one exercising a particular *charism* or role was distinct from the *laos* in some other category. Any authority conferred by Jesus was owned by the whole body rather than by particular individuals in it, and any offices that developed were exercised on behalf of the whole body. No individual (apart from Jesus himself in the letter to the Hebrews) is called a "priest", but the whole body of believers enjoys a collective priesthood, since described as the "priesthood of all believers".[17]

The development and standardisation of a hierarchy of offices took place as the Church institutionalised, a process which began within the New Testament period. The change from "itinerant" to "resident" leadership by heads of households probably contributed to this process. By the time the "Pastoral Epistles" were written, towards the end of the first century, the original apostolic leadership had passed on and the earlier variety of charisms were in the process of being superseded by two (later three) roles which were becoming regular offices. The roles of overseer (*episkopos* or "bishop"), and elder (*presbyteros*), are referred to, sometimes interchangeably,[18] and some people are also described as servants (*diakonoi*).[19] In time the most senior elder, acting as chairman or president amongst the council of *presbyteroi,* particularly as presiding over the Eucharist, became identified as the *episkopos.* Deacons probably assisted at the Eucharist. Later use of these terms should not be read back into the earliest period; a "bishop", for example, was the head of a local Christian community. The diaconate was first identified with the "seven" of Acts 6 and with charitable work by Irenaeus only late in the second century.

The late first-century *Didache* also suggests that the charismatic offices like that of the prophet were in the process of being superseded by the election, by the *laos*, of presbyter-bishops and deacons. Permanent office-bearers succeeded each other, designated by formal acts of ordination.

---

16 1 Corinthians 10:7-10.

17 1 Peter 2:4-5,9; Revelation 1:5,6; 5:9, 10; 20:6.

18 E.g. Titus 1:6-7.

19 1 Timothy 3:10, 13.

Clement of Rome (c.96) and Ignatius of Antioch (c.110), whose letters have survived, were such officers and were concerned for the proper ordering of such offices. Their authority was still delegated to them by the church, to represent the church; they did not claim to derive it from any independent historical succession from Christ or the apostles. Clement still uses the terms bishop and presbyter interchangeably. Ignatius is the first to describe the three-fold hierarchy with a definite monepiscopate. Hans Küng sums it up:

> The fellowship of believers, the collegiality of all believers, of all those who had charisms and fulfilled their own ministries… gave place to the collegiality of a special ministry within the community: the collegiality of the leaders of the community, the *episkopoi* or elders, who increasingly began to see themselves as distinct from the community, from the "people"; this is where the division between "clergy" and "laity" begins.[20]

By early in the second century the three-fold structure of one bishop, presiding over a council of presbyters and supported by deacons was becoming common. The role of the bishop was further reinforced as a focus of unity in the face of the Gnostic threat and the fact that correspondence between churches took place through their leading presbyters or bishops also tended to emphasise the leadership and marginalise the laity.

With the increase in numbers of Christians in urban centres and the spread of Christianity into the countryside, a further development took place in the second century. The presbyters, rather than remaining simply the council of elders around the bishop in a congregation, began to take pastoral and liturgical responsibility for outlying congregations. They became "little bishops" themselves, while representing the one bishop. This further distanced the ordinary laity from the bishop.

By the third century the various offices of the church were beginning to be seen as a *graded* hierarchy, a ladder up which clerics could climb rather than being ordained to an office for life, though this progression did not become an invariable rule until much later.

It was early recognised that one of the effects of these developments was to reduce the laity to a more passive role. In the third-century Pseudo-Clementines, the Church is likened to a boat owned by God, whose pilot is Christ. The mate is the Bishop, the deacons the sailors, the catechists the midshipmen. The "multitude of the brethren" (i.e. the faithful) are the passengers, who are advised not to rock the boat.[21] The structure had established clear distinctions. In sociological terms, what had taken place is described as the "*routinization* of charisma…a process which also involves

---

20 Hans Küng, *The Church* (London: Search Press, 1968) p. 410.

21 *Epistle of Clement to James*, 14, "The Vessel of the Church;" 15, "Incidents of the Voyage."

the *containment* of charisma."[22] Under this heading we can also refer to the gradual restriction of the preaching and teaching role in the Church. While the gifts of evangelism and teaching were taken over by the clerical role at an early stage along with the other *charismata*, notable lay Christians continued to exercise great influence. Some of the early Fathers, like Origen, were laymen. However the church progressively restricted this possibility, so that only bishops could exercise a magisterial, teaching role, and presbyters by delegation, and deacons if licensed. In the ferment in the Church of the eleventh century, the laity sought opportunity to teach and preach, but Gregory IX (1227-1241) prohibited lay preaching. The Barbarian invasions (which left the clergy as the only educated people) and the Protestant Reformation (which left the Church unwilling to trust lay enthusiasts) were other influences.

Priests

A second factor in the clericalisation of ministry was the adoption of the "priestly" language. Several things helped bring about this change. In the mid-second century Marcion's rejection of the Old Testament led to its favourable reappraisal by the Church and its priestly institutions began to be seen as models. The Levitcal priesthood, holy, wholly devoted to and knowledgeable about God, appeared an appropriate model for Christian leadership.

Analogies between Old Testament and Christian worship fostered the idea of offering "spiritual sacrifices," at first without specific or exclusive reference to the Eucharist, but the tendency is for metaphorical language to be taken increasingly literally. Justin Martyr (died c.165), Irenaeus (died c.200) and later writers saw the Eucharist in terms of a sacrificial meal, which contributed to the development of the idea that the one presiding over it had a priestly role. This may have been encouraged by the Roman idea that a legal religion should have sacrificial rites.

No separate Christian ministry is clearly identified as a "priesthood" until about the year 200 AD, when Tertullian refers to the bishop as *summus sacerdos* (high priest) and holds that the bishops, presbyters and deacons together comprise a clerical order as distinct from the laity.[23] But the bishop was *high* priest because *all* Christians were priests. Tertullian allows that even a layman could baptise in the absence of clerics.[24] Hippolytus of Rome,

---

22 Thomas O'Dea, *The Sociology of Religion* (Englewood Cliffs NJ: Prentice-Hall Inc., 1966) p. 50.
23 Tertullian, *On Monogamy*, 11, 12; *Exhortation to Chastity* 7, in Henry Bettenson (Ed.) *Documents of the Christian Church* (London: OUP, 1956) pp. 100-1.
24 Tertullian, *Baptism*. 17.

within twenty years, is found defending his episcopal office in priestly language and claiming succession from the apostles, though priesthood appears to have involved the helping and governing of the people rather than being associated particularly with the Eucharist.

However the priestly role became more entrenched with the progressive theological development of the idea of the Eucharist as sacrifice. Cyprian of Carthage in the mid-third century is the first known to have seen the priest offering the Eucharist as "acting in Christ's place",[25] and may also have implied that the priest thereby re-enacted Christ's sacrifice rather than merely portraying it. By the sixth century the Eucharist came to be seen as a means of "renewing" that event, with the elements being identified with Christ. The priest's ordination was seen as giving the power to make that happen, further separating him from lay Christians. The fourth Lateran Council of 1215 finally insisted that only an ordained priest had the power to turn bread and wine into the body and blood of Christ in the Eucharist.

After the fifth century the advent of private masses also emphasised the priest's power in isolation from what had always been a community event. By the tenth century the laity usually took communion only on great festivals; generally they were reduced to a spectator role in the liturgy.

Originally the line between the world and the church was drawn at baptism which was the decisive mark of all believers, changing their "character", their very being. Gradually ordination came to be seen as conferring a further distinct personal mark on the cleric. Augustine of Hippo (d. 430) distinguished between the grace of the Holy Spirit, which can be lost, and the unlosable grace of the sacrament of order. Ordination gave an "indelible character" to the ministerial order as something that could exist in isolation from the church as a whole. The *character indelebilis* or "indelible mark" was described authoritatively by Pope Eugene IV in the Bull "Exultate Domino", 1439, as applying to the sacraments of baptism, confirmation and orders.[26]

In Canon Law ordination became finally restricted to priests and deacons, while all other vocations and ministries – such as those of the minor orders of acolyte, lector, sub-deacon, porter – in the Church were jobs done by the laity. The change in location of the boundary between the world and the church from baptism to ordination was entrenched towards the end of the first millennium because of lay reaction to the general decline of spirituality in the Church, leading to a revival of monasticism. This led to the taking of monastic vows being seen as a new kind of baptism at a time when nearly everyone in society was already baptised. With more monks becoming

---

25 Cyprian of Carthage, *Epistle* 63.14.4.

26 J. Neuner and J. Dupuis, *The Christian Faith: The Doctrinal Documents of the Catholic Church* (Bangalore: Theological Publications in India, 3rd edn 1978) p. 350.

priests and the pressure on ordinary clergy to adopt monastic spirituality, priesthood became identified with a more spiritual way of life. The laity for example put pressure on the clergy to adopt celibacy – resisted at first but eventually made mandatory late in the eleventh century. All of this strengthened the medieval concept of the church as divided between the "order of the laity" and "order of the clergy". The boundary between world and church now lay at ordination.

In general we can also say that the general consequence of the development of the idea of the special "priesthood of some believers" was the attenuation of the concept of the general "priesthood of all believers". In David Wright's image, "like the proverbial cuckoo in the nest, the two will not comfortably co-habit".[27]

The Church in Society

A third factor in institutionalisation was the church's accommodation to the patterns of society. O'Dea points out that "founded religions tend to repudiate, at least implicitly, the stratification differences of society, but after a time they come more or less to accept these social distinctions. Important people in society consequently come to be looked upon as important in the religious group as well."[28] The concept of "order" was taken over from Roman society in which the senatorial and equestrian orders were the elite ruling classes by Imperial appointment or *ordinatio*, and people without rank were relegated to the role of *pleb*. Tertullian applied the same structure to the church: clergy were *ordo*, laity were *plebs*. His division between the ordo and the plebs was for the organization and administration of the church; it did not yet reflect special powers that belonged only to the clergy. However, with the growth of the Church in the third century, its leaders' authority was augmented as they gained in wealth and distinction within the community, gaining some power of patronage, and so came to be regarded as belonging to a superior social order, above other Christians. The structure of the Church also increasingly mirrored the administration of Empire, with metropolitan and provincial officials, and regional synods of bishops analogous to Imperial diets.

Within the third century it became more customary for clergy to be supported by church offerings rather than working at secular occupations. Even in the primitive church Peter and others had been supported, and Paul claimed to have forgone that right. (See 1 Cor. 9:3-14, 2 Thess. 3:7-10; 2 Cor.11:7-9; Gal. 6:6; 1 Tim. 5:17-18.) However it was probably as the local

---

27 David Wright, Foreword to Colin Bulley, *The Priesthood of Some Believers* (Carlisle: Paternoster, 2000) p. ix.

28 O'Dea, *Sociology of Religion*, p. 74.

bishops' responsibilities grew too large to manage as a spare-time activity that their support by the church became customary. Cyprian pronounced that "Everyone honoured by the divine priesthood and ordained to the clerical service, ought to serve only at the altar and sacrifices, and to have leisure for prayers and supplications."[29]

With the advent of toleration under Constantine Christianity gained equal rights with other religions and clergy gained special prerogatives. Even more significant change came with Theodosius I (379-395) when Christianity became *the* official religion of the Empire. The concept of *cursus honorum* (in which each order was seen as contained within its superior, rather like a series of Russian *maruska* dolls) was taken over from the model of Imperial organisation by the fourth century. Christianity was adapted to the late pagan conception of religion and the *clerici* became equated with the former pagan priesthood, charged with maintaining religion as a civic duty, exempt from all other civic responsibilities and salaried by the state. The higher clergy however increasingly served in government roles, as imperial delegates and counsellors, though the process had begun even earlier – witness the role of Hosius, Bishop of Cordova, under Constantine. Over the next few centuries, as the fabric of Empire unravelled under the impact of barbarian invasions, the civic magistracies melted away and the prelates of the church often inherited their functions under new over-lords.

In the eleventh and twelfth centuries the renaissance of Roman law also had a decisive influence on the Church's view of ministry in relation to community. This involved the detachment of the power of leadership from the concept of territoriality, and therefore, in the religious sphere, from the local church. A priest might not be leader of a community but still have "sacred power" to perform the Eucharist. At the Lateran Councils of the twelfth century, "absolute" ordinations (to priestly or episcopal status without any connection with an actual church community) had become acceptable, provided that the ordaining bishop accepted financial responsibility for the future maintenance of the ordinand, as a feudal overlord for his vassal.

Under social order we could include the comparatively minor line of demarcation between clergy and laity involved in the evolution of clerical dress. At first there was no such thing, and Pope Celestine rebuked some Gallic Bishops in a letter of 428 for wearing distinctive attire. "We should be distinguished from the common people (*plebe*) by our learning, not by our clothes; by our conduct, not by our dress..."[30] It was not until the fifth and sixth centuries that distinctive clerical garb became more common, and

---

29 Cyprian of Carthage, *Epistle* 65.1.

30 Mansi, *Concilia*, IV, 465, cited in On-line Catholic Encyclopaedia, downloaded 4 May 2006 from www.newadvent.org/cathen/04419b.htm.

then because Roman clergy adhered to the older style of long tunic and cloak while the laity increasingly adopted the short tunic, trousers and mantle of the new barbarian rulers. Conservatism was already the mark of the clergy. Architecture followed suit; the mysteries of the gospel retreated beyond the rood screen in the Gothic cathedral, and in modern Orthodox liturgy are still hidden from profane eyes.

What has been described here is the way in which the church's ministry became institutionalised into clerical status, a development reinforced by the development of "Christendom". As the Empire became Christian, the Church became Imperial. Thus structural, doctrinal and social developments over the first millennium of Church history all served to distance the clergy from the laity.

Chapter Two

Reaction and Counter-Reaction

When they shall read this clearly in your charge
New Presbyter is but Old Priest writ large.

John Milton,
On the new forcers of Conscience under the Long PARLAMENT.

Many times in the history of the Church when there has been a renewal of mission, some reaction against clericalism has been involved. Usually the movements involved have either been suppressed or have in their turn become clericalised.

Monasticism

Although Coptic monasticism goes back to people like Frontonius in the mid-second century, Monasticism is seen especially as a reaction against the worldly success of the Church in the fourth century. With Christianity's official Imperial recognition and role as a state religion, and the mass conversions of convenience which eventuated, some feared that true spirituality had to be sought in withdrawal from the world. Pachomius (ca. 287-346) in Egypt based a community Rule on obedience to a superior. He specifically forbade monks to become priests on the ground that "it is not good to covet power and glory", in itself a reflection of the growing status of clergy. St Benedict of Monte Cassino (480-543), still a layman, broke new ground for western community monasticism and his Benedictine Rule prevailed in Europe from the eighth to the twelfth centuries. Periods of decline and decadence led to periodic new and sterner foundations such as those of Cluny (910) and Citeaux (1098).

For the purposes of our study the point is that Monasticism was originally a lay movement, but became clericalised. The original hermit monks lived largely without sacraments, independently of clergy. Benedictine foundations tended to depend upon the nearest parish church unless they were too isolated in which case they had to either take in a priest or have some brothers ordained. Pope Gregory the Great, in the sixth century, drew on monasteries for ordinands, but even he believed that monastic and clerical vocations were incompatible. "No one can perform both ecclesiastical (clerical) duties, and remain by due order under monastic rule," he said.[1] This remained the general picture up until late in the first millennium when, paradoxically, monastic spirituality came to dominate clerical life at the same time as monastic life became increasingly clericalised. By the tenth century in some monasteries more than half the monks were ordained.

The growing commitment to the Eucharist at the centre of monastic spiritual life contributed to this gradual clericalisation. Social and cultural factors also helped, including the attempt, general within the church in the West, to replicate the Roman liturgy, which required many priests. The Cistercian economic system came to depend upon the manual labour of unlettered lay brethren. Monasticism came to reflect the feudal social order, with noble clerical monks and lay brother serfs.

New Movements

The late Middle Ages were a time of great ferment and change in Europe, not least in religion and spirituality. Revolt against an oppressive social system by marginalised workers has often characterised sectarian development. With the development of the middle classes, the identification of the church hierarchy with the seigniorial classes aroused resentment. While the movement of the official Church following the Gregorian reforms of the eleventh and twelfth centuries was towards centralisation, institutional conformity and a widening gap between clergy and laity, there was a counter mood amongst the laity, who became less willing to accept a passive role. This was characterised by a desire to return to evangelical living, partly in reaction against clerical decadence. Scripture reading, the imitation of Christ and the example of the apostolic church were frequently appealed to, indicative of the emergence of a better-educated and more self-confident urban middle-class.

Of the great variety of new religious expressions, some were passing occasions of mass excitement like crowds of flagellants rushing from town to town, leaving no organised association. Others coalesced about charismatic figures, like Arnold of Brescia, Lambert le Begue, Tanchelm of Utrecht or Peter of Bruys. Some were taken under the wing of the Church and became official "Orders" while others were fringe movements, drifting into heresy and schism.

---

1 Margaret Deanesley, *The History of the Medieval Church 590-1500* (London: Methuen [1925] 1979) p. 40.

Friars. Just as the Monastic Orders met and provided a means of expression for popular religious feeling at the various times of their foundations, the Dominican and Franciscan Mendicant Orders of Friars fitted the social pattern of the thirteenth century. They were an urban phenomenon and responded to and channelled religious aspirations of burgeoning urban life. The Dominicans were clerical from their inception but the Franciscans began lay. Francis of Assisi (1181-1229) reluctantly accepted deacon's orders from Innocent III but was not concerned about hierarchical status. Within a generation his order was becoming clericalised. This was partly because this made it easier to control and support and partly because the Franciscan tasks of preaching, evangelizing and spiritual direction required educated people – who were usually clergy.

Third Orders. Francis however recruited a further kind of follower in his last years; some lay people who professed a rule and made a commitment to an evangelical lifestyle but remained in their secular occupations, and could be married. These were known as a "Third Order". (The Friars Minor were the First, and women Franciscans comprised the Second.) The Dominicans and Carmelites also enrolled such Tertiaries. These associate orders have survived today in their "lay" condition.

The Brethren of the Common Life were the followers of Gerhard Groote (1340-84), a Dutch mystic who opted out of the ecclesiastical rat-race after becoming a deacon and gathered a following almost by default as an itinerant preacher. In his last years, silenced by the Church, he established small communities, including one for women. They had no rule or binding vow, worked at secular occupations for a living, and laymen lived together with clerks [clergy] in these communities. Despite their irregularity the Brethren somehow managed to escape juridical condemnation. Sadly they were no more successful than the "real orders" in maintaining their freedom from status. Opposition from the trade guilds restricted their occupation largely to book copying. Eventually the few layman left were cooks and servants, equality was lost and the distinction between clergy and laity was reinforced.

Waldensians. Many anti-hierarchical "Fringe Orders and Anti-Orders", as R. W. Southern[2] described them, rejected the institution and failed to make the transition to respectability. One of many such groups, Waldensians were the followers of Peter Waldo (d.1217), a French merchant who gave away his property and attracted followers as a mendicant missioner. These "Poor Men of Lyons" translated the Bible into vernacular Provençal and preached in their own words but were initially orthodox in doctrine until their exclusion from the Church caused them to develop their beliefs further. They encouraged both laity and women to preach and teach without being

---

2 R. W. Southern, *Western Society and the Church in the Middle Ages* (Harmondsworth: Penguin, 1970) p. 300.

incorporated in the Church's clerical and monastic structure or giving up their lay status. Centuries of persecution failed to destroy them and a remnant has survived, particularly in Northern Italy. Despite their view that any true believer could administer the Lord's Supper, they did evolve their own clergy in time, eventually having Bishops, Priests and Deacons. Here was another case of an initially anti-clerical movement becoming clericalised.

The Reformation

The precursors to the Reformation, Wycliff and Huss, while claiming that Christian people following the Bible and living in simplicity needed no priestly mediation, wanted to reform the ministry, not abandon it. The residual reform movements deriving from Huss in middle-Europe retained clerical roles.

The same is true of the main streams of the Reformation deriving from Luther and Calvin. Luther's reaffirmed the priesthood of all believers or the priesthood of the baptised, insisting that every Christian fulfils a mediating role between God and neighbour. He denied the traditional demarcation between a spiritual estate (pope, bishops, priests, monks) and a temporal estate (princes, lords, artisans, farmers). This did not mean that Luther believed that anyone in the Church could do anything. He made it clear that it was appropriate for ministerial functions to be performed by designated people in the Church, just as people could follow any other vocation in the world. He said that clergy acted on behalf of other believers when "commissioned in orderly fashion for preaching the Word, for administering the sacraments and for other pastoral ministrations."[3] A group of pious laymen in a wilderness could choose one of themselves for the task. "A priest is no longer a priest when he is deposed... *characters indelebilis* ... is mere talk and man-made law."[4]

Calvin, though himself a layman, stressed the authoritative teaching role of the clergy. He viewed all ministry as that of Christ, who chose to make men his substitutes,[5] delegating tasks to them but certainly not making them ontologically different. Examining Ephesians 4:4-16, Calvin described the ministries of Apostle, Prophet and Evangelist as "extraordinary" and not to be expected in day to day Church life, but said that those of Pastor and Teacher were regular and "ordinary". Of the offices of Bishop, Priest and Deacon, he claimed that the first two expressed the gift of government in the Church and that both were to be found in the office of Pastor (who also

---

3 Martin Luther, *On Councils and the Church*, 1539.

4 Martin Luther, *An Open Letter to the Christian Nobility of the German Nation*, 1520.

5 John Calvin, *Institutes of the Christian Religion*, Book 4, Ch. 3, Sect. 1, 1536.

served as Teacher). Deacons expressed the gift for the care of the poor and sick. Ordination was the Church's recognition and endorsement of God's call on the life of the Pastor; it did not create a different class of Christian.

Summarising the Reformers' position from a Catholic viewpoint, Yves Congar states, "The universal priesthood of all believers came to exclude all ministerial or hierarchical priesthood and, at any rate in principle, a purely synodal and presbyterian ecclesiastical system was set up."[6] From the "left wing", however, Emil Brunner, in a free church critique of the Reformers, claims that "Although it was precisely at this point that Luther attacked the structure of the medieval Church by preaching the priesthood of all believers and therefore not recognising an official priesthood, neither he nor any other of the reformers took this universal priesthood seriously in practice. Even in the Protestant Church, the clerical office – whether under the name of *ministerium* (the ministry) or *sacerdotium* (the priesthood) – continued in being as something constitutive for the existence of the Church."[7] It did not take long for the centre of gravity in the Reformation Churches to shift to the clerical end of the sea-saw. E. L. Mascall succinctly compared Reformation with pre-Reformation ministry by saying that "what Protestantism did to the religion of Western Europe was simply to substitute a clericalism of the Word for a clericalism of the Sacrament."[8]

The Radical Reformation

The Reformation, overturning so many previous certainties and placing the Scriptures in the hands of common people at a time when the invention of printing had made possible wide literacy, created the "religion of the mechanicks". All over Europe little groups of lay-people, from the 1520s on, met to study the Bible and determine for themselves the shape of the Church. Hugely diverse, and ranging from the mildly reformist to the certifiably revolutionary, they are known collectively as Anabaptists because most shared a belief in the need for adult baptism, whether or not they had, as everyone had, been baptised as infants. Beyond that, they tended to reject human authority, clericalism and hierarchy, resisting any connection between church and state. Their radical congregationalism provided the prototype for free churches of all descriptions since then, and they emphasised servant leadership, the responsibility of the individual believer to participate in ministry and the local congregation as the

6 Congar, *Lay People*, p. 36.

7 Emil Brunner, *The Christian Doctrine of the Church, Faith and the Consummation: Dogmatics* III (London: Lutterworth, 1962) pp. 98- 99.

8 E.L. Mascall, *The Recovery of Unity: A Theological Approach* (London: Longmans, 1958) p. 5.

appropriate context for biblical interpretation. Whereas the mainline Reformers in effect simply took over the "Christendom" model, with Church and State co-extensive, the Anabaptists rejected it.

Anabaptists rejected distinctions between clergy and laity. Rather than having no clergy, it could be said that they had no laity. However, even when a church polity attempts to exclude the possibility of clericalism, professionalism makes inevitable inroads and modern American Anabaptist congregations have not uncommonly reverted to a clerical pattern by emphasizing the need for pastors, pastoral counsellors, and psychiatrists so that the ministry roles in the community of faith have atrophied.

Most of the free churches descended from Anabaptism and the generally radical fringe of the reformation have maintained a clerical role even while making it clear that no clerical character is involved. The constitution of the Baptist Union of New Zealand for example insists of the pastoral role that "When the function ceases, the person is no longer a minister." The church's website admits that "Often other Christian traditions, their forms and thus implicitly their theology, can all too easily flow over to us. Here we need the courage of our biblical radicalism."[9] But for all practical purposes such clerics are indistinguishable from any of their colleagues at the local Ministers' Fraternal. The trend transcends the local level: Paul M. Harrison's 1950s study of the American Baptist Convention for example found that denominational officials had gained significant power not legitimated by the Baptist belief system.[10]

The Catholic Church

It would be appropriate to note that in the Catholic Counter-Reformation, both in the Council of Trent and in the whole ensuing direction of Catholic ecclesiology until the mid-twentieth century, the need to counter Protestant theology of ministry led to an unbalanced reaction, an increased emphasis on the juridical and hierarchical aspects of the Church. The pendulum has swung back the other way following the second Vatican Council of the early 1960s.

---

9 (http://www.baptist.org.nz/default.asp?id=37) Downloaded 20.12.05.

10 Paul M. Harrison, *Authority and Power in the Free Church Tradition: A Social Case Study of the American Baptist Convention* (Princeton NJ: Princeton University Press, 1959).

Methodism

Methodism was part of the eighteenth century revivalist movement which grew and flourished independently of any established church or effective parish system. John Wesley, however, was an ordained Anglican priest. "I live and die a member of the Church of England," he wrote in 1790, but by appointing lay preachers from 1740 on, he created what became in effect a parallel church. From the 1750s on he had at every Conference to fight against secessionist tendencies in his societies. In particular the local preachers wanted to give the sacrament to their societies, so that they did not have to depend on the willingness – not always forthcoming – of the Anglican parson to welcome Methodists to parish communion. However, despite even Wesley's usurping episcopal prerogative in 1775 by ordaining clergy for the American mission when the Bishop of London declined to do so, the final break with the established church did not come until 1795, four years after his death.

Concerned to ensure that his Methodists maintained his somewhat inconsistent status quo after his death, Wesley executed a "Deed of Declaration and Establishment of the People called Methodists" and enrolled it in Chancery in 1784. Methodism was to be ruled by a Conference of one hundred preachers, carefully chosen by Wesley from those who agreed with his policies. No laymen (that is, non-full time preachers) or women were included (although he had appointed his first woman preacher in 1761). Strictly speaking of course, almost all his preachers were lay; Wesley did not regard them as Ministers and did not permit them to use the title "Reverend".

With Wesley gone, the preachers soon began to style themselves "Ministers". Conference in 1795 permitted each Methodist society to have the Lord's Supper administered by an authorised person and to hold services at the same times as the established Church held its service – always forbidden by Wesley. While Wesleyan ministers were admitted to "connexion" with the Conference without ordination at first, ordination by the imposition of the hands of ministers was again adopted by the Conference in 1836. The New Connexion emerged in 1797 from disputes over "lay" representation at Conference and sacramental autonomy; the Wesleyan rump shed the Primitive Methodists in 1811 and the Bible Christians in 1815. Further agitation for lay-representation in government produced both the Wesleyan Reformers and the Wesleyan Reform Union between 1847 and 1852. Henry Rack says that "One of the tragedies of nineteenth century Wesleyanism was that it fossilised [Wesley's] pragmatism into a new ecclesiastical orthodoxy as dogmatic as the old ones."[11]

If tension between clerical and lay activism was at the heart of the process of schism in Methodism, clericalisation underlay the process which eventually brought together many of the splinter groups again in the twentieth century. Wilson notes that reunion "was largely a matter for the clerics in the movement rather than the laity... amalgamation was generally towards a greater recognition of ministerial authority and away from the priesthood of all believers."[12] The residual strength of the latter view, however, along with Anglican commitment to the historic episcopacy, was sufficient to abort attempts at Anglican-Methodist union negotiations from the 1960s to the end of the century. John Stacey enumerates the consequent variety of contemporary Methodist answers to the question, "What then is a minister?"

> One will tell him that he is simply a layman working full time; another that he is what he is because he has received a call from God, ratified by the Church, to exercise his particular gifts within a full-time ministry; another that what distinguishes him from a layman are the functions which he has to perform within the fellowship of the people of God; another that ordination means creation of an *ordo* and that he is therefore different in *being* from a layman.[13]

Other Sectarian Movements

Some other sects have determined to have no clerical roles.

Quakers: The Quakers, or Society of Friends, originated in England in the mid-seventeenth century. Although the Friends have almost invariably described themselves as without clergy, men and women who preached regularly, often as itinerants, were "recorded" and often described as "Ministers" from the early eighteenth century, despite being officially lay and without special training. Though in theory all were free to speak in meetings, those not recorded found it more difficult.

In the United States popular revivalism led to accommodation to the style of mainstream Protestant denominations. An American Quaker group adopted a professional pastorate by 1880 and at least in the United States it is now common. In England the recording of ministers was abolished in 1924 and the clerical tendency formally reversed. Despite this, a lay elite inevitably emerged to hold the real power.

---

11 Henry D. Rack, *Reasonable Enthusiast, John Wesley and the Rise of Methodism* (Nashville: Abingdon, 2nd edn., 1992) p. 250.

12 Bryan Wilson, *Religion in Secular Society* (London: C.A. Watts, 1966) p. 155.

13 John Stacey, *About Ministry* (London: Epworth, 1967) p. 34.

Plymouth Brethren: Although many of their early adherents in the 1830s were Anglican clergymen, their attitude was strongly anticlerical. Despite, or perhaps because of, their principle of minimal organisation, a relatively small number of leading Brethren became the real and effective leaders of their communities. Disputes of the 1840s led to the division between Exclusive and Open Brethren. Schisms remained a way of life, especially of the exclusives, long afterwards. In the twentieth century the ascendancy of James Taylor senior, and later of his son, over the Exclusives presented a curious paradox for a movement asserting local autonomy and without formally legitimated leadership – like having an infallible Pope without having a priesthood. However, there exists an informally institutionalised, non-professional, volunteer speaking ministry or local leadership.

On the other hand a growing number of Open Assemblies have invited full-time workers to associate themselves with a given assembly particularly, and these can become very much like conventional pastors although they rarely do all the preaching and they have no sacramental role.

Christadelphians: The Christadelphians, originating in the 1830s with Dr John Thomas, were also, like the Brethren, a lay movement, rejecting a trained ministry. Lay leadership by local officeholders and congregational decision-making notwithstanding, an odd development was the way in which Robert Roberts and his successors, editing *The Christadelphian*, an entirely private undertaking unconnected with any kind of central authority, assumed a de facto leadership role in the sect. Ecclesia which were "disfellowshipped" ceased to be reported. Efforts to secure exemption from military service in the first world war involved the appointment of a central registration authority for the sect, so that the principle of independence was sacrificed to safeguard the principle of pacifism.[14]

The Pentecostals

The Pentecostal churches regard all Christians as Ministers and reject the clergy/laity distinction as unbiblical. Nevertheless they have a place for "separated ministry" as the recognition of charismata and answering ordination by elders of a local congregation. Bryan Wilson drew attention to the role conflict experienced by Elim ministers as "guardians of a sectarian ethic in a denominationalizing organization".[15] Pentecostalism in fact offers

---

14 See Bryan Wilson, *Sects and Society: A Sociological Study of Three Religious Groups in Britain* (London: Heinemann, 1961).

15 Bryan Wilson, "The Pentecostalist Minister: Role Conflicts and Status Contradictions", *American Journal of Sociology* 64 (March 1959) p. 494.

yet another example of the sectarian emphasis on the priesthood of all believers gradually accommodating to clerical control.

Tracing the history of the "indigenous" churches of New Zealand as they evolved into the New Life denomination, Brett Knowles identifies the development whereby the

> ...charismatic authority of the Spirit was increasingly channelled and moderated by the pastor and the right to speak became specialised and restricted to those who were "recognised" by the leadership as "having a ministry". While spontaneous spiritual gifts continued to feature in the worship of the Indigenous Churches, the effect of this regulatory function was to replace the charismatic freedom of the Spirit with an "official" mode of leadership.

The shift from a "charismatic" to a more "official" form of authority was reinforced by an upward social mobility and by the acquisition of institutional authority as the pastors acted as "spokespersons" for the movement.[16]

Knowles outlines abortive negotiations for union amongst Pentecostal Churches in New Zealand in 1979:

> ... discussion was initially conducted at a senior leadership level, and only later involved the rest of the pastors in the movement... At no stage were the movement's congregations brought into the discussion. This demonstrated the penchant of the movement for discussing matters *in camera* and its perception of the role of the pastor as the institutionalised authority over the congregation.[17]

From being an informal, spirit-called ministry, the leadership was clearly professionalising and growing apart from the laity.

The Ecumenical Movement

Ecumenism of the twentieth century, described by Bryan Wilson as "the turning in on itself of institutionalised religion, as its hold on the wider social order has diminished",[18] was a different kind of phenomenon from the revival movements already discussed. However, some of the great founding leaders, people like John R. Mott, J.H. Oldham, and William Paton were lay,

16 Brett Knowles, *New Life: A History of the New Life Churches of New Zealand 1942-1979* (Dunedin: Third Millennium Publishing, 1999) p. 162, 164.

17 Brett Knowles, *The History of a New Zealand Pentecostal Movement* (Lewiston: Edwin Mellen Press, 2000) p. 274.

18 Wilson, *Religion in Secular Society*, pp. 175-6.

not clerics. With the setting up of the Department of the Laity in 1947 and the Ecumenical Institute at Bossey under Hendrik Kraemer (also a layman) great new impetus was given to the development of a theology of the laity. Over the years however this emphasis was diluted and the Department of the Laity dissolved. One document has confessed, "When we gather in ecumenical meetings the preponderance of laity no longer is evident. Clergy are often the representatives in ecumenical gatherings, regardless of the ecclesiological self-understandings of particular churches. In fact, in these contexts we sometimes talk about laity as objects to be trained, rather than people in partnership."[19] The focus of interest in the discussion of faith and order drifted back to clerical concerns – especially about who could do what, and be recognised by whom.

These examples, soundings taken in Church history, all illustrate how reactions have usually reverted to type within a short time, and demonstrate the cyclical process of institutionalisation of which clericalisation is one aspect.

19 World Council of Churches, "Towards a Common Understanding of the Theological Concepts of Laity/Laos: The People of God" (Consultation Statement, 7-10 May 1997).

Chapter Three

Pattern and Problem

> It seems, as one becomes older,
> That the past has another pattern, and ceases to be a mere
> sequence –
> Or even development: the latter a partial fallacy
> Encouraged by superficial notions of evolution,
> Which becomes, in the popular mind, a means of
> disowning the past.
>
> T.S. Eliot,
> *The Dry Salvages, Four Quartets*

Sociological Laws

Yves Congar has already been quoted concerning the probability that "sociological laws" may be discerned behind the events and movements outlined in the first two chapters, the presenting issues of function and status, of roles and ontological character of the church leadership. David Martin explains that "Sociology seeks to give an account of the patterns and sequences of social action. Human activity is not random. It gives rise to observable regularities which are susceptible to systematic statement and so allow modest anticipations concerning what is likely to happen next."[1]

Some might claim that the sociology of religion provides an interpretative framework which should form the starting point for a study like this one but it is not the only conceptual structure possible. For example, a well-known Salvation Army explanation for its history is "the guiding hand of the Lord".[2] These, as Martin puts it, are "different maps of the same ground".[3] Neither the poet's moon nor the astronomer's makes a nullity of the other. Explanations are not necessarily reductionist. The various levels of explanation for religious phenomena might be compared

---

1 David Martin *Reflections on Sociology and Theology* (Oxford: Clarendon Press, 1997) p. 1.
2 Wilfred Kitching, Foreword to Arch. W. Wiggins, *The History of The Salvation Army*, IV (London: Nelson, 1964) p. v.
3 Martin, *Reflections*, p. 74.

with the anatomical drawings in a medical text, in which successive transparent sheets, each inscribed with a particular system – skeletal, vascular, muscular etc – are all overlaid to show their relation. The Body of Christ does not exist on some abstract, spiritual plane, but is incarnate. This chapter therefore sketches some of the sociological patterns proposed to make some sense of the church's past.

The life-cycles of organisations, including religious ones, follow a sigmoid curve from movement to institution as they grow. They tend to plateau and enter a period of decline, from which they may or may not recover. Commonly, with the onset of decline, some schismatic or renewal movement strikes out upon a new trajectory of growth before eventually repeating the pattern. In the Catholic Church, various orders and groups from monasticism in the second century to Opus Dei in the twentieth, as well as heretical fringe movements, have been the loci of such renewal. In Protestantism, itself such a movement in origin, sectarian groups have flourished. Sometimes, usually in response to the new offshoot, a large segment of the church experiences a measure of rejuvenation, as in the sixteenth century Counter-Reformation or with the "third wave" of the charismatic movement of the twentieth century.

We have traced the way in which the church accommodated to society, successively Roman, Barbarian, Mediaeval, taking on characteristics incompatible with its founding vision. Such a vision nevertheless remained, in David Martin's terms, the "iconographic repertory of the church… a store of explosive materials capable of fissionable contact with social fragmentation" so that "schism is inevitable and rooted in the nature of Christianity itself as well as in the nature of society."[4] Movements for renewal in the Church have therefore usually coincided with ferment or major disruption in society as a whole and commonly expressed the dissatisfaction of marginalised groups, while such waves have in their turn been absorbed as new orthodoxies and hegemonies have become established.

Twentieth century sociologists of religion have described and analysed in particular the sectarian groups descended from the Reformation, and proposed "laws", to use Congar's term, to explain them. Max Weber employed the terms "church" and "sect" to distinguish groups to which people belonged by "birth" or by "decision" respectively.[5] The theologian Ernst Troelsch expanded the options of this typology to "churchly", "sectarian" and "mystical" behaviour.[6] H. Richard Niebuhr took Church and

---

4 Martin, *Reflections*, pp. 42-3.

5 Max Weber, *Sociology of Religion* [1922 and 1956], trans. Ephraim Bischoff (Boston: Beacon Press, 1963).

6 Ernst Troelsch, *The Social Teaching of Christian Churches* [1911] trans. Olive Wyon (New York: Macmillan, 1931).

Sect as the poles of a continuum, showing how sects emerged from churches but also evolved into denominational churches.[7] Later writers, such as Howard Becker,[8] Milton Yinger[9] and Bryan Wilson have elaborated on this scheme. Wilson summarised the characteristics of the sect as:

> A voluntary association; membership is by proof to sect authorities of some claim to personal merit – such as knowledge of doctrine, affirmation of a conversion experience, or recommendation of members in good standing; exclusiveness is emphasized, and expulsion exercised against those who contravene doctrinal, moral or organisational precepts; its self-conception is of an elect, a gathered remnant, possessing special enlightenment; personal reflection is the expected standard of aspiration…; it accepts, at least as an ideal, the priesthood of all believers; there is a high level of lay participation; there is opportunity for the member spontaneously to express his commitment; the sect is hostile or indifferent to the secular society and to the state.[10]

The Salvation Army would admit to many of these descriptors, though not all.

The various descriptions of sects tend to be "typological", and encounter the difficulty that very few religious bodies neatly fit the types, so that an ever more complex picture of mixed types and sub-types evolves. Benton Johnson drew attention to this difficulty, alternatively suggesting simply "rejection" of the world and "acceptance" of the social environment as the polarities of sects and denominational churches respectively.[11] Building on this, the "rational choice" protagonist Rodney Stark and his associates have elaborated a dynamic model to explain the behaviour of church members and bodies, and applied this template to religious groups across the board.[12] Sherkatt and Ellison summarise: "At the heart of all rational choice perspectives is the market analogy applied to religion… that religious markets involve exchanges for general supernatural compensators –

---

7 H. Richard Niebuhr, *The Social Sources of Denominationalism* (New York: Henry Holt) 1929.

8 Howard Becker, *Systematic Sociology* (New York: Wiley) 1932.

9 J. M. Yinger, *Religion and the Struggle for Power* (Durham, N.C: Duke University Press) 1946.

10 Bryan Wilson, "An Analysis of Sect Development", *American Sociological Review* 24 (February 1959) pp. 3-15,.

11 Benton Johnson, "A Critical Appraisal of the Church-Sect Typology", *American Sociological Review* 22:1 (February 1957) pp. 88-92; "On Church and Sect", *American Sociological Review* 28:4 (August 1963) pp. 539-49; "Church and Sect Revisited", *Journal for the Scientific Study of Religion* 10 (1971) pp. 124-37.

12 Rodney Stark and William Sims Bainbridge: *The Future of Religion: Secularization, Revival and Cult Formation* (Berkeley: University of California Press, 1985); Rodney Stark and Roger Fink, *Acts of Faith:Explaining the Human Side of Religion* (Berkeley: University of California Press, 2000).

promises of future rewards and supernatural explanations for life events and meaning."[13] While writers like Wilson set this discussion within a context of increasing secularization and the decline of formally religious life in Europe in particular, the exponents of rational choice, writing out of the American milieu, find evidence of a conservative religious renewal and somewhat contentiously extrapolate their findings to other parts of the world.[14] As a very broad generalisation, one way in which this argument may bear upon our theme is that where religion itself is thought to be in eclipse religious hierarchies may be perceived as increasingly irrelevant, while holders of conservative religious views may be more likely to maintain their significance.

The tendencies observed and models proposed by these and other writers provide helpful windows on the origins and development of the Salvation Army – however uncomfortable today's Salvationists may feel at Wilson's typecasting them as a "conversionist sect" – and are referred to again in these pages.

Benefit of Clergy

Common to all these analyses, and central to the subject of this work, is that in sectarian movements (including the primitive church) we find an egalitarianism, while the more institutionalised the body becomes, the greater the degree of clericalisation. The emerging ministers are not yet priests but are more than laymen. In time democracy gives way to bureaucracy and hierarchy. Most sectarian and denominational groups in the end evolve some clerical group or leadership, whether formally or informally, even though this development is in tension with the sectarian emphasis on equality and undifferentiated ministry. And although non-Christian religions lie outside the scope of this work, it is obvious that spiritual hierarchies have emerged there too, even when they are not of the essence of the particular faith. While Islam for example knows no clerical class, it is commonplace to refer to Muslim clerics, Mullahs, Imams, Ayatollahs, Grand Muftis and other dignitaries. The tendency towards

---

13 Darren E. Sherkat and Christopher G. Ellison, "Recent Developments and Current Controversies in the Sociology of Religion," *Annual Review of Sociology* 25 (1999) p. 378.

14 Rational Choice theory has been subject to sustained critique. See e.g. Stephen Sharot, "Beyond Christianity: a critique of the rational choice theory of religion from a Weberian and comparative religions perspective", *Sociology of Religion* (Winter 2002, pp. 1-20); J. M. Bryant, "Cost-benefit accounting and the piety business", *Method & Theory in the Study of Religion* (2000, 12) pp. 520-48; Steve Bruce, "Christianity in Britain, R.I.P.", *Sociology of Religion* (Summer 2001) pp. 191-203.

clericalisation appears to be universal, particularly so but not exclusively amongst revelatory religions.

Various explanations may be offered for this tendency within the overall process of institutionalisation, some to do with the internal dynamics of religious belief and others arising more generally from human behaviour and sociological process (recognising that all these are interdependent).

Richard Schoenherr argues that all religions, and especially monotheistic ones, have two paradoxical centralising tendencies. One, an externalising process, derives from the need for authoritative structures to safeguard the original vision, and leads to the elaboration of priestly hierarchies. The other, an internalising and egalitarian trend, emphasises the individual's personal relationship with the divine so that the mediating role of the structures is questioned.[15] Schoenherr observes that "one centralising tendency cannot exist without the other and each pulls in the opposite direction... Theoretically the movement between externalization and internalization can be viewed as a potentially infinite dialectic with no final synthesis."[16] The cyclical historical process reviewed in this chapter supports that conclusion.

On the other hand, as a sociological process, clericalisation can also be identified as a struggle for power, associated with social conservatism. The Pastoral Epistles and other sub-apostolic writings reveal the early shift from itinerant to local leadership in the household code material which legitimated the role of local male leadership in the household structure.[17]

Robert Michels' "iron law of oligarchy" offers five factors leading to the centralisation of power in organisations – originally proposed concerning political groups but equally applicable to religious ones.[18] These are (1) the felt inadequacy of ordinary members, leading to limited participation and apathy; (2) the experience of leadership enhancing leaders' knowledge, expertise and indispensability; (3) the tendency of leaders to use their power to retain the rewards of office; (4) the tendency of organizations to become co-dependent with their leadership, providing resources for their continued monopoly of power; (5) the way in which tenure of leadership establishes a customary right to office.

Michels' arguments support the theory of "mixed motivation", posited by Thomas O'Dea as the key to the clericalising process, as one of the "five dilemmas of institutionalisation" he discerned in the life of the Church.

---

15 Richard A. Schoenherr, "Power and Authority in Organised Religion: Disaggregating the Phenomenological Core", *Sociological Analysis* 47: S (March 1987) pp. 52-71.

16 Schoenherr, "Power and Authority", p. 60.

17 David Horrell, "Leadership Patterns and the Development of Ideology in Early Christianity", *Sociology of Religion* 58:4 (Winter 1997) pp. 323-41.

18 Robert Michels, *Political Parties* (New York: Colliers, [1911] 1962).

While leadership in the earliest stages is characterised by single-mindedness, the elaboration of offices provides opportunity for other motivations such as desire for prestige or power and the need for security within a professional structure.[19] This bureaucracy comes to impose its agenda, not always identical or even compatible with the founding vision, on its religious community as a whole. This mixed motivation in time characterises the membership as well as the leadership of the body.[20] Mixed motivation is also congruent with the "rational choice" schema, where the accrual of status and authority to those in leadership roles in the church can be seen as a commodity or reward. Stark therefore attributes the falling off of vocations to priesthood and orders in the Catholic Church in the West after Vatican II to the diminished respect and status afforded the clergy with the Council's renewed emphasis on the "priesthood of all believers".[21]

Role theory also offers some light on the way in which clergy come to be seen and to see themselves as a caste distinct from laity. Theodore Sarbin has argued that the roles people play and the narratives they tell serve to construct their sense of identity.[22] Thornton and Nardi describe how "the role is internalised and assimilated so that in a sense the person and the role become inseparable."[23] A Salvation Army officer's saying, "I don't know who I am if I'm not the Corps Officer," provides a striking but not untypical expression of this tendency. The officer role and narrative helps create a caste identity which becomes entrenched.

Andrew Abbott sees clericalism as an example of professionalisation, with particular reference to the "meaning of life" as a professional concern. Professions claim sole possession and control over the training, qualifications and skills required for the exercise of their role – a development observable from within the first centuries of the Church's life. Abbott uses the term "jurisdiction" for a profession's area of activity and says that it makes an exclusive claim.[24] He explains this in terms of a "continuum of instrumentation" – the varying distance between immediate

---

19 Thomas O'Dea, "Five Dilemmas in the Institutionalisation of Religion", *Journal for the Scientific Study of Religion* 1:1 (October 1961) p. 33.

20 Thomas O'Dea, *Sociology and the Study of Religion* (New York: Basic Books, 1970) p. 245.

21 Rodney Stark and Roger Finke, *Acts of Faith*, pp. 169-90.

22 See for example: Theodore Sarbin and Vernon L. Allen, "Role Theory" in Gardner Lindsey and Elliot Aronson (eds), *The Handbook of Social Psychology* 2nd ed. (Reading, Mass.: Addison-Wesley 1968); Theodore Sarbin (ed.), *Narrative Psychology: The Storied Nature of Human Conduct* (London: Praeger 1986).

23 Russell Thornton and Peter N. Nardi, "The Dynamics of Role Acquisition", *American Journal of Sociology* 80 (1975) pp. 870-85.

24 Andrew Abbott, *The System of Professions: An Essay on the Division of Expert Labour* (Chicago: University of Chicago Press, 1988) pp. 35-7.

result and ultimate value – and finds Catholic and Protestant theory at opposite ends of this continuum.

> The Catholic Eucharist is legitimated by revelation; it is grounded in itself. Protestant liturgy, and Protestant ministerial work generally, is by contrast more instrumental: the pastor aims to teach and lead, thereby enabling others to find God... Professions generally attempt to move towards the consummatory legitimation of the Catholic clergies.[25]

A functional role usually seeks to establish a claim to spiritually legitimated status; laicism nearly always gravitates back towards clericalism. The fact that clericalism is the default position of the church, Protestant as well as Catholic, argues that it is another case of a profession defending its jurisdiction in a permanent state of turf war with the laity.

Although the Salvation Army has not, like some conversionist sects, had a strong anti-ministerial ideology, it will be shown that this element has always been present. Some of these explanations for the clerical tendency may therefore resonate with Salvationists and help shed light on the development of officership in the Salvation Army.

In Brueggemann's schema, the alternative, prophetic community of Moses is set against the "royal consciousness" of the Egyptian Empire. The establishment of the Solomonic Empire, within 250 years of the Exodus from Egypt, represented a rejection of the free association of Israelites and a return to the structures of Empire.[26] In the same way, the process of institutionalisation and clericalisation in the church can be seen as a successful reconquest of the new community by the old structures of domination and power. These are in turn subverted in due course by a renewed egalitarianism.

Any human society needs some form of order to avoid falling into either anarchy or tyranny. A society called into being around some founding vision requires some means of maintaining what in the church is described as "apostolicity" – an authenticity derived from faithfulness to that founding vision. The danger with leadership, however, is that rather than being merely a means of maintaining authenticity; it can come to identify itself as central to it, the means becoming the end.

Faced with the reality of this context, the questions to be faced afresh in every generation of the ecclesia, are those posed by Ken Booth in a 1999 paper.

> The first question is:
> How is apostolic leadership to be given structural form in the church?

---

25 Abbott, *System of Professions*, p. 185.
26 Brueggemann, *Prophetic Imagination*, p. 23.

And the second question is:
How can we overcome the tendency to clericalisation in the church?[27]

One answer to the first of those questions occupies the major part of this book. In particular, it shows how the development of the Salvation Army illustrates the process of the development of apostolic leadership, and how it corresponds to the pattern suggested in this introductory section. The Salvation Army, in many respects exemplifying sectarian development, recapitulates the history of the church. It arose in a context of deprivation, was subject to a degree of persecution, and threw up walls against "the world". At the same time, the Booths cultivated secular society and its power brokers, and their Army has accommodated to society to the point that a survey recently conducted amongst American academics by an international think-tank could number it among the world's "ten most enduring institutions".[28] Its officer corps has shared the same ambiguity, both resisting and embracing clericalisation. The polarities present in the ministry of the early church and throughout its subsequent history, such as those between the charismatic and the institutional, the prophetic and the priestly, the functional and the sacerdotal, informal and formal, dispersed and centralised authority, even non-stipendiary and stipendiary, are all present and played out in the pages which follow.

Ken Booth's second question is touched on in the final chapter.

---

27 Ken Booth, "Something about Ordination" (Unpublished paper read at a seminar arranged by the Ministry and Training Division of the Christchurch Diocese, New Zealand, held at Bishop Julius Hall, 31 July, 1999).

28 Survey conducted by consulting firm Booz Allen Hamilton, 2004. http://www.ameinfo.com/56439.html, downloaded 14 December 2005.

Part Two: The Army's First Century

For much of its history few of the Army's leaders, teachers or writers have been interested in ecclesiology and for most of the movement's first hundred years there was little engagement with classical or contemporary ecclesiologies. This has meant that the Army's position on such matters remained largely undefined and ambiguous, which also adds to the interest and significance of the generally clericalising tendency found in its history.

This second Part gives an account of the Salvation Army's origins and development, with particular attention to the way in which its officers assumed clergy-like functions and status. The founders resisted these changes – while at the same time they facilitated and endorsed them.

At the end of this Part, Chapter Nine, "Transitions", follows the effects of "routinisation" during which the Army became less sect-like and more like a denomination, consolidating the clerical status of officers.

Chapter Four

Booth Led Boldly

Booth led boldly with his big bass drum.
(Are you washed in the Blood of the Lamb?)
The saints smiled gravely, and they said, 'He's come!'
(Are you washed in the Blood of the Lamb?)

Vachel Lindsay,
General William Booth
Enters into Heaven.

Of Sects and Sectarians

Booth did lead boldly, as Vachel Lindsay's poem declaims. Without him, Rider Haggard wrote in 1910, "the Salvation Army would not exist today, for it sprang from his brain like Minerva from the head of Jove, and has been driven to success by his single, forceful will."[1] At the same time, like Abraham, the bold leader was not always sure where he was going, and like Columbus, sometimes not sure where he had arrived when he got there. In a letter to *The Revival* dated the 17 August 1865, reporting on his East End activities, Booth informed readers that, "We have no very definite plans. We shall be guided by the Holy Spirit..."

So, whence were they guided? What did they become? A question at the heart of this study is whether the Salvation Army is, or was intended to be, a Church in the denominational sense. Traditionally the leadership of the church has been in the hands of an ordained clerical class. However, if the Army was not to be a church, its leaders could hardly be clergy. Such categories were not so much even repudiated by most early Salvationists – rather, unsuspected or ignored as irrelevant.

It was not the Booths' intention that the Salvation Army should become a church. In fact, Booth said, "From the first, I was strongly opposed to forming any separate organisation..."[2] Once he had, however unwillingly, an organisation on his hands, Booth still denied that it was a church or sect. "We are not and will not be made a Church. There are plenty for anyone

---

1 H. Rider Haggard, *Regeneration* (London: Longmans Green, 1910) p. 212.
2 Introduction to George Scott Railton's *Twenty-one Years Salvation Army* (London: SA, 1886) p. 22.

who wishes to join them, to vote and to rest."[3] Thus he dismissed churches as characterised by democracy and a passive laity, neither of which he intended would have a place in his Army.

In an article in the *Contemporary Review* in August 1882, Booth expressed his hope that the Army would never grow into a sect. He felt that Wesley had been wrong to permit Methodism to become another denomination. This was unfair to Wesley, who unlike Booth had tried to prevent any such thing. Booth's armour-bearer, George Scott Railton, inveighed against sectarianism in *Heathen England*.

> Shall we ever sink into a sectarian spirit of selfish care about our own, and cease to spend all our strength for the good of others?" Answering the hypothetical objection, "But this is making a new denomination – a new sect," he responded, "Well, and supposing that it is. Is there any harm in doing so? Is there not a need for just such a 'sect' in many cities?... But we deny that we are in any proper sense a sect... We are a corps of volunteers for Christ, organised as perfectly as we have been able to accomplish, seeking no Church status, avoiding as we would the plague every denominational rut, in order perpetually to reach more and more of those who lie outside every Church boundary.[4]

When interviewed by Sir Henry Lunn in 1895 on the Salvation Army position on the sacraments, Booth claimed, perhaps a little disingenuously, that "we came into this position originally by determining not to be a church. We did not wish to undertake the administration of the sacraments and thereby bring ourselves into collision with existing churches."[5] This glossed over the fact that the Christian Mission, and the Salvation Army until 1883, had in fact practised the sacraments. Begbie also quotes Randall Davidson, later Archbishop of Canterbury, as saying of Booth (*a propos* negotiations between the Salvation Army and the Anglican Church in the early 1880s), "He certainly gave me to understand, and very emphatically, that he did not seek to establish a new sect."[6]

By "sect", Booth perhaps meant what we would describe as a denomination – the sociologists had not yet taken responsibility for these terms. However, his use of the word suggests a pejorative sense, implying more than the mere nonconformity that was its conventional application. The fractured history of Methodism in the near century following Wesley's death and the arguments of the sectaries offended the Booths, not primarily

---

3 *Orders and Regulations for The Salvation Army* (London: SA, 1878) p. 4.

4 George Scott Railton, *Heathen England* (London: S.W. Partridge, 2nd edn, 1878) pp. 143-4.

5 Harold Begbie, *Life of William Booth, Founder of The Salvation Army* (London: Macmillan, 1920) I, pp. 468-9.

6 Begbie, *Booth*, II, p. 29.

because of the loss of unity and charity but because they meant distraction from the work of saving the lost. "The chief sorrow to me in connection with the sects of the past, had ever been their divisions on the subject of practical Godliness and immediate results… I constantly put from me the thought of attempting the formation of such a people."[7]

That the Army was not a church was the official position throughout the early years and well beyond. In a catechism-like pamphlet explaining the Army in the United States, one question asked, "Will not this movement result in the making of a new sect?" The answer: "Not in the sense in which a new sect is usually understood. It is not a Church, after the fashion of Churches, but an Army, that is aimed at – this is a force as real, as self-sacrificing, and as much under control for soul-saving purposes as the ordinary military armies are for slaughter and destruction. There is at present nothing after this model in existence; and if it be desirable and Scriptural, it does not matter much what it is called."[8] Maud Booth wrote, "There are sects and denominations enough. This is an Army, a band of aggressive men and women, whose work of saving and reclaiming the world must be done on entirely new lines…"[9]

The recollections of the Rev. F.S. Webster suggest that some recruits may still have had the impression at a comparatively late date that the Salvation Army was intended to be only a kind of para-church organisation. Webster describes how in about 1877 or 1878, Wilson Carlile showed him his "soldier's certificate", "explaining that it was an Army and not a Church, that people could be banded together for the purposes of evangelization and soul-winning, as they were in connection with the Moody and Sankey missions, and yet remain, for the purposes of worship and edification, in connection with their own churches." Carlile's understanding of the situation would seem to have been anachronistic for as late as 1878 but it is possible that he had received this impression from Booth's claims that the Army was not a "church". Webster also expressed his regret that, "Unfortunately – and, I think, most unwisely – General Booth deemed it necessary to make his Army into an independent Church."[10] Webster and Carlile went on to found the Church Army.

Another even later witness to the Army's ambiguous ecclesiastical status was Brigadier Susan Swift, notable early American officer and close associate of the Booth family. Swift resigned in 1897 to become a Dominican nun as Sister Teresa M. Imelda. Writing in that year about her

---

7 Railton, *Heathen England*, p. 22.

8 Frank Smith, *All About the Salvation Army* (New York: SA, 1885) p. 20.

9 Maud B. Booth, *Beneath Two Flags* (New York: Funk and Wagnalls, 1889) p. 271.

10 F.S. Webster in *The Life of General Booth*, anon. editor (London: Nelson, no date) pp. 153-4, 168.

second conversion, Swift looked back to her introduction to the Army in Glasgow in 1884. "The Army taught in those days that it was 'not a church but a mission' and placed no obstacle in the way of my receiving the 'sacraments' of my own or any other denomination."[11] An editorial in *The Field Officer* for July 1901 (p. 282) stated that "A Corps is neither a Church nor a Mission" – a negative version of having it both ways. As late as the 1950s, General Albert Orsborn still denied emphatically that the Salvation Army was a "church", preferring to describe it as "a permanent mission to the unconverted".[12]

In some European countries, where membership of the State Church was a corollary of citizenship, the fiction that the Army was not a church was also maintained. With his Swedish background, Colonel Karl Larsson, when Commander in Russia during the First World War, allowed Salvationists to remain in communion with the Orthodox Church.[13] Swiss Salvationist Victor Kunz, writing in 1947, stated that "the S.A. itself does not desire to be a church" and described himself as "a local officer of the Salvation Army and a convinced member of the Evangelical Swiss Church. All members of The Salvation Army, including Officers, without exception pay the Church tax..."[14]

One of the ironies of Booth's history is that although he was determined that the Army would never become a sect, it did of course become just that. Cardinal Manning, noting Booth's protests on this point and giving him credit for his intention, commented that the Army did not have much choice – "Nevertheless we have a conviction that the Salvation Army will either become a sect or it will melt away. This world is not the abode of disembodied spirits."[15] As Ronald Knox remarks of Zinzendorf, "it is an old dream of the enthusiast that he can start a new religion without starting a new denomination."[16] William Swatos notes of Methodism that it "is best understood as an order in origin, working firmly within the Church of England. Only after explicit schism is it properly treated as a sect or denomination. Likewise, the Salvation Army became sectarian, while the Episcopal Church's Church Army remained an order."[17] General John

11 Susan Swift, *The Conversion of Susan Swift* (1897) p. 5. Quoted by Norman Murdoch in *Soldiers of the Cross* (Alexandria Va.: Crest Books, 2006).

12 *The Officer* (March-April 1954) p. 74.

13 Information courtesy of T. G. Aitken.

14 Victor Kunz, "The Salvation Army – Its Origin, Spirit, Work" (Unpublished paper, 1947).

15 Cardinal Manning in *The Contemporary Review*, quoted by Begbie, *Booth*, II, p. 31-32.

16 Ronald Knox, *Enthusiasm* (Oxford: Oxford University Press, 1950) p. 403.

17 W.H. Swatos, "Church-Sect and Cult: Bringing Mysticism Back In", *Sociological Analysis* 42:1 (1981) p. 21.

Gowans recalls the Methodist Dr Gordon Rupp greeting Salvationist delegates at a British Council of Churches conference in the 1960s with, "You are our Franciscans. We Methodists began as a mission. We have become a Church. May the Army always remain a mission."[18]

In fact the Army's founders were willing to think in terms of denomination when it suited their practical needs. Even in 1870 the Christian Mission had a rule that "Persons belonging to *other Churches* [my italics] seeking membership with us shall be admitted on presentation of their note of transfer if such can be obtained,"[19] which implies that the Mission already saw itself in a sectarian light. The Salvation Army soon began to claim denominational status when legal considerations suggested advantages. For example, the Salvation Army in Australia, presumably with the founder's blessing, claimed legal status as a church as early as 1884.[20] Gordon Moyles notes that from 1892 Canadian Salvation Army officers could officiate at marriages, prior to which year the vows were administered by a clergyman of another denomination.[21]

Only with the twenty-first century, however, have Salvationist leaders explicitly and officially laid claim to denominational status. While the organisation's mission statement has until recently invariably described it as "an evangelical part of the universal Christian Church", there is now a tendency for it to be described as "a world wide evangelical Christian church". General John Larsson, addressing a 2001 International Theology and Ethics Symposium in Winnipeg, Canada, stated that "A key question for us is how we make the transition from a movement to a church in such a way that we do not lose the original dynamic that brought the Army into being. Or if we have lost something of that dynamic, how do we regain it?"[22] Unfortunately "loss of original dynamic" may describe an essential difference between "movement" and "church". Finke and Stark comment, "When successful sects are transformed into churches, that is, when their tension with the surrounding culture is greatly reduced, they soon cease to grow and eventually decline."[23]

---

18 Quoted by Denis Hunter, *While the Light Lingers* (privately published 2005) p. 36.

19 Minutes of the Christian Mission Conference, 1870, V:17.

20 Thomas Hubbard, *Officer* (November 1978) pp. 516-7. Hubbard cites, "*Regina* v Darling (1884) 5 NSWR 405. Martin, CJ, found in favour of the Army's position, Fawcett and Innes, JJ, concurring."

21 R. Gordon Moyles, *Blood and Fire in Canada: The History of the Salvation Army in the Dominion 1882-1976* (Toronto: Peter Martin Associates, 1977) p. 289.

22 Quoted in background papers to the 2006 International Theology and Ethics Symposium, Johannesburg.

23 Roger Finke and Rodney Stark, *The Churching of America 1776-1990* (New Brunswick NJ: Rutgers University Press, 1992) p. 148.

Whatever its ambiguity about terminology, the Army had by this time long since become a church, or denomination, in the sense that its local congregations bore a resemblance to those of other non-conformist denominations, and its members did come to think of their leaders as the equivalent of clergy. The remainder of this chapter traces why and how this began to happen.

The influences that chiefly shaped the Booths' religious outlook, particularly their view of the roles of clergy and laity, were firstly Wesleyan and secondly "revivalist".

Wesleyan Genes

Converted in the Methodist church at the age of 15, Booth claimed in a speech on his 60th birthday that he "literally worshipped Methodism. To me there was one God and John Wesley was his prophet."[24] Wesley's example inspired Booth's evangelical zeal. Like Wesley, Booth took to the fields and the streets (and circuses, skating rinks and theatres) when the churches were closed to him. Like Wesley's, Booth's followers tended to be of the lower classes and they suffered similar persecution from mobs and vested interests. Wesley's Arminian faith and his teaching on "Christian perfection" or "holiness" were Booth's creed as well. The doctrines and conference polity of the Christian Mission were entirely Methodist.[25] The Salvation Army retained the doctrines but not the Conference.

Methodism carried forward into its church phase the ecclesiological ambiguities of its para-church ethos. Colonel Earl Robinson notes that "Our lack of precision in responding (to the question of to what extent is The Salvation Army an ecclesia) may be considered to be part of our Wesleyan heritage." He quotes David Smith's suggestion in *A Contemporary Wesleyan Theology* that Wesley did not think of his followers as being incorporated into a separate church, but rather forming a group of societies within the Anglican church, an *ecclesiola in ecclesia*.[26] Robinson writes that the "same ambiguity existed in the early days of The Salvation Army, and to some extent exists still."[27]

---

24 St. John Ervine, *God's Soldier, General William Booth* (London: Heinemann, 1936) II, p. 735.

25 John R. Rhemick, *A New People of God: A Study in Salvationism* (Des Plaines, Ill: SA, 1993). See also Roger Green's *The Life and Ministry of William Booth* (Nashville: Abingdon, 2005) which I did not see before this book was completed.

26 "A little church within a church", a term coined for small home groups by the Lutheran Pietist Philip Spener in his *Pia Desiderata* of 1675.

27 Earl Robinson, "The Salvation Army – *Ecclesia?*", *Word and Deed*, 2:1 (November 1999).

As the quintessential pragmatist, Booth inherited Methodism's ambiguities. The "off again, on again" Methodist approach to ordination suggests that he may not have derived from Methodism any really strong convictions on the subject. His account of his own ordination, in a letter, was fairly perfunctory. "The service was an interesting one," he noted. He was particular, however, to ensure that, faced by a bevy of ex-Presidents of Conference about to lay hands upon him, he was nearest "some of those in whose piety and devotion he thoroughly believed", to "reap whatever advantage might accrue from their faith and prayers, while there were others whom he studiously avoided..."[28] Whatever significance the service held for Booth, he clearly believed that the character of the ordainer affected the validity of the sacrament.

Whatever uncertainties Booth entertained on the ordination of clergy, he shared Wesley's conviction that the laity were called to an active role in ministry. They were not merely pew fodder or spectators at religious ceremonies. The great strength of Methodism lay in the "classes" which were lay-led, and in the training and appointment of lay preachers. The Christian Mission, and in its turn the Salvation Army, also pressed every available man (and woman) into service.

William Booth wrote that one of the "principles with which I believe my heart was inspired in the earliest days of my spiritual life", was "our employment of the people – out of which has grown our varied classes of officers, opportunities for testimony, and the open door and continued encouragement to every man, and every woman, and every child, to use and exercise whatever gifts they may have received from God for assisting Him in subduing and winning this rebellious world to Himself."[29] Catherine Booth's vigorous claim was, "Yes, thank God, we are teaching the Churches that others besides clergymen, ministers, deacons and elders can be used for the salvation of men. The multitudes have too long been left to these. As a clergyman said to me the other day, 'There are 35,000 souls in my parish, what can one do?' What indeed! Set the carpenters and the washerwomen on to them, saved and filled with the Spirit!"[30]

The Booths, then, wholeheartedly adopted the Wesleyan model of lay ministry. That was however only half the story. Wesley, for all his fostering of lay ministry, was less willing to share the government of the church with the laity. Booth, like Wesley, was an autocrat by temperament and conviction. Ervine puts the similarity strongly: "When Wesley, in his old age, surveyed his society and appraised his preachers, he realized that the

---

28 Frederick Booth-Tucker, *The Life of Mrs Booth* (London: SA, 1892) I, pp. 221-2.

29 Railton, *Heathen England*, p. 23.

30 Catherine Booth, *The Salvation Army in Relation to Church & State* (London: SA, 1889) p. 75.

whole organization was his, as the whole Salvation Army, more than a century after Wesley's death, was to be William Booth's: a foundation largely, if not entirely, the personal possession of its founder."[31]

As we have seen, continuing power struggles between Methodist clergy and laity led to further schisms. William and Catherine had some brief involvement with the Methodist Reform Movement. In that case, the pendulum had swung too far towards anti-clericalism for the Booths' taste, as Catherine explained in a letter. "The discipline of the Reform Society was very unsatisfactory to us both, in denying the minister his proper authority they went over to regard him as nothing, denying him every shadow of authority, and only allowing him to preside at their meetings when elected for the purpose, and speaking of him in public and in private as their 'hired' preacher..."[32] Ervine summed up Booth's attitude on the question of authority: "... his instincts were conservative, but he also had a natural hatred of committees and interfering laymen and a deep belief in the authority of the minister."[33] The shadow of the coming Army may be discerned in which the foot soldiers would certainly share the fighting but the officers would issue the orders.

In brief, then, the Wesleyan influence on the Booths can be seen in their emulation of Wesley himself and in parallels between the situation, ethos and doctrines of Methodism and Salvationism. As far as the argument of this work is concerned, it can also be traced in a degree of ambiguity about the nature or importance of ordination, in their conviction of the importance of lay-participation, and paradoxically, in their equally strong conviction of the value of authoritarian rule.

American Nurture

The other main influence on the Booths was the American Revivalist movement, itself the child of Methodism. This tended to be non-sectarian (what we would today call non-denominational) and lay led and controlled. One of the best known nineteenth century evangelists, Dwight L. Moody, chose not to be ordained, even although he had in the course of his ministry, established and led more than one church congregation.[34] The influence of Charles Finney, James Caughey and Phoebe Palmer in particular, the latter two themselves children of Wesleyanism, helped shape the Booths' style of

---

31 Ervine, *God's Soldier*, I, p. 178.

32 Begbie, *Booth*, I, p. 138.

33 Ervine, *God's Soldier*, I, p. 80.

34 J.C. Pollock, *Moody Without Sankey* (London, Hodder & Stoughton, 1963) pp. 58-9

evangelism. All three visited Britain and Finney's books in due course became textbooks for Salvation Army officer-trainees.

Caughey's British campaign from 1841 to 1846, organised largely without reference to the official structures of the church, led to a vigorous controversy within Methodism about revivalism and lay authority. As a fledgling teenage preacher, Booth was impressed by Caughey's "straightforward conversational way of putting the truth, and the common-sense method of pushing people up to decision, and the corresponding results that followed".[35] Caughey later gave the Booths counsel on a visit in 1858 when they stood at a crossroads in their career – and also baptised their son Ballington. It is interesting that Caughey, while sympathising with Booth's frustration at the reluctance of the New Connexion to give him liberty to work as an itinerant evangelist under their aegis, nevertheless urged caution. William should wait until he was ordained before leaving so as to resign "from a position of strength" as a fully accredited and recognised minister.[36] There were mixed messages there about the clerical-lay relationship and the significance of ordination. Phoebe Palmer and her husband, both lay, evangelised together, but Mrs Palmer was the preacher and Dr Palmer's was a support role. Catherine Booth took up cudgels in 1859 in defence of Phoebe Palmer's right, as a woman, to preach. This led towards Catherine's own destiny as an advocate and exemplar of female ministry and so to the Salvation Army's precept of the equality of the sexes in ministry.

The non-sectarian character of the revivalists' missions was important for the Booths. It must have seemed to them that most really effective evangelical work was happening outside the official church structures, while churches tended to be self-absorbed and complacent. Certainly the official bodies strongly rejected the revivalist movement of the late 1850s, though some Anglican and non-conformist clergy supported it. Describing their freelance work in the early 1860s, when the various Methodist Conferences had closed chapels against them on the ground that evangelistic movements were "unfavourable to church order", Booth recalled that, "undenominational work was just then coming into fashion. The theory was, save the people outside the churches and then send them to the churches to be trained and cared for."[37]

The "Hallelujah Band", a kind of prototype Salvation Army exercise in the Midlands, was a short-lived English lay-movement in 1862-1863. Through Booth's influence perhaps it could also be described as a child of American revivalism. Converts, especially those with colourful reputation as formerly notorious sinners or people of note amongst the working class –

35 Railton, *Twenty-one Years*, p. 8.

36 Roy Hattersley, *Blood & Fire* (London: Little, Brown, 1999) pp. 95-6.

37 William Booth, in Railton, *Twenty-one Years*, p. 15.

pugilists, former poachers and jailbirds who could draw a crowd to a salvation "freak show" – were set up as the preachers and open-air rallies were held. They attracted thousands of people. "Many of the most notorious characters in the district were converted."[38] Booth's presidential address to the 1877 Christian Mission Conference claimed that "with the origin of this movement I had something to do." He described how he had got together a "collection of people" for a Camp Meeting at Walsall. "Directly after this much the same set of brothers held meetings all through the Black Country… I never had the opportunity of taking part in it…"[39] Their Garibaldi-like red shirts may have inspired the Salvationist red guernsey.

At any rate the Hallelujah Band's example not only confirmed Booth's views on the mobilisation of the laity. Their longer-term fate also confirmed his predilection for authority. "In course of time," he noted, "the leaders disagreed. Divisions crept in. There being no acknowledged authority, all did pretty much what was right in their own eyes. The work gradually died out, or, at best, left only the monument of a few half-and-half Methodist societies behind."[40]

From the American revivalists, then, we see that Booth not only learned about evangelical methods and concluded that there was more freedom in their use outside the control of denominational structures, but also had confirmed his convictions both about the importance of lay-participation and about the need for strong government.

We conclude from our sampling of these influences and experiences that ecclesiastical tradition and authority were not of great significance to the Booths. They took what they inherited, used what worked for them and discarded what did not. The key was the engagement of the laity. This, along with Booth's own disinclination to accept anyone else's authority, led them to work outside the existing denominational framework, and that led to their having to create an alternative framework, simply in order to organise what was happening and to secure its effectiveness and survival. We now come to trace the steps by which that was done.

Becoming a Sect

The period from 1865, when Booth began working in the East End of London, to 1878 when the Christian Mission became known as the Salvation Army, could be seen to encompass the transition from non-sectarian work to sect; from a parachurch agency to a denominational church.

38 Railton, *Twenty-one Years*, pp. 16-17.
39 *Christian Mission Magazine*, July 1877, p. 182.
40 Railton, *Twenty-one Years*, p. 16.

In a modern parachurch agency, working alongside the churches, the workers conventionally retain their membership of their original community of faith. Where the agency recruits individuals, rather than working with existing groups, and its main concern involves the holding of religious missions and services, the agency itself tends to become in practice a new and autonomous community of faith for its workers and their converts. It is not merely the vehicle for their work; it becomes the source of their own support and training, the locus of their fellowship and absorbing interest. James Packer suggests that "...these agencies of God's kingdom draw interest, prayer, enthusiasm, and money away from the wider-ranging, slower-moving, less glamorous realities of congregational life, so that the parachurch body comes to have pride of place in supporters' affections and in effect to be their church."[41] Forty-five years ago Salvation Army Commissioner A.J. Gilliard less charitably and more pungently described Youth for Christ as "religious parasites".

This certainly happened with Methodism. This is also what happened with Booth's mission, whatever Booth's intention at first.

> My first idea was simply to get people saved, and send them to the churches. This proved at the outset impracticable. 1st. They would not go when sent. 2nd. They were not wanted. And 3rd. We wanted some of them at least ourselves, to help us in the business of saving others. We were thus driven to providing for the converts ourselves.[42]

Such provision marked the birth of a new faith community, although in his 1868 Report of the East London Christian Mission Booth informed its readers that "this is an unsectarian mission. Our creed is the Bible, our work is to publish the gospel, and we welcome as co-workers all who hold the Word of God as the standard of faith and practice, and whose hearts are in sympathy with revival work."

History is usually a seamless garment and the transition from one stage to another with such an organisation is difficult to pin down. The Salvation Army has always regarded 1865 as its founding date – Railton published *Twenty-One Years Salvation Army* in 1886, even although that name was unheard of before 1877. However the point at which the Mission became the de facto community of faith for its adherents probably came earlier rather than later, probably 1867, despite Booth's "unsectarian" claim of the following year.

---

41 J.I. Packer, "A Stunted Ecclesiology? The Theory and Practice of Evangelical Churchliness", *Touchstone* (December 2003) Downloaded 17 February 2004 (www.latimer.org.nz/morecomment.asp?CoID=13).

42 William Booth, in Railton, *Twenty-one Years*, p. 22.

The steps on the way are well documented by Sandall's official history. The Home Mission revival movement of the late 1850s spawned many small agencies and missions. Reginald Radcliffe formed the East London Special Services Committee in 1861 to try to co-ordinate their activities in London. Booth talked with representatives of this group in 1861 but it was not until 1865, after the Booths had moved to London for the sake of Catherine's speaking engagements that William became actively involved. His first regular engagement with the Committee began in July 1865, with meetings held in a tent on a disused Quaker burial ground.

Pressed to continue his successful leadership of the "tent group", Booth informed the *Revival* (in the same number in which he denied having any definite plans), that, "In order to carry on this work we propose to establish a Christian Revival Association in which we think a hundred persons will enrol themselves at once. We shall also require some central building in which to hold our more private meetings, and in which to preach the gospel when not engaged in special work elsewhere." Nothing is plain sailing but after a year, there were 60 members.[43]

Sandall describes 1867 as "the turning point" as far as establishment of a distinct body is concerned. In that year the East London Christian Mission

- was named,
- acquired its first headquarters,
- hired a theatre for Sunday meetings and increased its number of "preaching stations" to six in the course of the year,
- began to hire workers (nine by the end of the year),
- established a system for processing converts (1st ensure a definite decision, 2nd give them instruction, 3rd train them and set them to work),
- printed its first document (combined Articles of Faith and Bond of Agreement, direct forbear of the "Soldier's Covenant" signed by Salvationists today),
- embarked on social relief for the hungry poor,
- organised its funds, issued its first financial statement and received a grant from the Evangelisation Society.

Sandall points to another significant development, a substantial change in membership. People left for various reasons, some because they didn't like the way things were going or the Booths' methods, and others because once the new mission was established they returned to their home churches which had loaned them. Booth set about building those who remained, and their

43 Robert Sandall, *The History of The Salvation Army* (London: Nelson, 1947) I, pp. 42, 46-7.

converts, into a fighting force.[44] The East London Christian Mission, like Methodism before it, was on its way to becoming a sect.

Clergy in the Making

For the purposes of our study, out of the innovations of 1867, the hiring of staff marks the beginnings of the development of a full-time, paid ministry. The first paid helper, Mrs Eliza Collingridge, herself a convert, was described as a "Biblewoman". She later became Superintendent of the Shoreditch circuit when expansion required such organisation and was therefore the first woman to hold office in the Christian Mission.

By 1868 *The Revival* recorded that "Twenty persons are wholly employed, assisted by a large band of devoted helpers." In the *East London Evangelist* of February that year, William Booth stated "not a single official salary is paid," evidently meaning "office staff" as distinct from the Mission field force. "One hundred and twenty services outdoors and in are held weekly, at which the gospel is preached on an average to 14,000 people." Most of the "twenty persons" were presumably evangelists, though some were doubtless involved in relief work and one appears to have been responsible for a sewing class. At first the various preaching posts or "stations" (Salvation Army officers are still described as "stationed" at their appointments today) were controlled centrally and evangelists rostered. James Dowdle was the first to be appointed to the charge of a particular centre, though in a voluntary capacity; he became a full-time, employed evangelist in 1873. Fixed (though still very brief) appointments soon replaced itinerancy; by 1874 there were eight district superintendents.

After some stagnation the Mission was entering a period of rapid expansion and thereafter was always "growing out of its clothes", in Bramwell Booth's phrase.[45] In 1874 there were 10 "Districts".[46] The 1875 Report lists 23 stations and their District Superintendents.[47] The first issue of *The Salvationist* gives 30 stations and 36 evangelists for 1877[48] and 81 stations and 127 evangelists for 1878. By the beginning of 1883 there were 442 Corps and 1067 officers operating in 13 countries. Three years later, there were 1,749 Corps and 4,192 officers.[49]

---

44 Sandall, *History*, I, pp. 46-7.

45 Catherine Bramwell Booth, *Bramwell Booth* (London: Rich & Cowen, 1932) p. 90.

46 *Christian Mission Magazine* (August 1874) p. 226.

47 *Christian Mission Magazine* (July 1875) p. 191.

48 *Salvationist* (January 1879) p. 4.

49 Sandall, *History*, I, pp.170, 2, p. 338.

With such growth the Mission inevitably entered also a period of reorganisation and constitution-making. The first Christian Mission Constitution, 1870, is described as a "self-denying ordinance" by Sandall – Booth made Conference the final authority in the Mission's affairs. Modelled on that of the Methodist New Connexion, it was largely composed of the evangelists in charge of districts and, according to Sandall, "two elected lay delegates from each district".[50] The 1876 Minutes do not use the word "lay" in connection with delegates, but say "That each district having a membership of 100 or upwards on 7th November next send their evangelist with one delegate if thought desirable to a meeting of the Conference Committee."[51] The word "lay" may be Sandall's anachronism, reading back a later clerical-lay distinction between officers and soldiers, or perhaps he intended it simply in the sense of not being professionally engaged. After all, the evangelists were also "lay" in the sense of not ever having been ordained. Never the less they were on the way to becoming the de facto clergy of a de facto church. A major break from Methodist tradition was that women were admitted to full participation – in government as well as in ministry. Wesley had appointed women as local preachers, though the practice declined amongst the Wesleyans after his death and Conference prohibited it in 1803.

Conference rule proved too inhibiting for Booth, and for his band of enthusiasts, a delegation of whom asked him to assume more direct control. A deed-poll enrolled in Chancery in 1875 provided that the Mission should be "under the oversight direction and control of some one person", giving Booth a veto over any proceedings of Conference, the power of appointment, office for the term of his natural life and also the power to nominate his successor. He was also sole trustee for financial purposes. Endless talkfest and the unreality of trying to organise a rapidly expanding organisation by annual decision-making and government by committees were still seen as inhibiting progress. A meeting of "Conference Committee" in January 1877 abolished Conference rule, this being ratified by the last Conference, styled a "Council of War", in July. Thus by something like a palace *coup d'état*, Booth resumed full control of the Mission. A new deed poll in 1880 gave legal sanction to these arrangements, along with the new style of "Salvation Army".

Wilson's comment on the tendency of sects to clericalise is apt here:

> The emergence of a paid ministry, and then of a central council which effectively ceases to maintain lay control, just as it ceases to permit local control, is a danger which all persisting sects have to face.[52]

50 Sandall, *History*, I, pp. 178-9.
51 *Christian Mission Magazine* (July 1876) p. 171.
52 Wilson, *Religion in Secular Society*, p. 209.

Not surprisingly, Booth was popularly supposed to be claiming greater powers than the Pope, an accusation that dogged him all his life despite denials, such as Catherine's in an address on "The Probable Future of The Salvation Army" in 1883.[53] Booth himself had no illusions on this score. Announcing his position on the sacraments, he commented that any order he might give for the general administration of the sacraments would probably be ignored – hardly consistent with the absolute obedience to his orders generally thought to be exacted.[54] Of course, this was an order Booth may not in any case have wished to give. There is an endearing vignette from the drawing up of the 1880 deed poll. The lawyer, Cozens-Hardy, later Master of the Rolls, protested, "Mr Booth, you want me to make you into a Pope, and I do not think it can be done!" To which Booth retorted, "Well, Mr Cozens-Hardy, I am sure that you will get as near to it as you suitably can!"[55] Not that he suffered delusions of grandeur; he put the military title after his name because he felt that "General William Booth" looked pretentious.[56]

Like Wesley's Lay Preachers, Booth's Evangelists were forbidden to use the title "Reverend".[57] Quite apart from the missioners' lay status in conventional church terms, this was part of the whole avoidance of conventional religiosity, which would be an obstacle to any effective approach to the unchurched masses. Ironically, Booth himself retained the clerical usage long after it was superseded by his quasi-military title. Publications as late as the 1910 *Year Book* bore his name as "Rev. W. Booth, General".

Between 1868 and 1878, then, the process took place whereby an independent mission staffed by volunteers from a variety of church backgrounds evolved into a highly centralised, sect-like organisation, a people with a distinct and common identity, and its own full-time, employed leaders, analogous to clergy.

---

53 Catherine Booth, *Church and State*, p. 66.

54 *WC* (17 January 1883) p. 4, col. 3.

55 W. Bramwell Booth, *Echoes and Memories* (London: Hodder and Stoughton, [1925] 2nd edn 1977) p. 184.

56 W. Bramwell Booth, *Echoes*, pp. 60-1.

57 Christian Mission Conference Minutes (1870).

Chapter Five

Clerical Roles

> The Commanding Officer, no matter what his or her rank, not only directs the movement of the Corps and carries out a more or less widespread plan of evangelistic campaign, but he must raise the money, spend it on certain approved lines, care for the sick both in body and soul, help the poor, push the sale of our literature, look after our property, and generally work like a slave of Jesus Christ for the moral, social and spiritual well-being of the people among whom he is appointed to live.
>
> Bramwell Booth[1]

The clerical class in the church has tended to be associated with specific functions – the administration of the sacraments, pastoring of the flock, the preaching and teaching of the Word and the government of the church. What can we say then about the roles of the Missioners, the Evangelists, later Officers, under these headings?

Administration of the Sacraments

The monopoly of this function became the distinctive mark of the emergence of priesthood in Christianity. The Christian Mission and, until 1883, the Salvation Army, practised infant baptism and celebrated the Lord's Supper, and there are indications that officials of the mission led these rites. The discontinuance of the practice could also have implications for the "clerical" role of officers, and requires some explanation at this point.

The earliest reference to sacramental practices in the Mission is in a printed report of the East London Christian Mission (c. Sept/Oct 1867). A list of meetings held at the Whitechapel Mission Hall, 188 Whitechapel Road included, "Sunday 3pm. Breaking of bread, or experience meeting, and service in the open air." Perhaps it is significant that this was the year in which, as we have seen by Sandall's account, the Mission developed many indications of an independent existence. At the same time there was a significant change in membership, in which it is suggested that many who had supported the Mission as a parachurch agency returned to their own

1 W. Bramwell Booth, *Servants of All* (London: SA, 1899) p. 80.

denominations. Perhaps those who remained therefore held "breaking of bread" together as part of their consciousness of belonging to a new entity.

Bramwell Booth's memoirs claim that when he "came on the scene as a responsible official of the Mission, in 1874, the Lord's Supper was administered monthly at all our stations to all members of the Mission and to such other Christian friends as were known to be in good standing and desired to join us."[1] And in fact Rule 39 of the Christian Mission in 1870 said that the Lord's Supper was to be observed once a month in each station unless two thirds of members desired it more often. On the other hand we have a reported explanation by William Booth to an Anglican clergyman "that some of his people on their own responsibility had had a very simple 'breaking of bread' together but that this was no part of the 'Army' – as an evangelistic agency."[2] The 1878 *Orders and Regulations* refer to the sacraments only in passing, in connection with the "Formation of Corps", a subsection of "How to Capture a Town", which suggests that their occurrence was taken for granted but not considered of central importance. "The Sacrament should be administered during the latter part of this meeting, and if it can be prolonged to midnight or an unusually late hour, it will make all the deeper impression upon all."[3]

The 1881 *Doctrines and Disciplines* catechism included a brief section on Baptism, indicating that by "adult, or Believers baptism", "the person baptised declares that he wishes it to be known that he is converted." However, it is "DECIDEDLY NOT... a duty that must be performed... The Army considers only one baptism essential to salvation, and that is, THE BAPTISM OF THE HOLY GHOST." Likewise in response to the question, "What is the teaching of the Army on the subject of the Lord's Supper?" (all within the section on Baptism) the book says that "When such an ordinance is helpful to the faith of our Soldiers, we recommend its adoption." It is "certainly not... essential to membership of the Army, or to Salvation."[4] Such a position naturally made the abandonment of the practices much easier in due course.

Reports of observances appear in the Mission's papers. At the conclusion of the "War Congress" of August 1878, "The usual unintoxicating wine having not been prepared for the sacrament, we managed uncommonly well with water... After the sacrament only a quarter of an hour remained for the love-feast, if we were to conclude, as intended, at six..."[5] *The Salvationist* reports an officers-only celebration when "at the house of Captain

---

1 W. Bramwell Booth, *Echoes*, p. 201.

2 Begbie, *Booth*, II, p. 26.

3 *Orders and Regulations for the Salvation Army* (London: SA, 1878) p. 72.

4 William Booth, *The Doctrines and Disciplines of The Salvation Army* (London: SA, 1881) Section 26.

5 *Christian Mission Magazine* (September 1878) p. 252.

Broadbent... we took the sacrament together" after an all-night meeting in the hall ended at 5.00am.[6] Later, advertisements appeared in the *War Cry* for special meetings: "At Headquarters on the morning of Good Friday, at nine o'clock, there will be a workers' breakfast; and, at ten, a consecration and sacrament service. Miss Booth will speak."[7] A similar service was advertised in the *War Cry* for Easter 1881.

War Cry reports from various other parts of the world confirm the practice. An 1886 Wanganui, New Zealand, report on Christmas Day activities included, "11a.m., Sacrament service, when 50 or 60 partook of the emblems of the Saviour's dying love. It was a heart-searching time."[8] This was nearly four years after the official cessation of such observances. Contemporary Australian editions of the *War Cry* carry similar reports. Movement of people between denominations would have been a factor. Primitive Methodists, relocating to an Australian outback town with no Methodist congregation but a Salvation Army Corps in evidence, could have brought their sacramental practice with them without any sense of incongruity.

Bramwell Booth recalled that one of the arguments for the discontinuance of the sacraments in the 1880s was the disagreement over who should administer them. "There arose the question whether the Evangelists alone should be the administrators. Great exception was taken in some quarters to the administration by others, even by the principal local officials; indeed in some places the people absented themselves from the service unless the 'bread and wine' were offered by 'the regular preachers'."[9] The very disagreement indicates that at least sometimes lay people, not Evangelists, presided. It also suggests that the polarisation of views in the ranks about the status of the ministry had already begun. That this relatively minor problem should have weighed against an apostolic practice at all could suggest both the relative unimportance attached to the sacrament, and also perhaps how unwilling the founders were that any distinction between clergy and lay should be institutionalised within the Salvation Army.

William Booth announced a new policy, abandoning the sacraments, at a council of London officers on 2 January 1883 and his statement was printed in the *War Cry* two weeks later.

The main points he made were that, (1)"The 'Sacraments' must not, nay, they cannot, rightly be regarded as conditions of Salvation;" (2) that any order he gave for their observance "would be likely to produce grave dissensions" on account of the wide variety of practices followed amongst

6 *Salvationist* (1 December 1879) p. 325.

7 *WC* (27 March, 1880) p. 3.

8 New Zealand *WC* (10 January 1886) p. 4, col. 2.

9 W. Bramwell Booth, *Echoes*, p. 203.

the churches; (3) that "we are not professing to be a church, nor aiming at becoming one"; (4) that it is wise for us "to postpone any settlement of the question, to leave it over to some future day, when we shall have more light, and see more clearly the way before us".

In the meanwhile, (5) "we do not prohibit our own people... from taking the Sacraments... if this is a matter of conscience... the churches and chapels around will welcome you for this." (6) He also urged Salvationists to "remember His love every hour of our lives, and continually feed on Him – not on Sundays only..." and that they all agree on "one baptism – that is the Baptism of the Holy Ghost". (7) Finally, having also announced the introduction of a new "formal service for the Dedication of Children", he concluded, "Let us keep off all mere forms, and do nothing in which, as far as possible, the hearts of our Soldiers do not go with us."[10]

Sandall quotes Booth as saying on this occasion, "I cannot accept any obligation as binding upon my conscience, neither will I seek to bind any upon yours, to do, or believe, or teach anything for which authority cannot be furnished from the Word of God, or which God Himself does not reveal to us by His Spirit, as our present duty."[11]

Some disapproval must have been expressed, whether from within or without, because Booth responded in an Exeter Hall meeting on 16 April 1883. "The great charge against us is that we depreciate the sacraments because we say that baptism with water and the taking of bread and wine at the Lord's Supper are not conditions of salvation. If it were proved that they were so, you would shut out from heaven some of the best and holiest that ever walked the face of the earth..."[12]

Was the fear of "grave dissensions" because of the variety of possible practice a present danger or a hypothetical one? There is no strong evidence that existing practices were causing strife within the Army or that many deserted the ranks in consequence of the change. A few senior officers, resigning for various reasons, mentioned the sacraments as contributory factors – Major Thomas Moore, when setting up his short-lived secessionist Salvation Army in the USA in 1884, re-instituted sacraments; a Colonel Keppell, resigning in 1898, referred to the Army's sacramental theology as "shifty and unexplainable".[13]

This was in the period of the Army's very rapid expansion, particularly amongst people with little or no previous church experience. The sacraments

---

10 *WC* (17 January 1883) p. 4, col. 2.

11 Robert Sandall, *The History of The Salvation Army* (London: Nelson, 1950) II, p. 130.

12 *WC* (25 April 1883) p. 2, col. 2.

13 Edward H. McKinley, *Marching to Glory: The History of the Salvation Army in the United States of America 1880-1980* (San Francisco: Harper and Row, 1980) pp. 74, 78.

had no meaning for them, and the majority of salvationists were, if not all illiterate, then certainly theologically illiterate; they were not going to argue with Booth about anything so apparently inconsequential. Schillebeeckx makes the point that throughout the history of the Church whenever there has been any significant change, "on each occasion official documents sanction a church practice which has grown up from the grass roots."[14] Perhaps Booth's passing comment that any general order he might give enforcing sacramental observances would probably be ignored also indicated an instinctive reading of his times and people, and Schillebeeckx's rule may be observed here in Salvationist microcosm.[15]

The fullest explanation Booth himself gave for his decision was in response to questioning by Henry Lunn, published in *The Review of the Churches*, April 1895:

> In the first place, we do not consider that the Sacraments are essentials of salvation…
> Secondly. With reference to the question as to our Lord's intention to institute these as permanent ceremonies in the Church, we reply that there are other ordinances that are apparently commands of a similar character which the Church has universally agreed in not observing. The most striking example of that is the command to wash one another's feet.
> Thirdly. We came into this position originally by determining not to be a Church. We did not wish to undertake the administration of the Sacraments and thereby bring ourselves into collision with the existing churches.
> Fourthly. We were further driven to take up our present position by clergymen of the Church of England refusing to administer the rite to our soldiers because they had not gone through the form of confirmation. This created difficulties which seemed to me only to be solved by the declaration of my own conviction that these Sacraments were not essential to salvation.
> Fifthly. We have found the existing notions with reference to these ordinances seriously interfering with the right views of penitence and holy living. Men and women are constantly in danger of putting their trust in ordinances, and thinking that baptised communicants must be in a secure position, no matter how inconsistently they are living…
> Sixthly. Moreover I should like to emphasise the fact that this with us is not a settled question. We never declaim against the Sacraments. We are anxious not to destroy the confidence of Christian people in institutions which are helpful to them.[16]

Regarding his father's third point, Bramwell Booth recalled that while Dean Farrar "made a great effort to persuade me to ask for the

---

14 Edward Schillebeeckx, *Ministry: A Case for Change* (London: SCM, 1981) p. 3.
15 *WC* (17 January 1883) p. 4.
16 Henry S. Lunn, *Review of the Churches* (April 1895).

reintroduction amongst us of the supper", Dr Westcott had said "they approved of the stand we took... as this meant a refusal to embark on what was, in their view, a 'schismatic procedure'."[17]

Lunn's final two questions about the sacraments concerned firstly whether anything was substituted for the Sacraments, and secondly whether Salvationists would still be free to be baptised and take communion if they so desired. To the first, Booth suggested that every meal was an occasion to remember Christ's sacrifice, and to the second, "the General gave an unqualified answer in the affirmative." Begbie, who copies out the whole exchange, prefaces his chapter with the cautionary tale of Lady Henry Somerset. Lady Henry wanted to become a soldier but asked the General if she might still "be allowed to go for Holy Communion to the Church of England. The answer was a negative."[18]

Other reasons were subsequently offered – at various times – and repeated in various Salvation Army publications. For example Sandall claims that "a very practical consideration was that its orthodox administration was a snare to the poor souls who had been slaves to drink." He also refers to William Booth's desire to avoid controversy, quoting Booth as writing in the *Contemporary Review* of August 1882 that controversial questions should be avoided as "the poison of hell".[19] This seems a bit rich, coming from so controversial a figure as Booth.

Bramwell Booth noted that "the idea of women administering the sacraments at that time was almost unthinkable to many good people, in spite of our stand, from the beginning, on the perfect equality of men and women in the Kingdom of Christ."[20] Mrs Carpenter also suggests that one of the reasons for discontinuance was that "William Booth was not willing to surrender the principle of perfect equality of men and women in every activity of the Kingdom of Christ."[21] The evidence is not conclusive: a letter writer to the *Non-Conformist and Independent* of 9 February 1882 drew attention to the fact that in the Salvation Army for the first time in Christian history the sacrament had been administered by women.[22] We do not know if that had occasioned dissension.

Not mentioned publicly at the time but later suggested as significant was the issue of whether sacraments required "priests". George Scott Railton had attempted to persuade William Booth to acquiesce in the abandonment of the sacraments on these grounds. In a paper written for this purpose in 1881 (in Begbie's words, "set forth with a speciousness and a plausibility which

---

17 W. Bramwell Booth *Echoes*, p. 207.

18 Begbie, I, p. 459.

19 Sandall *History*, II, p. 133.

20 W. Bramwell Booth, *Echoes*, p. 203.

21 Minnie Lindsay Carpenter, *William Booth* (London: SA, 1942) p. 78.

22 Sandall, *History*, II, p. 134.

are more curious than persuasive") Railton urged that "there must be no Lord's Supper 'administered' by anybody in such a way as to show anything like a priestly superiority of one over another – every saved person being a 'priest unto God'."[23] Harry Dean included this in a list of reasons for discontinuance in a 1960 *Yearbook* article: "The sacraments had been linked, in the main, with systems necessitating a separate priesthood for their administration; this suggested a double standard for Christians, and contradicted the New Testament emphasis on the 'priesthood of all believers'."[24] Dean argued that the Salvation Army's dispensing with the sacraments was an indication of its standing in the prophetic, over against the priestly, tradition.

The influence and example of the Quakers has sometimes been mentioned as a factor in the Army's decision. It was claimed that a member of the Fry family had been an influence on Booth in this respect,[25] but I do not know of any contemporary evidence for this. While Railton and Catherine Booth may have been influenced by Robert Barclay's "inner light" theology, the truth is probably that, in Rightmire's words, "the influence of the Society of Friends on the Salvation Army was more implicit than explicit" and that "the Quaker position on the sacraments provided the early Army leaders with a theological precedent for justifying their non-sacramental practice."[26]

This is not the place to discuss the validity of Booth's arguments or explore the subsequent history of Salvation Army apologetics. However it will be obvious that none of the reasons alleged above, individually or taken together, amount to insuperable difficulties or provide irrefutable arguments for abandoning the nineteen-hundred-year practice of Christianity. To understand why the Army ceased to baptise or celebrate communion we need to look behind the immediate explanations and the arguments of later Salvationist apologists, to the theological mind-set of the Booths and their associates.

The most comprehensive account of their approach to the sacraments is David Rightmire's 1990 work. He places the Army's early theology in the

---

23 Begbie, *Booth,* I, p. 462.

24 Harry Dean, "The Founders and the Sacraments", reprinted in *Another Harvest of the Years* (London: SA, 1975) p. 36. See also his *The Sacraments – a Salvationist Viewpoint* (London: SA, 1960) pp. 71-5).

25 "Henry William Fry, last surviving grandson of Elizabeth Fry, the Quaker Prison Reformer, who recently passed away at San Francisco at the age of ninety-one, was an intimate friend of the Army Founder. It is said that it was largely owing to H. W. Fry's influence that the Founder decided that The Army should be like the Quakers in not outwardly observing the Sacraments." *WC* (5 August 1939) p. 7, col. 4.

26 R. David Rightmire, *Sacraments and the Salvation Army: Pneumatological Foundations* (Metuchen NJ: The Scarecrow Press, 1990) pp. 117-8.

context of Victorian society, the Wesleyan revival and the nineteenth century holiness movement. He makes the point that by the mid-nineteenth century Wesleyanism had lost touch with its founder's sacramental theology, maintaining the forms but subordinating other means of grace to the Word. William Booth had been taught William Cook's subjectivistic sacramental position while Catherine Booth especially was influenced by her reading of church history by people like John Lorenz Mosheim and Augustus Neander and a range of seventeenth and eighteeenth century "radical restorationist" and "spiritualising" writers like Isaac Newton and Madame Guyon. The American holiness revival teaching of Caughey, Finney and Phoebe Palmer also "emphasised a pneumatological ecclesiology that needed little continuity with historical institutions". Phoebe Palmer claimed that "the full baptism of the Holy Ghost" is "the act of ordination on the part of God".[27] Rightmire's argument is that once the Booths' "Holiness" or "Second Blessing" theology was fully developed, it provided a spiritualised substitute for sacramental theology.

George Scott Railton's views have been mentioned. He and Catherine Booth were most influential in persuading William Booth to make the break with sacramental practice. Catherine's most public statement is found in a lecture reprinted in her Popular Christianity, where she attacks four "mock salvations" – theory, ceremony, mere belief and unbelief. "Another mock salvation is presented in the shape of ceremonies and sacraments. These were only intended as outward signs of an inward spiritual reality, whereas men are taught that by going through them or partaking of them, they are to be saved. Amongst these may be classed Baptism, the Last Supper, and the ceremonials of ancient or modern Churches."[28]

William and Bramwell Booth were less willing to change. Bramwell described himself as possibly the last officer to officiate at the Lord's Supper, his father having given him "a freedom in this matter which, so far as I am aware, he gave to no one else, and which he gave me on no other subject of importance on which our views were for the time out of accord. But gradually I, too, realised how prone the human mind is to lean upon the outward."[29]

The issue possibly came to a head in 1882 at the same time as discussions with the Anglican Church and perhaps because of them. The Church was divided in its view of the Army. Some elements of the Church were interested in taking over the new religious movement that seemed to offer a means of rapprochement with the alienated working classes – while others regarded the Army with disgust because of its sensational and vulgar style. In May 1882 the Upper House of Convocation, Canterbury, appointed a

27 Rightmire, *Sacraments and the Salvation Army*, pp. 150, 155, 158.
28 Catherine Booth, *Popular Christianity* (London: SA, 1887) p. 42.
29 W. Bramwell Booth, *Echoes*, p. 204.

committee consisting of Dr Benson (Bishop of Truro) as Chairman, Dr Lightfoot (Bishop of Durham), Canon Westcott, Canon Wilkinson and Dr Randall Davidson, Dean of Windsor and Chaplain to Archbishop Tait, to negotiate with General Booth.

According to Sandall, the negotiations foundered on four issues: the role and authority of General Booth, with the associated matter of the doubtful status of Salvation Army officers as clergy (and their likely subordination to each local vicar); the matter of female ministry (the most the Church would concede was training as Deaconesses); and the matter of the sacraments.[30] Of these, Randall Davidson viewed the first as the most serious. "Booth was determined to keep control, and a very autocratic control, of the Army… We could not get anything in the nature of control over the organization, and so we had to let it go."[31] Benson reported to the House in April 1883 that his impression was that the Army was in a state of transition and that they should continue to gather more information. Over his objections, however, the committee was dissolved.[32]

For a brief period there were signs that the Army might assume the character of an *ecclesiola*, a church within a church, rather as Wesley had thought of Methodism, because there are recorded instances of Corps attending parish churches to take the sacrament. This was suggested by Canon Wilkinson as a way forward, and it was already happening in some places. For example, 400 Salvationists attended communion at St Paul's Hogate in March 1882 at the invitation of Archbishop Thompson of York. The *War Cry* of 20 April 1882 reported a combined service at St. Mary's, Halifax, where 315 Salvationists participated in Holy Communion. The House seriously debated Wilkinson's proposal, to the indignation of the *Church Times*, and Bramwell Booth admitted that it "afterwards for a time bore some fruit".[33] Sandall records various instances of Salvation Army Corps and Anglican parish churches participating in each other's services in the early 1880s.

The practice was not without difficulties; in his interview with Lunn, as already noted, Booth recalled that some clergymen "refused to administer the rite to our soldiers because they had not gone through the form of confirmation".[34] He did not want his soldiers divided at the Church door, with those of non-conformist background or no church history at all, diverted to another table.[35] Wesley's Methodists had suffered similarly in their time.

30 Sandall, *History*, II, p. 148.

31 Begbie, *Booth*, II, p. 29.

32 Sandall, *History*, II, p. 148.

33 Bramwell Booth, *Echoes*, p.77; Sandall, *History*, II, p. 147.

34 *The Review of the Churches* (April 1895) quoted by Begbie, *Booth*, I, p. 469.

35 *WC* (17 January 1883) p. 4.

It is interesting to compare the course of the Salvation Army's relationship with the Church of England with that of its Wesleyan original. Methodism grew out of the established Church and the question was whether it could be contained. Salvationism was an independent entity and would have had to be grafted on to the Anglican stock – a more difficult exercise. With Methodism, the preachers, who had not hitherto been permitted to officiate at the sacraments, assumed this role. Salvation Army evangelists and officers, who had enjoyed this privilege, relinquished it. Could the Army's abandonment of the practices have been seen as an accommodation to the Church, preparatory to closer association, though this was not stated explicitly? It seems likely that there were several crosscurrents involved in this meeting and parting of streams.

The history of the Salvation Army also illustrates the maxim that if the sacraments did not exist it would be necessary to invent them, to adapt Voltaire. Forms and ceremonies have been substituted. The *Directory* or catechism for children included the question:

> "What are the FIVE ORDINANCES of the Army?
> The Army's Five Ordinances are: -
> The Dedication of Children to God and the Army.
> The Mercy Seat.
> Enrolment under the Army Flag.
> Commissioning of Officers.
> Marriage according to Army rules."[36]

The very term "ordinances" implies sacramental usage. Even furniture attracted an aura. Booth took over from his American revivalist exemplars the practice of the "altar call" when penitents were invited to kneel at the front of the hall. At first a simple form or row of chairs sufficed to kneel at, but despite protestations that the place itself was of no merit, the "Mercy Seat" became sacred furniture. A 1908 article on "The Proper Use and Care of the Penitent Form", described the new style introduced at the recently opened West Green Citadel in London. "The floor surrounding the Mercy Seat is slightly raised and enclosed by heavy red cords, which are easily removed when the form is in use."[37]

It could be argued that if officers only rather than soldiers administer these ceremonies, they make of the officers a priesthood in the old sacerdotal sense. Soldiers sometimes dedicate infants but Officers would always conduct the enrolment of soldiers. For a while it seems that this function may have been reserved for Divisional Officers, rather like an episcopal confirmation rite. A contemporary witness claimed there was a

---

36 *The Salvation Army Directory, No II* (London: SA,1900) p. 62.
37 *Field Officer* (September 1908) pp. 327-8.

rule that "All soldiers must be SWORN IN PUBLICLY by the Divisional Officer, the Officer in charge of the corps having previously, at the soldiers' roll-call, read and explained the doctrines and the articles of war."[38] The Commissioning of Officers likewise became, once the practice was established, the prerogative of the General, or in his stead, Commissioners or Territorial Commanders.

It is interesting that the list of "ordinances" did not include the wearing of uniform, which certainly serves as an "outward and visible sign of an inward and spiritual meaning." It also provides the medium for the nearest the Salvation Army comes to a form of excommunication. For such lapses as immorality (sex out of wedlock), smoking tobacco or drinking alcohol, incurring a criminal conviction or suffering a marriage break-up, a soldier might be "stood down" – relieved of duties and temporarily removed from the Soldiers' Roll for a period of amendment of life, and so obliged to cease wearing uniform.

For the purposes of this analysis however it would have to be said that although after 1883 the Officers did not have a sacramental role in the conventional sense, they were regarded as the focal figures of the faith community in matters of public worship, specifically for Salvation Army rituals which came to be regarded as substitute sacraments, such as those mentioned above, and for funerals. Lt.-Colonel Fred Hoyle writes, "I believe it is the prerogative of the officer to officiate on the occasion of dedications, weddings and funerals. The officer is also the unifying factor in corps life."[39]

Well out of our period, but in linear development, is the comparatively recent (introduced in the 1980s by General Burrows) custom of "installing" officers in certain positions – particularly Corps Commanding Officers, Divisional Commanders and Territorial Commanders – in public gatherings. Whereas once the individual simply arrived, was extended words of welcome, and got on with the job, now a church-like liturgy of charge and acceptance marks the occasion. In the case of Territorial Commanders, someone with the rank of Commissioner usually presides at their installation – and their later retirement. Possibly a similar ritualisation of initially informal custom contributed to the original elevation of the presbyteral role in the early church; doctrine follows praxis. In due course, unchecked, such customs could affect the Salvation Army's nascent ecclesiology. At the same time, officers in less public roles continue to arrive and get on with it.

All of this also indicates that although sacramental observances are usually taken as the initial catalyst for the process of clericalisation in the

38 [Abner Sumner]"An ex-staff officer, A.S.", *The New Papacy: Behind the Scenes in the Salvation Army* (Toronto: Albert Britnell, 1889) p. 63.
39 *Officer* (May 1982) p. 223.

Church, the Army's clericalisation gathered momentum after their abandonment (apart from the substitute sacraments described above), suggesting that clericalisation is a sociological process independent of a theological base. Schillebeeckx likewise argues that the development of the priesthood was bound up with the Eucharist only because the leader presided.[40]

Pastoring

Pastoring of the flock was not the original function of the Christian Missioners – they were pre-eminently itinerant evangelists. The gradual assimilation of evangelist into pastor in the role of the individual Salvation Army officer has paralleled the gradual metamorphosis of the para-church sect into denominational church. That trend has been accompanied by the gradual loss of the individual and corporate sense of responsibility of the ordinary members or soldiers to exercise the pastoral role. Within the early Salvation Army there was strong emphasis on the "lay" pastorate, with the appointment of Visitation Sergeants with pastoral responsibility. The area included in a Corps' boundaries was divided geographically into "Wards", with a sergeant responsible for the nurture of all Salvationists (and the salvation of all the sinners) in each.[41] The system was also overlapped by the appointment of Brigade Sergeants, responsible for the welfare of members of their Brigades, such as the brass band, or the slum brigade specialising in relief work, or those who sold the *War Cry* in public houses. It is not clear how well or for how long the Ward System actually worked, although the Brigade system still operates to a limited extent.

With pastoral care undertaken by those with a more settled existence, the Evangelists or Missioners, and subsequently the officers, were itinerant. Itinerancy was a tradition inherited from Methodism in any case, with frequent changes of pastorate for clergy, but taken to another level, so to speak, when combined with the more limited role of the evangelist. Railton, already quoted as wanting no priests in the Army, wrote that, "we refuse to allow our officers to stay long in one place lest they or the people should sink into the relationship of pastor and flock, and look to their mutual enjoyment and advantage rather than to the salvation of others..."[42]

Appointments tended to be for a matter of weeks only or months at most in the early days. This was facilitated by the youth of the overwhelming majority of officers. Many were still teenagers. Catherine Booth stated in

---

40 Schillebeeckx, *Church with Human Face*, p. 145.

41 *Orders and Regulations for Field Officers* (London: SA, 1886) pp. 179-82.

42 Railton, *Heathen England*, p. 144.

1883 that most were under 25.[43] Single and almost without possessions, they were highly mobile. In 1883 two men aged 19 and 20 were sent to pioneer the Army in New Zealand. Marriage, families and the accumulation of personal effects made such mobility more difficult to sustain.

As time went on, officers became under increasing pressure to exercise a pastoral role in addition to the evangelical one. An article entitled "The Work of a Soul Nurse" in *The Field Officer*, for example, encouraged the following up of new converts, the practice of visitation and the need for care in arranging for the "transfers" of Salvationists moving from one district to another.[44] Likewise, Bramwell Booth's 1899 book on officership included a section on "Shepherds and their Flocks".[45] Whatever Railton's fear of a pastor-flock relationship developing, it was inevitable; nurturing of new converts would establish expectations for continuing care.

Teaching and Preaching

Clergy have usually assumed the magisterial role, the responsibility for teaching, in the Church. Although the *Orders and Regulations for Officers* prescribed instructing and drilling the troops as a significant officer-role, Booth saw preaching as the definitive clerical task ("one who had nothing else to do but preach") and in his movement there was no thought of reserving this task to any special group. The reverse was his intention. The Minutes of the Seventh Christian Mission Conference record one Corbridge wanting "all our people [to] be praying and preaching men and women", while Bramwell Booth agreed; "Let us make all our people parsons!" The success of the movement in achieving this is shown in the exponential growth in the number of "voluntary speakers".

By the turn of the century, a debate was beginning to surface on the viability of longer appointments – a year or even two years at a time. Writers in *The Field Officer* discussed how it was possible to sustain a preaching ministry for such a protracted period.[46] A Field Officer of that day would probably have to preach half a dozen times on Sunday and every weeknight as well, both in-doors and in the open-air.[47] For many decades *The Officer* provided "Outlines of Addresses" or "Subject Notes" and "The FO's Armoury" and stocks of sermon illustrations as aids for this task. It is significant that preaching rather than pastoring, whatever Railton's reservations about the latter, was felt to be the difficulty with longer terms.

43 Catherine Booth, *Church and State*, p. 77.
44 *The Field Officer* (January 1901) pp. 21-2.
45 W. Bramwell Booth, *Servants*, pp. 93-9.
46 For example, *Field Officer* (March 1904) pp. 104-7.
47 Maud Booth, *Two Flags*, p. 149.

The limited educational background of most officers, the brevity and inevitable superficiality of their training and the relentless pressure of work to be done and money to be raised would exacerbate that difficulty.

Whatever the theory, the Evangelists and then the Officers became the main speakers and preachers as time went on. A rearguard action against this trend has been fought ever since. In 1928 Bramwell Booth wrote to an officer in charge of a corps he had visited, advising him to, "Rope in your own people in so far as it is at all possible to take part in platform [i.e. speaking, preaching] work. If the soldiers and locals felt the responsibility of speaking to the people the words of life and truth they would fit themselves for this work. This would relieve you of some of your platform responsibilities, and thus enable you to tackle other work."[48] And General Edward Higgins wrote, "I am afraid the idea has sometimes got abroad that Officers are intended to be like parsons and preach sermons, to monopolize all the time of a meeting while the people they are supposed to lead in fighting do nothing."[49] But many officers still jealously guard their prerogative in this respect, to the neglect of the gifts of their soldiers.

Government

On the fourth task, government, it is significant that only the full-time, employed evangelists or missioners attended the Council of War in 1878, whereas "lay" delegates had attended earlier Conferences. The rank and file of the Salvation Army ceased to participate in the organisation's government. At the same time as the Mission metamorphosed into the Salvation Army, it constitutionally reverted to Wesley's original Methodist model of benevolent dictatorship. There must have been some dissenting voices, for in an address on June 18 1880, Booth complained,

> There is a growing spirit around us in favour of no government at all. All masters and no servants is the motto... the children don't want any authority; the work-people don't want any authority; sinners don't want any authority; saints don't want any authority. "There ought to be no submitting of one Corps to another," says one. A step further and there will be no submission of one man to another, and you will have, with individual independence, weakness, confusion, disorder, and destruction.[50]

---

48 Catherine Bramwell Booth, *Bramwell Booth*, p. 492.

49 Edward J. Higgins, *Stewards of God* (London: SA, undated but early 1930s) p. 16.

50 Th. F.G. Coates, *Prophet of the Poor* (London: Hodder & Stoughton, 1905) p. 133.

Booth made no bones about the fact that he insisted that things would be done his way. He wrote to his son in 1877, "...controversy is useless ... I am determined that evangelists in this Mission must hold my views and work on my lines." Thirty-four years later his beliefs on this subject had not altered: "I feel as if I had a call from Heaven to make my officers and soldiers understand what I want in The S.A. and make them feel that they have got to work to my plans and not to ___'s or their own conceits."[51]

The government of the movement was clearly concentrated in the hands of a leading group, though always as a delegated authority derived in the end from the General himself. This remains the case today. Only at the highest level in the Army is decision-making by majority vote. The High Council, by which the General is now elected, is the only council not simply advisory in function, and it may vote for that purpose only, after which it automatically dissolves. For ordinary purposes, however, it may be seen that the role of an officer is to command, to direct the government of the organisation at a particular level. The post-1877 polity certainly left the way open for the elevation of an "officer class" in the all-lay Army.

Railton defended the Army's "military order and system".

> The question is how men and women, hitherto averse to all religious control, and indeed, control of any kind, are induced to submit themselves without fee and reward to the orders of those who are often in every way their inferiors. Look at that young lad, not out of his teens, commanding a corps in some large city. His every sign is obeyed by men and women old enough to be his grandparents, by tradesmen who were accustomed to manage business affairs before he learned arithmetic (what little he knows of it), by sergeants and soldiers of the Army, who have served several years longer than himself in it, and some of whom know more of God and mankind, more of the work and literature of the Army, than he does... It is easy to explain all upon "the love of Christ constraineth" us principle, "submitting yourselves to one another in love"; but take that away, and what becomes of the Army's discipline?[52]

In sum, then, of the four clerical roles of officiating at rites, pastoring, preaching and government, it would seem that Christian Missioners became Salvation Army officers with only the fourth of these fields unambiguously as their largely exclusive prerogative. Their other roles were in the process of development. Officers were not yet clergy in any generally recognised sense at this time, any more than the Army itself was regarded as a church. They were not ordained even in free-church terms, much less in any formally recognisable apostolic succession.

---

51 Catherine Bramwell Booth, *Bramwell Booth*, pp. 96, 217.

52 Railton, in Catherine Booth, *Popular Christianity*, p. 193.

This chapter has looked at how the Army became, despite the intentions of its founders, a sect, and how their helpers began to assume some kind of ministerial role. It is helpful in this connection to review next what the founders thought they had done.

Chapter Six

What the Founders Said

Cleric before, and Lay behind;
A lawless linsy-woolsy brother,
Half of one order, half another.

Samuel Butler
Hudibras I iii 1226.

The founders' and their contemporaries' words again betray an essential ambivalence as far as clericalism is concerned. Pragmatism, under the banner of Catherine Booth's dictum of "adaptation of measures",[1] became the Army's leading principle. The pragmatic origins of its ministry and polity have meant that the Army has championed the concept of the priesthood of all believers and rejected the clerical role. The Revivalist movement to which the Booths belonged tended to exploit English anti-clericalism and their mentors, Finney and Caughey, sometimes made invidious comparisons between lay and ordained ministry. At the same time the Army has claimed ministerial status for its officers whenever that has seemed advantageous. Thus it has inherited and carried forward the ecclesiological contradictions of Methodism.

All Lay Together

Like Wesley before him, Booth did not see his Evangelists as clergy. He complained in 1877 that some had resigned because "they rub up against some Baptist or Primitive preachers and get ministerial notions."[2] Much later he complained that the Corps officer was being "left to imitate the Ministers of Religion around him; and does he not often fall into their lifeless style, without possession of their knowledge of the theory of

1 Catherine Booth, *Aggressive Christianity* (London: SA, 1891 [1880]) p. 43.
2 *Christian Mission Magazine* (July 1877) p. 172.

religion, or their general intelligence and education?"[3] Railton quotes Booth, addressing young officers, as saying,

> ...my conversion made me, in a moment, a preacher of the Gospel. The idea never dawned on me that any line was to be drawn between one who had nothing else to do but preach and a saved apprentice lad who only wanted "to spread through all the earth abroad," as we used to sing, the fame of our Saviour. I have lived, thank God, to witness the separation between layman and cleric become more and more obscured, and to see Jesus Christ's idea of changing in a moment ignorant fishermen into fishers of men nearer and nearer realization.[4]

Catherine Booth, in a letter to an early associate, Mrs Billups, wrote, "You need no human ordination, no long and tedious preparation, no high-flown language, no towering eloquence: all you want is the full baptism of the Holy Spirit in your heart, the Bible in your hand, and humility and simplicity in your manner."[5]

William Booth wanted to disabuse his officers of the notion that there is any "exclusive order of preachers" or that ministry was

> confined to a particular class of individuals who constitute a sacred order specially raised up and qualified... on the ground of their ancestors having been specially set apart for it, and authorised to communicate the same power to their successors, who are, they again contend, empowered to pass on some special virtues to those who listen to their teaching ... I deny the existence of any order exclusively possessing the right to publish the salvation of God... I honour the Order of Preachers; I belong to it myself... but as to his possessing any particular grace because of his having gone through any form of Ordination, or any other ceremonial whatever, I think that idea is a great mistake.
>
> And I want to say here, once and for all, that no such notion is taught in any authorised statement of Salvation Army doctrine or affirmed by any responsible officer in the organisation... the duty in which I glory is no more sacred, and only a few degrees removed in importance, from that of the brother who opens the doors of the Hall in which the preacher holds forth... As Soldiers of Christ, the same duty places us all on one level.[6]

For Booth the preaching role was the only one that sprang to mind – the sacramental role was perhaps too distant and the governmental role too close

---

3 William Booth, *Letter to Commissioners and Territorial Commanders* (London: SA, 1900) p. 16.

4 George Scott Railton, *General Booth* (London: Hodder & Stoughton, 1912) p. 17.

5 Norman S. Murdoch, *The Origins of The Salvation Army* (Knoxville: University of Tennessee Press, 1994) p. 57.

6 *Officer* (June 1899) pp. 202-3.

at hand to recognise. However, he clearly denied that any apostolic succession or clerical character was needed to authenticate his officers' functions.

Railton, leading the invasion of the United States in 1880, admitted that he was not ordained when told that only an ordained clergyman could apply for a licence to preach in the open air in New York.[7] Railton's initial scepticism about uniform-wearing (though his invasion-force were in fact the first Salvationists to don a regulation uniform) was because of his fear that it would "'create a hindering separateness,' to put the soldiers apart from the people, as a priest, by his garb, is put apart from his congregation".[8]

Negotiations for some kind of association with the Church of England, initiated by the Church in the early 1880s, foundered on ecclesiological questions. Commenting on the likely outcome in 1882 under the heading "Proposed Alliance Hopeless", the *Nonconformist and Independent* pointed to the difference over clericalism as the main impediment. "The Church shuts up its pulpit against the layman and suffers not a woman to usurp the authority of teaching; insists in fact upon the necessity of 'orders', or at any rate, upon their supreme virtue. Now here is a divergence which goes to the very root of the two systems."[9]

A book published pseudonymously in 1882 commended the Army for its avoidance of clericalism. *The Question of Questions* by "Caractacus" is subtitled "Church Communities of the Present and Past Contrasted with the Church Communities of the Apostolic Age". It outlines the development of monarchical government in the Church in place of charismatic fellowship and universal Christian priesthood, denounces the idea of Apostolic Succession as a "profane fiction" and claims that "there is no warrant in Scripture for an exclusive caste."

The final chapter, "The Remedy", offers the Salvation Army as the ideal model for a modern apostolic church. "I suppose there is not another people beside the Salvation Army that really and entirely seeks implicitly to follow the Apostolic practices and principles, in making the one thing needful the business of their lives, preaching and teaching a full Gospel." Much of the book is a rambling attack on Roman Catholicism and Puseyism, which might explain reticence about Salvation Army ownership. However, while the book was not published by the Army, the London Heritage Centre's copy has a Salvation Army crest embossed on its cover. This implies some kind of official support for the opinions expressed in it even though there is no evidence that the writer was a Salvationist. Possibly the Army helped

7 Dianne Winston, *Red Hot and Righteous* (Cambridge MASS, Harvard University Press, 1999) pp. 27-8.

8 Ervine, *God's Soldier*, I, p. 449.

9 Sandall, *History*, II, pp. 149.

market the book. It sometimes published Salvation Army editions of books of which it approved or wanted to use, such as Wesley's New Testament Commentary and Finney's lectures and autobiography (often without acknowledgement), and adorned them with a crest, though in this case the Army was not the publisher. It is interesting that the publication date coincided with the period of Anglican-Salvation Army discussions.[10]

According to McKinley, Booth's rejection of suggestions that officers should be ordained was one of the sources of tension with his son Ballington, commander of the Army in the United States before the latter's resignation in 1896 and his forming of the rival Volunteers of America.[11] Six months after leaving the Salvation Army Ballington Booth was ordained a "Presbyter of the Church of God in General" in an unusual interdenominational ceremony at the hands of Bishop Samuel Fallows (Reformed Episcopal Church) assisted by Methodist, Presbyterian, and Congregational clergy.[12]

William Booth is also quoted as delivering to his officers "an exhortation to devote ourselves to the work of lay apostles... We all are 'a royal priesthood, an holy nation'. Even though we have not been anointed sacramentally by the laying on of hands by a bishop, we have all been consecrated *lay* [my italics] apostles by the sacrament of the Holy Ghost."[13] Booth's son-in-law, Frederick Booth-Tucker, editorialised in *The Officer*, "There is a danger of the old clergy and laity idea creeping in amongst us. The common church idea is that of a minister doing all the fighting and feeding, while his congregation does all the looking on and swallowing. We are an Army. Every soldier is expected to fight. We teach this as a duty. It is for us, as officers, to create the opportunity."[14]

William Booth himself addressed the same theme in a "Farewell Charge in the Royal Albert Hall" before setting off on a trip overseas in 1898. He hoped that soldiers would not shirk their duty "by any talk of not being an officer".

> You cannot say you are not ordained. You were ordained when you signed Articles of War, under the blessed Flag. If not, I ordain every man, woman and child here present that has received the new life. I ordain you now. I cannot get at you to lay my hands upon you. I ordain you with the breath of my mouth. I tell you what your true business in the world is, and in the name of the living

---

10 "Caractacus", *The Question of Questions* (London: S.W. Partridge, 1882) pp. iv, 95-6, 104, 106.

11 McKinley, *Marching to Glory*, p. 74.

12 *The Outlook* (3 October 1896) pp. 618-9.

13 *The Staff Review* (February 1930) p. 77.

14 *Officer* (June 1893) p. 176.

> God I authorise you to go and do it. Go into all the world and preach the gospel to every creature![15]

Booth was clear that if any were ordained, all were ordained. That sympathy for these views was not unknown in some other churches is evidenced by an editorial from *The Methodist*, as early as 20 May 1881.

> It may only have been called into being yesterday; it may be without a history, without prestige, without worldly power; but if the fire be there which transfigures and cleanses, it stamps it as divine. On the other hand, if the fire be wanting, no ecclesiastical pretensions, or far-stretching history, or scriptural creed, or sanction, or state, or boasted majorities can constitute a "true church". It is with this canon in our hand that we turn to The Salvation Army. The Salvationists have reared their altar; best of all, the fire has fallen! The question of questions today is, "Have ye received the Holy Ghost?" Oh, the infinite littleness of silly squabblings on such subjects as "orders", "apostolic succession", "connexionalism", "congregationalism" – when placed by the side of a question like this! Show us the bright flame upon your altar, and that settles your claim to the apostolicity.[16]

Early publications of the Army did not appear to demarcate very strongly between commissioned and non-commissioned, "local" officers. For example, in the 1881 *Doctrines and Disciplines* section on "Officers", the question, "How then is The Army governed?" is answered, "By a Commander-in-Chief, Chief of Staff, Lieutenant-Generals, Generals of Divisions, Captains, Lieutenants, Treasurer or Paymaster, Secretary or Paymaster Secretary, Sergeants, Colour-Sergeants, and other officers."[17]

Interesting evidence is provided by an Officer's commission for the first officer commissioned for Australia and appointed to a Corps in Adelaide (held in the Australian Eastern Territory's Archives). The commission, dated 5 January 1881 and signed by William Booth, appears to be a standard form used for the commissioning of people to a variety of offices. Dotted lines provide spaces for the handwriting in of not only the name of the office-bearer and his appointment, but also his function, in this case "Captain". Examples of the identical form held at the Heritage Centre in London are made out for people with the local officer role of "Treasurer" or "Secretary". Such a scenario suggests a relative equality of status for full-time, commissioned officers and lay functionaries or local officers.

Testimony to the equality of all ranks is also offered by La Comtesse Agenor de Gasparin, who published a pamphlet against the Army in 1883. She quotes the *Orders and Regulations* as saying, "Our plan, moreover,

---

15 *WC* (22 January 1898) p. 9, col. 3.

16 Sandall, *History*, II, p. 126.

17 William Booth, *Doctrines and Disciplines*, p. 110.

makes every soldier in some degree an officer, charged with the responsibility of so many of his townsfolk, and expected to carry on the war against the streets, street or part of a street allotted to his case..."[18] The sentiment is wholly Boothian though the words do not appear to be from the 1878 regulations. Bramwell Booth, reflecting fifty years later on the negotiations with the Church of England, opined that, "the idea that Jesus Christ in some way instituted a society with set orders of worship, and appointed the times and manner of sacred things, such as sacraments and sacrifices, or settled an order of ministers who should be the exclusive channel of grace, has no particle of authority in the New Testament."[19] Quoting Clement of Rome on the Apostles appointing their converts as bishops and deacons, Bramwell points out that "It will be noted that no reference is here made to 'ordination', but to appointing..."[20]

In his journal for 19 April 1920 Bramwell Booth noted, reading the Report of a Free Church Ministers' Committee on the Lambeth Bishops' appeal for unity, that "the chief difficulty lies in the question of ordination." He replied to the Secretary of the National Free Church Council, "I am rather outside the deliberations referred to... I am not sure that I feel so enthusiastic with regard to the subject of Reunion... We of The Salvation Army look for important changes in the near future. If, for example, the Anglicans were to follow us all the way in giving full authority to women, that might have a very important result in modifying their whole position with regard to ordination and bring them again nearer to the practice of the Early Church, which seems to have made little of 'Ordination' and much of 'Appointment'." He went on to write, "Just as Paul said in speaking of the old Jewish system: 'Neither circumcision availeth anything, nor uncircumcision but faith which worketh by love', so I feel like saying to the Confirmed and the Unconfirmed – to the Ordained and to the Unordained – to the Baptised and the Unbaptised, "If any man have not the Spirit of Christ, he is none of His."[21]

Florence Booth, wife of Bramwell, published a book entitled, *Wanted – an Elite*, being collected addresses she had made to British officers in the 1920s. However, her point was not that such an elite was provided by the officer corps – rather, the reverse. "The kingdom of Satan and sin will never be overthrown by a body of officers, as officers only. Our Founders raised the Salvation Army because they saw clearly there should be an army of fighting men and women. The churches have erred by shutting out the laity

---

18 Agenor de Gasparin, *Read and Judge The (So-Called) Salvation Army* (London: Griffiths and Farran, 1883) p. 26.

19 W. Bramwell Booth, *Echoes*, p. 79.

20 W. Bramwell Booth, *Echoes*, p.81.

21 W. Bramwell Booth, *General Booth's Journal*, 1921-2 (London: SA, 1925) p. 30.

and making God's work depend on the leaders only; and the Army was raised up as a protest against this very mistake. Do not ape the parson. Do not imitate the Church. Let your great aim be to raise an Army that shall glorify God by fighting His battles."[22] Retired Commissioner John Carleton contrasted the "military system with its very strict line of demarcation between officers and soldiers" and the Salvation Army. "Such a distinction is contrary to the spirit of all our teaching."[23]

Finally, Catherine Bramwell Booth, in summing up the distinctive marks of the organisation, "the militant church", established by her grandfather and father, includes among them, "ministers who were not ordained".[24] All of the above quotations make it clear that the founders did not see officers as ordained.

Ministers Who Were Not Ordained

At the same time as we have these very clear statements that the Salvation Army was an essentially lay movement, we find the development of an assumption that officers did enjoy a distinctive and special role – or status. The specialness of the officer role was emphasised on two counts; firstly because of the need to foster and encourage the *esprit de corps* of officers in order to promote the effectiveness of the Army's leadership, and secondly from the desire to secure recognition of the officers within the wider community. Both would inevitably contribute to the process by which function would assume status.

Perhaps a straw in the wind is suggested by a footnote to statistics provided in *The Salvation War* of 1885. On the "Field State of The Salvation Army" it is explained that "Our grand total of officers does not show so great a growth in proportion to those abroad, because we last year had included employees in our grand total, whereas this year we exclude them at home and abroad."[25] This suggests that a clearer line was being drawn between those commissioned and those not.

Although not claiming any ordination for their officers, the Booths regarded them as in every way equal to the clergy of other denominations. Sandall reports a statement by William Booth, made in 1894: "The Salvation Army is not inferior in spiritual character to any organization in existence... We are, I consider, equal everyway and everywhere to any other Christian organization on the face of the earth (i) in spiritual authority, (ii) in spiritual intelligence, (iii) in spiritual functions. We hold 'the keys' as truly

22 Florence Booth, *Wanted – An Elite* (London: SA, 1928) p. 8.

23 *Staff Review* (July 1924) p. 242.

24 Catherine Bramwell Booth, *Bramwell Booth*, p. 221.

25 *The Salvation War, 1885* (London: SA, 1886) p. 170.

as any church in existence."[26] While these claims were made of the Army as a whole, the exercise of "authority" and the holding of the "keys" could be taken as peculiarly clerical or leadership roles. Booth was in no doubt that the Army would rise or fall on the quality of its leadership. His first *Orders and Regulations*, written particularly for officers leading a growing movement, noted that "The work must, of course, depend mainly upon the officers…"[27] Bramwell agreed with this, writing, "Officers … they are the spinal column of the affair and their tone and spirit is its spinal marrow."[28]

In a circular to senior commanders, William Booth spoke of the role of officers as akin to a priesthood: "Indeed, the fact is ever before us – like Priest, like People; like Captain, like Corps."[29] "More and more as I have wrestled with the [new] regulations this week," he wrote to Bramwell in 1903, "it has been borne in upon me that it is the Officer upon whom all depends. It has always been so. If Moses had not made a priesthood, there would have been no Jewish nation. It was the priesthood of the Levites which kept them *alive*, saved them from their inherent rottenness… and perpetuated the law which made them."[30]

Perhaps such a statement shows that Booth's own views were changing. Ervine comments that "This was a far different note from any that he had hitherto sounded. Priests had never previously been much esteemed by him who was more ready to admire prophets than priests… The Soldier-Prophet was about to leave his command to a Lawyer-Priest. A younger William Booth would have known that this was dangerous, but Booth was old and solitary and tired, and old men want priests more than they want warriors."[31] Robertson attributes this change to Booth's anticipation of a possible leadership crisis during the "period of routinisation" by his Supplementary Deed of 1904 (which provided for the deposition of a General adjudged unfit for office and the election of a replacement by a High Council). "Further, he came to the conclusion that the priesthood of all believers, although already effectively dropped in practice, had to be attenuated as an ideal."[32]

In his Foreword to a book by Hulda Friederichs, Booth paid glowing tribute to "My Officers, as a whole one of the most remarkable and I think, important facts about The Army there has not been a single year without its

---

26 Sandall, *History*, II, p. 126.

27 *Orders and Regulations* (1878) p. 8.

28 Letter of 24 February 1899, in Catherine Bramwell Booth, *Bramwell Booth*, p. 218.

29 William Booth, *Letter to Commissioners and Territorial Commanders*, p. 15.

30 Begbie, *Booth*, II, p. 306.

31 Ervine, *God's Soldier*, II, pp. 777-8.

32 Roland Robertson, "The Salvation Army", in Bryan Wilson (ed.) *Patterns of Sectarianism* (London: Heinemann, 1967) p. 80.

increase, not only in quantity, but in quality…As a body the men and women who make up the sum total of our leadership are a signal evidence of the presence of Christ in our midst, proving themselves to be no mean successors of the Apostles…"[33]

In one of his "Letters to Soldiers" from the *War Cry* and the *Social Gazette*, reprinted in book form, Booth promotes the enlistment of the children of Salvationists as officers, asking, "Ought not a soldier's children be trained for officership? To this I reply, Most certainly they ought, if they make it manifest that they possess or are likely to possess, gifts that will qualify them for such an important position. Every Salvationist father ought to foster in the hearts and minds of his children – boys and girls alike – that to be Officers in The Salvation Army is the highest and most useful position to which they can hope to aspire in this world, and so create the ambition in their hearts to reach it. And every Salvationist mother ought to do the same, only more so…"[34]

In an address to Staff Officers, reprinted after his death, William Booth said that

> The Salvation Army also claims possession of certain authority – authority received from God and man adequate for the work required from it, and equal to that of any other Christian organisation in existence, if not superior to that of many which pass under that name. I claim such authority for myself as an ambassador of Christ, and I claim it also on your behalf. I claim for the Army all the authority necessary for the ruling of its people, their admission to its ranks or their exclusion from it… When I am asked to state the grounds on which the Army claims authority over the consciences and conduct of men, I reply that we do these things not on the authority of man, or of any outside organisation of men, but by the authority of God Himself.[35]

Even Railton, enemy of the concept of the priestly class, wrote, "The work of the ministry is another thing altogether. Let no one suppose that The Salvation Army at all underrates the 'separation' unto His work of those whom God has chosen for entire devotion to some task, whatever it may be."[36]

Bramwell Booth echoes similar sentiments in his memoirs.

> In this, we humbly but firmly claim that we are in no way inferior, either to the saints who have gone before, or – though remaining separate from them,

---

33 William Booth, in Hulda Friederichs, *The Romance of The Salvation Army* (London: Cassells, 1907) pp. 12-4.

34 William Booth, *Letters to Salvationists on Religion for Every Day* (Atlanta: SA, 1987, [1902]) p. 31.

35 *Officer* (September 1915) p. 579.

36 Railton, *General Booth*, pp. 21-2.

> even as one branch in the vine is separate from another – to the saints of the present. We, no less than they, are called and chosen to sanctification of the Spirit and to the inheritance of eternal life. And our officers are, equally with them, ministers in the church of God, having received diversities of gifts, but the one Spirit – endowed by His grace, assured of His guidance, confirmed by His word, and commissioned by the Holy Ghost to represent Him to the whole world.[37]

In one of his "Talks with Officers" series of articles in *The Officer*, later reprinted in book form, Bramwell notes that

> even now many religious authorities deny our claim to minister to the souls of men because of an alleged lack of human accomplishments in our people. Some Christian bodies, Protestant as well as Roman Catholic – deny the claim even of our Officers to be ministers of Christ, and with a narrow and hateful sectarianism refuse them the hand of fellowship. That they should do so all the more surprises me because I know quite well on what slender ground the authority of their own ministers rest... But whatever may be the views of others, for any sake, do not let us have any lack of faith in God inside our own borders. The days of the fishermen and gardener, who were also disciples and apostles and evangelists, are not passed![38]

The issue became of more practical importance in the First World War. In Britain, because of uncertainty as to whether the Salvation Army was a *bona fide* church, obstacles were placed in the way of soldiers attesting as members of the Army. Salvation Army officers were not at first exempt from conscription, because of the unwillingness of the War Office to recognise them as Ministers of Religion. Bramwell Booth battled hard and eventually successfully for this. He also joined with other churchmen in opposing a proposal to call up clergy – pointing out that breeding horses and brewing beer were also reserved occupations.[39] He forbade officers to volunteer for military duty, saying

> It seems to me that the consecration of their lives to the things of Christ, which all our officers have made, is inconsistent with their voluntarily drawing the sword in earthly warfare. There can be no doubt that they are as truly ministers of Christ's gospel as were the apostles themselves, and as ministers of God they are covenanted to approve themselves in patience, in affliction... And so I say I cannot approve their taking the sword, or any other carnal weapon.[40]

---

37 W. Bramwell Booth, *Echoes*, p. 82.
38 W. Bramwell Booth, *Talks with Officers* (London: SA, 1921) p. 15.
39 Catherine Bramwell Booth, *Bramwell Booth*, p. 361.
40 *WC* (19 September 1914) p. 7. Cited by Shaw Clifton, "The Salvation Army in War Time" (PhD thesis, King's College London, 1984, p. 215).

In the United States the Judge Advocate General determined in September 1917 that the Salvation Army was a religious denomination, and that its officers were clergy, regularly ordained within the meaning of the statutes – exempt from conscription but eligible as chaplains to the forces. The question arose from the discovery that a Salvation Army officer had been for some time already acting in the capacity of military chaplain, his Californian National Guard unit having been called up.[41] Chaplains were also appointed from amongst Salvation Army officers from New Zealand (in 1915), Australia and Canada. It was not until April 1918, however, after considerable political influence was brought to bear, that the British War Office relented and four Salvationists were appointed chaplains with British troops. On the Continent, Salvation Army Officers were conscripted both by Allied countries and by the Central Powers – some of those conscripts then being assigned to chaplaincy duties with the German troops.[42]

All of these examples, in contrast to those in the previous section, would support the view that the Army and its leaders progressively tended to claim a clerical role and status for officers.

A reminiscence by Edward Joy, an officer who served under both the founder and his son, serves however to underline the essential and continuing ambiguity of the Army regarding ordination. In 1944 he wrote:

> During the last war there was some argument among a certain section of religious folk in Britain on the right of Salvation Army officers to regard themselves as "ministers of the Gospel" within the meaning of the Act of Parliament. At a ministers' fraternal I attended, a minister of one of the (then) minor Methodist Connexions contended that we had no such right, never having been ordained.
>
> "Oh, but we have been ordained, as you call it, according to the practice of our denomination," I exclaimed, "just as truly as you have in accordance with the custom of your church."
>
> He, however, vehemently asserted that ordination could only be by the laying on of hands by a duly ordained minister. Such is the practice of the British Free Churches; Anglicans and Roman Catholics adhere to the belief that only a duly consecrated bishop – in what is called the "Apostolic Succession" – can perform the ceremony of ordination.
>
> After some argument with my friend I turned to the chairman, a Nonconformist minister of high standing in his denomination, and asked for

---

41 *Officer* (May-June 2005) p. 8.

42 Shaw Clifton, Thesis, "War Time", pp. 148, 150, 197-204, 263, 271-3; Herbert A. Wisbey Jr., *Soldiers Without Swords: a History of The Salvation Army in the United States* (New York: Macmillan, 1955) pp. 167-8; F.L. Coutts, *The Better Fight: The History of The Salvation Army* VI (London: Hodder, 1973) pp. 22, 27.

his ruling. For a moment or two he seemed nonplussed, then he said whimsically, "Let us ask the bishop next week."

"Good enough," said I. If he agrees that _____ is properly ordained, I'm sure he will admit that I am." I knew full well that the Bishop, a High Anglican, would never admit the validity of my friend's ordination, and most certainly not of mine. No more than the Roman Catholics would allow his!

I told this incident to my dear old leader, Commissioner T. Henry Howard, during a shipboard conversation, and asked him if my argument was sound.

"I'll answer it in this way," he said. "Kneel down." (We were in his cabin.) I knelt before him, a feeling of solemnity taking possession of me as I realised his intention. Placing his hands on my head, he said something after this manner (I do not remember his exact words): "Receive thou the Holy Ghost for the office of a minister of the Gospel. In the name of the Father, the Son and the Holy Ghost I declare you to be ordained to the office of the Christian ministry."

"But Commissioner," I asked, "who gave you the authority to ordain me?" And then he told me this:

In one of the early-day Exeter Hall "Two Days with God" Meetings Commissioner Howard made a reference to his not being an ordained minister, but as truly called to the preaching of the Gospel as any such. Whereupon the General – the Founder – jumped to his feet and exclaimed: "Not ordained? It shall be done now!" And placing his hands on Howard's head, he said: "Thomas Henry Howard, in the Name of the Father, the Son and the Holy Ghost, I ordain thee a minister of the Gospel." Some time later the Founder said to the Commissioner, "Don't you trouble about the validity of the matter; I am an ordained minister of the Gospel, and as such fully qualified to perform the rite in your case."

Now, am I an ordained minister, or am I not?"[43]

So, the Salvation Army, in attempting to maintain a sectarian equality of believers, resisted the idea that its officers were clergy like other clergy. At the same time, because of the autocratic temperament of its founder, it adopted a military, hierarchical structure which served to expedite the process of clericalisation. In the process of coming to terms with the fact that it was becoming a church amongst other churches, even while denying the fact, it claimed for its officers a distinctive status difficult to distinguish in any practical sense from that of other clergy.

---

43 Edward H. Joy, *Officer's Review* (April-June 1944) pp. 103-4.

Chapter Seven

What Manner of Men... and Women

WANTED ALWAYS
TO BECOME OFFICERS IN THE SALVATION ARMY
MEN AND WOMEN OF GOD

Anxious to devote their lives to the work of saving souls, Whose characters will bear any amount of investigation; Who can talk to a crowd of people out of doors and in, so as to wound sinners' hearts; Who can lead a band of godly men and women to do anything likely to win souls; Who are perfectly ready to speak, pray, visit, sit still, travel a hundred miles; Who have given up drink, tobacco, and finery for Christ's sake, or are willing to give up anything and everything for Him; Who are willing to be led and taught, and to be sent home again if they do not succeed. Who are willing to be evil spoken of, hated and despised, and even to be misrepresented, misunderstood, and undervalued at headquarters.

THE FOLLOWING NEED NOT APPLY:

Persons who, "being out of employment, desire to give themselves entirely," &c., &c.; Who "do not think they can be expected" to exhaust all their strength in labouring day and night to save souls; Who, "if engaged, will endeavour to give satisfaction to their employers"; Who will take any notice of the fact that their "friends object" to their going or living anywhere or doing anything they are asked to do; Who desire "light employment," "find their work begin to tell on them," &c., &c.; Who would like to know "particulars as to salary, hours, home, &c., before engaging"; Who "are sometimes troubled with doubts" about the inspiration of the Bible, the Divinity of Christ, the Atonement, election, the possibility of falling from grace, eternal damnation, or the personality of the devil. Who "having had considerable experience" in our kind of work, think they know how to do it.

G.S. Railton[1]

A Peculiar People

If the founders' attitude to the ecclesiastical status of Salvation Army officers was ambiguous, they entertained no doubts at all about the qualities that should characterize those officers' lives, or the functions that they should discharge, or the conditions under which they should work.

---

1 *Heathen England* (5th edn 1883) p. 192.

Early Salvation Army theology of officership was not couched in traditional ecclesiastical terms. Rather it was motivational, descriptive and prescriptive of function. Any theoretical justification it took from (1) Biblical models, such as the claim that General Booth occupied in respect of the Salvation Army a position analogous to that of Paul in the early church,[2] and (2) practical necessity – the exigencies of the war. "The power of a movement is in proportion to the force of its government," it claimed.[3] It was in no way interested in questions of authenticity and authority in relation to the historic ministry of the church. Questions of ecclesiology could be lived with, with a degree of imprecision and uncertainty that would not have been acceptable concerning doctrines considered more central to the Salvationists' faith. The Eleven Points, the statement of Salvation Army belief, contain no doctrine of the Church. Salvationist doctrinal publications made few explicit references to the matter before *Salvation Story*, the 1998 version of the *Handbook of Doctrine*. It was probably not until the 1960s that some officers began to discuss such matters with more than casual interest; not until the mid 1970s that the expression, "theology of officership" actually appeared in the pages of *The Officer*.

The principles established in the time of the first two generations of Salvationists determined the nature of a tradition, of which some elements have been perpetuated as a cultural mythology even when the reality has drifted from that ideal. Chapters Seven and Eight look at "what manner of men", and women, the officers of Booth's day were required to be. Again, the question is raised as to whether the people described under these headings enjoyed a particular status separate from that of other Salvationists, or whether they merely exercised one function within the organisation. These chapters do not refer to that one thing that seemed to most distinguish Salvation Army Officership from almost every other contemporary clerical institution – the equality of sexes in ministry. This is treated separately in later chapters.

The Military Model

The most obvious thing about the Salvation Army is that it is an Army – an authoritarian religious organisation structured on quasi-military lines and employing military terminology. This has implications for the status and function of officers within such a hierarchy. As Booth's small, London-based Mission expanded he first attempted to organise it on Methodist conference lines, which involved a measure of democratic

2 *Orders and Regulations for Field Officers* (1886) p. 162.
3 *Orders and Regulations for Field Officers* (1886) p. 159.

participation. In his words, he "launched the Conference on a sea of legislation and it all came to nothing."[4] Both Booth and his closest associates found this frustrating. A delegation of close supporters told Booth in 1876, "We gave up our lives to work under you and those you shall appoint, rather than under one another."[5] Close examination of the Mission's structure through to 1877 suggest however that Booth's control was never less than authoritarian and the eventual reorganisation along even more autocratic lines in 1877-79 "marshalled it in the way that it was going". The iron hand discarded an ill-fitting velvet glove.

A certain spontaneity nevertheless attended the adoption of military ranks and terms. Booth followed rather than led in this respect so it was in a way a manifestation of grass-roots democracy. Militarism and jingoism were in the air; Britain was fighting small colonial wars; the Volunteers were a contemporary British phenomenon – although a somewhat risible one. The church also employed the fashionable language of war; it was the age of "Onward Christian Soldiers". Railton wrote to Booth as "General" and signed himself as "Lieutenant" as early as 1873.[6] Elijah Cadman of Whitby first used the expression "salvation army" to describe the mission. Booth made it official when he corrected a printer's proof of the title page of the 1878 Christian Mission Report, by crossing out "Volunteer" in "Volunteer Army" and substituting "Salvation". Cadman had styled himself a captain and Booth as "General of the Hallelujah Army" in posters in 1877 and first proposed uniform as "a suit of clothes that would let everybody know that I was for God and the Salvation of the world".[7] Booth became General, Evangelists became captains and members soldiers. Regulations, flags, bands and all the panoply of war followed.

With the organisation of the Army into Divisions under Divisional Officers in 1880 a quasi-episcopal structure came into being.[8] International expansion soon brought about the three levels of Command that still exist – Territorial, Divisional and Corps. (The Salvation Army was sometimes a bit hazy about the precise application of military terms and managed to make Corps a subset of Division rather than the reverse.) Not quite the traditional three-fold order of the Church, but interesting to compare this with Hans Küng's comment: "But even in non-episcopal missions in many cases an office corresponding to that of bishop, though bearing another

---

4 *Christian Mission Magazine* (July 1877) p. 147.

5 Sandall, *History*, I, p. 198.

6 Bernard Watson, *Soldier Saint: George Scott Railton* (London: Hodder, 1970) p. 26.

7 Humphrey Wallis, *Commissioner Cadman* (London: SA, 1928) p. 75.

8 *WC* (18 September 1880).

name, has been established to meet the requirements of ecclesiastical life."[9]

Leadership, as the whole military metaphor would insist, would be the principal aspect of the officer's role. A vigorous note from William Booth to Bramwell in March 1877 encapsulates his theology of officership: "You must have a leader, and you must have a band of men who are 'alive'. Let us pour contempt on our 'ministerial helpers' and end them or mend them... Give me godly, go-ahead dare-devils and anybody may have the preachers!"[10] His closest spirits shared his vision. Railton lauded the "superiority of a personal directorate over a divided management..." "By this means above all," he claimed, "can our members be preserved from the tendency to sectarianism and kept continually moving on to the fulfilment of the great evangelistic enterprise for which alone the Army exists. The supremacy of one who is pledged to an invariable and unalterable programme is guarantee for the perpetual prosecution at every station of the same system, which has proved so blessedly successful hitherto."[11]

The Orders and Regulations spelled it out in Chapter VI, "The Government of the Army". Section 1 was about "Strong Government"; "Where prompt, decided, forcible action is being continually required, there must be a form of government proportionately strong and determined." Section 2, on "Leadership", showed how such command, and corresponding obedience, was natural, Scriptural, universal and effective. Section 3, "Description of the Government", claimed that "The Army has been modelled substantially after the fashion of the most powerful form of human government, a military one." Because, "to rise in the Army, a soldier has only to prove himself proportionately good and able... It is really the administration of government by the wisest and best... If the value and utility of a government be proved by its success in attaining the ends for which it is instituted, the unprecedented successes which have attended the career of The Army, taken alone, establish its claim to be considered not only wise and useful, but Divine."[12] Commissioner Allister Smith in opposing The Salvation Army Act of 1931, told a Parliamentary Select Committee that the General held office "by Divine Right".[13] (Smith had voted against the deposition of Bramwell Booth by the 1929 High Council.)

Discipline has to be seen in the nineteenth-century context when even ordinary conditions of employment would be judged harsh by twenty-first

---

9 Hans Küng *Structures of the Church* (London: Burns & Oates, 1965) p. 134.

10 Catherine Bramwell Booth, *Bramwell Booth*, p. 90.

11 Railton, *Heathen England*, p. 180.

12 *Orders and Regulations for Field Officers* (1886) pp. 159-163.

13 Ervine, *God's Soldier*, II, p. 1007.

century OECD-country expectations, and the Booths were leading a force many of whom were unused, as Railton noted, to discipline of any kind. An 1879 report announced that "Four officers were reduced to the ranks in December. 2 for light and frivolous conduct and conversation, 1 for contracting a matrimonial engagement immediately after appointment and without the consent of Headquarters. 1 for misbehaviour in the presence of the enemy."[14] Discipline could also be perceived as arbitrary or capricious. Colonel Henry Edmonds, once William Booth's ADC and later a Territorial Commander, evidently fell from favour for exhibiting too great an independence of mind. In his unpublished memoirs he wrote of "...the extent to which, at a certain period, the General and Headquarters carried their spying and persecuting propaganda against those whom they suspect of seeking reforms in the Army system, or criticising any department of the Army, or any member of the Booth family, or their administration of their responsibilities, would be incredible but for the knowledge and experience of those who have suffered it."[15]

Orders and Regulations

The earliest ecclesiology for Salvationists is found in the *Orders and Regulations*. At first all evangelists, and later all officers, were engaged by the Founder and heard from his own lips what character and duties he expected of them. As the organisation grew, William Booth, Bramwell and Railton all spent much of their time on peripatetic inspections, encouraging and correcting the workers and their work. This proved increasingly unmanageable. Booth recalled that for a time he resorted to issuing "these instructions in the form of correspondence; but this also I soon found to be a task beyond my ability... I was therefore compelled to print such special directions as I had formerly issued in other forms."[16]

The Orders and Regulations of The Salvation Army, prepared by Railton under Booth's supervision and first published in October 1878, were the result. In it Booth claimed that "our system corresponds so closely to that of the Army and Navy of this country that we have been able to use even the very words of many of their regulations, and of Sir Garnet Wolseley's *Soldier's Pocket-book.*"[17] This first edition majored on the practical issues to be addressed in seizing and holding posts for the

14 *WC* (29 December 1879) p. 4.

15 Henry Edmonds, unpublished memoirs, quoted by Glenn K. Horridge, *The Salvation Army: Origins and Early Days 1865-1900* (Godalming: Ammonite, 1993) p. 88.

16 William Booth, in Preface to Hulda Friederichs, *Romance*, pp. 7-8.

17 *Orders and Regulations*, 1878, p. 9.

Army and establishing Corps. The much larger and more detailed *Orders and Regulations for Field Officers* appeared in 1886.[18] Additional volumes for the guidance of Soldiers, Secretaries and Treasurers, Staff Officers, Social Officers, Territorial Commanders and Chief Secretaries, and anybody else appointed to do anything at all, followed. Their multifarious revisions continue to order the life of the Army today, providing cohesiveness and a legal framework.

Because they preceded any form of training – the most rudimentary form of which began in 1879 – and because in Booth's words, "a very large proportion of my officers were uneducated and comparatively ill-trained,"[19] the "O's and R's" became very comprehensive. The more than 600 pages of the *Orders and Regulations for Field Officers* ranged over diverse matters from doctrine to book-keeping; "how to capture a town" and dealing with persecution; behaviour on board ship and the "construction of the Army", how to talk with Mohammedans and how to march in formation; the need for fresh air in bedrooms at night and the application of hydropathy to such illnesses as scarlet fever and "difficulties of the bladder and urine".

The Regulations prescribe the character and role of the officer. The expectations were high: "The F.O. [Field Officer], by virtue of his position, stands out before his Soldiers more prominently than any other man. To them he is the Ambassador and Representative of God. He is their Captain, their brother, and friend. Their eyes are on him night and day. They regard him as the pattern expressly set for them to copy, the leader who at all times it is their bounden duty to follow."[20] It is difficult to imagine a description of function more likely to inspire perceptions of status.

Chapter One also explains that the Officer's teaching must be accompanied by his personal example, that the Officer must be a "Divine Man" – must have been converted and possessed by God – and must be "Holy", which holiness will be expressed in every aspect of his life. The groundwork having thus been laid, Chapter Two devotes 27 pages to the Officer's "War Qualifications", these being outlined under the headings of a Soldier's Spirit, Compassion for the Perishing, Intelligence, Improvement, Responsibility for Success, Humility in Prosperity, Perseverance in Adversity, Obedience, Manner, Loyalty and Business.

According to Bramwell, William Booth's "anxiety was to compile in that book a set of regulations which would perpetuate the Salvation Army, and preserve it from the mistakes and confusions which have befallen so

---

18 Sandall, *History*, II, pp. 33, 35.

19 Friederichs, *Romance*, p. 11.

20 *Orders and Regulations* (1886) Part I, Chapter I, Section 1, No. 4.

many other societies in the religious sphere."[21] Against that, the elder Booth confessed that "I have never placed too great a reliance upon either these laws or the methods of their application."... "I have ever been deeply impressed by a vivid sense of the utter powerlessness of any mere system, however wisely it may have been framed, which has not in its application that Spirit of Life which alone can impart that vital force without which no extensive or lasting good can be accomplished. God forbid that any regulations which I have issued, no matter how effective for their immediate purpose, should go to swell the number of dead forms and powerless systems already in existence."[22]

Recruiting

Not discussed in the Regulations but another general principle to which attention has already been drawn was Booth's conviction "that the best way to reach ... [those] lying entirely outside the influence of the Churches was by means of those who had themselves belonged to those classes. Therein lay what may be called the germ of The Salvation Army. From that point everything else, or nearly everything else, in our peculiar propaganda, has proceeded."[23] He concurred with and quoted Lord Shaftesbury (who detested him, and his Army) as saying that "The working classes will never be reached but by an agency provided among themselves."[24]

Some of the most notable of the first generation of Salvation Army officers were firstly taken prisoner from the ranks of the "Skeleton Army", the organised bands of roughs that persecuted Salvationists in the English tradition of "rough-musicing" during the 1880s. Popular attention was focussed on such recruits. "It should not be forgotten that many of the officers of the Army have been recruited from the lowest strata of society, and some from the ranks of the most dangerous and criminal classes."[25]

Glenn Horridge has shown however that "while the majority of officers continued to be recruited from a wide social range across the working class [he gives the figure of 93% in the period 1878-1883] few actually came from the 'submerged tenth'" – the class to which Booth felt especially called. A high proportion had had some previous religious affiliation – two thirds of them Wesleyan or Primitive Methodists. Some

21 Begbie, *Booth*, II, p. 158.

22 Friederichs, *Romance*, p. 9.

23 Friederichs, *Romance*, pp. 4-5.

24 Sandall, *History*, I, illustration opposite p. 228.

25 Emma Booth and Herbert Booth, *Called Out! And what comes of it* (London: SA, 1886) p. 11.

came from what Sandall described as "'the Christian unemployed' – men and women already converted for whose service there was not provided any outlet in their own sphere." "Between the recruits who came from the 'dangerous classes' [Booth counter-culturally applied this term to the middle and upper classes] and the comparatively few 'preachers from the pub', ... were the ever-growing large number of ordinary men and women..." Horridge also notes that Anglican and Methodist women were attracted by the Army's policy of equality of opportunity for women.[26]

Booth tried to discourage the middle and upper classes from joining because he did not think they would fit in or accept his discipline. In fact they usually rose quickly to prominence and high rank. William Booth's "first gentleman", and subsequently his son-in-law, was Frederick St. George de Latour Tucker, sometime Indian Civil Service magistrate. Tucker's ancestors included a secretary to Elizabeth I and a grandfather who had been Chairman of the Court of Directors of the Honourable East India Company. He had a head start in the Salvation Army, by-passing training in 1881 and with the initial rank of major led the invasion of his native India in 1882. He was made a Commissioner the following year.[27]

However, Bramwell Booth assured his readers that, "All, or practically all promotion is from the ranks. Less than ten in a thousand of our leaders have reached that position without having first served as followers."[28]

The Call

One identifiable strand in the Army's officership ethos, a characteristic inherited from its non-conformist, sectarian forebears, is the "call". William Booth spoke of his own call when interviewed in 1894: "I have heard a great deal about the 'call to the ministry' since those days, but my call to follow my Saviour and save as many sinners from the pains of Hell as I possibly could, came to me at the beginning of my career... I never needed either my Bible or my minister, or any special movement of the Holy Spirit on my heart to press this truth home upon me. It appeared to me self-evident that the religion of Jesus Christ could not be possessed without the Christ-like hunger for the Salvation of men."[29] Booth here regards a call to evangelism as inseparable from being a Christian.

In Salvation Army usage however the call came to be associated particularly with officership. A frequently quoted saying by William

---

26 Horridge, *Origins*, pp. 76, 80-6, 225-7; Sandall, *History*, II, p. 59, 64.

27 Harry Williams, *Booth-Tucker, William Booth's First Gentleman* (London: Hodder, 1980.)

28 W. Bramwell Booth, *Servants*, p. 22.

29 Begbie, *Booth*, II, p. 196.

Booth – "'Not called, did you say?' Not heard the call, I think you should say..."[30] – was by its context evidently addressed to all Salvationists concerning their responsibility for evangelism, but became associated with the call to officership. Bramwell Booth refers to "that direct and definite impulse, born, I believe, of the Spirit of God, which is usually described by those who recognise it as 'the call to the work.'" "There is sometimes, I admit, an illusion... element of selfish ambition... a mere impression. But in the majority of cases that call is a very real, a very beautiful, a very powerful occasionally a very terrible, visitation... an overwhelming conviction of duty." He goes on to say that, "Rarely is one asked to become an Officer. The proposal comes to us in the form of an 'offer' for service from the candidate, and is usually addressed to the Captain of the Corps of which the proposer is a soldier."[31]

Whatever Bramwell's disclaimer, this is not to say that there was not aggressive recruiting. Apart from the constant need for money, the ever-expanding war was hungry above all for officers. In 1878 Booth was already demanding "1,000 recruits, 1,000 evangelists, to join the salvation army," initial letters not yet capitalised.[32] In 1919 Bramwell Booth launched "a great call for two thousand candidates... Will each officer secure at least one offer of a life in 1919? I want those two thousand almost immediately – a thousand men and women at once, and another thousand in six months or so."[33]

Heart Training

The onset of special training by a sect may mark a significant step towards denominationalising. In Wilson's words,

> Training implies a lack of parity between leaders and members, it compromises the radical democracy of the sect and the ideal of the priesthood of all believers. Spontaneity disappears, and leaders begin to employ the status symbols of their profession, seeking equal esteem with the pastors of other movements.[34]

At first the only training available for Christian Mission Evangelists or Salvation Army Officers was of the apprenticeship model, and there was little enough of that. Bramwell Booth was painfully aware of the lack. He

30 *Officer* (August 1921) p. 93.
31 W. Bramwell Booth, *Servants*, p. 27, 32.
32 *Christian Mission Magazine* (November 1878) p. 305.
33 *Officer* (January 1919) pp. 1, 8.
34 Bryan Wilson, "An Analysis of Sect Development", *American Sociological Review* 24 (February 1959) p. 9

confided to his diary in February 1877, "Oh this miserable hunt for men ... we must take in and make our own men." And to his mother he wrote in May of that year, "If this ship is going to live out the storms, ought not the whole strength and skill of everyone aboard be concentrated on the one great want, organisation of the rank and file, and training of the officers? ... Here is no plan for training these women. After all we have said and seen and suffered, we are daily taking out girls without any previous training or education whatever."[35]

The earliest systematic attempt was made when ten young men were sent to assist Captain Ballington Booth in the establishment of the Manchester Temple Corps, as reported in *The Salvationist* of May 1879.[36] "Training Homes" were subsequently opened in London, firstly for women under Emma Booth in April 1880 and then for men under Ballington and later under Herbert Booth in October that year. Emma, only 20 years of age at this time, remained in this work for eight years and became known as the "Training Home Mother". A basic catechism, *The Doctrines and Discipline of The Salvation Army*, "prepared for the Training Homes by The General" was published in 1881.

In 1881 the London Orphan Asylum in Clapton was acquired and this remained the "International Training Home" until 1930, when a new College was opened at Denmark Hill, South London. By the end of 1882, more than 400 cadets had been sent out as officers after training for a few weeks, or months at most.

A new system was instituted in 1886, whereby instead of entering and being commissioned in "driblets", cadets came into training at half-yearly intervals. Three months were spent in the classroom, with practical work in the immediate vicinity, after which the cadets were sent out for a further three months "brigading" in various parts of the country under the Training Officers. Commissioning and appointment to the "Field" followed. By June 1886, some 2,600 cadets had passed through the system.[37]

The system was further modified in 1894, when Candidates began with prescribed local training in their home Corps, followed by seven weeks in the Training Home, four months in twos and fours out at Corps, then a final three weeks back at Clapton. A year's probation followed their commissioning.[38] The length of training was increased to ten months in 1903.[39] That term remained the norm until the mid-1960s.

---

35 Catherine Bramwell Booth, *Bramwell Booth*, pp. 132-3.

36 Sandall, *History*, II, p. 67.

37 Sandall, *History*, II, p. 70.

38 *Officer* (April 1894) pp. 114-7.

39 Wiggins, *History*, IV, p. 209.

Training majored on three books: the *Bible*, the *Orders and Regulations for Field Officers* and the *Doctrines of The Salvation Army*.[40] Reading, writing and elementary mathematics also needed to figure in the curriculum for some. The main purpose of training was not, however, academic. William Booth had a horror of academic learning for its own sake, fearing that ministerial education would cause his officers' zeal to evaporate. In this he was supported by Railton, who wrote to Bramwell in 1877, "I shall always I trust continue dead against any approach to a college sort of thing which cannot ever be justified from scripture or experience, and can never produce anything but parsons. We want to train men to be like us, without time for self, always at it, and yet always being stoked and fed up as they fly."[41]

The real purpose of training was "officer formation". In his *Servants of All*, Bramwell Booth identified the task as "character-building" and "the training of the heart"; the Training Home as a "manufactory for the making of men."[42] "The main aim was to influence the spiritual life of the cadet. Personal contact with the leader, by interviews and meetings, loomed larger than anything else in the curriculum. That and the cadet's own contact with sinners constituted the chief objectives…"[43] T. Henry Howard, erstwhile Training Home Principal, described the aim as helping the cadets to "get a fairly good knowledge of themselves, and also to set up right standards by which they can measure their future life and work."[44]

Terms of Engagement

Commission, Covenant and Undertakings: these three instruments define and document the relationship between the officer and the organisation, although the Covenant is, strictly speaking, an agreement with God rather than with the Army.

Rank is conferred with a "commission", which constitutes the officer's authority to act. At first the appointment of officers was fairly informal but it became more formalised with the development of institutional training. The *War Cry* reported commissioning meetings from the 1880s on and the 1886 inauguration of "sessions" with definite commencement and commissioning dates gave more scope for public commissioning exercises. At first a fresh commission was issued for each new

40 "One of the Scholars", *A School of the Prophets* (London: SA, 3rd edn, 1901) p. 67.

41 Quoted by Bernard Watson, *Soldier Saint*, p. 38, from the Railton Papers.

42 W. Bramwell Booth, *Servants*, pp. 51-2.

43 Catherine Bramwell Booth, *Bramwell Booth*, p. 133.

44 "One of the Scholars", *School*, p. vii.

appointment but from 1898 "new and artistic" commissions were provided as a "permanent certificate of officership" while a "special form of 'Marching Orders'" was provided for changes of appointment.[45] Distinction was soon made between Staff and Field ranks, providing different ladders for promotion as well as differing benefits and emoluments. These caused much heart-burning until their abolition in the early 1930s.

The "Undertakings", pertaining to the acceptance of Orders and Regulations for Officers, included promises to work a certain number of hours per day, that gifts would not be accepted, that no other trade or moneymaking activity would be engaged in and that courting and marriage regulations would be observed. Early versions in North America at least, according to some sources, included a promise to "never, without having first obtained the consent of the Commissioner, to take part in opening any place for religious services, or in carrying on services in any place within three miles of any then existing station of the Army, under penalty of forfeiting $250 to the Commissioner for the benefit of the Army if I should in any way prove unfaithful to this solemn pledge."[46] Undertakings appear to have been supplied at first as part of the application form for appointment as an officer, and were later also signed, as the "Field Officer's Bond", at the conclusion of training, before commissioning. The application form also included the Salvation Army doctrinal statement and marriage conditions for officers.

Early forms of Undertakings seem ambiguous about the non-contractual nature of an officer's engagement. "I fully understand that he (the Commander) does not undertake to employ or retain in the service of the Army anyone who does not appear to him to be fitted for the work, or faithful and successful in it..." could imply that those who met the standard were considered to be employed, even although they also undertook to "discharge the Army, and you or the Commissioner for the time being, from all liability in respect of salaries, acknowledging that I fully understand that you do not engage to pay me or guarantee that I shall be paid any salary while holding an appointment..."[47]

The modern version is quite explicit: "I understand and agree that there is no contract of service or employment nor any other legal relationship between the Army and me."[48] The Undertakings "spell out very clearly that there is no contractual relationship between the officer and The

45 *WC* (19 March 1898) p. 5.

46 "A.S.", *New Papacy*; p. 62; "Norah Marks", *Facts About the Salvation Army* (Chicago: Rand McNally, 1889) p. 156.

47 1891 American form of Declaration, cited in "A.S.", *New Papacy*, p. 64.

48 Minute by the Chief of the Staff, 2001/IA/09.

Salvation Army. It follows therefore that the officer is not an employee nor is The Salvation Army his employer."[49]

A test case was Rogers v Booth which involved a claim by an officer under the workers' compensation legislation in force in Britain at the time. The court found,

> It is a relationship pre-eminently of a spiritual character. They are united together for the performance of spiritual work and, in order to carry out efficiently the end they have in view, they submit to a very strict discipline, and a very strict command... the necessary contractual element which is required before a contract of service can be found is entirely absent. The parties, when they enter into a relationship of that kind, are not intending to confer upon one another rights and obligations which are capable of enforcement in a court of law.[50]

The Covenant was the brainchild of Bramwell Booth, and was signed by cadets on the final "Spiritual Day" (a day spent in religious services intended to inculcate personal consecration to the cause) before commissioning.[51] The earliest *War Cry* report for a Covenant Day is in the issue of 13 May 1922.

A brochure on training first published in 1923 provided a former cadet's account of the commissioning events. Referring to the final Spiritual Day, she wrote,

> In the afternoon meeting all received the Covenant form to pray over and sign. Towards the end of the evening meeting we repeated the words of the Covenant after the General:
> "I give myself to God, and here and now bind myself to Him in a solemn covenant. I will love and trust and serve Him supremely as long as I live. I will live to win souls, and will not allow anything to turn me aside from seeking their salvation as the first great purpose of my life. I will be true to The Salvation Army and the principles represented by its flag, under which I stand to make this Life-Covenant."
> The colours were held over us, we sang...the General prayed that we might be true to the Covenant which we afterwards signed.

The Commissioning Day was also described.

---

49 Major Peter Smith, "Current and Future Legal Issues" (unpublished paper for International Conference of Leaders, Melbourne, 1998) p. 1.

50 Rogers v Booth (1937) 2 All ER 751 p. 754, quoted by C.J. Jamieson of Bell Gully Buddle Weir, "Status of Officers" (Unpublished legal opinion for New Zealand SA, dated October, 1992) p. 8.

51 Catherine Bramwell Booth, *Bramwell Booth*, p. 136.

> The Afternoon Dedication Service, held in the Congress Hall, transformed us all into officers, and when we marched into the crowded hall, at 6pm, to receive our appointments, our hearts beat with unusual rapidity. The General's message to the Cadets began, "In the name of the Lord, I receive you into our Ranks as Officers of The Salvation Army."

The booklet also described another occasion, when the Commissioning and Appointment evidently took place together:

> "To be Lieutenant and appointed to Camlachie, and may God bless you, and give you a long life of soul-winning," said the Training Commissioner, as he handed an officer's commission to a girl, 19 years of age.[52]

It was on the basis of these documents that Salvation Army officers could be described as clergy, and like other clergy fell within the category of "employed by God". Up until now this has secured the Army against legal action by officers in common law legal jurisdictions.

---

52 Anon., *The Training of Salvation Army Officers: Glimpses of the work at the International Training Garrison, London* (London: SA, 1927) pp. 27- 31.

Chapter Eight

The Work of an Officer

> We have no hobbies... unless it be a hobby to want to save the largest number of souls with the highest possible salvation in the quickest space of time by the best imaginable methods.
>
> Frederick Booth-Tucker.[1]

The Work

The activity and employment of an officer was described as "the work", in a manner comparable with St Luke's use of "the way" for being a Christian. In *Servants of All,* written to explain and promote the role of officers, Bramwell Booth quotes letters from officers using the word in this manner: "I was sorely tempted to leave the work..." and, "I value the work too highly to leave it..."[2] In expressions such as to "enter the work", to be "still in the work", to "leave the work", this remains a Salvation Army idiom for officership to this day. The title of Booth's book echoed John Wesley as well as St. Paul: Wesley described a clergyman as "the Servant of All."[3] Bramwell Booth evidently thought of his officers as clergy.

Bramwell Booth noted that "little by little the conception of a Salvation Army officer has grown until it has come to include very much. A servant of God, and a servant of the common people living amongst them, such a one must be a fisher of men, in touch with them and yet above them, an example to them, a friend, an advisor, confessing their sins, pleading for them at the Throne of Mercy, sharing their sorrows, rebuking and warning them in truth, albeit, with tears, a faithful messenger of the Cross, a shepherd of the sheep, caring for the household of faith, patient, kind, a leader of the Lord's host, the servant of all."[4]

It is true that the general expectation of workplace ethic was more strenuous in the Victorian era than in OECD countries today. Longer hours and fewer holidays were the norm. The Booths were however classic

---

1 *Officer* (February 1893) pp. 1-2.

2 W. Bramwell Booth, *Servants*, pp. 105, 112.

3 John Wesley, "An Address to the Clergy", in *Wesley's Works*, Ed. Thomas Jackson, [London: Wesleyan Methodist Book Room, 1872] (Grand Rapids: Baker, 1978) X, p. 485.

4 W. Bramwell Booth, *Servants*, p. 18.

workaholics with a spiritual imperative, and a similar commitment was expected of anyone enlisting in their Army. The Orders and Regulations insisted that "Holiness also supposes the F.O. [Field Officer] to be saved from idleness. Idleness in a Salvation Army officer is sin. Idleness means broken vows. It means hypocrisy, it means heartlessness, and such things cannot be imagined where the Spirit of Holiness reigns."[5]

Bramwell confessed in a letter to his father, "This feeling that you are a poor sinner loaded with guilt if you stop work for ten minutes, even in a railway train, is really dreadful."[6] In retrospect, Bramwell's daughter expressed regret that this had been perhaps too extreme. Of Bramwell she wrote, "It was a flaw in his well-balanced mind that he did not take the need for relaxation seriously. He never learned to relax ... It would not be an exaggeration to describe his life as an orgy of work." She notes that in fifty years he never took a holiday in which any one complete day was free from work. When his doctors urged him in his seventies to relax, he "could not easily break the bondage of mental habit."[7]

Would-be Candidates for Officership were certainly urged to count the cost. "To come here," warned an early recruiting pamphlet,

> means to throw yourself into a life where shadows and gloomy disappointments are plentiful, where misunderstanding and misinterpretation of friends and foes will bring to the heart many a sting hard to be borne – a life from which the gratification of self, the pleasures of ease, comfort or wealth have for ever been banished, and in which the ceaseless pulling against the tide of popular feeling and worldly ambition will lead to isolation, derision and contumely. It means care on behalf of the souls of others, and sorrow on account of their sins. A little of the great burden on behalf of a lost world, which crushed the great heart of the Saviour of mankind until it broke, shall be laid upon your shoulders.[8]

Bramwell Booth illustrated the "work", the Field Officer's way of life, by quoting a diary, "supplied to me by an old Field Officer".

> MONDAY
> Arose at 7a.m. – a good night's rest after yesterday – hard but happy fight. Began the week in faith for a time of great blessing.
> 9a.m. – Visited Sunday's converts. Saw them during the breakfast hour. We had cheer and prayer. Then went visiting Soldiers and Recruits who were prevented from attending meetings. Found three sick.

---

5 *Orders and Regulations* (1886) pp. 7-8.
6 Catherine Bramwell Booth, *Bramwell Booth*, p. 199.
7 Catherine Bramwell Booth, *Bramwell Booth*, p. 100.
8 Emma and Herbert Booth, *Called Out*, p. 12.

1p.m. – Hour for dinner. Found wife had been dealing with a backslider – a poor woman who appears to be very easily driven back.
Afternoon resting.
7p.m. – Open Air - Boro' Lane – great impression made by one of last night's converts, who testified.
8p.m. – Indoor Meeting. The converted Irishman and two saved footballers testified – spoke myself on Prodigals – had two at the Mercy-seat – one from a Lodging house – found he was a poor backslider.
9.45p.m. – On way home from Meeting visited two backsliders – they were very grateful for my visit.

TUESDAY
After breakfast and family prayer answered correspondence from D.O. – went to see Mr. Thompson concerning work for last night's Lodging-house man – got him fixed up.
10.30a.m. – Went to see a gentleman with reference to the taking of a small room down among the navvies who are opening up the new line – took building.
Afternoon. – Visited from door to door – saw twenty-five families and prayed with them.
Evening. – Soldiers' meeting – spoke to them on responsibility for the drunken classes.
9.30p.m. – Held Census Meeting to consider condition of Roll Book – found it was necessary to specially look up several backsliders and to follow down one or two offended. Local Officers appear to feel the burden of the Corps.

WEDNESDAY
After breakfast visited Soldiers and Recruits.
Afternoon. – *Crys* delivered. Wife and self busy with them – folding, etc., until 4.30p.m.
Night. – Children's special Band of Love Meeting at 6.30 – gave tea and drills.
Senior Meeting. Spoke on 'God's open door' – also had good powerful three-minute addresses from six Bandsmen – finished at 9.30 with one good case at the Mercy-seat.

THURSDAY
Was called up about 3 o'clock in the morning to visit a dying man – often been to our barracks – was with him until he died at 7. After breakfast went visiting.
Afternoon. – Held Cottage Meeting amongst some old cottagers – had sixteen present – one old woman converted.
Evening. – Salvation Meeting – got a runaway girl – just starting a life of ill-fame – took her back to her home 16 miles off by last train tonight. Tired, but happy.

FRIDAY
10a.m. – Attended Officers' Council – Divisional Officer gave explanations *re* New Scheme and told me the Target for my Corps – saw Divisional Officer on important question.
Afternoon. – Visited the navvy quarter and managed to have a word with several of their wives – sold *Crys* and got a promise from several that they would attend Saturday night's Free-and-Easy.
Special preparation for Holiness Meeting.
7.15p.m. – Local Officers' Meeting.
8 p.m. – Holiness Meeting.
9.30 p.m. – Made up Corps books. Found soldiers were doing much better in giving, as a result of a talk a few weeks ago.

SATURDAY
Assisting wife with house-cleaning till mid-day – gave special attention to Barracks windows.
Afternoon. – Went with four Soldiers to gates of football-field. Sold 65 *Crys*, and spoke to several persons about Salvation.
Special thought and reflection *re* Sunday's Meetings.
7 p.m. – Open Air, Market-place.
8 p.m. – Free-and-Easy. Had several navvies present – got one converted.
9.45 p.m. – Had an hour's special dealing with God *re* Sunday.

SUNDAY
7 a.m. – Knee-Drill.
8.15 a.m. – Breakfast.
10 a.m. – Open-Air Meeting.
11 a.m. – Holiness Meeting.
12.45 p.m. – Dinner.
2 p.m. – Four Company Open-Airs – ten Soldiers in each. Wife conducted Open-Air with Converts.
3 to 3.30 p.m. – Attended Junior Meeting – examined Register.
3 p.m. – Wife did first part of Adult Meeting.
3.30 p.m. – I conducted the latter part of Adult Meeting – had 45 testimonies.
4.15 p.m. – Met three Corps Cadets and gave them counsel.
5 p.m. – Tea.
5.30 p.m. – Met Bandsmen and had special prayer with them.
5.45 p.m. – Open-Air.
6.30 p.m. – Salvation Meeting.
8 p.m. – Prayer-meeting. Held on until 9.45 – got five persons to seek Salvation. Accompanied two Converts home, and reached quarters at 10.30. Rather weary, but cheered.[9]

The only trick unturned in this recitation was an encounter with a backsliding but repentant ex-officer.

---

9 W. Bramwell Booth, *Servants*, pp. 88-90.

At the heart of the Work was the imperative, "Go for souls and go for the worst!" – a saying attributed to William Booth. Booth summed it up with, "The end of The Salvation Army Officers is to convert men, to change their hearts and lives, and make them good Saints and Soldiers of Jesus Christ."[10] Bramwell Booth described "fighting" as the "Central Idea of The Salvation Army", to which "the selection, the consecration, the separation, the training of our Officers... are but preparatory".[11] Officers today are still reminded that "The primary purpose of corps officers is to bring the message of salvation to the unconverted in their district, and to lead and train the soldiery to win souls for the kingdom of God."[12]

Poverty, Suffering and Sacrifice

The theme of poverty and willingness to sacrifice oneself for the cause is too frequently touched on to be ignored. Begbie admitted that "It was a charge against (Booth), ... that he underpaid his Officers and condemned them to lives of inordinate hard labour. The fact was, that William Booth believed in poverty and feared riches."[13]

Bramwell Booth named poverty as one of the problems to be "faced by the would-be Life-Servant of the Army". He stated that "There is no guarantee of salary or other emolument – not for a single day – no, nor of a single penny... Theirs must be a very real life of faith." He claimed that one of the benefits of this regime that, "We have been very little troubled with those who are in the service of the Temple for a piece of bread!" He quoted with approval the assessment of Sir Walter Besant, writing of Salvation Army officers: "But they must remain poor. They must always remain poor. That is essential. They must never let the world suspect that the old passion of devotion is decaying. The last words of the dying Catherine Booth were a command. 'Self-Denial,' she said, 'will prove your love to Christ.' Therefore they must remain poor."[14]

Quite early Booth became concerned that his officers' survival was at stake, and issued an "Order against Starvation".

> He had learned with great concern that the bravest officers who had gone to the towns recently entered, had endured the greatest privations, going, in fact, to the very brink of starvation without informing him, and this, even in cases where they actually had money in their possession, which they had intended to use for the payment of rent or other debts. Such devotion, however noble, was

10 William Booth, *International Congress Addresses 1904* (London: SA, 1904) p. 86.

11 W. Bramwell Booth, *Servants*, p. 64.

12 *Orders and Regulations for Corps Officers* (London: SA, 1976) p. 1.

13 Begbie, *Booth*, II, p. 177.

14 W. Bramwell Booth, *Servants*, pp. 40-3.

> to be avoided and condemned, especially because it not merely exposed the strength and life of the officers to great risk, but was likely to bring great discredit upon the Army.[15]

Nevertheless, the *Orders and Regulations* prescribed suffering as part of the commitment: "The F.O. must choose not only the Salvation of Souls as the end of his existence, but that suffering, without which they cannot be saved. He embraces not only the end, but the means by which alone this end can be accomplished."[16] Bramwell adverts to Paul's words in Colossians 1:24 to provide Biblical underpinning for this expectation: "Christ gave himself for the world. He asks that those who have given themselves to Him will do the same thing and fill up the measure of His sufferings. That is the root idea of every true Salvation Army Officer."[17]

In his memoirs, Bramwell Booth referred to the experience of Colonel Jacob Junker in Germany, when arraigned before the local Schiedsrichter on a charge of treating his officers with undue severity after complaints were made by some "deserters". In his defence Junker referred to his military career and the privations endured for king and Fatherland.

> "And sir, shall I not suffer some little hardship and privation and pain in warfare against the powers of darkness? Shall I not press on to the end, to save some souls for whom my redeemer died?..."
> The court was silent. The judge wiped a tear from his cheek: the defendants [*sic*], ashamed, withdrew the charge, and, as a result of the incident, throughout the Rhineland the purpose of the Salvation Army was understood as never before. [18]

An outsider's viewpoint is provided by "Norah Marks", the pseudonym of a Chicago reporter told off by her editor to infiltrate the Salvationists. Presented with an application form for officership, "I was absolutely dumbfounded by the picture it presented of complete renunciation of self, hopes, plans, ambitions, prosperity... The Trappist monks give up scarcely less, because while immolated it is with the reverence of the world. With these Salvationists there is poverty perpetually enjoined, scorn, ridicule, a crushing of every part of the nature but the religious, and what seems a heartless abandonment of their bodily welfare by those with whom they

15 *Christian Mission Magazine* (December, 1878) p. 317.
16 *Orders and Regulations* (1886) p. 9.
17 W. Bramwell Booth, *Servants*, p. 17.
18 W. Bramwell Booth, *These Fifty Years* (London: Cassell, 1929) pp. 131-2.

serve."[19] Booth was in fact dogged by accusations of heartless ill-treatment and neglect of his officers.[20]

The "suffering" alluded to arose not only from the Army's ascetic discipline; it also followed the reactions of both mobs and the civil authorities to the Army's activities, particularly in the open-air. In 1882 alone, 642 soldiers were assaulted in the United Kingdom, one third of them women and 23 of them children... sixty Army buildings were damaged."[21] In Britain, some 600 Salvationists had been imprisoned by the end of 1884, and as late as 1912 the last British officer spent time in prison for preaching in the street.[22]

Obedience

The section on "Obedience" in the Orders and Regulations begins with the F.O.'s need to "obtain a cheerful and willing obedience from those under his command," and to "secure (it) without the display of any domineering, masterful spirit... To make his Soldiers serve him, an officer must be willing to serve them." Further, "the F.O. must be an example of obedience to his soldiers ... A proper respect for those in authority over him and a ready compliance with their wishes will do much to beget in those under him all necessary respect for his own authority."[23] Booth boasted that the Salvation Army

> is the only religious body founded in our time that is based upon the principle of voluntary subjection to an absolute authority. No one is bound to remain in the Army a day longer than he pleases. While he remains there he is bound by the conditions of the Service. The first condition of that Service is implicit, unquestioning obedience... We were told that in a democratic age the people would never stand the establishment of what was described as a spiritual despotism... Despite the alleged unpopularity of our discipline, perhaps because of the rigour of military authority upon which we have insisted, the

19 "Norah Marks", *Facts About The Salvation Army*, p. 160.

20 J.J.R. Redstone, *An Ex-Captain's Experience of The Salvation Army* (London: Christian Commonwealth Publishing, 2nd edn, 1888); John Manson, *The Salvation Army and the Public* (London: Routledge, 1906).

21 K.S. Inglis, *Churches and the Working Classes in Victorian England* (London: Routledge & Kegan Paul, 1963) p. 192.

22 Frederick L. Coutts, *No Discharge in This War* (London: Hodder, [1975], 2nd edn, 1981) p. 94.

23 *Orders and Regulations* (1886) p. 32.

> Army has grown from year to year with a rapidity to which nothing in modern Christendom affords any parallel.[24]

Such obedience Bramwell Booth characterised as "The Yoke" in his *Servants of All*, and described "as one of the happiest results of our system... the growth of the habit of obedience to superiors". He quotes a fragment of correspondence to illustrate its value: "I shall never be able to repay you, my dear leader, for the labour and patience you have expended on me. I feel I can at last say, by God's grace, that my self-seeking and pride are really broken down... Your tears and prayers with me, and your determined mastering of my unwillingness has won the day."[25]

Defending the "despotism" of which the Army was accused, Railton compared it with the general acceptance of the orders of a policeman in directing traffic – "all were fully aware that without just such acts of despotism in our city thoroughfares traffic would become utterly impossible... We have already seen that the extent of the Army's victories has always kept pace with its advance in the direction of thoroughly military organization."[26]

Obedience was expected firstly in respect of the methods of evangelism espoused by Booth. In a letter dated 7 March 1877, he gave an account of his dealings with a missioner who preferred different tactics: "I wrote him very frankly and told him that the only way in which he could walk in harmony with me was in carrying out my wishes... I told him he must go in and do Mission work on Mission lines, or move off."[27]

The yoke proved most irksome to some however in its application to the power of appointment. As noted previously, itinerancy was part of the Army's Methodist inheritance. Maud Booth wrote that

> officers in the Army are liable to removal, promotion, or any other change of circumstances without a moment's warning or any reason assigned. This is quite true, and is known to every Candidate, and yet they multiply rapidly, even among those whose faces have been set like flint against it... Nothing human ever could do work such as this, and, if not human, its results being eminently Christian, what can it be but the Holy Spirit that can so change multitudes of human hearts, that they yield perfect obedience, that rarest of all fruits in this age, and especially in this land of self-assertion and independence.[28]

---

24 William Booth, *In Darkest England, and the Way Out* (London: SA, 1890) pp. 242-3.

25 W. Bramwell Booth, *Servants*, pp. 70, 72.

26 Railton, *Twenty-one Years*, p. 175.

27 Catherine Bramwell Booth, *Bramwell Booth*, p. 90.

28 Maud Booth, *Two Flags*, pp. 127-8.

Ironically, it was in that land, the United States, that Maud and Ballington Booth resigned rather than accept a change of appointment in 1896.

Bramwell Booth recalled that, "In the early days of the Army's expansion in the United Kingdom, one of the most anxious problems which concerned the Founder... was the unwillingness of a certain proportion of the first leaders to be moved from one place to another – from one appointment to another... Here was a serious question of principle..." Apparently the principle was the occasion of some disagreement in 1878, when Booth resumed autocratic powers and a minority of missioners parted company with him. "Twelve or fourteen years later the question again came to the front... Two men, both holding important positions... agitated for a change in the Army system." The Founder resisted the move. "His pronouncement was accepted throughout the then Army, to the immense gain of the movement. Several officers resigned... in particular the two men referred to promptly took their departure. They both came back a year or two later acknowledging their mistake..."[29]

Others were more malleable:

> "Since receiving my appointment to South Africa, I have never for a second doubted the divinity of that appointment.' This expression of Commissioner Rees at the recent farewell meeting which took place at International Headquarters, undoubtedly voices the feelings of the nearly 1,600 officers who have just farewelled in Great Britain. But that it is possible to arrange such a changing over of officers, the magnitude and influence of which can scarcely be conceived, without difficulty, shows on the part of those officers affected by the change, their reliance on God and the confidence of their leaders."[30]

Enduring to the End

The killing pace of the Work most likely contributed to the high turn-over of personnel. Horridge gives figures of about one third and one half for the loss of "workers and members" respectively in the 1880s but notes that in the 1890s officer resignations decreased to about one quarter per annum.[31] John Manson in his *The Salvation Army and the Public* (1906) computed the number of "worked-out" Salvationist men and women officers amongst the public at over 5000.[32] Nevertheless the expectation was that officership would be a life-long vocation – a fiction not yet laid to rest in official

29 W. Bramwell Booth, *These Fifty Years*, pp. 142-8.

30 *Officer* (August, 1894) p. 240.

31 Horridge, *Origins*, p. 225.

32 Brian Lunn, *Salvation Dynasty* (London: Wm. Hodge, 1936) p. 183.

documents in the twenty-first century.[33] This was not due to any doctrine akin to the indelibility of priestly character but in practical terms the moral implications were similar.

The language used at times would not have been out of place in a Roman Catholic publication concerning priestly character:

> The ex-officer, no matter what was the cause that resulted in his loss to our fighting forces, is still a child of the Army. He entered the sacred circle. He became one of us, sharing our joys and sorrows, losses and crosses. He received the commission of a divinely-appointed authority to proclaim Salvation, build up men and women in their most holy faith, and help to win someone to God. He received the spirit of officership, whereby he mingled amongst us, for a season, as one of us, and go where he likes, and do what he likes, the imprint of the life he lived will remain. Time will not efface it; sin even will not blot it out. So that in a sense which we ought ever to remember, the ex-Officer still belongs to The Salvation Army.[34]

Asked about those who had left the ranks of officership, William Booth claimed that, "We remain in sympathetic and friendly relations with the great bulk of them … a large proportion – in this country nine out of ten – remain with us, engaged in some voluntary effort in our ranks."[35] The seriousness with which such lapses were viewed is evidenced however by the frequency of cautionary articles in Army publications, usually in the form of letters from ex-officers. In his *Servants of All*, Bramwell Booth quotes three such letters, one from an officer who was tempted to give up but hadn't done so, and two from people who had resigned – one to become a soldier again while the other had "become a castaway".[36] At least nineteen contributions on this subject were printed in *The Officer* and *The Field Officer* between 1894 and 1917. These ranged from short letters like the "confession by an ex-officer" which concluded with a call for "life-long endurance"[37] to two-part articles like that by the General on "Conservation of Officers".[38] Putting one's hand to the plough and then turning back was considered a serious matter and a cause for great anxiety.

Fortunately some saw the errors of their ways and returned – an editorial writer in 1900 observed that, "it must be gratifying to the General and Field Officers alike that the year now closing has been marked by the return of a larger number of ex-officers to the ranks, in different capacities, than has

---

33 W. Bramwell Booth, *Servants*, p. 17.
34 *Field Officer* (December 1900) pp. 453-4.
35 William Booth in Friederichs, *Romance*, p. 13.
36 W. Bramwell Booth, *Servants*, pp. 105-8.
37 *Field Officer* (November 1905) p. 401.
38 *Officer* (March and April 1897).

any previous period of our history."[39] The actual numbers were not given however.

An earlier issue shared

> that Brigadier Miles, after resigning and going to take work in America, has given up that work and come back again to the Army, expressing his deep sorrow for having, in a fit of depression and discouragement, left its ranks. He has been re-accepted, with the rank of Major, and is in charge of a Division. His advice to people who think they can be happier or better off under any other flag is that it is all a lie of the devil, and that they should stick to the Yellow, Red, and Blue. Ex-Commissioner Adams has also returned to the fold. He has acknowledged his sins and unfaithfulness, and confessed, with tears, to have wrongly done and said many things against the Army, its leaders, and his comrades, which he now regrets and acknowledges to have been untrue. He is re-accepted, with the rank of Captain. Pray for him.[40]

Evidently the higher they climbed, the further they fell. Too delightful to omit is the following:

> We regret to report the resignation of Colonel Boon. He has left the Army with a view to joining the Independent Labour Party, in the hopes of securing by direct political agitation and law reform the results which we believe can best and indeed *only* be achieved by salvation. We can only say that we believe our comrade has made a fatal mistake, which he will regret both in time and in eternity... Who can doubt that a drunkard-saving, slum-visiting, people-converting F.O. ranks far higher in the *Heavenly* scales than any M.P. in the land.[41]

A Clayton's Priesthood?[42]

A distinct leadership or officer caste was established in the Salvation Army during the "Booth" period of Army history – from the 1870s up to the deposition of Bramwell Booth in 1929. The Army resisted the notion that it was a church, which would have implied that its officers were clergy. In practical terms, however, this is what came about, and when it suited its purposes, the Army was quite happy to accept and take advantage of this implication.

---

39 *Field Officer* (December 1900) p. 453.

40 *Officer* (January 1898) p. 12.

41 *Officer* (August 1894) p. 232.

42 "Claytons: Proprietary name of a substitute for hard liquor... Usu. as a quasi-adjective indicating a pretence to or a largely unsuccessful imitation of the 'real thing'." Harry Orsman, *Oxford Dictionary of New Zealand English* (Oxford: Oxford University Press, 1997).

This chapter has described officership as revealed in the character and functions expected of officers and the conditions under which they operated over this same period. The question is whether or not these also indicated a distinct clerical group within the organisation. The ambiguity already observed applies here too.

On the one hand, the qualities of life prescribed by the founders – being thoroughly saved and sanctified, eager to save sinners, filled with compassion for the lost and suffering, loyal, humble, perseverant, endued with the spirit of enterprise – would be expected to some degree of any Salvation Army soldier, officer or not. Leadership is exercised at many levels, and not only by officers. All Salvationists are subject to some form of the Regulations. All Salvationists as Christians are regarded as having a "call" to some vocation and we have seen that the Founders believed in the call of all Salvation Army Soldiers to ministry. Some form of training for their particular role would be recommended for every sphere of service – officers were tasked with training their soldiers. All soldiers sign a form of "Covenant". Responsibility for the "lost" of their own neighbourhood is expressly enjoined on all Salvationists. The standard of living at which early officers were supported was assumed to be about that of the average of their soldiers. Obedience "to the lawful orders of my officers" was a pledge in every Soldier's *Articles of War*. "Enduring to the end", with a life-long commitment to service in the Army, was always held up as an ideal for all ranks, whether in a voluntary or a professional capacity, however honoured in the breach.

The distinctive quality of officership could not therefore be located in any or all of these features per se. Neither would it ever have been accurate to generalise that officers would have these characteristics or qualities to a higher degree than possessed by non-officers.

On the other hand, we can see that all these qualities would naturally be expected to be most characteristic of officers, and it came to be assumed that officers would meet a higher standard than soldiers. T. Henry Howard wrote that, "when Cadets are made to perceive the standards by which they must measure their work and conduct, they not only see how far short they fall, but ceasing to measure themselves, their abilities, and their doings, by one another as Soldiers, they aim at far higher success than would be possible if they did not adopt the standards presented to them."[43]

The conditions of officers' service would constitute their professional milieu in a way that could not be true of non-officer, volunteer Salvationists. The mystique of the Call to officership, the spiritually intensive nature of officer-formation in training and the sessional group bonding with peers, the extent of personal commitment involved in the Covenant and Undertakings, the ranking system, the distinctive functions and roles of officers and the

43 "One of the Scholars", *School*, Introduction, pp. vii-viii.

intensity of the all-absorbing work, together with the sense of corporate identity and *esprit de corps*, gave officership a character which could be described as clerical compared with that of the rank and file.[44]

This was naturally a process. The first officers were already Evangelists; they simply added ranks. Later candidates for officership were pressed into service without training or special recognition of their roles, or were given a few weeks on-the-job apprenticeship assisting in a corps. With the introduction of training and commissioning, the elaboration of "Army" practices, customs and rituals, and the steady accretion of tradition, a mystique gradually became associated with officership. This process was probably accelerated by the tendency to sentimentalise and romanticise everything to do with the Army. Booth was the "dear old General" at 48 years of age.[45] The "dear old Congress" (Clapton Congress Hall), the "dear old flag" and the "dear old days" in training are all quoted in a letter from an officer "who had not been long in the field."[46]

This ambiguity over the status of officers arose in part from the Methodist theological roots we noted in a previous chapter, and in part from the fact that traditional ecclesiastical and canonical distinctions were of little interest or relevance. Salvationists were, as far as they were concerned, *sui generis*, needing no external ecclesiastical validation or referencing. Bramwell Booth felt this:

> We had no precedent to go on, very little experience to guide us... We had to build the ship while we were at sea, and not only build the ship, but master the laws of navigation, and not only master the laws of navigation but hammer sense into a strangely assorted crew! ...The character of the work was so new in religious history that many decisions, even though they seemed at the time to involve only minor points of policy and method, proved to be of great importance.[47]

Pragmatic decisions beget principles. An interesting light on the Army's pragmatism is offered by research done by John Niles Bartholemew, who compares the policy-making and policy-implementation of congregations ascribing to three different polities, which he describes as "Local Autonomy", "Collegiality" and "Titular Hierarchy". Bartholemew analyses

---

44 For a recent analysis of the effect of training, see Roger Finke and Kevin D. Dougherty: "The Effects of Professional Training: The Social and Religious Capital Acquired in Seminaries", *Journal for the Scientific Study of Religion* 41:1 (2002) pp. 103-120, who "illustrate how seminaries provide clergy with social and religious capital that is distinctive from that of the laity."

45 W. Bramwell Booth, Letter of 8 September, 1877, in Catherine Bramwell Booth, *Bramwell Booth*, p. 79.

46 W. Bramwell Booth, *Servants*, pp. 74-5.

47 W. Bramwell Booth, *Echoes*, pp. 22-23.

these in terms of "use of theologically legitimated authority" and "use of institutionally legitimated authority". In the case of "the titular hierarchy, institutional authority was so sufficient that theological authority was never explored." Perhaps then the Army's military structure has contributed to a paucity of theological reflection.[48]

The founders set out to do just whatever appeared the most practical thing to do next. Rather than intentionally taking the historic pattern of the church as a model they positively eschewed any such intention. They fought against it as repugnant to their view of the ministerial role of Christians in general. For all that, they could not avoid bringing with them from their church background ways of thinking about how the church should be organised. The irony is that they ended up with a similar model of clergy and laity and an episcopal system of government under different names. And the Army chose for practical reasons to stake out legal grounds for having its officers recognised as clergy.

This analysis of the character and tasks of officership confirms that it is difficult *in practice*, leaving aside ecclesiastical distinctions of legitimacy and apostolic provenance, to distinguish officership from the clerical status in any church.

---

48 John Niles Bartholemew, "A Sociological View of Authority in Religious Organizations", *Review of Religious Research* 23:2 (December 1981).

Chapter Nine

Transitions

> "Fortunately I didn't go to any place of devotion, though I did get mixed up with a Salvation Army procession. It was quite interesting to be at close quarters with them, they're so absolutely different from what they used to be like when I first remember them in the eighties. They used to go about then unkempt and dishevelled, in a sort of smiling rage with the world, and now they're spruce and jaunty and flamboyantly decorative, like a geranium bed with religious convictions. Laura Kettleway was going on about them in the lift in Dover Street Tube the other day, saying what a lot of good work they did, and what a loss it would have been if they'd never existed."
>
> "Saki" (H.H. Munro),
> *Louise.*[1]

Routinisation

William Booth was "Promoted to Glory" in 1912. In accordance with the Deed Poll of 1878, a sealed envelope was opened by the Army's solicitor and to no-one's surprise was found to contain the name of William Bramwell Booth. Then 56 years of age, he had in reality run the Army for the previous twenty years while his father had returned to his first love of peripatetic evangelism and made imperial progresses around his far-flung dominions.

Bramwell had a prodigious capacity for work, and continued to keep his hand on the day to day affairs of the organisation. The first part of his Generalship was overshadowed by the Great War, which almost overtook his International Congress called for June 1914. He sought to preserve the Army's internationalism and maintain links with his forces amongst the Central Powers, setting himself against anti-German hysteria. His Christmas message for 1915 included, "Every land is my Fatherland for all lands are my Father's" and soon after the end of the war he called upon a German officer to address a meeting in Westminster Central Hall. He gave special attention to youth work and promoted missionary expansion – the flag was raised in 23 new countries between 1913 and 1928. Under his leadership the

1 H.H. Munro, *The Short Stories of Saki* (London: John Lane The Bodley Head, 1930) p. 449. "Louise" was first published in *The Toys of Peace* in 1923.

number of Corps and Outposts increased from 9,415 to 15,163, and the number of commissioned officers from 15,988 to 25,427.[2] It is interesting to compare these figures with the 15,339 corps and 25,716 officers recorded in 2003.[3]

Bramwell lacked his father's charisma however and his profound deafness isolated him to some degree. His senior commanders grew restive at the closeness of his control and the suspicion that he promoted and favoured his children above long-serving officers. Opposition was led by his sister, Evangeline, Commander in USA from 1903, and his brother-in-law Frederick Booth-Tucker, who resented being deprived of active command and retired at the age of seventy-three. Bramwell resisted in particular the suggestion that he forgo the right to nominate his successor and allow election by senior commanders. "[William] Booth, after long consideration and constant seeking for the guidance of God," wrote Bramwell, had decided that the appointment of a General by his predecessor "was on the whole the safest and best."[4] "[The General] is not the maker or unmaker of the original Trust. He is the Trustee, the servant of the Trust. His great duty is to conform to its terms, preserve its integrity and spirit, to guard and fulfil it, and to hand it on in complete and unimpaired efficiency to his successor."[5]

Bramwell Booth's stubbornness on this point, claiming that he could not relinquish a sacred trust God had inspired the Founder to institute, is interesting in the light of Bryan Wilson's comment on the "absoluteness" of sectarian ideology. "Revealed truth being God's will, cannot readily be countermanded… 'Reform' is not possible in a sectarian organisation, since it must cast doubt on present and past arrangements which were ordained by God."[6] Was Bramwell still a "sectarian" while his subordinates were becoming more flexible? When he fell gravely ill in 1928, fears that his daughter Catherine would succeed him prompted a number of Commissioners to requisition a High Council in terms of the 1904 Deed Poll which provided for the removal of a General who became "unfit for office." Bramwell was deposed by 52 votes to 5 in February 1929, made a Companion of Honour by George V in April and died in June of that year.

Edward Higgins, Bramwell's Chief of Staff for ten years, was elected to replace him, and secured the passage of the Salvation Army Act through the British Parliament in 1931, regularising the election of successive Generals by High Council, setting a retirement age for the General and vesting

2 Ervine, *God's Soldier*, II , p. 851.

3 *The Salvation Army Yearbook* (2004) p. 33.

4 Ervine, *God's Soldier*, II, p. 908.

5 Letter from Bramwell Booth to Evangeline Booth, 24 November 1927, quoted by Catherine Bramwell Booth, *Bramwell Booth*, p. 488.

6 Wilson, *Patterns of Sectarianism*, pp. 10-11.

Salvation Army property in a Trustee Company instead of in the General as sole Trustee. Evangeline Booth finally had her turn at the top 1934-39 but by this time the fire had gone out and the Army was in retreat in the land of its birth. The Australian George Lyndon Carpenter (1939-46) struggled to hold the international Army together – it was progressively proscribed in the Axis nations, money was in short supply and travel restricted – and Albert Orsborn (1946-54) faced mounting tasks in the post-war reconstruction period with diminishing resources. In these years Europe especially began turning away from religion in general and the Army's well-tried methods failed to connect with an increasingly secularised society.

In one of Conan Doyle's Sherlock Holmes stories, Holmes draws Dr Watson's attention to the curious incident of the dog in the night-time. Watson protests that the dog did nothing; it did not even bark. *That* was the curious incident, Holmes rejoins.[7] The close on forty years of near silence on the theology of officership in Salvation Army publications up until about 1960 are similarly informative: they suggest that Salvationists did not spend much effort or time in thinking further about the theological implications of decisions made about these matters. In the words of Lieut-Colonel Fred Hoyle (commissioned in 1941), "Looking back on my training days I cannot remember anything being taught on this subject (officership and the 'priesthood of all believers'), or anything being said in any of the many councils I attended."[8] The slender record could also indicate that there were limited opportunities for the expression of opinion, and little use of the one forum for discussion, the pages of *The Officer*, seems to have been made to discuss this issue.

There is a discontinuity between the concerns of the period described in the last chapter, and those of the later twentieth century and the present day. Interest in the earlier period was centred on the personal qualities and work of officers, but less concerned with how they stood *vis-à-vis* the ministries of the churches. The attitudes and parameters established in the nineteenth century continued to provide the intellectual and spiritual framework and the regulatory expectations for officership through most of the twentieth century. The literature does not reveal any significant development or florescence of new thinking in the intervening period. The principles espoused by the founders were still taken for granted, and largely unexamined.

During these middle years there are few, mostly oblique, references to the theme of this work. There were some contributions of the spiritual and motivational kind, largely reiterating the views of the previous generation. General Edward J. Higgins' little book *Stewards of God* from the early 30s, consisting of advice to Corps officers, might be taken as representative of

---

7 Arthur Conan Doyle, "Silver Blaze".

8 *Officer* (December 1987) p. 549.

this genre. Higgins did suggest a tentative distinction of roles: writing of "things for which all alike have responsibility – time, opportunity, gifts, influence..." and then of "the further trust to officers: responsibility for affairs not our own – care of Corps or Social Institutions or wide field; embraces care of immortal souls, the glorious gospel... committed to my trust (1 Timothy 1.11)".[9]

In the 1925 *Year Book*, an article on "The Salvation Army officer and his work" stated that "Salvation Army officers are divided into two main classes, the Local Officer and the fully commissioned officer. The first class... voluntarily devote their spare time... Commissioned officers are drawn from the rank and file of soldiers and Local Officers... Upon completion of their training the young officers are commissioned and drafted to suitable appointments." This statement links commissioned and local or non-commissioned officers and implies no essential distinction in character between them. The only difference lies in the training and full-time availability of those commissioned.[10]

Staff-Captain Carvosso Gauntlett reviewed two German Catholic works, *Der Salutismus* by P.A. Classen, and *Catholic Salvationism: The Salvation Army and its World Propaganda* by Martin Fassbender, in 1928. He made "a call to maintain these Army methods that have led to victory in all lands ... to maintain and advance throughout our ranks what they [the German authors] have termed the *Lay Apostolate* - the royal priesthood which, our Founders taught us, included all from the General down to the latest convert; an Apostolate of deeds, of prayer, of sacrifice, of good example, and of the love that seeks the lost: the Apostolate of Salvationism!"[11] Catholic writers, however well disposed towards the Army, would naturally see all Salvationists – officers and soldiers alike – as lay, like lay members of an Order in the Church. That very ascription assumed that there was also an alternative, non-lay status to which Salvationists did not aspire. This was tantamount to imputing second class ecclesiastical status to officers, although it is doubtful whether Gauntlett would have been content with that interpretation. Indeed, the fact that he found it necessary to emphasise the Lay Apostolate might indicate that he realised this was in danger of neglect in favour of a more professional/specialised officer cadre. The dog may not have barked, but Gauntlett appeared to be sniffing the air.

General Wilfred Kitching (1954-63), at the end of this period, avoided the imputation by not using the word "lay" at all. Writing in a series of *War Cry* articles in the 1950s on the character of Salvation Army soldiership, Kitching said that

9 Higgins, *Stewards of God*, pp. 6-7.
10 *SA Year Book* (1925) p. 23.
11 *Staff Review* (April 1928) p. 220.

> The usual distinction between officers and soldiers is obviously useful at certain levels, but the nomenclature can be misleading, and at times there may be danger in the distinction. There is in God's sight no different order of believers, even though there are different callings. All believers – and to us that means soldiers as well as officers – belong to the "community of God", and have gifts according to their calling.
>
> The corps that revolves too much around the officer is a corps which is falling short of its calling. Soldiers who fail to realize their obligations as co-workers with those who have been appointed as their leaders can well be "out of step" in the march. In the set-up of our corps life the relationship of soldiers with their officers is something different and apart from the usually understood relationship of a congregation with its minister... He (the soldier) sees in his officer a God-called man or woman needing the assistance of others in his task.[12]

Kitching possibly intended to suggest that Salvation Army soldiers were expected to be more active in the affairs of the Army than church members were assumed to be in those of the church. He also probably wished to imply that the soldiers would be more active in mission, in evangelism and deeds of service than were the majority of church members. He gave the impression that officers were officers and soldiers were soldiers because of their differing gifts, although he did not elaborate on the nature of those gifts. However, those of the soldiers were evidently more appropriate for followers than for leaders, and the officer role took precedence if the function of the soldiers was to support it.

These three writers in any case presented with some authority the Army's official commitment to the "functional" view of Salvation Army officership. That is, officers differ from non-officers only in their role and not in any ministerial or priestly character or status.

There was still, however, that other strand in the Army's thinking about officership – that it did enjoy some special status, and that officers were different from clergy but equal. In an article on preserving the Army's distinctiveness, Brigadier Bramwell Taylor noted that "we take pride in the fact that we are different from other members of the 'Ministering Fraternity'... We are not 'ecclesiastics' according to the accepted interpretation of that term, although we qualify under its most sacred meaning."[13] The nature of the differences or similarities was not spelt out.

---

12 Wilfred Kitching, *Soldier of Salvation* (London: SA, 1963) p. 49.

13 *Staff Review* (January 1926) p. 113.

Upward Mobility

The extract from the story by "Saki", given at the head of this chapter, reminds us that although the Army's conscious ecclesiology appeared to undergo little development in this period, sociological changes of significance for its future direction were inevitably taking place. Upward mobility had long been a feature of sectarian life in Britain. The oft-quoted judgement of the 84-year-old John Wesley on Methodism could have been repeated of Salvationists by Bramwell Booth:

> The Methodists in every place grow diligent and frugal; consequently they increase in goods. Hence they proportionately increase in pride, in the desire of the flesh, the desire of the eyes, and the pride of life. So although the form of religion remains, the spirit is swiftly vanishing away...[14]

Likewise Bryan Wilson's comments on the Nazarenes could have applied to the Army:

> They were recruited mainly of the lower classes. As their members rose in social status and as the discipline and orderliness of religious commitment led to habits of frugality and responsibility which increased opportunities for economic gain and social responsibility, so the Nazarenes ceased to be so dominantly identified with the very lowest sections of society. They gradually came to manifest a concern for status, prestigious buildings and display which characterised other denominations.[15]

Salvationists may not have risen to the same degree as the Methodists but the same process will have been taking place as for the Methodists and Nazarenes. While the social structures and class patterns differed from the British model, Salvationists in countries like New Zealand likewise participated in the general rise in the standard of living with increased opportunities for education and diversification of occupation. I am not aware of research on the socio-economic status of Salvationists in the twentieth century but it can be surmised that the proportion of blue-collar workers in the ranks diminished and that of business and professional people increased. Some Salvationists of course sought the shelter of more respectable and less socially embarrassing religious groups and others drifted from any religious profession, but many took the Salvation Army with them as they rose. The Army therefore may be seen as conforming to many of the characteristics the sociologists attribute to a "conversionist" sect or movement consolidating or denominationalising.

---

14 Quoted by J.H. Plumb, *England in the Eighteenth Century* (Harmondsworth: Penguin, 1950) p. 97.

15 Wilson, *Religion in Secular Society*, p. 108.

One of these is a change of focus from a mission to maintenance, from a crusade to change the world to a preoccupation with the interests, needs and desires of the existing members. The Salvation Army probably began this journey even before the period under consideration here. This development did not necessarily involve a change in activities at first, but rather subtle changes in the way those activities were addressed. For example, brass bands were originally pressed into service within the Salvation Army in order to augment open-air witness – to support hymn singing, drown out the opposition and, because brass banding was a fashionable element in popular culture, to attract attention. The evangelical intention was gradually subsumed by the social and cultural needs of the bandsmen themselves, even though the ostensible rationale and rhetoric was unchanged. In time the actual music reflected this change of purpose; what William Booth called "soul-saving" music – inseparable from the words of the hymns and songs it accompanied – became music for the sake of the music. The musicians became much more presentable (as "Saki" observed) and the composers more inventive. The genre became in some sense decadent: the arrangement of themes from Tchaikovsky might do people good as music but was unlikely to touch their conscience with the memory of words of hymns they once learned in Sunday School.

Over this period the Army's practical theology also began to drift from its doctrinal moorings. Niebuhr says that "By its very nature the sectarian type of organisation is valid for only one generation... Rarely does a second generation hold the convictions it has inherited with a fervour equal to that of its fathers, who fashioned these convictions in the heat of conflict and at the risk of martyrdom."[16] The children and grandchildren of those who had experienced the miracle of the changing of beer into furniture did not necessarily enjoy a vital conversion experience of their own. They grew up within the world of the Salvation Army and it was their familiar sub-culture, but they did not necessarily inherit the evangelical imperative. The fact that Salvationists have in general become less inclined or likely to be motivated to engage in personal evangelism probably indicates a slackening commitment to the doctrines underlying such activity. A diminished conviction that their neighbour is going to hell perhaps renders them less inclined to risk giving offence by trying to save him from it. Allen Satterlee also draws attention to disillusionment following the First World War as a factor contributing to loss of evangelical zeal.[17]

This doctrinal "cooling off" can also be seen in connection with the Army's characteristically sectarian "perfectionism". The Army had inherited the Wesleyan theory of holiness, as mediated through the nineteenth century

16 H. Richard Niebuhr, *Social Sources of Denominationalism* (New York: Meridian, [1929] 1957) p. 20.

17 Allen Satterlee, *Turning Points* (Alexandria Va.: Crest, 2004) pp. 76-80.

holiness revival and expounded by the Booths and notably by the American Commissioner S. L. Brengle (1860-1936).[18] This held that the believer may be "sanctified", enjoying a "second blessing", a distinct and instantaneous work of grace subsequent to conversion, by which the tendency to sin is removed and power given for living a holy life. By mid-twentieth century a new generation of Salvationists found this doctrine difficult to reconcile with their experience and Brengle's books were being neglected. At the 1960 New Zealand Local Officers' Conference Bandmaster H.H. Neeve asked why holiness was no longer being preached.[19] Frederick Coutts endeavoured to reinterpret the doctrine in more accessible form, with greater emphasis on the "process" of sanctification than on the "crisis" entry experience.[20] Such diluting of perfectionist expectations was perhaps another sign of a denominationalising tendency.

If one of the presenting characteristics of the sectarian ethos was the holding of the "world" at arms-length, the early Salvation Army certainly conformed to type in that respect, but the period from the Booths to the 1960s saw a steady, if slow, retreat from the ghetto. Early female converts had feathers snipped from their hats at the Mercy Seat. In 1929 a New Zealand officer, Ensign Bennett, so misguided as to mention in speaking at a youth meeting that she had attended a cinema found the rest of her remarks drowned out by energetic singing led by the senior officer presiding. In the 1930s it was still reprehensible to attend a football match – the advent of a Salvation Army rugby club team in Christchurch in the late 1930s greatly perturbed the Englishman serving as Chief Secretary in New Zealand.[21] In the 1950s it was still daring to attend a dance. Today salvationists still take the pledge to abstain from alcohol and gambling, but the "world" is now on their side as far as tobacco is concerned. Robertson sums it up in observing a shift "from abstention from worldly amusements and fashions to the injunction to be judicious and selective in such indulgences".[22]

It is instructive to review such changes described above in the light of Dean M. Kelly's 1972 survey and analysis of declining mainline churches and growing evangelical churches in the United States. Kelly concluded that

---

18 Wm. Booth et. al., *Holiness Readings from "The War Cry"* (London: SA, 1883); Wm. Booth, *Purity of Heart*, (London: SA, 1902); Samuel Logan Brengle, *Heart Talks on Holiness* (1896); *Helps to Holiness* (1897); *The Way of Holiness* (1902); *The Soul-Winner's Secret* (1903); *When the Holy Ghost is Come* (1909); *Love Slaves (1923); Resurrection Life and Power* (1925); *The Guest of the Soul* (1934). See also R. David Rightmire, *Sanctified Sanity: The Life and Teaching of Samuel Logan Brengle* (Alexandria VA: Crest Books, 2003); Chick Yuill, *We Need Saints!* (London: SA, 1988); Shaw Clifton, *New Love* (Wellington: Flag, 2004).

19 Minutes in New Zealand Salvation Army Archives.

20 Frederick L. Coutts, *The Call to Holiness* (London: SA, 1957).

21 Cyril Bradwell, *Touched with Splendour* (Wellington: Flag, 2003) pp. 49-50.

22 Robertson, in Wilson, *Patterns of Sectarianism*, p. 74.

"strict" churches (doctrinally and ethically), making significant demands on their members, were strong and grew, while declining churches asked less of their members.[23] The Salvation Army was tending towards the "declining main-line" profile in these years. The question remains as to whether churches decline because they are less demanding, or demand less as they decline, or whether both tendencies are part of the wider "denominationalising" process, the one feeding the other.

The Salvation Army has displayed a sectarian tendency to provide an all-embracing social milieu for its members. This period from the 1920s on saw a change from most activities being evangelical in intention (if not in achievement), and directed outward, to more activities being provided for the entertainment of the Salvationists themselves. This probably took place in two stages. At first the same activities, like brass banding, served both purposes, while later new activities which had no explicit evangelical rationale, such as "socials" (games, as an alternative to dancing) were introduced, along with youth groups, Baden Powell organisations and other recreational activities.[24] These did serve as points of entry for potential converts but they also served to hold the members together and make it unnecessary for them to seek diversion elsewhere. The very smallness of the movement (consistently about six and a half thousand soldiers in New Zealand from the 1920s until recent years), and the practice of holding regional and national meetings, congresses, band festivals and sports meetings, fostered a significant sense of community. These activities, plus the tendency for officers' children to leave home and marry into the local Corps when their parents were appointed elsewhere, led to a situation where many Salvationists had relatives and friends, or at least acquaintances, throughout the country.

Joan Hutson's loving but warts-and-all account of the Gisborne Corps in the 1930s describes how

> The Salvation Army buildings were also the centre of the corps' social life. Banquets, concerts, engagement parties, socials, twenty-first birthdays, wedding anniversaries, welcomes and farewells, all took place within these walls.

---

23 Dean M. Kelly, *Why Conservative Churches are Growing* (New York: Harper and Row, 1972). Roger Finke and Rodney Stark explain this in terms of rational choice theory. "Why Mainline Denominations Decline" in *The Churching of America 1776-1990*. Extract in Susanne C. Monahan (ed.), *Sociology of Religion, A Reader* (Upper Saddle River NJ: Prentice-Hall, 2001) pp. 236-241.

24 See articles like "Gymnastic Equipment in our Young People's Corps" by Adjutant James Fookes (USA), *Officer* (October 1923) pp. 322-4; "Saturday Afternoon Cinema Matinees for Children: Suggestions for Counter Attractions", by Capt. Wm. Ware (Great Britain), *Officer* (September 1925) pp. 243-6.

> Almost without exception, faith in their God as expressed through The Salvation Army took precedence over all other loyalties, and there were many other loyalties. Somehow work and families and sport had to be fitted in around Army commitments. In addition most soldiers belonged to some kind of lodge, the Oddfellows Lodge, the Rechabites or the Masonic Lodge. Some became Grand Masters, giving the Lodge their loyalty second only to their Salvationism…
>
> The feeling of "family", with all its ups and downs, extended way beyond the borders of Gisborne. A Salvationist could walk into any corps throughout the country, indeed throughout the world, and feel welcome. There was even a distinctive Army whistle used primarily in New Zealand from about the time of the Great War. Thought to have been the opening bars of a once popular march, it was used to attract the attention of a fellow Salvationist whether in a military canteen, across the street or at a rugby match – all immensely tribal. The strong Army culture meant that the uniforms, the belief system, the rituals, the jargon and, yes, even the whistle all loudly declared that Salvationists were "at home" even if they knew not one person present. At the deepest level of consciousness, they belonged.[25]

In Tom Aitken's words, in 1964,

> The smallness of the group, coupled with a sense of the peculiarity of the Army's customs, has tended to make the Army an "in-group" for its members. This tendency towards exclusiveness has probably weakened since the war, for the Army now co-operates far more than it did with other organisations, but the Army is still tightly bound together as a social group.[26]

However, in terms of Wilson's observation that "sects have a totalitarian rather than segmental hold over their members,"[27] this hold was in the process of relaxing in the period under review. The tendency observed amongst Methodists in the nineteenth century, when "the 'Means of Grace' were fighting a losing battle to rival 'the social party, the secular concert, or the tennis club' as a claimant for the time and energy of members," was now to be found amongst Salvationists.[28] Werner Stark sees this as part of the sect's coming to terms with the fact that "the conflict of the sect with society must be solved somehow, for it is an acute crisis which cannot be turned

---

25 Joan Hutson, *As for Me and My House: A Salute to early Salvation Army families of Gisborne, 1886 to 1952* (Wellington: Flag, 2004) p. 227.

26 T.G. Aitken, "Aspects of the History of The Salvation Army in New Zealand, 1929-1963: A Study in Adjustment" (MA thesis, Victoria University of Wellington, 1964) p. 29.

27 Wilson, *Patterns of Sectarianism*, p. 24.

28 A.D. Gilbert, *Religion and Society in Industrial England: Church, Chapel and Social Change 1740-1914* (London: Longman, 1976) p. 181, citing Minutes of the Wesleyan Conference, 1890, pp. 354-5.

into a lasting state… it must either withdraw from society or learn to live with it."[29]

A fear of being "led astray" by "worldly" education – an offer to pay for a university education for Bramwell Booth had been declined by his parents – might also have been a matter of class attitude amongst some New Zealand Salvationists before and even after the second world war. Another indicator of change might therefore be found in the increased number of Salvationists accessing higher education. From being rare, Salvationists obtaining tertiary education had become sufficiently numerous to be perceived to require some special pastoral support lest they be lost to the movement, and Salvation Army Students' Fellowships became established in countries like the United Kingdom and New Zealand in the 1950s. By the 1970s higher education was sufficiently common for this organisation to have outlived its usefulness and fade away, in New Zealand at least.

Such observations need not be confined to the Army in Western countries. In countries with entrenched class or caste systems, upward mobility might also be observed, within limits. In India for example, the Army recruited chiefly amongst the lowest castes; the higher castes might often admire and support its work financially, much as the aristocracy did in Britain, but few of them were prepared to sign up. The Army itself, however, offered the means of rising in status. In many third world countries the Army, along with other churches, has undertaken to provide schools, and mission-school education has been the key to advancement. (Conversely it has been suggested that the relative weakness of "Corps life" in the United States territories today derives from a failure of the Army there to establish a strong middle-class presence, so that in many places the soldiery also double as a client base while the role of active "laity" in the "church" has devolved upon employees, who may not be Salvationists or even professing Christians, a growing trend in Western countries).[30]

The processes of institutionalisation and clericalisation naturally affected the character of the Army's leadership as well. Ervine believed that "the success of the Army… was the cause of the change in the spirit of its officers. Formerly, they were men of God: now they were men of affairs… [Commissioner Elijah] Cadman did not care whether he was a corporal or a commissioner so long as he saved souls. His successors wanted to save souls, but they also wanted to be commissioners…"[31] Inevitably the second and third generations of leadership differed in attitude from the pioneers. George Bernard Shaw predicted in 1905 that

---

29 Werner Stark, *The Sociology of Religion, Vol. II: Sectarian Religion* (London: Routledge and Kegan Paul, 1967) p. 235.

30 The *SA Year Book* (2005) reported 85,570 senior soldiers and 65,259 employees nationally in the USA.

31 Ervine, *God's Soldier*, II, pp. 862-3.

> its present staff of enthusiast-commanders shall be succeeded by a bureaucracy of men of business, who will be no better than bishops, and perhaps a good deal more unscrupulous. That has always happened sooner or later to great orders founded by saints; the order founded by William Booth is not exempt from the same danger.[32]

Shaw, as an observer of human nature, anticipated the sociologists here. Wilson says that,

> ...the Churches have increasingly adopted the same style of operations and similar methods of organization as the large concerns of business, education and recreation in modern society... Administration has in some measure superseded spirituality, and rational business organisation has replaced the distribution of grace or the reception of divine inspiration... There can be few human activities on which rational planning, administrative co-ordination and the regulations of bureaucratic organization have such deleterious effects as religious movements.[33]

This is not to say that Salvation Army officers in administrative roles inevitably become less "spiritual" but particular spheres of responsibility shape the responses of the individual – we see from where we stand. The Army's early leaders tended to be out front leading the charge; their successors, the *apparatchiks*, became more cautious about counting the cost.

These changes did not affect just the higher echelons of command of course. Thomas O'Dea commented that when a professional pastorate emerges,

> there comes into existence a body of men for whom the clerical life offers not simply the "religious" satisfactions of the earlier charismatic period, but also prestige and respectability, power and influence... and satisfactions derived from the use of personal talents in teaching, leadership, etc. Moreover, the *maintenance* of the situation in which these rewards are forthcoming tends to become an element in the motivation of the group.[34]

It must be admitted that the demands of ministering to an established congregations naturally shape the role, outlook and expectations in ways quite different from those of the pioneer and itinerant evangelist – and may attract a different candidate.

It would be fair comment to say that rising standards of living, improved educational levels and the progressive secularization of western society,

---

32 George Bernard Shaw, Preface to "Major Barbara" in *The Complete Prefaces* (London: Paul Hamlyn, 1965) pp. 126-7.

33 Wilson, *Religion in Secular Society*, pp. 138-140.

34 O'Dea, *Sociology of Religion*, p. 91.

combined with the general diminution of evangelical zeal almost inevitable amongst the second and third generations of a movement, impacted upon the Salvation Army's self-understanding and behaviour in the post-Boothian era. However, rhetoric often persists long after conviction has faded and we no longer walk the talk. The cinematic cartoon roadrunner character, charging well over the edge of the precipice before suddenly realizing that the void has opened below, might be analogous to the way the Army's sectarian persona was maintained long after many Salvationists had ceased to take it seriously, except for a niggling and ritualised sense of guilt. The sectarian mind-set enjoyed a long twilight. At the tail end of the period, however, many Salvationists would have struggled to recognise themselves in Robertson's mid-60s summation:

> In essentials... the Army remains the same as in the early years of the present century – an authoritarian organisation, demanding extensive commitment and obedience to its rules and regulations, which also extend to matters of private thought, conversation, socialisation of children, work and leisure, financial expenditure, dress and physical health.[35]

Gordon Moyles offers a critique of Robertson, suggesting that he has been misled by the traditional rhetoric of the Army's "stated policies and doctrines", and that "he ignores the beliefs of the Salvationists themselves, never acknowledging that there might be a vast difference between the formalized beliefs of the organization and of lay Salvationists."[36] Formal statements thus tend to be left behind in the wake of a sectarian community accommodating to the wider world. Werner Stark offers a similar reflection on Wilson's and Yinger's use of the term "established sect", terming it a "*contradictio in adjecto*... unjustified if the group's inner history is taken into account... A sect that ceases to be an elementary expression of passionate protest is a sect no more... It is in effect a denomination."[37] At the same time, the Army continued – as it still does – to retain *in some measure* such distinctively sectarian characteristics as "tests of merit on would-be members, ...discipline, regulating the declared beliefs and the life habits of members, prescribing and operating sanctions for those who deviate, ...demands ...for commitment from its members."[38]

It may be observed during the forty or fifty years up to 1960, that the Army's language and official line remained sectarian, while in practice its

---

35 Robertson, in Wilson, *Patterns of Sectarianism*, p. 89.

36 Moyles, *Blood and Fire*, pp. 228-244.

37 Werner Stark, *Sectarian Religion*, pp. 266-7.

38 Bryan Wilson, "The Persistence of Sects", *DISKUS* 1:2 (1993) p. 2. (www.Uni-marburg.de/religionswissenschaft/journal/diskus/Wilson.html). Downloaded 10 November 2004.

general tendency might be described as "denominationalising". The corollary of this was that the soldiers were more likely to regard their officers as clergy and the officers to see themselves in that role. The inevitable tension between these two continental plates moving in opposite directions began to surface as the movement entered its second century in the 1960s.

Metamorphosis

A.F Walls taught Patristics in a West African Anglican theological college in the 1950s. Visiting local churches in his district he realised that the things he was teaching about during the week, he could observe actually happening at the weekend. The same kind of consolidation and reflection he described taking place in the second century churches, was in progress in West African churches in their second century.[39] The second century seems to have a similar significance for the Salvation Army. Roger Green, referring to various late twentieth and early twenty-first century initiatives in Salvationist theological discussion, comments that "these are still tenuous efforts for a denomination yet in its primacy. The Army is only now coming into an understanding of what it means to have a corporate theological life."[40] General Paul A. Rader acknowledged in 1998 that "The Salvation Army is passing through a critical metamorphosis of self-understanding."[41]

The Salvation Army entered its second century in the 1960s. Its first great age of expansion was well and truly over; it was now becoming more self-conscious, and beginning to clarify and rationalise what it had been doing, as well as adjusting to the fact that it was now operating in a world strangely different from that in which it had taken shape. Salvationists were becoming more aware of the rest of the church, and some more informed about theological issues and more likely therefore to question the Army's own position. This can be illustrated by the publication in 1960 of Brigadier Harry Dean's *The Sacraments, The Salvationist's Viewpoint*. There had been earlier a few articles in *The Officer* or pamphlets on this subject, or the odd chapter in a book here and there, by that time long out of print or inaccessible to most. In the words of A.J. Gilliard, commissioned in 1922, "For a good many years the matter was never in the average Salvationist's thinking. I cannot recall ever coming across it until after I was an officer and

---

39 A.F. Walls, *The Missionary Movement in Christian History: Studies in the Transmission of Faith* (Maryknoll NY/Edinburgh: Orbis/T&T Clark, 1996) p. *xiii*.

40 Roger L. Green, "The Salvation Army and the Evangelical Tradition", *Word and Deed* (May, 2003) p. 61.

41 *Word and Deed* (Fall 1998) p. 1.

then only casually."[42] Dean's new booklet marked the opening of new phase of self-awareness and questioning.

The election of the scholarly Frederick Coutts as General in 1963 probably encouraged as well as adding some cachet of respectability to theological thinking. John Gowans (General 1999-2002) comments in his memoirs that "Frederick Coutts was regarded by some as a dangerous liberal. When Commissioner Coutts was elected to the office of General, one leader was overheard to say that this particular High Council's selection heralded the end of The Salvation Army."[43] A.J. Gilliard observed of IHQ in 1965 that "There is a decided spirit of release and change here, but I get the idea that we do not yet know what to do with the new opportunities thus provided."[44] Writers such as Fred Brown, Bernard Mobbs and Harry Dean took up the task of earlier intellectuals like Alfred G. Cunningham and Carvosso Gauntlett in trying to widen Salvationists' theological horizons. *The Officer*, edited in turn by Eric Coward, William Burrows and William Clark, entered a halcyon period, with a significant educative role.

The Salvation Army was also affected to some extent by a new wave of radical, popular theology associated with writers such as John A.T. Robinson, Harvey Cox and Paul Tillich, and for perhaps the first time began to develop some conscious pluralism of theological outlook. For example, some tension can be remarked between more liberal and the more conservative outlooks. At the 1958 Commissioners' Conference, Lt.-Commissioner Alfred J. Gilliard, Principal of the International College for Officers (an advanced training centre in London) "spoke of the problems of theological 'idiom' involving officers from various countries". He was obliged to defend his College against claims by "a number of Commissioners that some officers had been disturbed at some teaching which they regarded as 'the infiltration of liberalism'."[45]

Commissioner Norman Marshall, an American officer who served as chairman of the International Doctrine Council in the 1980s, wrote of the "London bias" as a "liberal bias which must be confronted carefully". He attributed this in part to Commissioner Alfred G. Cunningham who "has cast an influence passed down through the Literary Department that has been damaging for many in his train have occupied positions of influence and have been writers of Army literature. Also, there has been an influence of London University cast upon some officers who have studied there."[46] Some of this related to differing emphases on matters like Biblical

42 Letter dated 3 May 1963.

43 John Gowans, *There's a Boy Here* (London: SA, 2002) p. 57.

44 Letter dated 22 February 1965.

45 Unpublished Reports and Recommendations of the 1958 International Conference of Commissioners.

46 Norman S. Marshall, unpublished letter dated 13 January 1990.

inerrancy, or what Marshall called the "authenticity of the Scriptures" and views on creationism/evolution. Just sometimes shades of emphasis and indications of polarised assumptions became apparent, as when a British reviewer damned with faint praise ("could have some value...") an American Commissioner's book on the Bible, suggesting that "a simplistic view is in danger of creating some pitfalls for the uninitiated reader."[47] Again, there was a perception of differing interpretations of the Wesleyan doctrine of entire sanctification – like the Corinthians, some said "I am of Brengle" and others "I am of Coutts".

To some degree the different emphases were represented respectively by the British (International Headquarters) Salvationist literary establishment and that of the United States. The International Training College in London would be more likely to encourage the use of Biblical commentaries published by SCM and the American Schools for Officer Training to prefer work of more conservative provenance. Escott quotes Captain John Read, senior tutor at Denmark Hill in the early 1990s, as referring to the "liberal woolly tendency" of the educational syllabus before he instituted "a radical revision of the syllabus which is now more recognisably evangelical".[48] However, lest it be thought that this was simply an Atlantic divide, a letter to the American *New Frontier* accused its editor, Dr Robert Docter, of pursuing a "liberal agenda".

Very little in it – certainly nothing like a full-scale public liberal-fundamentalist breach, and the administration was unwilling for major differences of theological opinion to become widely debated in print. The "Fred Brown affair" of 1970, when a well-known British officer was suspended and eventually compelled to resign over the refusal of the hierarchy to approve publication of work deemed too radical, demonstrated that the institution would not bend too far. The case attracted embarrassing public notoriety in Britain.[49] Even at the end of the century, John W. Hazzard was able to write of the American Salvationists he sampled that even though there was some tension between a "traditional orientation" and

---

47 Fred Hoyle in *Officer* (January 1982) p. 26.

48 Philip Escott, "Church Growth Theories and The Salvation Army in the United Kingdom" (PhD thesis, University of Stirling, 1996) p. 145.

49 *Secular Evangelism*, by Fred Brown (London, SCM: 1970); Gordon Batten and others, letter in *Battlepoint* 29 (September 1970) pp. 13-15; Harold Hill, "The Fred Brown Affair", *Battlepoint* 30 (December 1970) pp. 1-6; *The Guardian* (18 September, 9, 10, 13, 17 October 1970); *The Times* (9 June 1970); *The Daily Telegraph* (15 and 19 October 1970); *The British Weekly* (17 September, 16 October 1970). *The War Cry* did not report the matter at all.

a "progressive orientation," that "my impression … is that these orientations are not manifested in opposing political camps organizationally."[50]

The Salvation Army Students' Fellowship provided a semi-official but semi-independent forum for slightly radical discussion in these years and spawned a variety of periodicals, usually quarterly: *Magazine* in Great Britain, *Battlepoint* in New Zealand, *New Soldiers* in the USA and *Impact* in Australia. These were mostly short-lived although *Battlepoint* survived for 25 years, until 1988. The novelty and difficulty of achieving any forum for free discussion is illustrated by the appearance of the February 1963 number of *Magazine* with several pages featuring only the word "censored". However the Students' Fellowship Council, meeting without the official Headquarters representative, had the offending articles printed and circulated to subscribers independently. One of the Army's occasional underground reform movements or ginger groups, the Salvation Army Renewal Group, was stillborn in the late 1960s. A short-lived broadsheet, *Crossfire*, appeared in London in March 1971, describing itself as "The electric organ of the radical centre".

Membership of the World Council of Churches and of local and national ecumenical bodies, helped broaden Salvationist understanding. In the early 1980s the organisation responded to the World Council of Churches' "Lima" Document on *Baptism, Eucharist and Ministry*. Territories were asked to set up working parties to contribute to that response.

From the 1980s on there were a number of indicators of increasing interest in academic theology:

- Literary activity: such officers as John Coutts, John Larsson, Philip Needham, William Clark, Shaw Clifton, John Rhemick and Chick Yuill continued to broaden Salvationists' theological horizons with relatively accessible, popular writing. They were joined by non-officer writers, a new generation of Salvationist academics like Roger Green, David Rightmire, James Read, Jonathan Raymond and Donald Burke – all North Americans.
- Increasing numbers of tertiary-educated Salvationists and officers obtaining theological qualifications.
- More extensive Biblical and theological training for officers, which in most "Western" countries and some others has involved formal relationships between Salvation Army Training Colleges and external, degree-conferring institutions.
- The establishment of institutions like the Catherine Booth Bible College[51] and the Ethics Centre in Canada.

---

50 John W. Hazzard, "Marching on the Margins: An Analysis of The Salvation Army in the United States", *Review of Religious Research* 40:2 (December 1998) p. 138.

- The holding of international symposia and commissions on educational and theological themes.
- The publication of the American biannual *Word and Deed* since 1998 and the *Practical Theologian* in Australia since 2003.

Most of the above do not relate directly to the debate on officership or the Army's ecclesiology, but they do indicate an increasing interest and relative openness (a Salvationist *glasnost*?) in which such discussion could emerge. The next part of the book outlines the course of this discussion.

51 Since re-named the *William and* Catherine Booth College.

Part Three: Into the Second Century

This Part documents the Salvation Army's internal debate on clericalisation, showing that its official ambivalence has been reflected in polarised opinions. The Army's official attempts to explain and delineate its ecclesiology have been fraught with continuing ambiguity.

Chapter Ten

Putney Debates of a New Model Army

> How do wee know if whilst wee are disputing these thinges another companie of men shall gather together, and shall putt out a paper as plausible perhaps as this? I do nott know why it might not be done by that time you have agreed upon this, or gott hands to itt, if that be the way. And not only another, and another, butt many of this kinde?
>
> Colonel Henry Ireton,
> Putney, 1647.

The "Putney Debates" is the name historians have given to the series of discussions held by the Council of Cromwell's New Model Army, at Putney in October-November 1647. At the end of the English Civil War they were trying to reach agreement on a political settlement which might take into account the aspirations of the Levellers, the extremist element which wanted to abolish not only the monarchy but also the class structure of English society and its political expression. The Salvation Army has not been playing in such major league, and yet it is an Army, and its debate has been in part about whether there should be "classes" within it, a debate ultimately sharing the same religious roots as the Levellers' vision. Although "debate" is perhaps not the best word for a forty-year long exchange of views, the word does recognise that for the first time in Salvation Army history there has been scope for significant expression and exchange of personal opinion in print.

Previous chapters have traced the formation of a professional ministry, officership, in the Salvation Army and explored what was believed about that ministry. A strand of uncertainty and ambiguity about the Army's attitude to the character of its clerical group has been noted. On the one hand the Army was reluctant to describe itself as a church or to regard its officers as clergy, while on the other it was willing to do both of these when they might appear to be to its practical advantage or made its members feel better about themselves. The intention of this chapter is to trace the movement's subsequent internal discussion of the nature of officership.

A word of explanation is necessary to put this "debate" in context. The General's Advisory Council was inaugurated in March 1947 and the institution of regular Commissioners' Conferences, later International Leaders' Conferences, from 1949, both of them involving only the most senior level of command. Apart from these, and the International Doctrine Council (discussed in Chapter Thirteen), the Salvation Army has not had any other formal, constitutional provision for discussion of significant issues since William Booth abolished government by Conference. It was assumed to be unnecessary – everyone knew what had to be done, and had only to get on and do it, under the direction of those God had raised to command. That basic principles, or their application, might be open to widespread discussion, let alone doubt, was beyond surmise. People who did not like it, left.

For officers, now a body of about 25,000 people internationally, *The Officer* in its various forms was for a hundred years the only forum in which issues might be raised for discussion. Even then, the extent of censorship, whether editorial or self-imposed by contributors, at least in the earlier decades, is difficult to determine. Nevertheless the pages of *The Officer*, particularly over the past fifty years, provide a rare opportunity for taking the pulse of the Salvation Army, at least from the officers' point of view. For much of the period, there is no other public record. (Non-English editions of *The Officer* have been published in various countries from time to time; the English language edition is made available to all English-speaking officers in the world.) For rank and file Salvationists there were no means of raising issues publicly until the launching of periodicals like the student publications already mentioned, or official organs like *The Salvationist* in Britain and *New Frontier* in USA Western Territory in the 1980s, and the IHQ Website Discussion Page in the 1990s.

What follows in these chapters is a survey of contributions on the theme of the "theology of officership" over the last forty years of the twentieth century, chiefly in *The Officer*, and since its inception in 1986, of *The Salvationist*, and most recently of *Word and Deed*. (These chapters do not touch on articles or correspondence on the role of women officers, which are treated separately.) This section reviews a total of 53 articles (including Editorial columns) and 57 letters. Many of the letters were part of discussion following articles. *The Officer* ran 42 articles and 32 letters, and *The Salvationist* 8 articles and 22 letters on this theme. By decades, the 1960s saw 10 articles and 4 letters, the 1970s 10 articles and 8 letters, the 1980s 10 articles and 12 letters, the 1990s 19 articles and 27 letters. While hardly indicative of a deluge of controversy, these figures suggest that with the mid-80s advent of *The Salvationist*, the British weekly not restricted to officer-readers, the debate gathered some momentum. It is interesting that *The Salvationist*'s American contemporaries carried very little discussion on such matters – one relevant editorial comment, in *New Frontier* of May

1988, and some discussion arising from the reprinting (from *The Officer*) of a contentious article by Lieutenant Minna Karlström of Finland in 2000.[1]

More than half of *The Salvationist* correspondents on this subject were officers. The debate has been conducted largely amongst officers because until comparatively recently the majority of Salvationists have not been greatly concerned – possibly because most twentieth century Salvationists have regarded the Army as their church, simply viewed their officer as their minister, and not been interested in the small print. For example, a lay correspondent in *The Salvationist*, David Stirling, expected his officer to be the professional ministerial person, "my God-appointed priest".[2] Officers on the other hand have obviously felt a greater need to understand and interpret their role in changing times.

The subject of debate over this period was firstly about the nature of officership in the Army. Were officers clergy? The obvious answer was yes – officers in most countries enjoyed that legal status and recognition in the community, and exercised a role within their community of faith similar to that of other ministers.

Some officers clearly felt the need for some distinct recognition of their higher calling, even though they may have been slightly uncertain about how this ought to be expressed. Against this was the other, earlier, Army tradition that the Army was a movement rather than a church and that all its members shared an equality of status, distinguished only by variety of function. We have already seen both these points of view expressed by the founders of the Army. In either case, the second question follows as to the function of officership: what are officers supposed to do? As time went on, as the number of officers in many Western countries has declined, and work formerly done by officers was seen to be done increasingly by non-officers, this second question gained greater urgency for some.

The first ranging shots were lobbed in the "Captain's Diary", a regular column in *The Officer*. The writer referred to the priesthood of all believers, which was to become a leitmotif in the ensuing years. Pointing out that this phrase meant the corporate "priesthood of *all the believers*" rather than of "*each believer*" individually, the writer called for "more teaching in our ranks about the nature of the Body of Christ on earth, the doctrine of the church and its consequent need to make some apostles, some pastors and teachers."[3] In the June 1963 issue an article by Captain Cecil Waters also proposed greater attention to the doctrine of the ministry. In 1974 Major William Clark introduced the expression "Theology of Officership" for the first time, asking,

---

1 *New Frontier* (2 June 2000 and 19 September 2000) p. 2. Karlstrom's article was reprinted from *The Officer* of October 1999.

2 *The Salvationist* (12 September 1998) p. 19.

3 *Officer* (January-February 1960) pp. 47-8.

> Do we accept that there is a theology of Christian ministry and therefore of Army officership, and if we do, how should we define it? ... Dialogue on the subject within the pages of THE OFFICER is hereby encouraged.[4]

The articles and letters of the early 1960s introduced most of the themes to which correspondents would refer for the next few decades. Writers were no doubt sometimes unaware that the ground had been fought over previously. While the recurrence of themes shows that these were matters of continuing significance, it also makes for it difficult to establish any sort of chronological development in the debate.

"Debate" implies some dialogue, of which there was in fact not much at first. Although there was a series of spirited exchanges in *Magazine* on the matter of "clericalism" in the Army between June 1962 and October 1963 involving Max Cresswell, Roy Terry, Hazell Langley and John Coutts, none of those writers believed that officers ought to have clerical status. For the most part, however, the debate consisted of a series of solo manoeuvres and untidy skirmishes rather than a set battle. Simply summarising the various views presented tends to obscure what process of interaction did occur but to establish some order in presentation, the contributions may be subsumed under these main headings:

1. Those ascribing some special character, status or quality to officership, "different from the churches but equal to them".
2. Those maintaining a simple, functional view of ministry.

Officership with Status

This rather diverse group all thought it important to establish that officership enjoyed a special status, even if some expressed it in terms of "function". For some this was simply to establish equality with clergy of other denominations, while others seemed to attach a mystical significance to the officer role. Commissioner Edgar Grinstead, writing on "Spiritual Doctrines of Command", stated that "We believe in the divine origin of the Army and that its pattern of leadership is inspired by God." He referred to the "spiritual authority vested in God-called officers" and claimed that "such power to command and act is given in the name of the Father, the Son and the Holy Ghost."[5] Captain Douglas Hillborne similarly asked, "Is officership a Higher Order? ... For the Ministry and officership, is there not a special anointing? We detract from officership and our place in the Church of Christ at our peril. There must be no self-importance, pomposity or 'Lording it'

---

4 *Officer* (January 1974) p. 47.

5 *Officer* (January-February 1961) p. 2.

over the flock of God, but how sad to lack the priestly expression of spiritual authority, and the spiritual elevation of privilege." He was anxious that "If you detract from the ministerial function of officership, what have you (or our people) left? You cannot state that the Army is not a church on the one hand and be upset if the officer is not recognised as one of the ministers at a civic gathering."[6]

General Frederick Coutts in his "General's Affirmation", a kind of policy manifesto after his election as General, referred to the subject.

> To spell it out with such courtesy and clarity as public circumstance may require so that none shall have any cause not to acknowledge every officer man or woman, married or single – as "a good minister of Jesus Christ, nourished up in the words of faith and of good doctrine." To insist on such recognition is not to want to turn our officers into ministers (in the denominational sense of the word), but to save any from grasping at a clerical collar as if it were a lifebelt which alone could win a more perfect acceptance of their service in the sight of God. No blessing – episcopal or non-episcopal – can make us more truly what by divine ordination we now are: ministers of grace.[7]

Captain Michael Pressland adduced support for the Salvation Army's functional view of ministry from contemporary New Testament and Patristic studies, while at the same time following earlier Salvationist claims that Salvation Army commissioning was every bit the equal of church ordination.[8] The corollary, that ordination was no more significant than commissioning, was left unstated.

Captain Philip Williams of Canada was concerned to explain that "the 'priesthood of all believers' does not teach the equality of minister and layman in the Church" but that "every man and woman has direct access to God..." He went on to say that "the role of the Minister, set aside and ordained to preach the Word, is scriptural and a fundamental and integral part of the Church. No layman is commissioned to do that..."[9] This opinion is certainly far removed from the historic Salvation Army position laid down by William and Catherine Booth, as outlined in earlier chapters.

Colonel John Hunt quoted John 15:16 to support his sense of the special significance of having been "chosen by Jesus". The implication would appear to be that, as Christ was addressing his inner group of disciples, the call could be seen as constituting a special ministerial group.[10] This illustrates a tendency to limit the application of such passages in this way

---

6 *Officer* (January-February 1962) p. 46.

7 *Officer* (January 1964) p. 3.

8 *Officer* (June 1969) p. 373.

9 *Officer* (February 1971) p. 128.

10 *Officer* (March 1974) p. 112.

and begs the question of whether Christ's words might also be taken as addressed to "all who will believe through their message" (John 17:20). Hunt was in good company; the Church has always done it. The Second Vatican Council adopted the same device in, for example, restricting to bishops the application of Jesus' words in Luke 10:16.[11] A number of contributors to this debate employed the same kind of argument.

Editorial comment in July 1976 also belongs under the heading of "special ministerial status". William Clark acknowledged the influence of John Macquarrie, whose two-article series on "The Church and the Ministry", I Ministerial Functions and II Ministerial Character, had recently appeared in the *Expository Times*, January and February 1976. Clark claimed that because of

> a direct call from God into the ranks of Salvation Army officership, we have been given particular spiritual authority... Whatever our role ...happens to be for the time being... we are primarily spiritual leaders...Our spiritual authority lies not only or chiefly in what we do, but in what we are... Our calling is to be a certain kind of person and not ... to do a certain kind of job... The "ordained" ministry of the Church – to which body we belong by virtue of our calling, response, training and commissioning – is a distinctive ministry within the body of the whole people of God, different from that "general" ministry of the Church which is defined in the New Testament as "the priesthood of all believers".[12]

Clark appeared to be feeling his way towards a definition of clerical status derived not from historic apostolic succession, but based on the personal spirituality of the officers. He was careful to deny that this was the case, saying, "by 'a particular quality of character' is not meant a higher spirituality than those who have not been so called." However, when he came to answer the question, "what characteristics should mark those who are called to fill our particular place in the church", the three characteristics proposed appeared to relate to the area of 'spirituality'. Only the first is a description peculiar to officers. That is "a particular kind of sacrifice" by which he means a self-denying life-style; specifically, availability for appointment "at the disposal of the divinely-directed Movement, The Salvation Army". The only other marks he suggested are "our attitude to success and rewards" and "our readiness and ability to be supporters of needy people", neither of them necessarily true of every officer, nor confined to officer ranks.

---

11 "Lumen Gentium" Chapter 3, No 20, in Austin Flannery (ed.), *Vatican Council II*, p. 372.

12 *Officer* (July 1976) pp. 289-90.

A two part *Officer* article by Lieut-Colonel Fred Hoyle (British Territory) was entitled "Priesthood and Officership".[13] Within the context of the priesthood of all believers, and while discounting any sacerdotal role for officers, Hoyle thought that officership had much in common with the Catholic or Anglican conception of priesthood. He referred to the priestly character of the New Testament community, and said that priesthood must emerge from that Christological and pneumatological base. He believed that the priest's role was to represent Christ to the people, being co-opted by Christ for this role, which involved an element of aloneness and special responsibility for leadership.

Major David Pickard insisted that "Officers do have a distinctive function and it is surely not one that can be shared by all. If it were so, then the concept of officership would be redundant and we would not need officers at all. I, too, think that we might need to reassess the idea of officership, but those who have been given this special ministry should seek to elevate officership to the high calling we know it to be."[14] Lieut-Colonel Alan Atherton, also British, wrote, "Officership must be seen in the context of the whole Christian Church... Because the Army is of the Body of Christ, it is within the line of spiritual apostolic succession... Officers are among those ministers, separated to a sacred and spiritual office. As long as the Church exists, officers will be called into ministry."[15]

All these clearly see officership as a higher calling of some kind, although they would differ as to what kind.

Officership as Functional

The 1960 writer of "The Captain's Diary" noted that, "The distinction we make between officer and soldier is one of function and not of essense [*sic*]. There is no essential difference in quality (except as it resides in completeness of consecration) between the service of the officer and the service of the soldier. We know of no ecclesiastical ordination bestowing peculiar gifts."[16] The assumption that officership required a more "complete consecration" than did a secular vocation is interesting. By this expression presumably the writer meant an officer's willingness to be available for appointment, so this implies consecration to the Army rather than to God. (God and the institutional Church are easily confused.)

In the number following Commissioner Grinstead's article on "Spiritual Doctrines of Command", whether or not by design, the Editor expressed

---

13 *Officer* (December 1987) pp. 549-52; (January 1988) pp. 28-30.

14 *Salvationist* (13 July 1996) pp. 12-3.

15 *Salvationist* (3 August 1996) p. 13.

16 *Officer* (March-April 1960) p. 117.

concern about the tendency to clericalism. He quoted approvingly F. D. Barry, Bishop of Southwark, as suggesting that "clericalism was one of the worst disasters to befall the Church... based on a false division between clergy and laity ... beginning with the mistake of identifying the Church with its office-bearers, as in the phrase, 'Going into the Church' – i.e. taking the part for the whole." The Editor compared this with the Army expression, "Entered the Work" as evidence of a similar tendency, and argued against accepting a passive role for the soldiery. He concluded, "Perhaps we are at fault for narrowing the meaning of The Call: for every sanctified man is called to be a priest and every seeking heart is a holy place where he can minister."[17]

Later that year Major Oliver Clarke weighed in on the same theme, with a complaint which also helps cast light on William Booth's views.

> Of recent years I have noticed a growing tendency to pronounce what we call the Benediction ... in the pontifical manner: "The Blessing ... be with YOU all..."
> We do not claim endowment by apostolic succession in the sacerdotal sense. We believe in "the priesthood of all believers". It was against this practice that the Founder remonstrated ... when Commissioner Jeffries, asked to pronounce the Benediction, merely said: "The blessing of God Almighty be with us all." Note, he even did say us instead of you; but he gave the appearance of administering something instead of invoking the same by saying "*May* the blessing of Almighty God be with us all."
> We have already gone far enough already for the good and safety of our Movement in the direction of classifying officership as a higher ORDER. Does this seem to be pedantic? To my view a vital issue is at stake, namely: a Clericalism versus Laity; Ecclesiasticism versus an Evangelical non-conforming Movement...[18]

Brigadier Eric Coward asked if there was not "some confusion here between function and status". He pointed out that many officers discharged their vocation in servant roles – "mere hostel managers, nurses, office-workers" – and would never enjoy clerical or civic status and recognition, but be accepted as ministers by those they served. He also referred to the anti-clericalism that for centuries had marked the "lower classes" for which the Army was raised up and was anxious lest "keeping up with the cloth" would mean deepening alienation from "our people". He wrote "the 'priestly expression of spiritual authority' has little to do with status or official duties. Our authority is in our acceptance as servants of all. In this ministry there is no priestly class or higher and lower orders. But officership is a higher vocation because we have obeyed the call to place our whole present and

17 *Officer* (March-April 1961) pp. 142-4.
18 *Officer* (September-October 1961) p. 339.

future in the hands of God and the Army."[19] Coward thus took up the key polarity of function and status, and came down on the side of the former. At the same time he muddied the waters in that a "higher vocation" sounds very like a matter of status.

Major William Burrows repudiated "any suggestion of an officer possessing any peculiarly priestly sanctity" or role as mediator. He cited Emil Brunner's characterisation of the formation of priesthood as a retrograde step in the history of the Church, reverting from New Testament transcendence of the opposition between the profane and the holy, to the Old Testament conception of a sacrificial cultus. Asking "What, then, is the distinction between officer and soldier?" he replied that "It is a distinction of function rather than of capacity. The officer is being financially supported so that, with all of his time, he may represent his soldiers in caring for the flock and in promoting the evangel. It is their task as well as his; only he is set free to do tasks impossible to a man who has to earn his own living."[20]

Burrows devoted a December 1964 editorial comment to "Lay Ministry", suggesting that rather than taking exception to some cleric's appellation of this term to Salvation Army officership, "we ought to fasten on such a designation as the highest compliment that could be paid to our movement." Having cited examples of non-officer Salvationist leadership, Burrows asked,

> Could it be that a yearning for ecclesiasticism, felt in some quarters, is to be seen as a yearning for status...? If so, the attempt will fail. Election is never to special favour but only to greater responsibility... Jesus undertook a "lay" – a practical, unclerical – ministry.[21]

Writing on Salvationist principles, Commissioner Hubert Scotney, an Australian, included this under the "Principle of Equality":

> Officership indicates special functions within the structure, rather than superior status.[22]

Later he wrote,

> The distinction made today between clergy and laity does not exist in the New Testament... The terms layman and laity (in the current usage of those words) are completely out of character in a Salvation Army context... It is foreign to

19 *Officer* (May-June 1962) pp. 188-9.
20 *Officer* (June 1963) pp. 356-7.
21 *Officer* (December 1964) pp. 861-2.
22 *Officer* (April 1969) p. 254.

> the entire concept of Salvationism to imagine two levels of involvement. Any distinction between officers and soldiers is one of function rather than status.[23]

Another contribution under this heading was an article by A. Skevington Wood, a Methodist, on the "Priesthood of All Believers". Reprinted from *The Christian Graduate*, this article traced the development of Methodist ministry as a lay phenomenon. It was written as a protest against what the writer saw as "the astonishing and disturbing" Methodist capitulation to "historic Romanism" in negotiations with the Anglican Church on ministry.[24] The inclusion of such outside writing in the pages of *The Officer* was uncommon and clearly signalled editorial, and therefore official, disagreement with clericalising views in the Salvation Army.

Major Hubert Boardman (Great Britain) observed that the lack of theological definition had resulted in "a great deal of confusion in our thinking". After surveying New Testament teaching, he noted that, "It was only when the Early Church had begun to settle down and felt the need to protect the institution, that it sought to do this by founding a special professional religious caste, who would protect and preserve it and, unfortunately in the process, often impede its progress." In each age, as new expressions of Christian life similarly became more established, the same process could be seen. He quoted David Jenkins in *Protestant Ministry* as saying that the Church forgot its function of this total ministry of the whole Church and proceeded on the assumption that its primary function was "to provide a milieu in which professional ministries could exercise their gifts".

> As the Army evolved and took on forms of establishment so the development of its professional officer caste, with a corresponding separation between officer and laity, became increasingly apparent... More and more did officers begin to assume a "special (priestly?) role", assuming greater responsibility, while increasingly congregations opted out of their own responsibilities and adopted an attitude of "paying an officer" to do the job! ... In this unfortunate evolution, I would contend that our ranking system has been one of the greatest contributory factors, for it has tended to emphasise an officer's status rather than his true function.[25]

William Clark's 1974 Editorial quoted the contemporary *Orders and Regulations for Officers* to describe Salvation Army officers: they are

> men and women who (a) have left ordinary pursuits and occupations; (b) have consecrated their lives to the service of God and the people; (c) have

---

23 *Officer* (July 1969) p. 452.
24 *Officer* (September 1965) pp. 621-6.
25 *Officer* (August 1972) pp. 345-50.

undergone a course of training; and (d) are, unless retired, engaged in full-time service as leaders in the Army's ranks.

Clark notes that (b) applies to every Salvationist, and that (a), (c) and (d) concern function, with the proviso that every Christian also engages in full-time service.[26] *The Orders and Regulations* therefore provided no grounds for claiming any special spiritual status for officers.

Letters from Brigadier Ernest Yendell, claiming that "officership...had been regarded from the very beginning as being in a privileged apostolic succession... a term that must never be devalued... both priestly and apostolic... denoting spiritual commission and privileged position by all who respond to this special calling of God"[27] and Major Stanley Richardson holding that "our superiority is surely to be found in two aspects – privilege and *responsibility*,"[28] drew a response from Lieutenant Shaw Clifton. Describing the context and summarising the argument of Luther's *Address to the German Nobility*, Clifton noted that Luther rejected any clergy/laity division, saying that the cleric acts on behalf of all Christian people and distinctions are derived not from qualifications but from function. The implication for Salvation Army officership was that "the doctrine of the priesthood of all believers is incompatible with the idea of there being any difference in kind between officers and others. Had Luther been asked... to pronounce upon a theology of officership, he would not have been able to reply in terms of "privileged apostolic succession" or "privileged calling"... Luther could never have used theology to point up any distinction between clergy and laity save one of function."[29]

Richardson, responding, was surprised that Clifton ignored "the evidence that almost without exception the churches that sprang from the Reformation accept a doctrine of the Ministry."[30] Clifton replied that his article had been written out of concern "that participants in the 'officership' debate might lack basic information on the history of Protestant thought" and that "Major Richardson's comments ... confirmed my worst fears. I take it (from his previous letter on the subject) that when he speaks of a 'doctrine of the ministry' he means a doctrine that affirms the existence of a priestly virtue not available to lay Christians. If so, his statement that 'almost without exception the churches that sprang from the Reformation accept a doctrine of the Ministry' is factually incorrect." Quoting from Methodist, Baptist, Congregationalist and Presbyterian traditions, Clifton showed that these all rejected any sacerdotal status for ministry, and

26 *Officer* (January 1974) p. 47.
27 *Officer* (March 1974) pp. 112-3.
28 *Officer* (March 1974) p. 114.
29 *Officer* (September 1974) pp. 408-10.
30 *Officer* (November 1974) p. 498.

contended that Anglicanism was in a different category, being a compromise between Roman and Reformation thinking. "Salvationists should feel ill at ease at any suggestion that it be applied to their officers."[31]

Major Paulo W. Rangel, Brazil, attempted to "demonstrate that the concepts 'laity' and 'clergy' constitute an anti-biblical classification, contrary to the concept of the Church and contrary to its nature... Our position as officers has to do with our pastoral functions, which do not include superiority...." He was concerned that "there is still too great a distance between Salvationist people and the leadership... Decisions, as a rule, are still centralized, giving little or no opportunity of participation for soldiers, recruits and friends..."[32] "Time to lay aside the priest concept" was the message of a letter from John and Kathleen Lowther. Disagreeing with an article by Commissioner Dinsdale Pender equating officership with priesthood, the Lowthers believed "that introducing the concept of Salvationists being either priests or laymen is not only an affront to our origins in the reformed wing of the church and bad theology, but one reason for the priesthood of all believers not functioning as it should in staffing our Army." They noted that "when the pastorate pulls all functions of leadership and ministry to itself the result is an overworked officer/pastor/priest and a passive soldiery/congregation /laity."[33]

John Coutts, United Kingdom, long a spokesman for reforms in the movement, writing in the *Salvationist,* welcomed General Gowans' world-wide consultation in 2000 about the future of officership. Noting that "for the Salvationist, the Christian Church is defined by faith, not by Church order", John Coutts repeated that "this means that our view of ministry is 'functional' ... Some hold that ordination to the priesthood is indelible – 'once a priest always a priest'. But the Salvation Army view is 'captain is as captain does'."[34]

The exchanges quoted in this chapter, however, suggest that both views were variously and strongly held by members of the Salvation Army.

---

31 *Officer* (January 1975) pp. 33-4.
32 *Officer* (May 1996) pp. 229-32.
33 *Salvationist* (12 April 1997) p. 7.
34 *Salvationist* (27 May 2000) p.7.

Chapter Eleven

Ordination

> We have here met on purpose, according to my engagement, that whatsoever may be thought to be necessary for our satisfaction, for the right understanding one of another, might be done, that we might go on together. For, though our ends and aims be the same, if one thinks this way, another another way, that way which is the best for the subject is that they both may be hearkened unto.
>
> Trooper Robert Everard
> at Putney, 1647.

The following exchanges concerning "ordination" suggest that Trooper Everard's sage advice has been followed by this later Model Army – both points of view were "hearkened unto". A 1966 Editorial on "Qualified or Commissioned" had rejected the concept of "ordination". "Perhaps because in some communions the word 'ordination' carries the idea of the conferment of special 'grace' but also (and primarily) because our word more nearly describes what we mean and also has a military connotation, we use the word 'commissioning'."[1] The words "ordination" and "ordain" were in fact rarely used in a Salvation Army context prior to 1978. Some examples are given in the next chapter.

However, in 1978 General Arnold Brown provided for the word "ordain" to be used in the Commissioning of officers. The circumstances attending this decision, and its sequelae, are discussed in Chapter Twelve. This innovation seemed at first to pass without comment. It was not until 1985, seven years after the introduction of ordination, that signs of disquiet appeared. One wonders whether earlier expressions of opposition were not published or whether it just took a long time for the significance to dawn. Following this somewhat delayed reaction, responses and contributions dealing specifically with ordination could be grouped under three headings: some opposing the innovation; some supporting, or at least accepting it; and

1 *Officer* (September 1966) pp. 645-7.

some concerned to explore the function of officership, whether or not ordained.

Against Ordination

Most opponents of this innovation did so because of their commitment to the traditional, functional view of officership.

In his regular 1985 column "Matters Arising", Scottish officer Captain Chick Yuill described his "discomfort" on hearing at commissioning the words, "It is my privilege to commission you as officers of The Salvation Army and ordain you as ministers of Christ and his gospel." Admitting that "it might be argued that it has been inserted simply to amplify and explain the meaning of our commission as officers," he noted that "'mere words' have a life of their own, and I fear that this one might lead us along a pathway which God never meant us to tread."

Yuill went on to set quotations from Luther on the priesthood of all believers alongside extracts from the World Council of Churches "Lima" Text on *Baptism, Eucharist and Ministry*. (This also appears to be the first time this document had been commented on critically in *The Officer*.) He claimed that "the whole tenor" of Lima "is governed by a view of the ordained ministry as possessing a priestly status... it is to the ordained ministry that the Church looks for 'an example of holiness', and it is the ordained ministry who 'signify and represent' the presidency of Christ at the Eucharist." He reminded readers that "William Booth saw his officers, not as an ecclesiastical caste with a calling to the holy life beyond that of the rank and file soldiery, but as ordinary men and women, singled out for leadership and service... Moreover he saw the 'presidency of Christ' as a reality in the midst of his people, a reality which required neither ordained clergy nor Eucharistic celebration..."

"May I suggest'" wrote Yuill, " that we need to re-emphasise the truth that there is no real distinction between officers and soldiers, that the difference is simply of function... If that little word 'ordain' has crept in because of a subconscious desire that other Christians should realise that we are as 'important' as the clergy of other denominations, ... in the end it matters not a jot where we stand in the estimation of any who would compile a league table of ecclesiastical importance."[2]

Yuill's comments provoked more reaction than any other single contribution to *The Officer*, six letters appearing in the following ten months, with further articles and letters on the subject being printed from time to time.

---

2 *Officer* (October 1985) pp. 438-40.

Mrs Major Sandra Dalziel of London "feared that it [ordination] had been copied from elsewhere for reasons that have little to do with theology" ... to "make us feel 'one above', extra special."[3] Colonel Hubert Boardman likewise believed the word to be an "attempt to identify ourselves more closely with practices which our Founder abandoned for the sake of the mission... and do not benefit our cause."[4]

A first mention of ordination from a non-officer perspective is found in *The Salvationist* of the same year. David McKenzie wrote,

> The Salvation Army's contribution to the debate about women priests would carry more weight had we not introduced the concept of "ordination" into the commissioning ceremony a few years ago. The arguments in the Anglican Church are not about whether women should be allowed to preach or do pastoral work; the church already has "women in ministry" as deaconesses. The argument is about the mystical – dare one say magical? – nature of the priesthood, and about the *fitness of* a woman to represent Christ in this role... "Ordination", with its unfortunate connotation of grades of spiritual authority rather than differences of function, has eroded this fundamental principle. If all are priests, then all are ordained. What we have done is not to exclude women, but to exclude all who have not passed through a Salvation Army training college![5]

Another non-officer comment came from Robert Docter of California, writing editorial comment in *New Frontier*. He expressed disquiet over the use of "ordination" in commissioning, lest it imply "an increasing separation of the officer corps from the laity of Army".[6]

The Officer's regular columnist for 1988 was an American, Major Joseph Viola, who noted that "the 'ordination' service will create the usual perennial debate as it did when the terms 'ordination' and 'ordained' were first introduced into our commissioning festivities." (Evidently all had not been silent between 1978 and 1985 after all.) Viola observed that "in America most officers with whom I have spoken seem very comfortable with these words", because American Salvationists were tired of being thought of as "a glorified YMCA" and wanted to be recognised as a church. However he believed that if that was the purpose of the change, it was not working, "in this country at least", and that if they really wanted to carry that argument they should re-introduce baptism and communion as well.

He drew attention to the fact that the Army was clearly not using the term ordain to denote a special character, "an external sanction" for the officer, in the way other churches used it. "When an officer decides to leave the

---

3 *Officer* (January 1986) p. 15.
4 *Officer* (January 1986) pp. 15-7.
5 *Salvationist* (2 August 1986) p. 3.
6 *New Frontier* (11 May 1988) p. 7.

work... he or she immediately loses all the rights and privileges of ministry (conducting weddings ceremonies, dedications, etc)" whereas "in the majority of major denominations the principle 'once a minister always a minister' applies, unless the individual is defrocked...". He noted that amongst many other churches, a reciprocal recognition of ministerial credentials is granted. Our standing aside from this principle "does not completely invalidate our use of these words – it merely makes them quite unnecessary." He concluded, "we should review why we use these words and ask if their use really accomplishes the intended purposes." Viola believed that it was pointless to use a word generally used for conferring a priestly character if it was not in fact used that way.[7] The same point was made by Colonel Gordon Sharp. Referring to the fact that "the Army does not differentiate between officership and appointment", that... "no officer may be unavailable for appointment and retain his officership", Sharp contrasts this with "most other denominations, [in which] ordination is a distinct state... This point of view has never found acceptance within our movement. It is only recently that the words 'and ordain' have been added to the ritual of commissioning officers. That change seems a little pointless so long as the link between officer-rank and appointment remains an unaltered concept."[8]

Lieutenant Martin Howe wrote, "We must continue to reject the sacrament of ordination with its consequences of distinction between 'special' and 'average' Christians."[9] Lieut-Colonel David Guy also reiterated that "the restriction of priestly ministry to the *ordained*, commissioned, official, trained, salaried ministry departs from the New Testament insight."[10]

Another non-officer contribution is found in Andrew Watkinson-Trim. "I am not and never have been a lay member of The Army and wish to dissent from this creeping churchification. Our Founders accepted and implemented the New Testament doctrine of the priesthood of all believers. Officers were not ordained and soldiers were not laymen (in itself a sexist term). I understand that 'ordination' was imported into the Army to demonstrate that our officers are just as much ministers as the leaders of any other church. How sad! Such a concern for status and respectability would have horrified the first Salvationists."[11]

Captain Cecil Waters was one of three who wrote about ordination in February 1993. He felt that "the increasing, formal use of the word 'ordain' may well encourage misconceptions – for instance that some are, by virtue

7 *Officer* (May 1988) pp. 222-4.
8 *Officer* (November 1992) p. 488.
9 *Officer* (July 1988) p. 314.
10 *Officer* (April 1990) p. 178.
11 *Salvationist* (11 July 1992) p. 12.

of being 'ordained', be able to do things which the rest of the church cannot do for itself... We must be sure that it does not carry any suggestion of imputed grace or spiritual status." He followed this up with a study of New Testament words, showing that "while Biblical usage does not require us to understand ordination... as imputing special grace... there is no biblical reason to prevent us using the word 'ordain' interchangeably with 'appoint' or 'commission'". However he concludes that "because the term has a different significance for the rest of the church, we should avoid using it."[12]

Cadet Stephen Court of Canada wrote in May 1993, dissenting from the views expressed by Lt. Colonel Earl Robinson in explanation of "ordination".

> He claims that the function of an officer can be distinguished from those of other soldiers by the covenant that, "I will live to win souls, and I will not allow anything to turn me aside from seeking their salvation as the first great purpose of my life." This statement is offered as justification for ordination. But what of the soldier? ... A good soldier makes war his business. He may do something in other lines of duty ... but after all, fighting is his trade... There is no difference between the two functions, there is no distinctive, and so there are no grounds to justify ordination by this argument. The emphasis on ordination and the professional nature of officership only serves to widen the artificial gap existing between officers and soldiers. Note I use the term "soldier" rather than the insidious term "laity".

He concluded by warning against "the gradual abdication of our characteristic birthright in 'favour' of a mainstream church identity."[13] Major Laurence Hay, New Zealand, trenchantly noted

> that cadets are still to be ordained as well as commissioned. I have not been ordained. What then do I lack for my ministry? If I do lack something, what is it, and how do I acquire it? If I lack nothing, then ordination is an empty charade and should be abandoned forthwith. In my view, no convincing justification has yet been put forward for this radical change in our theology of ministry. Or have I missed something?[14]

Hay was supported by Lieutenant Paul M. Waters, Norway, who observed that no-one appeared to know what "ordination" meant, that the word "minister" in the ordination/commissioning ceremony was very confusing in Norway as there was no parallel other than "priest", and that no-one had adequately rebutted objections raised. "Either 'ordination' is the

---

12 *Officer* (February 1993) pp. 71-6.
13 *Officer* (May 1993) pp. 214-5.
14 *Officer* (July 1994) p. 336.

same as 'commissioning' – in which case why bother with it or else it means something which at least some officers cannot accept."[15]

A letter from Major David Pickard in March 1995, claiming that officer-ordination conferred spiritual authority and constituted a priestly class, was also refuted in the April number of *The Officer* by Colonel William Clark and Major Cecil Waters.

"We Don't Need an Ordained Clergy" was the headline for an article in a 1996 number of *The Salvationist* by Major Ian Barr. Reacting against the use of "lay Salvationists" for "non-officers", Barr noted that its increasing use was "mirrored by an increasing use of the sixteenth century word 'ministry' to describe the work of officers and the equally loaded word 'ordained' to describe their status." Reiterating the functional base of any difference between officers and soldiers, he protested against the "churchification" of our language.[16] Barr returned to the fray in May 1997, quoting an article by the Rev. Dr Janet Wootton, a Congregational Minister, that raised the question of "How do we square ordination with the priesthood of all believers?" Dr Wootton had asked, "Why not ordain caretakers too." Barr agreed "with the premise that in theological terms there are no functions open to ministers (officers) that are closed to members (soldiers)".[17]

For Ordination

Commissioner Victor Keanie, commented on Yuill's strictures on the Lima document, "as one closely involved in this matter" (the Army's response to Lima). He defended the Army's use of term "ordained". "The term 'ordained' was introduced into the commissioning formula by General Arnold Brown as a result of representations from a number of territories in which the concept of an 'ordained ministry' was becoming necessary to give The Salvation Army and its officers the place in church and state relationships which we rightly claim. In some countries where the word can be translated only by the equivalent of 'laying on of hands' it is not used. The concept of our 'ordained ministry' is still distinctively our own…" He quoted the dictionary definition of "ordination" – "admission to the ministry" – suggesting that it was an appropriate term for the description Yuill gave of entering upon officership. He felt that Yuill's use of the expressions "'singled out' and 'the sense of divine calling' surely tend to demolish the argument developed on 'the need to re-emphasise the truth that

15 *Officer* (September 1994) p. 432.
16 *Salvationist* (21 September 1996) p. 5.
17 *Salvationist* (10 May 1997) pp. 8-9.

there is no real difference between officers and soldiers…'", and urged "that we do not swing to the opposite extreme from that envisaged in this (Lima) document."[18]

Another retired British officer to respond was Brigadier Norman Gothard, who although also "uneasy about anything that sounds 'churchified'", felt that "the word 'ordained' in this connection does not rule out the 'priesthood of all believers'". He quoted a number of examples of the use of the word from the AV translation. He pointed out that the conduct of the office-holder, rather than the name of the office, commends its holder. Like Keanie, he appeared to come down on the side of some special status for officers however: "All believers have access to God through Jesus… but all are not called to the ministry of the Gospel. Those who are, are privileged responsible beings, separated and consecrated to stand between God and the people, and as such are 'ordained to preach the word of the Lord.'"[19] Major Arthur Brown, Great Britain, also came down on this side of the argument, claiming support from Old Testament priestly distinction (as reflected in the AV's Hebrews 5:1 – "taken from among men" and "ordained for men in things pertaining to God") and modern English usage of "professionals" and "laymen". On this rather shaky exegetical base he could claim, "herein lies the essential difference that sets us apart from those to whom we minister and endows us with the authority to do what we do and be what we are…"[20]

Major Clifford Hurcum, Great Britain, argued that the principal requirement for officership – or ministry in any other church tradition – was always the conviction of having received a call from God, and described this as scripturally based, giving Biblical examples of "call". This "remains central to the whole concept of ordination." Like Clark in July 1976, he distinguished between the general "call" to all believers to participate in the priesthood of all believers, and a "specific 'call' to some, for full-time commitment. "Whilst we do not give support to the sacerdotal doctrine, we nevertheless believe that for some, there comes a direct call to be 'set apart' to offer all their time and minister as: 'Apostles… prophets… evangelists… pastors and teachers, to equip God's people for work in his service' (Ephesians 4:11)."[21] Along with a number of contributors, Hurcum looked for a middle way, a functional ministry with special character. He also, like most others, seemed to assume that a Biblical call to ministry was, *ipso facto*, a call to full-time professional ministry, which overlooked the possibility of "tent-making", worker-priest model of ministry as exemplified by Saint Paul.

---

18 *Officer* (February 1986) pp. 76-7.
19 *Officer* (April 1986) p. 167.
20 *Officer* (February 1993) pp. 81-3.
21 *Officer* (March 1989) pp. 134-7.

Commissioner Stanley Walter, adroitly fence-sitting in a paper given at the 1988 International Conference of Leaders, made a number of references to ordination in the course of a general survey of "Officership, its Meaning and Theology". He quoted John Stott as claiming that "the Pauline doctrine of 'every member ministry' does not mean that ordained clergy are irrelevant", and confining the application of the pastoral injunction of Ephesians 4:11,12 to such a clerical group. Further on he used the anachronistic AV translation of Mark 3:14 ("And he ordained twelve...") to read a "special call and ordination" into the calling of the disciples. Walter (a Canadian) expressed himself as "quite comfortable with the use of the additional word 'ordain' in our commissioning service... [it] helps our soldiers to realise that our officers are as fully accredited and accepted as ministers of the gospel as are those of other churches". However he did not want the word stressed "at the expense of that peculiarly Army sense of the word 'commissioning'."[22]

Lt.-Colonel Earl Robinson described the officer, as a result of God's calling, as "ordained by God just as surely as are any who, since the first century of the Church, have thought of themselves as serving in the apostolic succession." Robinson described the Commissioning ceremony as "parallel to the act of ordination". The three steps in the ordination to Salvation Army officership – signing of a covenant, the commissioning and the prayer of dedication – he saw as "in keeping with the traditional meaning of ordination in the Church as a whole."[23]

Major David Pickard, United Kingdom THQ, argued that the definition of officership in the Orders and Regulations ("have left other pursuits and occupations; have dedicated themselves to the service of God and the people") suggested that "officers belong very much to a 'special spiritual caste', a priestly class, and by virtue of our calling and consecration, set apart from those whom we lead. The divine ordination... gives us spiritual authority..."[24]

Brigadier Bramwell Darbyshire, was emphatic about the status of officers.

> In spite of all the stuff about the priesthood of all believers, ordained and commissioned officers are different from non-officer Salvationists. They are not cleverer, wiser, more loved of God than their fellows, but they are special, set apart for Jesus in a way that involves sacrifice and often great inconvenience to their families... No one is more grateful for the Army's dedicated lay staff than this old warrior; but let's get it right. They may be as

22 *Officer* (September 1989) pp. 396-402.
23 *Officer* (February 1993) pp. 77-81.
24 *Officer* (March 1995) p. 143.

> much involved as officers, but there is for an officer a sacramental dimension and if we lose sight of this the Army is finished.[25]

Finally, Lt. Colonel Evelyn Haggett (Canada), basing her argument on God's gift of priesthood to Aaron (Numbers 18:7), saw officership as a "gift of ordination to a sacramental life..." and found it "awesome to be called by God to the priesthood." Officers were "of the cloth" like clergy and priests.[26]

Ordination as Functional

It would be incorrect to say that all protagonists for "ordination" belonged to the "status" school. Some were, and, as we have seen, obviously welcomed its introduction as an additional support. Others, realising that the word would not now go away, sought to explain or use it in such a way as to secure the "functional" view and play down any implications of "status".

In 1989 Major Raymond Caddy, International Headquarters, defended ordination's introduction to the Salvation Army on the grounds that "one of its meanings is closely tied to the idea of organisation which underlies all military structures... means to categorise, to place in a particular ranking... the specific ranking, then, has something to tell us about function." In Church terms, "this is the classification of people ... to carry out certain roles. These duties are restricted to people of that rank, otherwise there is no point in separating them from the rest."

He went on to distinguish two kinds of ordination in the Church, one of all Christians, and the other to the exercise of certain spiritual gifts (see Romans 12, 1st Corinthians 12), "vocations given so that the Church may be governed and served... Particular ministries are recognised and encouraged when the Army commissions or warrants its officers and local officers. However, every Salvationist is ordained to the greater vocation of Christian. There is no higher calling than this."[27] Caddy thus safeguarded the Army's traditional functionalism while accommodating the new use of ordination. Secondly, he lined up Pauline passages about spiritual gifts with this functional use of ordination; as all Christians were recipients of spiritual gifts, this meant that all were ordained. This broke new ground in this discussion.

In 1995 Major Clifford Kew, International Headquarters, published a series of articles on "A Theology of Officership", again accepting the use of ordination but making it clear that he saw its meaning as functional only. In Part One he asked, "Does an officer belong to a special spiritual caste,

25 *Salvationist* (18 April 1998) p. 6.

26 *Officer* (January-February 2006) p. 23.

27 *Salvationist* (20 May 1989) p. 5.

which makes him different from all other Salvationists and gives him 'ex-officio' special rights and authority and privileges and, in a special sense, grace?... It is rather strange that spiritual ministry has so often come to be seen in terms of priesthood, often ritual priesthood. There seems to be a built-in tendency for spiritual calling to revert to religious office." He noted that this made it all the more important "to examine our theology of officership, to ensure that we are not following outdated patterns of ministry."[28]

In Part Two, Kew set the prophetic against the priestly tradition, and noted that New Testament ministry cut across the priestly emphasis. New Testament offices of evangelists, pastors, deacons, presbyters and bishops were descriptions of the work people did, not priestly office.[29]

In Part Three he traced the development of "an exclusive monopoly of ministry" by a clerical caste, while the function of the laity was depressed in the second and third centuries, and the influence of Augustine's doctrine of indelible ministry, the idea of apostolic succession and priestly authority to administer sacraments. Passing on to the Army's use of ordination, he said "we can live with the word as an added explanation of ministry but not as a ritual qualification for ministry in any exclusive sense..."[30]

Eric Welsby wrote that "lay" was "quite appropriate when referring to Christians who although committed to full-time service, are serving in a non-professional capacity – that is, without financial reward." He felt that the dictionary definition, "to set apart for an office or duty", gave sufficient justification for the use of ordain, "although some may feel it to be elitist or at least seeking parity with other denominations."[31]

Colonel Shaw Clifton, by now Territorial Commander in Pakistan, published *Who are These Salvationists?* in 1999. In the course of a general description of the Salvation Army, Clifton described the priesthood of all believers as the basis for the Army's functional approach to church order. It did not touch "... upon the question of who does what in the life and affairs of the church" but allowed "the recognition of distinctive roles for both the laity and the clergy". He noted that

> some non-ordained members of the church are allowed to take up wider responsibilities and to carry out the same functions in a corps as an ordained and commissioned officer. I refer here to sergeants, envoys and auxiliary-captains. (In Pakistan we also use the term corps leader for such a person.)... We believe the grace that energizes the ordained clergy is the same grace and of the same order as that which empowers and sustains the ministry and

---

28 *Officer* (February 1995) pp. 87-90.
29 *Officer* (March 1995) pp. 131-4.
30 *Officer* (April 1995) pp. 173-6.
31 *Salvationist* (21 December 1996) p. 20.

service of lay persons... Any distinction between them is one of role or function, not one of priestly or spiritual status.[32]

Clifton thus combined the use of clergy and laity terminology with a functional view of ministry. It is unclear however, why "corps leaders" were not ordained when there was no distinction of "role or function" between them and corps officers.

Exploring the Function of Officership

Some writers sought to define officership in terms of tasks or roles appropriate to officers. Lieut-Colonel David Guy asked, "What is the function that explains and identifies an officer; that differentiates him, in practical terms only, from a soldier; that provides the clue to his calling and effectiveness or otherwise in pursuing it?" He pointed out that the tasks of preaching, pastoring or representing the Army in the local community, are all discharged by soldiers as well as by officers, along with the "somewhat hazy concept of spiritual leadership".[33] Other writers were more sure that they could identify certain tasks as peculiarly officer ones. Lieutenant John G Merrit[34] Captain Anthony Stone[35] and Captain Louis Kinsey[36] all offered variations of the "primary function of every Salvation Army Corps officer" as being "the equipping of the saints for the work of service, to the building up of the body of Christ...".

An official American definition suggested that the role was *sui generis*. "All of God's people are equally called. The call to officership is the call to a particular role in Christian work. Strictly speaking, this role is neither altogether that of minister nor of social worker. It includes most aspects of both roles but can only properly be described as the role of the Salvation Army officer, the primary purpose of which is to reach the spiritually and physically impoverished with the gospel of Jesus Christ."[37]

Some also saw the officer as the focus or representative figure for the congregation. Major Cliff Ashworth's 1996 article, "Yes – officers are still needed!" suggested the two ideas of "focussing" and "enabling" as descriptive of the officer-role. "The officer ... represents the work which

---

32 Shaw Clifton, *Who Are These Salvationists?* (Alexandria VA: SA, 1999) pp. 27-9.

33 *Officer* (January 1986) pp. 15-8.

34 *Officer* (June 1970) p. 375.

35 *Officer* (August 1986) pp. 365-6.

36 *Officer* (July 1990) pp. 315-6.

37 "The Role of the Corps Officer in the United States of America: Guidelines for CO's in the USA", Approved by the Commissioners' Conference, USA. October, 1972.

properly belongs to the whole body.... Does not supersede the work of the whole community... the officer enables the community itself to fulfil the mission... does not abrogate the ministry... he/she facilitates it" in the manner of Ephesians 4:12.[38] Likewise Major Ray Harris (Canada), noting that "our own movement has a certain ambivalence about the meaning of ordination", contended that apart from the matter of function, we need to give attention to an officer's representational role. Like the captain of a hockey team or a Member of Parliament, officers of The Salvation Army represent something greater than themselves... to serve and equip that which we represent."[39]

Some saw leadership as the particular responsibility of officers. Colonel Harry Williams of Southern India in "The Priest and the People", said he used the term "priest" loosely to describe the "leader of a group of believers". Setting out four roles – ritualistic, sacerdotal, executive and "spokesman on religious matters", he observed that there were none that could not be performed by a layman. He concluded nevertheless that "the priest must, more than ever before, stand forth as a skilled and disciplined leader, meriting the respect and support of his congregation."[40] Captain David Radford said that it was "clear from Scripture that some people are called to have authority and responsibility for other believers".[41]

Lieut-Colonel Earl Robinson in an article on "Ordained to Spiritual Leadership", looked at functions of an ordained officership. In Part One he took the Pauline "leadership" and "government" from Romans 12:8 and 1st Corinthians 12:28 respectively, and explored the qualities of spirituality, knowledge of God, self-denial, humility, love and integrity required of "those called and ordained to a ministry of spiritual leadership" as well as the further requirements of 1 Timothy 3:17. Part Two dealt with the concept of "servant leadership".[42]

Some writers suggested a mix of roles, generally reflecting the usual run of clerical responsibilities in churches. Major William Burrows suggested "that there are four major responsibilities which are inescapable": the prophetic ("by which we mean the proclamation of the Word"), that of pastor, that of the priest and finally that of the evangelist. Burrows was a little obscure on the priestly role: "The priestly office involves the conveying of another's sins to God and the mediating of God's grace to them. In some communions this is interpreted sacramentally. Salvationists interpret it sacrificially."[43] From the explanation that follows it appears that

---

38 *Salvationist* (18 May 1996) pp. 8-9.

39 *Word and Deed* 2:1 (November 1999) pp. 43-4.

40 *Officer* (August 1970) pp. 550-2, 558.

41 *Officer* (November 1990) pp. 513-4.

42 *Officer* (May 1993) pp. 223-37; (June 1993) pp. 253-6.

43 *Officer* (September 1966) pp. 465-7.

he meant by this a sacrificial life-style. It is improbable that he was ascribing any priestly character to officership, as that would contradict his opinion already stated earlier in the article.

Lieut-Colonel Fred Hoyle suggested the officer-roles of leader, teacher, preacher and pastor; like many others he appeared to refer exclusively to people in a clerical role without considering whether the categories could apply equally to other Christians.[44]

Major Clifford Kew drew attention to the need for officers to find a balance between being a priest and being a dog's-body; not to be so immersed in the meeting of multitudinous needs that the prior responsibility to preach the gospel is neglected.[45] Major Jean Bradbury, United Kingdom, described the roles of an officer as: a spiritual leader, a communicator of the faith, a pastor, an enabler and a representative – for Christ, his gospel and for the Army.[46] David Stirling described the officer's "primary tasks" as "to preach the gospel and shepherd the flock" and to serve as a "spiritual mentor and confidant".[47]

For a number of writers, it was not what officers did that marked them out – such narrow terms as those offered really excluded all except Corps Officers. Rather, it was the conditions under which officers served that gave them a distinctive character, and in particular the officer's availability for appointment. A 1976 editorial mentioned being at the "disposal of the... Movement", elsewhere described as "availability" or "appointability", as a particular mark of officership.[48]

"Officership is Availability" headed an article by Colonel Wesley Harris in Australia. Having described officership as "a miracle and a mystery" and "sacramental", Harris said, "the essence of officership is availability." Admitting that "availability to God" and "availability to the people" should mark all Salvationists, he said, "officers are called, in a particular way, to be available to The Salvation Army."[49] This was not a new argument, but Harris made it particularly his own, returning to it in 1987 and in 1998.[50] Lieut.-Colonel Kenneth Manson referred to the same concept in addition to that of the "call", in "Change of Function": "I am an officer by the calling of God. I bind myself in a covenant with Him to serve Him within the Army. I am commissioned by God to be an officer. My appointments given and

44 *Officer* (December 1987) pp. 549-52; (January 1988) pp. 28-30.
45 *Officer* (May 1995) pp. 233-5.
46 *Salvationist* (9 May 1998) p. 16.
47 *Salvationist* (12 September 1998) p. 19.
48 *Officer* (July 1976) p. 290.
49 *Officer* (June 1979) pp. 243-5.
50 *Officer* (August 1987) p. 371, *Salvationist* (5 December 1998) p. 15.

received within that framework are settled by another. Our calling never changes but our function does."[51]

Colonel Gordon Sharp said that for him personally the elements were 1. A sense of calling; 2. Working out that calling in appointments; 3. His role in relation to fellow Salvationists; 4. The role of the Army in the particular circumstances in which an officer was called to work. He noted that the "act of appointing is a human act... mistakes are possible." He quoted an officer as saying, nevertheless, that "No place was the wrong place, no time the wrong time, to do God's will."[52] An Australian officer, Captain Howard Davies, drew attention to the unspoken assumption that "availability" assumed a close connection between the will of God and the decisions of appointment boards. He argued that the need to fill "the more secular" Headquarters appointments with non-officers, presumably to free up people with a "spiritual" call and training for spiritual work, also raised questions about the accountability of the senior Army administration for the deployment of officer-strength. "At what point or level," he asked, "does administrative decision become the 'divinely-directed Movement'?"[53]

Other writers again looked beyond the officer-conditions to the attitude required to accept them, and the sense of vocation involved in making an officer-covenant. Reacting to suggestions that the doctrine of the Priesthood of all Believers left no special significance for officership, Colonel Dinsdale Pender, Scotland, asked, "What Is Special About Officership? ... if any soldier can do what an officer can do..." Pender believed that the officer's calling was unique – to specific tasks, to full-time service and professional development, to a vision of the needy world and what they could do to meet those needs (= a "call"), and by virtue of the covenant, a sacred vow with a life-time commitment. He saw this not as a matter of elitism but of special privilege and responsibilities. Pender provided a list of supporting Scripture references, none of which could be applied exclusively to officers.[54]

Given that an Army needs leaders and strategists, Major Ian Barr agreed that the Army needed officers and that officership needed "to be defined within the purpose and mission of the Army" rather than "in terms used by other churches... in order to prove some point of equivalency". He suggested three non-negotiable aspects of an officer's life style and role: firstly, the Covenant - a "perpetual thing", which "once signed could not be unsigned" – secondly the identity of the Salvation Army itself, which Barr

51 *Officer* (June 1990) pp. 274-5.

52 *Officer* (November 1992) pp. 486-8.

53 *Officer* (September 1976) p. 421.

54 *Officer* (February 1990) pp. 51-3.

describes as "a radical fighting force" rather than a "passive institution", and thirdly the mission of proclaiming the gospel.[55]

Answering "Just what is officership?" Barr suggested that it had "three dimensions: it is a mode of being, a function, and it is a lifestyle." By "mode of being", he meant "a matter of being rather than doing", "a sense of 'being' an officer in the realm of the spirit". He ascribed this to the conditioning or "spiritual foundations laid in training" and observed that former officers tended to retain it. (Shades of indelible character...) By "function" Barr did not necessarily mean an evangelist or leader-role, since many officers did not have those specific appointments, but rather, "being available to concentrate on the issues we signed up for. Our function is not defined by our appointment, but by our covenant." He was not referring here to "availability" as he included that under "Lifestyle" – in fact as "the only lifestyle necessity". Other outward expressions of lifestyle were incidental, "occasionally based on little more than the social conventions of a particular society at a particular time…"[56] Major David Pickard held, on the other hand, that "the call, the covenant and a sense of identification with the Army are not just the foundations of officership. They are the bedrock of salvationism. The role of officers is a separate issue."[57] He did not however enlarge on that role.

Those looking for qualities peculiar to officership in fact tended to stray into theological quicksand. Recognising this, Major Cecil Waters urged a return to an unabashedly Salvationist argument from simple pragmatism. Under the heading "Us and Them", he suggested that "we will go on looking for a definition of officership unless and until we recognise that officership exists firstly as a convenience by which we organise the Army and secondly as one function, among many, to which we feel 'called of God'." It was "impossible to define a concept of officership which is plainly and clearly distinct from that of soldiership". The usual arguments – the call to a specific task, to full-time service, to a covenant – all applied equally to some soldiers. The anomalies did not permit classification. He concluded "(a) That it would seem that the Army needs full time workers… Most, but by no means all, these workers are officers. (b) That we believe we may be called to be such workers – and this call may refer to officership (rather than employee or envoy status). (c) That to be so called and so engaged is sufficient to sustain our work, our spirit and our identity. I believe we need look for nothing more special than this."[58] Major Cliff Ashworth also acknowledged that "officership can be expressed in a variety of ways. Most officers are leaders of corps communities… Some… serve in caring or

---

55 *Salvationist* (10 May 1997) pp. 8-9.
56 *Officer* (December, 1998) pp. 26-7.
57 *Salvationist* (7 June, 1997) p. 7.
58 *Officer* (July 1992) p. 317.

medical fields, educational or administrative ones.... The reality of officership can be expressed in a variety of contexts."[59]

One of the more extensive contributions to this debate seems not to have been heard at all widely. Major Ian Cooper, a British officer (the quality of whose scholarship is indicated by his membership of the committee that revised the translation of the New English Bible) wrote an 8,000-word monograph, "A Theology of Salvation Army Officership" some time after Lima in the 1980s. Divided into sections of *Officer*-article length, it sadly does not appear to have been published but was accessed by the Heritage Centre Archives in 1989.

Writing from the functional point of view regarding officership, Cooper does indeed define, describe and clarify that role. Acknowledging that "Booth's doctrine of officership was a 'high' one, placing the officer in responsibility for fostering spiritual growth and guiding the mission...", Cooper also noted that Booth "felt no need to add ordination or apostolic validation at the hands of bishops". He concluded from this that definition of ministry in the Salvation Army "does not involve directly any attempt to meet the criteria of other churches for valid ministry".[60] Having based Christian ministry on that of Christ and traced its apostolic development, Cooper regretted that the emphasis on ministry by the whole body had been lost by division between ordained and lay, and the reintroduction of the title of priest. He observed that "the New Testament challenges... the inevitable tendency for human organisations to reflect human values which can operate on the basis of power rather than grace."[61]

With a passing glance at the development of the military rank system ("It would be interesting to bring to bear on this deeply entrenched aspect of our structure the theological principles which underlie Christian ministry"), Cooper said that by contrast the content of officership had always been deeply theological. In common with other Free Churches the Army esteemed vocation more highly than ordination and this call was validated by the congregation and the organisation's leadership. He quoted the definition of officership from the Orders and Regulations, but noted that this was a practical definition, omitting vocation and the relationship of officer to soldier, that it was not set within the context of the whole people of God and did not relate vocation to the mission and pattern of Jesus. The wording of the Officer Covenant and Commissioning service however supplied some of these. The Salvation Army has seen commissioning as the heart of ordination. Of the recently-added ordination, Cooper noted that it "does not

---

59 *Salvationist* (18 May 1996) pp. 8-9.

60 Ian Cooper, "A Theology of Salvation Army Officership" (Unpublished monograph, 198?) pp. 1-2.

61 Cooper, "Officership", pp. 5-6.

have the meaning of conferring a unique and indelible clerical character... officership is terminable." "Apostolic ministry" meant in accordance with the Apostles' teaching and being sent by Christ as they had been sent – "not ministry conferred by an unbroken chain of bishops".[62]

In addition to the primary evangelistic role, officership could involve a wide variety of other functions or ministries, many of which could also be discharged by laymen. It was difficult to draw clear boundaries. "Certain traditional aspects rest on their utility to the work rather than theological essentials – custom tends to sanctify practice." There was a need to review the life-style expected – such as the requirement that both spouses needed to be officers, and review the utilisation of married women officers. The Army had tried to avoid making a priestly elite. Officership needed to be kept as something which is *sui generis* in the realm of spiritual leadership. There was a danger that what had evolved would now be given sacred status, making us reluctant to change.[63]

Cooper then described the way in which all soldiers, not just officers, took responsibility for the mission. He pointed out that without needing to officiate at sacraments, officers lacked a clearly distinguished clerical role, though they did have representative and legal functions. However, there had always been a strong emphasis on the officer vocation. He felt that there were four elements that distinguished the role of officers from that of soldiers. Firstly, there were special sacrifices implicit in officership, not only those arising from obedience and appointability but also the proneness to misunderstanding and isolation of command. Secondly, the pastoral expectations went beyond those expected of Christians in general, as the Army invested particular responsibility in the appointed officer leader. Thirdly, the officer acted as the bridge between the local unit and the organisation as a whole, functions as the focus of unity and integrity of values for the group, and represents the Army in the district. Fourthly, the vocation demanded exemplary qualities of life and spiritual leadership.[64]

Cooper is mindful that the military style system could be abused, so warns that these roles needed to be exercised in a servant manner, and that the leader's task is to facilitate the ministry of those he or she leads. He refers to the difficulty of integrating the old style of command with the modern need for consultative leadership. He also identifies problems regarding the role of women in the Army, and says that "society has now gone ahead of a movement that once led the way in using the gifts and abilities of women; perhaps it is time for us to ask why."

62 Cooper, "Officership", pp. 7-10.
63 Cooper, "Officership", pp. 10-12.
64 Cooper, "Officership", pp. 13-15.

The final section concerns the relationship of the soldier to the officer, and here Cooper probes a number of issues that arise when the tradition of obedience faces the reality of the voluntary nature of lay participation.[65]

The Debate So Far

While our examination of the theology of officership in the earlier period was dependent largely on official publications, prescriptions and descriptions, or on the opinions of the founders and senior leadership of the Army, in the later period described in these two chapters we have been able to sample more grass roots officer (and, eventually, non-officer) opinion.

During the first forty years of the Army's second century, a major focus of discussion on the theology of officership has no longer been concerned primarily with the qualities and roles of the officer, but with the officer's status. Brown's introduction of ordination suggests that this preoccupation was shared by the senior hierarchy as well.

That basic ambiguity about the status of officers – whether they are distinguished from soldiers solely by their role and function or whether they enjoy some distinctive character or status – which we saw in the origins of the Salvation Army's professional ministry group, persists today in the minds of Salvationists. If the "denominationalising" tendency involves an increasing distance between lay and clerical roles, this was resisted by some and accepted or endorsed by others. It must be said that the latter more often revealed assumptions based on dubious exegesis or limited historical knowledge.

Where people did examine the roles or functions of officers, they generally covered the same ground we have seen traversed in earlier chapters. Officers were to lead, pastor, preach, teach and disciple, and equip the saints for ministry. Some saw the officer as being assisted in ministry by non-officers; others saw that the officer's role was to assist non-officers in *their* ministry. Some writers addressed officer conditions of service, such as appointability, as the distinctive mark of officership. A few called attention to officers' representative role, as head and focus of their community of faith.

Some people, while rejecting any spurious status equivalent to priestly character for officership, felt that an entirely functional description could not justify a separate officer role. They therefore looked for an internal, Salvation Army validation, a combination of the officer's own personal sense of calling and the objective fact that Salvation Army officer ministry was an existing reality to be taken into account.

---

65 Cooper, "Officership", pp. 18-21.

In all of this, except by implication as an aspect of the officers' "equipping" role, the function of Biblical and theological reflection did not attract comment. Historically this essential task has been dependent upon the emergence of specialists with time and opportunity to discharge it, and for the Salvation Army these have been until recent years mainly its officers.

Chapter Twelve

Official Words

> "I don't know what you mean by 'glory,'" Alice said. Humpty Dumpty smiled contemptuously. "Of course you don't – till I tell you. I meant 'there's a nice knock-down argument for you!'" "But 'glory' doesn't mean 'a nice knock-down argument,'' Alice objected. "When I use a word," Humpty Dumpty said in rather a scornful tone, "it means just what I choose it to mean – neither more nor less." "The question is," said Alice, "whether you can make words mean so many different things." "The question is," said Humpty Dumpty, "which is to be master – that's all."
>
> Lewis Carroll,
> *Through the Looking Glass,*
> Chapter VI.

The previous two chapters traced the unofficial debate that has taken place over the past forty years on the status of Salvation Army "orders". Chapters Twelve and Thirteen look at what the organisation has said officially on the same matter. No doubt the unofficial discussion helped prompt the movement to seek to clarify what Salvationists were intended to believe about ministry, just as the official pronouncements in their turn fuelled further debate.

This chapter looks firstly the use of the word "ordain" in Commissioning of officers, and then at the Salvation Army's response to the World Council of Churches' "Lima" Document.

Ordination

We have seen that there is some tension between the arguments of those who sought to identify officership with the historic ministry of the Church and those who, regarding this as irrelevant, seeing the Army as outside the traditional ecclesiastical arrangements. With the adoption of the language of ordination, the hierarchy came down on the side of the former – while at the same time attempting to keep a foot in both camps.

Traditionally, cadets were commissioned as officers. Although "ordination" was not in regular Salvation Army usage, isolated examples can be found, usually invoking Biblical precedents. In 1911 Colonel John Dean made a comparison between the Apostolic call and life with that of

Salvation Army officers. "From the general body of disciples there followed a special selection for the office of apostleship, the commission or ordination conferring new powers and new teaching." The terms of officer commissioning were those of Matthew Chapter 10.[1] Again, in a 1927 booklet on officer training, a section is headed, "Chosen and Ordained".[2] The use of the word in this context probably owes more to the AV translation of John 15:16 than to any claim to ecclesiastical status.

Some evidence of an informal use of the word is also provided by Colonel Frank Bell in a pamphlet of 1948. This included representations he had made to Generals and to members of the 1934, 1939 and 1946 High Councils as well as a general review of what he saw as weaknesses in the contemporary Salvation Army. Amongst signs of the "drift to Churchism, conventionalism, professionalism and secularism", Bell included "commissioning becomes ordination".[3]

Just occasionally the word was used when reference was made to Salvation Army ministry in comparison with that of other denominations. For example General Albert Orsborn, in an article on "The Office of a Bishop", claimed that "the apostolic succession is not in flesh and blood, not in the gift and power of men, but in the witness and work of the Holy Spirit ...spiritual ordination is in the gift of God, a conferment, not an attainment."[4] Later, in the course of an article on the World Council of Churches, he stated that "We cannot allow the effective ordination (commissioning) of our officers, including the women, to be challenged. We should never agree to their re-ordination at the hands of anyone."[5]

Another example is found in an article, "Ordained by God", written by Commissioner Frederick Coutts. Writing on the 100th anniversary of William Booth's ordination, Coutts noted that "Ordination as such meant recognition as a minister and provided him with accredited status within the Connexion. But the imposition of hands did not make William Booth a man of God." Arguing on the basis of Catherine Booth's "law of adaptation", Coutts went on to ask, "How can ecclesiastical garments which fitted in the third century, and possibly in the tenth, be deemed the only adequate attire for the twentieth?" Coutts cited Booth's contemporary, the Anglican scholar Hort: "The true apostolic succession means nothing more than the continual call of men to service by Christ Himself. No ceremony avails to effect it. 'The true succession,' to quote Cromwell, 'is through the Spirit.'"[6]

---

1 "Notes of an address to Officers" in *Field Officer* (November 1911) pp. 401-4.
2 Anon., *Training of Salvation Army Officers*, p. 31.
3 Frank Bell, *The Fight for the Flag* (privately circulated, 1948) p. 25.
4 *The Officers' Review* (November-December 1947) pp. 330-1.
5 *Officer* (March-April 1954) p. 77.
6 *SA Year Book* (1958) pp. 10-3.

An editorial writer in the Australian War Cry commented, under the heading "Truly Ordained", on the commissioning of officers in Sydney and Melbourne. Quoting an expression of Albert Orsborn's, the writer stated: "Although in these important ceremonies there is no laying on of hands, these young ministers of Christ are truly ordained: theirs is the 'ordination of the nail-pierced hands'."[7]

Captain Earl Robinson of Canada provided an extended comparison between commissioning and ordination in 1968, for a commissioning booklet in the Canadian Territory, and it was reprinted in *Servants Together* in 2002:

> There are three steps in the ordination to Salvation Army Officership in keeping with the traditional meaning of ordination in the Church as a whole:
> 1. THE SIGNING OF THE COVENANT:
> This involves the recognition that the essential basis of ordination is that Christ calls and ordains, so that the covenant is made between the individual and his Lord: 'Called by Almighty God to proclaim the gospel ... I give myself to God, and here and now bind myself to Him in a solemn covenant.'
> 2. THE COMMISSIONING:
> The Officer is given authority to manifest the saving grace of God in the ministry of leadership within The Salvation Army. This is the outward authentication of the inward summons, and, as with the laying on of hands, has to do with the symbol of the passing on of wisdom and authority by the one already ordained...
> 3. THE DEDICATION:
> The Officer is, by prayer, committed to the help and guidance of the Holy Spirit, and to the intercessions of the Church (the Dedicatory Prayer). This dedication follows the declaration by the Officer that he or she understands the implications of the signing of the Covenant and the commissioning, will be loyal to Scriptural truth, and, by living and word, be true to the apostolic succession of being Christ's messenger.
> The Salvation Army Officer is thus ordained a minister of the saving grace of God, a prophet and a priest, a pastor and teacher, a servant, as much as any minister of any denomination.[8]

Following, according to Commissioner Victor Keanie, "representations from a number of territories", the word "ordain" was introduced into the rubric for commissioning Salvation Army officers in 1978.[9] According to the explanation offered in *Servants Together*, the book on "Salvationist

---

7 *WC* (Australia) (16 January 1965).
8 International Doctrine Council, *Servants Together* (London: SA, 2002) pp. 77-8.
9 *Officer* (February 1986) p. 77.

Perspectives on Ministry" published in 2002, "it was believed by Salvation Army international leaders in the 1970s and 1980s that these signs of equivalence of standing with the ordained clergy of other churches might be aided by associating the historic Church term, 'ordain', with our traditional term, 'commission'."[10]

Could this sentence be taken as suggesting the writers' distancing of the present hierarchy from their predecessors' concerns?

The initiative was taken by General Arnold Brown in 1978. In his memoirs Brown explained that, "Some, I felt, did not fully understand that the granting of a commission not only admitted the recipient to officership, but also conveyed all that is commonly drawn from the term, 'ordination,' only the ceremonial form of conferment being different. As General I had full support in revising the wording of the commissioning statement so that the thought of 'ordination' was more explicit..."[11]

Brown evidently consulted the retired General Frederick Coutts as to a way forward. A letter from Coutts on 20 February 1978 suggested that the following sentence could be added to the commissioning ceremony:

> "In accepting these pledges which you each have made, I commission you as officers of The Salvation Army and ordain you as ministers of Christ and of His Gospel."[12]

On 28 February Brown wrote to the secretary of the Advisory Council to the General asking that the matter be tabled, beginning his letter with

> You will know my anxiety to secure in the minds of the cadets being commissioned as officers, and in the minds of those who attend the Dedication Service during a Commissioning Weekend, that the ceremony is in every way, and equals, an ordination.[13]

He also made the point, taken from General Coutts's letter, that by this addition, "ordination is not linked with any human movement but with Christ himself, following our Lord's own practice (John 15:16)". (We note again the tendency to restrict the application of Jesus' words to a "clerical" group.)

The Advisory Council seems to have been less than enthusiastic. It recommended that "in territories where the phrase 'ordained as a minister of

10 *Servants Together*, p. 73.

11 Arnold Brown, *The Gate and the Light* (Toronto: Bookwright Publications, 1984) p. 22.

12 Letter in IHQ Archives.

13 Letter in IHQ Archives.

Christ' seems to be required it might well be used", but hoped that the General "would not feel it should be made obligatory upon all".[14]

Their hope was not realised. Following this, the Chief of the Staff, Commissioner Stanley Cottrill, wrote to all Territorial Commanders on 30 May 1978 as follows:

> It is the General's wish that a slight modification should be made to the wording of the Dedication Service during the Commissioning of cadets, in order to emphasise the fact that Salvation Army officers are ordained ministers of Christ and of His Gospel.
>
> After the cadets have made their Affirmation of Faith, the officer conducting the Commissioning should then say: "In accepting these pledges which you each have made, I commission you as officers of The Salvation Army and ordain you as ministers of His Gospel." In countries other than English-speaking, and where the word "ordained" has no exact equivalent, a translation should be used which will give the nearest possible meaning to the English-language expression.[15]

General Brown's announcement of the change was an aside in an address to officers attending the 1978 International Congress. Reviewing the variety of "Covenants" into which Salvationists might enter, such as Soldiership and Marriage, he went on to speak of the "Covenant of Officership".

> For a few, in these days of ecumenical activity, the validity of officership is under scrutiny. Some of our clerical brethren seem fond of reminding us that there are three forks in the road where the Army marches one way and the historical churches another. The road along which we march, according to some, is the road of omission – we have no ceremony of baptism; there is no observance of Holy Communion; and our officers are not ordained in the episcopal sense of the term.
>
> But allow me to say that the swearing-in of a soldier demands no less a commitment to Christ than the rite of baptism; that for the Salvationist every meal is a "holy communion" and the whole of life is sacramental (nor is the penitent-form as an outward form of inward desire to be overlooked) and, in the commissioning of an officer, he – and she! – is in every sense of the word "ordained" to the ministry of Christ in the world. (The wording of the commissioning ceremony has just been extended to say so!)[16]

---

14 Advisory Council Recommendation 1078, 19 April 1978.

15 Letters in IHQ Archives.

16 *Officer* (October 1978) pp. 438-9.

This, in what was essentially a private gathering, appears to have been the extent of public announcement of the change. This low-key promulgation seems at odds with the desire to heighten public awareness of the real significance of Salvation Army commissioning, though it does reflect Brown's assumption that nothing of significance had changed.

The matter was reviewed ten years later, at the 1988 International Conference of Leaders (Lake Arrowhead), after which the Conference Implementation Commission minuted the following at its meeting of 25-28 October 1988:

> ORDINATION
> The introduction of the word had been important for the USA where it was desired to manifest equal status with the ministers of the Gospel. It had been helpful in India and generally accepted in Africa. However in some languages no direct translation was possible. There were territories, particularly in Europe, where the use of the word caused some distress. Territorial leaders in such situations should be sensitive to the feelings of their people. Generally it was felt to be difficult to withdraw the use of the word. A warning was issued that ordination might be legally construed as "ordination for life" making possible legal action against termination of officership in some instances.

The following recommendation was agreed:

> The Commission recommends that the use of the word "ordination" be confirmed. Any territorial variation deemed wise may be cleared through the International Secretary with the approval of the Chief of the Staff.[17]

This recommendation was accepted by General Eva Burrows and conveyed to Territorial Commanders in a letter dated 16 November 1988:

> Ordination
> It is confirmed that this word will remain as part of our commissioning ceremony. However, in the event that a variation to this rule is deemed wise in a particular territory a proposal should be submitted by the TC/OC to the IS for decision by the CoS.[18]

Just over three years later, by letter of 3 February 1992, Burrows requested that the Advisory Council to the General revisit the issue, saying:

---

17 Conference Implementation Committee Minute 1, 1988 Conference of Leaders. IHQ Archives.

18 International Conference of Leaders Follow-up letter 2, IHQ Archives.

> Because there continues to be some questioning in certain parts of the world about the use of the word "ordained" in the commissioning of cadets, I have looked into the origin of its introduction into the ceremony... I would value consideration of this matter by the members of the Advisory Council ... Also to enquire as to whether a clear statement should be sent out by the CoS as a Memorandum.[19]

The Advisory Council took into account a number of observations: that the initiative to use the word ordination was said to have come from the USA; that it was thought to give officers a status similar to that conferred on ministers of other churches; that it was loaded with theological implications considered by some to be incompatible with the concept of the priesthood of all believers; that it could imply "continuation" whether the officer remained an officer or not (though it was noted that in the USA officership and therefore ordination was rescinded by the same authority that conferred it); that General Brown had pointed out that ordination was not linked with any human movement but with Jesus Christ himself; that "ordination" could not always be exactly translated.[20]

Having discussed the matter, the Advisory Council reported:

> Acknowledging the differences of view and practice held in various parts of the world, it re-affirms Rec 1078 of the Council and the Rec on "Ordination" agreed by the CIC of 1988.
>
> It also recommends that it would be helpful for a clear statement on this issue to be sent out by the CoS to territorial and command leaders.[21]

Commissioner Bramwell Tillsley, Chief of the Staff, issued M283, "Commissioning and Ordination of Cadets" on 28 April 1992 and sent it to all Territorial Commanders and Officers Commanding under cover of a letter signed by General Burrows. It stated:

> By the issuing of this memorandum it is confirmed that the word "ordained" will remain as part of our commissioning ceremony. Therefore, after the cadets have made their Affirmation of Faith, the officer conducting the commissioning shall say:
>
> "In accepting these pledges which you each have made, I commission you as officers of The Salvation Army and ordain you as ministers of Christ and his gospel."

---

19 IHQ Archives.
20 Advisory Council Minutes, March 1992.
21 Advisory Council Recommendation 2043.

> Should a variation to this rule be thought wise in a particular territory, a proposal should be submitted by the TC/OC to the IS for decision by the CoS.[22]

In May 2000, General John Gowans rephrased the form when he commissioned cadets in London and in Atlanta a month later. He said, "Accepting your promises and recognising that God has ordained you to preach the Gospel, I now commission you an officer of The Salvation Army." Colonel Gudrun Lydholm, a member of the International Doctrine Council, felt that "this wording more clearly confirmed Salvation Army belief in God as the one acting" and corresponded with Gowans, proposing a further, explicitly Trinitarian, modification to the wording.[23] Gowans then asked the International Doctrine Council to recommend possible changes to the 1992 wording "that might more clearly reflect Salvation Army theology associated with ordination and commissioning." A meeting of this body on 2 November 2001 produced four variations that were then discussed by the newly instituted General's Consultative Council. As a result of this process a Memorandum from Commissioner John Larsson, Chief of Staff, was issued on 1 February 2002, and included the words:

> The commissioning officer will say to each cadet in turn: "Cadet (name): Accepting your promises and recognising that God has called, ordained and empowered you to be a minister of Christ and of his gospel, I commission you an officer of The Salvation Army."[24]

The significant change here, apart from the individual address, would appear to be that "ordination" was now seen as something already done by God rather than in this ceremony by a representative of the organisation. This reflects what Coutts had written in his letter of 20 February 1978, although the actual rubric he had suggested at the time did not convey this meaning. It remains to be seen if this compromise proves acceptable to protagonists on both sides of the debate that had clearly continued behind the scenes over the course of the subsequent twenty-four years.

As a postscript to this account of what had been intended as a decisive affirmation of officer status, it is interesting to compare the Army's experience with that of the Roman Catholic Church in the years following Vatican II. Rodney Stark and Roger Finke argue that the immense loss in numbers of clergy and religious after that event, at least in the Western world, resulted largely from the loss of status they were accorded *vis-à-vis*

---

22 IHQ Archives.

23 Colonel Gudrun Lydholm, letter dated 17 December 2002.

24 IHQ Archives.

the laity by the Council's decisions.[25] By that token one would have expected the increased status of ordination to have helped shore up the decline in the numbers of officers in Europe, the United Kingdom and the "Old Dominions". This has not however been the case.

Response to Lima

The 1982 Lima Document on *Baptism, Eucharist and Ministry* was produced by the Faith and Order Commission of the World Council of Churches, of which the Salvation Army was a founding member in 1948.

Some elements within the Salvation Army have always been wary of this association. General Albert Orsborn was reluctant to be involved when the World Council was formed. In an address on the Salvation Army in relation to Ecumenism, given to the 1969 Commissioners' Conference, Commissioner Hubert Westcott quoted Orsborn's memorandum to the Advisory Council in 1947 as concluding with, "I do not wish my period of leadership to be associated with the gravitation of the Salvation Army nearer to church life in faith and order." Having received the Advisory Council's recommendation, Orsborn commented, "It occurs to me to wonder why we should participate in the Assembly... but the majority of our leaders think that we should be represented and therefore I have told the Chief to arrange it." Orsborn later did not to replace the retiring Commissioner A. G. Cunningham on the executive council of the WCC Central Committee.[26] His successor, Wilfred Kitching, wrote concerning the WCC that "we may have at times lost something by seeking to withhold interest in the affairs of the Church."[27] Successive Generals or other leading Army figures involved in the ecumenical movement have been at pains to explain the nature and limits of this association over the years, especially at times of WCC General Assemblies.[28]

For some there was possibly a fear of absorption into some generic super-church, espousing modernist or possibly Roman doctrines (depending on the

---

25 Stark and Finke, *Acts of Faith*, pp. 177-90.

26 Albert Orsborn, *Officer* (March-April 1954) pp. 73-8; Arnold Brown, *Gate and Light*, p. 232; Hubert Westcott, Unpublished paper in Report on 1969 Commissioner's Conference, p. 1.

27 *Magazine* (December, 1961) p. 5.

28 See Albert Orsborn, *Officer* (March-April 1954) pp. 73-8; Wilfred Kitching in *Officer* (September-October 1961) pp. 289-294, 323-34, (November-December 1961) pp. 361-5; Reginald Woods in *Officer* (March-April 1962) pp. 109-13, (May-June 1962) pp. 167-72, (July-August 1962) pp. 257-60, (September- October 1962) pp. 289-94, (March 1963) pp. 125-8, (April 1963) pp. 161-4, 167; Harry Williams in *Officer* (April 1979) pp. 150-4, 178.

individual phobia), and the loss of identity and mission. At the extreme end some sympathised with the views of Dr Carl McIntire, an American Presbyterian minister who established an "International Council of Christian Churches" in 1948 and in his journal the *Christian Beacon* was wont to charge the WCC with being a Catholic-modernist-Communist conspiracy.[29] Commissioner Reginald Woods, the Army's representative on the WCC Central Committee in the 1960s, took his influence sufficiently seriously to rebut some of his allegations in an article in *The Officer*.[30]

Chiefly American anti-Communist fears and regard for the sensibilities of donors were certainly a factor contributing to the Army's withdrawal (suspension of membership pending discussions) from the Central Committee of the WCC in 1979 over the issue of aid to liberation movements in Africa.[31] Letters from Salvation Army Archives in USA support this allegation, and letters in London Archives show that leaders in London had tried unsuccessfully to mollify the American leaders' opposition to the World Council of Churches. The deaths of Army personnel in a 1978 guerrilla attack on a mission station in Zimbabwe-Rhodesia helped point the issue.[32]

The Army's concerns were not solely political however. The 1980 Report of a Commission also referred to a "change of emphasis", if not a change of policy, in the Council's approach to ecumenism. "The WCC has undoubtedly become more active in recent years in its quest for church union." Referring to the influence of the Faith and Order Commission's 1975 study booklet, *One Baptism, One Eucharist and a Mutually Recognised Ministry*, the Report says that "the emphasis on a 'mutually agreed ministry' has made it necessary for The Salvation Army to define more clearly the position of an officer in relationship to other ministers and in relationship to the soldiery... It would be fair to say that the Army takes 'the priesthood of all believers' more literally than most member churches and therefore gives its laity – at least theologically – a more important role than that accorded by most other churches... this is a position which the Army wishes to safeguard." The report suggested that "the Army will have to be prepared to find itself increasingly 'out of step' with other

29 See http://www.ptsem.edu/grow/Library/collections/McIntire.htm. Accessed 3 November 2005.

30 *Officer* (April 1963) p. 162.

31 Norman S. Murdoch, "In Darkest Africa: Martyrdom and Resistance to Colonialism in Rhodesia", *Journal of Third World Studies* (Spring 2005) p. 9.

32 Henry Gariepy, *The History of The Salvation Army* VIII (Atlanta GA: SA, 2000) p. 20.

denominations, even to the extent of becoming a permanent irritation to them."[33]

The Army eventually settled on maintaining its association by adopting non-voting "fraternal" status in 1981.[34] This relationship derived from the Army's new status as a "Christian World Communion", which it shared with such bodies as the World Methodist Council, the Lutheran World Federation and the Baptist World Alliance. This reflects the Army's international polity as distinct from membership of the Council by separate national churches of each denomination.[35] This association is now referred to as "advisor" status, a category shared by all participants in the Conference of Secretaries of World Communions, including the Roman Catholic Church and the Conference of Seventh-day Adventists.

The North American Army remained suspicious of the WCC. Commissioner Victor Keanie's Report on the 6th World Assembly (Toronto, July 24-August 10, 1983) commented, "We were aware of a lack of interest and in some cases antipathy regarding the WCC on the part of Canadian Salvationists (in common with their USA neighbours)... It seems obvious that our North American friends have not understood the relationship of the Army to the WCC and in general seem to be adversely influenced by the media interpretation of the Council's activities."[36]

The WCC produced its Faith and Order Paper 111, the "Lima" document on *Baptism, Eucharist and Ministry*, in 1982 (Footnoted as *BEM 111*). This end-product of many years of discussion by the Faith and Order Commission represented the areas of "theological convergence" among the major confessional groups as the conferences brought together not only the WCC member bodies but also representatives of the Roman Catholic Church and some other non-members. The document was transmitted to churches with a request for their official response. While the intention had been that churches would look for areas of agreement, the majority ended up by drawing lines around their own particular distinctives and the result pleased no-one. Catholics (in the broad sense) felt the document was Protestant in emphasis; Protestants felt "left out".[37]

---

33 "Findings of the Commission Appointed to Review the Relationship of The Salvation Army with the World Council of Churches", Unpublished Report, January, 1980.

34 Arnold Brown, letter dated 31 July 1981 to Philip Potter of WCC, in *Gate and Light*, p. 239.

35 *One Faith, One Church: The Salvation Army's Response to Baptism, Eucharist and Ministry* (London: SA, 1990) p. 1.

36 Victor Keanie, Unpublished Report, 1983, p. 2.

37 Contrast John Collins, *Diakonia* (Oxford: Oxford University Press, 1990) pp. 256-7, and Miroslav Volf, *After Our Likeness* (Grand Rapids: Eerdmans, 1998) p. 20.

To prepare a response, the Salvation Army asked all Territories to set up study groups "composed of theologically and experientially qualified Salvationists, ordained and lay".[38] The resulting paper contained the first extensive official statement on the Army's doctrine of ministry, even though it was necessarily reactive, taking its cues from the Lima document.

The responses were published as *Faith and Order Paper 137 – Churches Respond to BEM* (Footnoted as *BEM 137*); pages 230-53 of Volume IV contain the Salvation Army statement. Copies of the Army's response were distributed to officers in some territories at least, as it became available.[39] The Army also published its response separately in book form in *One Faith, One Church* in 1990.

Anxious to find what common ground it could, the Army welcomed the invitation to contribute, "despite the fact that the Army's traditional approach to the subjects dealt with differs significantly from the hypothesis on which the present study rests" and regretted that "the sincerely held views of non-sacramentalist Christians are ignored in this document."[40] Because of its non-sacramental stance the Army was inevitably out of step with the major groups represented and its response could probably be characterised as "Yes, but..." The Movement had not been comfortable with the 1975 revision of the Functions and Purposes section of the WCC constitution which gave "increased prominence to the World Council's role in encouraging church unity" and the introduction of the phrases "visible unity" and "Eucharistic fellowship". It regretted "the apparent elevation of apostolic tradition to the level of apostolic faith".[41]

Salvationist reviewers were "troubled by the apparent inference that we start divided and must see how we can achieve unity" whereas the Army's assumption was that "we are already 'one in Christ Jesus'" and that "the task facing the Church is to see how that can be realized and made visible..."[42] This distinction was probably intended to reinforce the Army's support for the 1950 WCC Toronto Statement that "no church... is required to give up its self- understanding or subscribe to one understanding of the Church".[43]

The passages dealing with baptism and the Eucharist are outside the scope of this essay but we are concerned here with the section on Ministry.

---

38 Max Thurian and Geoffrey Wainwright (ed.), *Churches Respond to BEM: Faith and Order Paper 137* (Geneva: World Council of Churches, 1986) p. 232.

39 Lt.-Colonel Trevor Standen, letter to all officers in New Zealand, dated June 1987.

40 *BEM 137*, p. 230. Note however that the "Canberra Statement", adopted by the Seventh Assembly of the World Council of Churches in 1991, included the concession that, "we gladly acknowledge that some who do not observe these rites share in the spiritual experience of life in Christ."

41 *BEM 137*, p. 231.

42 *BEM 137*, p. 233.

43 *BEM 137*, p. 232.

What follows is a clause by clause summary of salient points from Lima together with points made in the Army's response.

The Lima paper on Ministry opened with Section I: "THE CALLING OF THE WHOLE PEOPLE OF GOD." The Army agreed that the mission of the Church was vested in the whole community of the faithful and that "any consideration of ordained ministry" must work from the perspective of the whole people of God" and viewed its "commissioned and ordained officers" from this perspective.[44]

Section II: "THE CHURCH AND THE ORDAINED MINISTRY" provided a glossary defining charism, ministry, ordained ministry and priest. The Army agreed with the definitions given while dissenting from the significance invested in the laying on of hands.[45]

A: "The Ordained Ministry", outlined the need for church leadership, whose ministry "is constitutive of the life and witness of the Church". Its role was to represent Jesus Christ to the Community, proclaim his message of reconciliation, to be leaders, teachers and pastors, to build up the Community, to be examples of holiness and loving concern. The Salvation Army supported all this as coinciding with its own views on the "calling and status of its commissioned officers" and it supported "the need to avoid dogmatic claims regarding the ministry of any one church or any one form of ordination".[46] However, it dissented from "the assumption that our ministry is founded on that of the apostles. Like theirs, our ministry is founded on Christ."[47]

Short interpretative passages of "Commentary" were scattered through Lima. The Commentary on paragraph 14 held it appropriate for an ordained ministry to be given the task of presiding at the Eucharist, while admitting the absence of explicit New Testament evidence that this was required. The Army commented that "We read into this an acceptance of the fact that the Eucharist was not instituted as a form, ceremony or sacrament, which is the Salvation Army viewpoint."[48] This was probably not what the authors of Lima had in mind here.

B. "Ordained Ministry and Authority" stated that the authority of the ordained minister is rooted in Jesus Christ and conferred by the Holy Spirit, not as the possession of the ordained person but as a gift for the body, with whose co-operation it is exercised. The Army supported this.

C. "The Ordained Ministry and Priesthood" derived the priesthood of the whole community from that of Christ, but noted that ordained ministers could also be described as priests because of their service of edification and

---

44 *BEM 137*, p. 246-7.
45 *BEM 137*, p. 247.
46 *BEM 137*, p. 248.
47 *BEM 137*, p. 247.
48 *BEM 137*, p. 248.

intercession. The Army preferred not to use the term "priest", but said "the paragraph describes the function and relationship of our 'priesthood of all believers' and of our ordained and commissioned officers."[49]

D. "The Ministry of Men and Women in the Church" acknowledged that "there is in Christ no male or female" (Galatians 3:28) and noted that "the Church must discover the ministry that can be provided by women as well as that which can be provided by men."[50] However, it admitted that the churches differed on the admission of women to ordained ministry. The Salvation Army, "having at least twice as many ordained women officers as men"[*sic*], preferred "to accept the open door to the full involvement of women in the work of the Kingdom".

Section III: "THE FORMS OF THE ORDAINED MINISTRY"

On "Bishops, Presbyters and Deacons", Lima admitted that the New Testament showed a variety of forms rather than prescribing a single pattern of ministry. However it suggested that the three-fold pattern "may serve today as an expression of this unity we seek and also as a means of achieving it", even though the "present forms of the traditional pattern raise questions for all churches".[51]

The Salvation Army was happy with the three-fold pattern as three levels of ministerial authority, indicating that it had its own administrative levels, but found "attempts to give distinct theological meaning to these levels unconvincing and confusing".[52] It preferred to see the gifts of *episkope* and *diakonia* operating in and characterising all levels of ministry.

"Guiding Principles for the Exercise of Ordained Ministry" laid down that ordained ministry should be exercised in a "personal, collegial and communal" way, "constitutionally ordered", with "regular representative synodal gatherings" and "active participation of all members in the life and decision-making of the Community".[53] The Salvation Army's support for the latter concept, and its citing of Advisory Boards and Corps Councils as such bodies, might have given the impression that it possessed a more participative polity than was actually the case.

On the "Functions of Bishops, Presbyters and Deacons", uniformity was not required but the Commission made tentative suggestions. The Army claimed that its functionaries already "conformed in a general way to each of the categories described", but took the view that "functions rather than the title or form of ordination are of most importance" and that "the true ministry is unified, not compartmentalised."[54]

---

49 *BEM 137*, p. 248.
50 *BEM 111*, p. 24.
51 *BEM 111*, p. 25.
52 *BEM 137*, p. 249.
53 *BEM 111*, p. 26.
54 *BEM 137*, pp. 249-50.

"Variety of Charisms" should characterise the community, and "the ordained ministry, itself a charism, should not become a hindrance for the variety of these charisms."[55] The Army endorsed this, and felt that its own existence and history illustrated the need for the Church "constantly to receive new impulses from the Holy Spirit... unrestricted by ecclesiastical structures".[56]

IV: "SUCCESSION IN THE APOSTOLIC TRADITION"

"Apostolic Tradition in the Church" meant continuity in the permanent characteristics of the Church of the Apostles, which were then listed. The Salvation Army agreed, with the reservation that it did not see the celebration of baptism and the Eucharist as a necessary part of that tradition. The Army did not "give to apostolic or any tradition the same value as to the scriptures" and observed that "historical continuity alone does not guarantee apostolicity."[57]

"Succession of the Apostolic Ministry" was described as an expression of permanence and continuity of Christ's ministry, in which the ordained ministry has a particular task. It was suggested that general acceptance of the episcopate "will best further the unity of the whole Church if it is part of a wider process by which the episcopal churches themselves also regain their lost unity".[58]

The Salvation Army opposed the concept of "mystical transmission from one ordained minister to another" and suggested that "orderly transmission" was to be found in "faithfulness to the word of God and an openness to the Holy Spirit". It welcomed the acknowledgement that "continuity in apostolic faith, worship and mission have been preserved in churches which have not retained the form of historic episcopate... the reality and function of the episcopal ministry has been preserved ... without the title of bishop."[59]

V: "ORDINATION"

"The meaning of Ordination" was that "the Church sought to continue the mission of the apostles and remain faithful to their teaching" by ordaining certain of its members by invocation of the Spirit and the laying on of hands. The Lord was the true ordainer and the rite denoted action by God and by the Community.[60] The Army was gratified that Commentaries 39 and 40 recognised the validity of different ordination practices. It would not support episcopal re-ordination of ministers from non-episcopal traditions.

---

55 *BEM 111*, pp. 27-8.
56 *BEM 137*, p. 250.
57 *BEM 137*, p. 250.
58 *BEM 111*, p. 30.
59 *BEM 137*, p. 251.
60 *BEM 111*, p. 30.

The Army was happy that "The Act of Ordination" was placed by tradition in the context of worship, and particularly of the Eucharist, preserving the understanding that ordination was an act in which the whole Community was involved.

"The Conditions for Ordination" recognised that people were called in differing ways to the ordained ministry but that the Community must authenticate the call. They could be professional or remain in other occupations, and could be celibate or married. Study, preparation and training were required, and no time limit was generally envisaged in their commitment. Ordination could not be repeated, and need not be repeated after absence from the role. It was accepted that the disciplines of no one church could be seen as universally applicable. Discrimination on grounds of race or sociological group was inappropriate. The Army did not dissent from these.

However, the Army's responses to Section V appeared to miss some cues. On V, A, for example, the Army did not dissent from the implication of "classes" of Christian inherent in the derivation of ordination – possibly because its recent adoption of the term had cost it the high moral ground in this argument.

Again, on V, C, "Conditions for Ordination", the response also seems to miss the real issue as far as the Army's position was concerned. The Salvation Army supported the conditions suggested, including ordination for life and the unrepeatability of ordination, viewing its own officership as a life-long vocation. The current *Orders and Regulations for Officers* state that "There is no release from the calling of a Salvation Army officer, but provision is made for retirement from specific responsibility…"[61]

The Army found that its own appointment of lay-salvationists as "envoys" was analogous perhaps to that of lay-readers but it had no equivalent of non-stipendiary priests. The Army however evidently missed the significance of the implication that ordained persons were seen as having an indelible character, whereas no Salvation Army officer could retain his or her commission and rank if not in an appointment (except for a short period of special leave). This was perhaps a crucial difference but seemed to be glossed over, possibly because the Army confused its expectation of life-long commitment with the catholic church view that orders retained their validity even when the ordained person no longer functioned as a minister.[62]

VI: "TOWARDS THE MUTUAL RECOGNITION OF THE ORDAINED MINISTRIES."

The Commission called for churches to make deliberate efforts to examine their understanding and practice of ministry and make changes if required. The Salvation Army expressed disappointment in the emphasis on

---

61 *Orders and Regulations for Officers* (1997) Vol. 2, Part 7, Chap. 3, Section 1.1.
62 *BEM 137*, p. 253.

"the laying on of hands" and the "need to recover the sign of episcopal succession". It felt that Salvation Army officers could "claim the right to be accepted as part of the ordained ministry through which God has been pleased to perform all the essential functions outlined in this section of the Lima text".[63]

In sum, then, the Salvation Army identified with Lima where it could. Even in its response on Ministry, it appeared somewhat preoccupied with the issues of baptism and Eucharist. On the question of how Salvation Army ministry is perceived in relation to traditional Church belief about ordination, it appeared to be less sensitive and therefore, as we have noted, missed a significant area of difference under V, A, "The Meaning of Ordination", and C, "Conditions for Ordination".

When pragmatic decisions are made without having a clear theological principle, inconsistencies of policy and practice are not uncommon. Dr Alan Harley recalls that when he resigned from the Salvation Army and entered the Congregational ministry, he was not required to be ordained because his Salvation Army commissioning was accepted as equivalent. When however after a long and distinguished career in the church he rejoined the Army as an officer in Australia, he was required to be re-commissioned and to re-sign his covenant.

Comments on the Army's IHQ website discussion page cast further light on the recognition of credentials. Barbara Moulton of Canada wrote (19 February 2002) that she and her husband, after serving as officers for seven years, transferred to another denomination in the Wesleyan-Arminian tradition, which recognised their prior ordination. Thomas G. World of USA found that his Territory would not transfer his ordination even though requested by the Bishop of his new denomination, even though his Territory was stated to be a signatory to an agreement on transference of ordination. Of course we are not informed of all the circumstances which might have obtained.

In New Zealand the practice has been that officers whose period "out of the work" has been comparatively brief – perhaps two years or so – have been re-accepted as officers without re-commissioning. Others, after many years' absence, have been re-accepted as Auxiliary-Captains for a probationary period before restoration to substantive rank. In recent cases where people have returned after many years in secular employment, some have been warranted as Lieutenants – which title, since the 2001 revision of ranks, has been not counted as a commissioned rank. If later reaccepted as commissioned officers, they are not now to be recommissioned but must re-sign their covenant. This is curious, in that one would expect the covenant to be seen as the expression of a personal relationship with God, independent

---

63 *BEM 137*, p. 253.

of ecclesiastical role, whereas a commission seems to be for a specific officer role and is not valid when the holder is not exercising that role. This points again to the ambiguity associated with officership. Current policy seems to assume in practice a permanent ontological "character", related to the commission, which is denied in theory.

At the same time as the Army was dismissing as irrelevant the theological fine print on matters of faith and order, it had adopted a form of words, "ordination", that did not belong to its own tradition. It interpreted this term in a sense unacceptable to the mainstream of that tradition which held apostolic succession to be important. Possibly it was able to do this because its own ecclesiology had not been thought through.

Chapter Thirteen

Towards an Equilibrium

> In the case of a physical pendulum, you have a mass suspended somehow, and gravity acts on its center of mass. When the center of mass is directly beneath the point of suspension, the pendulum is in equilibrium, and will not move. When the center of mass is not directly under the point of suspension, gravity pulls on the center of mass and exerts a torque around the point of suspension, causing the pendulum to swing.[1]

The "official words" spoken since "Lima" have been different in tone, both from the response to Lima and from each other, setting new benchmarks for Salvation Army writing. The first, the book *Community in Mission*, is an assured and integrated essay in ecclesiology. The second, the work of the International Doctrine Council in *Salvation Story*, embodies a new approach to the exposition of Salvation Army doctrine. The third, *Servants Together*, also the product of a committee, is perhaps a trumpet blowing an uncertain sound, but paradoxically for that very reason indicative of a more mature recognition of the Army's diverse constituency. These three works represent an adjustment of the Army's ecclesiological centre of gravity, although it is not yet clear where the "centre of the mass" really lies.

Community in Mission

Their work on the Lima document on *Baptism, Eucharist and Ministry* evidently alerted the Salvation Army's leadership to its lack of a coherent ecclesiology, and its concluding comments in response to the Lima document referred to the preparation of "a clearer definition of our ecclesiology and the theology of Salvation Army officership". This was *Community in Mission, A Salvationist Ecclesiology* by an American officer, Major Philip Needham and published in 1987. The Foreword by General Eva Burrows explains that Needham had been "invited to produce a volume which would be a supplement to The Salvation Army's official response to the Lima Document, *Baptism, Eucharist and Ministry*".

1 (http://mathforum.org/library/drmath/view/63895.html) Downloaded 24 March 2005.

Needham's basic premise is that "a Salvationist ecclesiology stands as a reminder to the Church that its mission in the world is primary, and that the life of the Church ought largely to be shaped by a basic commitment to mission."[1] Within the elaboration of this theme, he refers to an ordained or specially designated ministry firstly in connection with the means of celebrating and nurturing the "pilgrim people" on their journey.

Describing the Mercy Seat, the swearing in of soldiers and the Love Feast as "key characteristics of ministry in the pilgrim Church", Needham says they are "celebrated primarily through ordination".[2] However, he is evidently not reserving the presidency over such celebrations to an "ordained class". Calling attention to the disparity between the New Testament accounts of initiation for specific ministries and the elaboration of orders along with the concept of clerical classes which subsequently developed, he claims that "the understanding of ordination which arises out of a Salvationist ecclesiology can best be described in the word commissioning... This emphasis on function or mission, rather than ecclesiastical status, broadens the concept of ministry to include everybody in the fellowship... In Salvation Army practice, soldiers are commissioned to specific responsibilities. This is true of both laymen and ministers..." He concedes that "Clearly there are 'status' overtones to the Army's military form of ecclesiastical government, and there have been those who have mistakenly viewed the officership calling as spiritually superior to that of the local officer."

However, he sees the commissioning concept as faithful to New Testament understanding in that "all God's people are called to specific ministries, that the Church is charged to give spiritual direction in discerning and developing individual gifts for ministry, and that each member is to be commissioned to carry out responsibilities which best utilise his gifts." The rite of commissioning is inclusive because it does not discriminate on the basis of social class or sex and the call to ministry is "addressed to all pilgrims in a Church which is on the move... It embodies the dynamic understanding of ministry because of its emphasis on mission rather than maintenance."[3]

Needham concludes this section with consideration of the question of Church structure and government. He notes that the New Testament does not prescribe any particular form of government but that these developed in response to social and cultural setting and the requirements of the mission. The Salvation Army opted for an episcopal form of government expressed in the language of the military, which "fostered decisive leadership, courage in times of trial, mobility, adaptability, focus of action and clear cut

---

1 Philip Needham, *Community in Mission* (London: SA, 1987) pp. 4-5.

2 The Love Feast is a Moravian custom, practised spasmodically within the Army.

3 Needham, *Community*, pp. 47-9.

goals...[and] lay participation". Needham acknowledges the weaknesses inherent in this form – "the monopoly of leadership by a hierarchy of professional soldiers... the insidious pull towards rigid hierarchy and immobile bureaucracy".[4]

Needham notes that Salvationist rites such as soldier-enrolment, commissioning of local officers ["lay leaders", meaning that this is not their full-time occupation] and ordination to the [full-time] ministry ought all to "emphasise a commissioning for battle". He reiterates the Army's opposition to "interpretations of ordination that stress the conferring of a unique spiritual status". He concludes, "We hold that all Christians are called to ministry and mission and that full-time ministry, while exceptional in some ways, is not essentially different from lay ministries... Ordination, then, is commissioning to specific ministries within the context of the Church's mission – ministries that require theological training, specialised skills, pastoral leadership and a full-time vocation...the ordained ministry can only be understood as functional..."[5]

Needham notes but does not elaborate on the fact that "lay participation" fostered by the military model historically has not included participation in government. As we have already seen, not only has this role in practice come to be restricted to the "officer class", but also the presidency at the rites of celebration for the embarkation on and nurturing of the soldier's pilgrimage. However, it must be said that this officially commissioned and promoted Salvationist ecclesiology, while accepting and employing the language of ordination makes it clear that this is seen simply in functional terms. One has the impression that Needham, while accepting the term as a *fait accompli*, is fighting a rearguard action to ensure that the traditional Salvation Army concepts are not lost sight of.

Further, a great strength of *Community in Mission* as an ecclesiology is that it deals pre-eminently with the ministry of the Army as a whole, and only *inter alia* with that of the officer corps in particular. In this it would have earned the approbation of Hendrik Kraemer, prophet of the *laos*, who urged that "the general plan of these books be: the Ministry of the Church as incumbent on the whole body, specified subsequently by a treatment of the Ministry of the Clergy and of the Ministry of the Laity, always keeping in mind their co-existence and inter-existence."[6] It also reflects the general recovery of the Church's appreciation of the basic "ordination of baptism" and concept of the whole people of God over the past forty years, across the whole denominational spectrum.

---

4 Needham, *Community*, p. 50.

5 Needham, *Community*, p. 65.

6 Hendrik Kraemer, *A Theology of the Laity* (London: Lutterworth, 1958) p. 155.

The International Doctrine Council

The Doctrine Council was instituted by General Higgins in January 1931, "to examine and report to him as to the correctness and harmony with Salvation Army principles and doctrines, as defined in our Deed Poll of 1878, of the teaching contained in all Salvation Army publications such as Song Books, Company Orders, Directories, Advanced Training, and similar lesson Courses and Text Books, and other publications in which doctrinal teaching appears in any form".[7]

Amongst subsequent tasks committed to this body, now styled the International Doctrine Council, has been the preparation and revision of successive editions of the *Handbook of Doctrine*. The latest version of this is called *Salvation Story*. More recently still, the Council has produced a book on the Salvationist understanding of ministry entitled *Servants Together*. This section concerns these two books, in so far as they touch on the theme of this work.

The Handbook of Doctrine

The Salvation Army arose as something akin to a parachurch movement, with a limited evangelical focus. The Eleven Points of doctrine, the formulation of beliefs based selectively on the articles of the Methodist New Connexion contained no doctrine of the Church or of ministry. It has been suggested that this lack of ecclesiology might be traced to the Booths' pre-millennial eschatology. Salvationist literature from the heady days of exponential growth sometimes gives the impression that the world was about to be won for Jesus in the very near future, largely through the instrumentality of the Salvation Army.[8] With the urgency of the task of mission, no time could be spared for hair-splitting about a dispensation and order that was in any case about to pass away.[9] Another consideration could be that the Army's ecclesiology was to be found in its disciplines rather than its doctrines; in the expanding body of regulation.

The first exposition of Salvation Army beliefs was contained in *The Doctrines and Disciplines of The Salvation Army*, prepared in 1881 for use in training officers. An identical public edition, hastily made available to

7 Unpublished paper in SA Archives, London.

8 "I believe that this movement shall inaugurate the great final conquest of our Lord Jesus Christ." (Catherine Booth, reported in *WC*, 21 February 1880 p. 1)

9 Jonathan S. Raymond, "The Implications of Wesleyan Theology for a Salvationist Understanding of Community", *Word and Deed* (November 2004) p. 25.

refute charges about a "secret book", was made available in 1883.[10] In 1885 *The Doctrines of The Salvation Army* appeared. A more extensive *Handbook of Salvation Army Doctrine* was published in 1922, the title being changed to *The Salvation Army Handbook of Doctrine* for the third edition in 1927 and an expanded version in 1940. A new, substantially revised, edition appeared in 1969.[11] This was the work of Colonel Gordon Mitchell and edited by Lt.-Colonel Cyril Barnes, and then re-written in part by General Frederick Coutts.

An abridgement of the 1969 version entitled *The Doctrine We Adorn* was written by Colonel Ernest Yendell for English Second Language readers and published in 1982. It was designed as a companion volume to *Chosen to be a Soldier* (the 1977 update of *Orders and Regulations for Salvation Army Soldiers*).

None of the pre-1969 editions of the Handbook made any reference to a doctrine of the Church. In the 1969 edition, and in *The Doctrine We Adorn*, the Church is discussed under the general heading of "The Ministry of the Holy Spirit" within the section on Trinitarian doctrine. No reference is made to a "separated ministry". Rather, it is stated that "men and women were called to be co-workers with God and were equipped by the Holy Spirit...", that "He still calls, appoints and equips believers to serve the Christian fellowship and to be nourished by it... to be witnesses for Christ in the world... to be concerned about the daily needs of his fellows."[12]

In 1992 General Eva Burrows asked the International Doctrine Council to prepare a new edition, which appeared in 1998 under the title of *Salvation Story*. This publication was a radical departure from earlier handbooks, written in narrative style rather than as a series of proof-texted propositions – the fish is alive and swimming rather than dissected on a slab; a post-modern exercise.

Although the doctrines as set out in successive deeds poll and in various Acts of the United Kingdom parliament remain essentially unchanged, *Salvation Story* does include for the first time a chapter on the doctrine of the Church, entitled "The People of God". It explains that "One very important change since the Eleven Articles were formulated and adopted is the evolution of the Movement from an agency for evangelism to a church, an evangelistic body of believers who worship, fellowship, minister and are in mission together."[13]

---

10 Catherine Booth, "The 'Secret Book' so called", Appendix to *Church and State*, pp. 78-92.

11 Information compiled by Colonel Earl Robinson. Letter to General Paul Rader dated 27 January, 1999.

12 *Handbook of Doctrine* (London: SA, 1969) pp. 70-3; *The Doctrine We Adorn* (London: SA, 1982) pp. 41-2.

13 *Salvation Story* (London: SA, 1998) p. 100.

With reference to Ministry, within a section headed "The Holy Spirit empowers the whole church for witness", a paragraph explains that all Christians are "ministers or servants of the gospel... share in the priestly ministry... In that sense there is no separated ministry." However the section goes on to say:

> Within that common calling, some are called by Christ to be full-time office-holders within the Church. Their calling is affirmed by the gift of the Holy Spirit, the recognition of the Christian community and their commissioning – ordination – for service. Their function is to focus the mission and ministry of the whole Church so that its members are held faithful to their calling.
>
> They serve their fellow ministers as visionaries who point the way to mission, as pastors who minister to the priests when they are hurt or overcome, as enablers who equip others for mission as spiritual leaders.[14]

The description of the role of those ordained corresponds generally to the functions that have come to be associated with the ministerial class in the modern church rather than to any single Biblical model. All of the tasks referred to are also regarded as incumbent upon all Salvationists, whether officer or not, although the "focus" function is more particularly and appropriately that of one in leadership or "command".

The expression, "the gift of the Holy Spirit", cannot refer to the general experience of the indwelling of the Holy Spirit, common to all believers, as that is not limited to those ordained. Nor can the gift be identified as one of those specific endowments described in the Pauline epistles of the New Testament. The writers presumably refer to a spiritual gift for the particular role of "full-time office-bearers" sought by specific invocation on the occasion of ordination. To say, "*the* gift" could however give the impression of referring to some generally recognised authority (Biblical? Historical?) for the concept of a separate ministerial group. This could amount to a claim to ordination in the historic sense; an acceptance of Lima's "ordained ministry, itself a charism..." This was not a Biblical category of gifting, but appeared firstly in Hippolytus in the early third century.[15] The ambiguity as to the status of this gift is the same as that we have traced throughout this work. It also illustrates the way in which the Army, while in theory maintaining its claim that the Scriptures alone "constitute the Divine rule of Christian faith and practice" (Doctrine One), also concedes in practice a normative value to Church tradition.

However, the important thing is that the statement establishes the principle that the ministry of particular persons arises from the ministry of

---

14 *Salvation Story*, p. 108.

15 Colin Bulley, *Priesthood of Some Believers*, pp. 263-4, cites Hippolytus, *Refutation of All Heresies* 6 and *Apostolic Tradition* 3.

the whole Christian community and it is at least an attempt to describe and justify what happens in practice.

Servants Together

Continued debate pointed to the need for further clarity on the Salvation Army's theology of ministry. The 1995 International Conference of Leaders meeting in Hong Kong recommended "that the roles of officers and soldiers be defined and a theology of the 'priesthood of all believers' be developed to encourage greater involvement in ministry (for example, spiritual leadership, leadership in general), worship, service and evangelisation".[16]

General Paul Rader committed this task to the International Doctrine Council, chaired by Colonel Earl Robinson. The Council produced the book, *Servants Together*, subtitled *The Ministry of the Whole People of God, Salvationist Perspectives*, and published in 2002.

The introduction to the book admits that Salvationist theology, despite the collectivist character of the military metaphor, has tended to be individualistic. Section One, "The Calling of God's People", therefore places the concept of ministry in the context of the calling of all God's people to worship, community and mission. Section Two the "Ministry of the Whole People of God", postulates three theological bases for this ministry: vocation, the priesthood of all believers and the gifts of the Spirit. Section Three considers "Leadership" and attends to the matter of Commissioning or ordination to specific tasks in the Church. Section Four deals with the character of such leadership, exemplified in Jesus Christ. Sections Two and Three are of particular interest for the theme of this work.

Section Two, Chapter Four, on Vocation, refers to the dangers of the medieval concept which implies that the primary vocation is holy orders while that of the laity is second best. "For those who grew up in the Army the implied message was often that the true vocation was that of the officer … being a soldier was second class." To counter this the writers set out the Biblical principle that all believers are called to the ministry of reconciliation (2 Corinthians 5:18-20), a ministry that "may be demonstrated by various means in the vocations to which God has called us"[17] At the same time, the writers note that "this doctrine of vocation does

---

16 *Servants Together*, p. 127.
17 *Servants Together*, pp. 39-40.

not in any way deny that some are called to the specific ministerial tasks of preaching, teaching or administration."[18]

In Chapter Five, the priesthood of all believers is presented as another way of breaking down the distinction between sacred and secular. The concept of priesthood is traced through Old and New Testaments, the Patristic period (in a sentence or two), and then in the thought of Luther and Wesley. The point is reiterated that the priesthood of all believers does not mean that all believers should hold the office of "priest" – this term now being used to denote preaching, teaching and leadership functions. The section applies this thought to the Salvation Army today with a warning against the tendency that "those with more public abilities ... may assume some special status or privileged place."[19] Chapter Six is given over to an exposition of the Pauline gifts as described in 1 Corinthians 12, Romans 12, and Ephesians 4, with reference also to 1 Peter 4. It is noted that the terms in these lists are not used to describe any hierarchy or ministerial status and any connection between ministry gifts and place or status in the church or Corps is denied. Unresolved is the problem that, at least in contemporary culture, the gift of leadership is likely to be recognised by status, (and that leadership status not accompanied by appropriate gifts is likely to be less effective). Having given an account of the twentieth century Pentecostal movement and its second and third "waves", the writers note that "charismatic renewal has not materially affected the structure of church government."[20]

Section Three is concerned with "The Leadership of God's People – its Scope". While vision-casting, teaching, administration and pastoring are not the sole concern of leaders, these roles are "so vital that they should be owned and guarded by those specially appointed". It is also acknowledged that "at a time of change, the Salvation Army is seeking to redefine its leadership."[21]

Chapter Seven deals with "Commissioning", the Army's traditional term for the act of recognising a ministry role. "It signifies a calling from God rather than some special status, and the assurance for those who are commissioned lies in that calling rather than in some privileged position." This is affirmed as a Biblical principle. It is frankly acknowledged that most of the early Salvation Army leaders were "lay" and that "distinctions between the laity and the clergy would arise only after the institutionalisation of the Salvation Army." A most significant paragraph suggests that "We now have the opportunity in The Salvation Army *to return to the Biblical principle that all are in ministry* [my italics]. While

---

18 *Servants Together*, p. 42.
19 *Servants Together*, p. 50.
20 *Servants Together*, p. 60.
21 *Servants Together*, p. 61.

distinctions between officers and soldiers may at times be useful and appropriate, we recognise that all officers are first and foremost soldiers in the Army and that everyone in the Army is in ministry both in the context of his or her daily vocation and in the context of life in the corps... We commission both officers and local officers to their respective ministries."[22]

The admission that the Army had strayed from a Biblical principle may refer especially to the loss of evangelical fervour amongst the laity, though the context could also imply that the widened gap between officer and soldier in terms of status was also to be deplored. The chapter goes on to suggest ways in which the practice of "commissioning" could be developed and extended to further "lay" roles to reinforce the understanding that all were equally in ministry.

Having warned that a "passive laity and a clergy defensive of its status and role" can inhibit the life and work of the Church, the chapter concludes with a warning against "an imbalance in another direction which devalues the role of so-called 'professionals'... The doctrine of the priesthood of all believers ... acknowledges the specific authority of those who are called and trained for ministries of preaching, evangelism or administration... The call for commissioning in this chapter does not negate the understanding that some are commissioned to the ministry of officership within The Salvation Army. Those who are commissioned to that office are also ordained to servant leadership."[23]

Chapter Eight goes on to explain what is meant by "Ordained to Servant Leadership". *Salvation Story* is quoted to affirm that all Christians share in ministry so that "in that sense there is no separated ministry", but also to insist that "within that common calling, some are called by Christ to be full-time office-holders within the Church. Their calling is affirmed by the gift of the Holy Spirit [that phrase again], the recognition of the Christian community and their commissioning – ordination – for service." It is tacitly assumed that the phenomenon of full-time office-holding is ordained by Christ rather than administratively determined by the Church. However, the writers go on to admit that "full-time office-holders could include any believer, not exclusively clergy or Salvation Army officers.... The term 'ordination' is, however, normally used specifically with reference to clergy or Salvation Army officers.... This does not mean that preaching, teaching and exercising authority cannot be part of the ministry of soldiers, but it emphasises that an ordination to spiritual leadership is especially integral to officership."[24]

---

22 *Servants Together*, pp. 65-6.
23 *Servants Together*, pp. 67-8.
24 *Servants Together*, pp. 69-70.

The writers note that questions arise concerning the ordination of Salvation Army officers because of comparisons with the practices of other denominations. One is whether the terms "commissioning" and "ordination" are interchangeable and carry the same meaning. Significantly, perhaps as a "first" for an official Army publication, it is admitted that people have different opinions on this. Some hold that there is no difference and others claim that the introduction of "ordain" indicates a change in mindset "from mission to maintenance" within the Army, and a change of perception of both officership and of the Salvation Army as a whole. However, the fear that ordination presupposes a priestly order foreign to the Army's ethos and theology is not alluded to. The writers conclude that it might be best to maintain the use of both terms, accommodating a range of views.

Explaining why the term "ordination" was introduced, it is suggested firstly that it was to "facilitate an understanding of how solemnly the commissioning of Salvation Army officers is regarded and understood". A second reason was the desire that a Salvation Army officer should be regarded as equal to any priest or minister of other denominations. There follows a brief historical survey of commissioning, showing that early leaders held this conviction, and a brief account of the process by which "ordination" came to be introduced into Salvation Army usage.

A further question addressed concerns the ways in which the ordination or commissioning of officers relates to the ordination of other clergy. A brief reference to the setting aside of some Old and New Testament characters for ministry is followed by a summary of Presbyterian Thomas F. Torrance's analysis of ordination in Protestant ministry in terms of source, end or nature and its act. Earl Robinson's notes from the 1968 Canadian Commissioning Brochure (referred to earlier) are quoted in full at this point.

The chapter goes on to say that despite parallels with the ministry of other denominations, officership differs because "in keeping with our tradition of not drawing rigid lines between officers and soldiers, it has been one of the distinctives of The Salvation Army to believe that there is no essential ministry exercised by a Salvation Army officer that could not also be carried out by a soldier." It has therefore to ask what is unique about a Salvation Army officer, and how the call to officership differs from the call to ministry incumbent on all Christians? The writers suggest that possible responses "have to do with an authority of office in terms of the officer's relationship to the movement, the expectations of the movement towards the officer, decision-making powers related to finances, property, worship leadership and availability. The officer has a particular function to be a focus for mission and ministry of the Army. He or she is responsible through life and by ministry to ensure that the Word of God is proclaimed and the grace of Christ is offered in all possible ways to a needy and suffering world."[25]

As already acknowledged, anything officers do that could be done – is at times done – by a non-officer, and there is no role from which a non-officer would be disqualified on theological grounds.

The writers then tease out the implications of some of the particular functions they have ascribed to the officer. They set out to show, within the same chapter and section as the "uniqueness of Salvation Army officership", the ways in which officers, like clergy of other denominations, are "set apart for the ministry of the Word and Sacrament." (Is the "uniqueness" then in relation to other soldiers rather than to other clergy? Perhaps the composite nature of the authorship is evident here.) The task of the preaching of the Word is comparatively straightforward – the officer's covenant refers to the calling to "proclaim the gospel". Difficulty with the parallel concerning sacramental usage is acknowledged; officers usually do not perform baptisms or preside over the Eucharist. However the writers refer to *Salvation Story* and the 1998 *Report of the International Spiritual Life Commission*, where it is asserted that "Christ is the one true sacrament, and sacramental living – Christ living in us and through us – is at the heart of Christian holiness and discipleship."[26] That experience is not unique to officers, however, so its relevance to the point at issue is unclear.

The writers do recognise that neither of these roles – preaching the word or living out the life of Christ – is assigned only to officers. However, they assert that, "In signing their covenants, Salvation Army officers, *particularly* [my italics] accept the call to live the life of Christ, who is the one true sacrament, in an exemplary and sacramental way as spiritual leaders in the Church of Christ and in the world, just as Christ called his first apostles for that purpose."[27] Perhaps the reference to the apostles is intended to assert a parallel leadership role for officers; a kind of virtue by association. As we have seen before, this could imply that the calling of the disciples established in perpetuity a special class in the church, rather than their being seen as a pilot scheme for emulation by all the faithful. The following paragraph goes on to expand on "sacramental living" as embracing the social service implications of the gospel.

It has to be said again that the insertion of words like "especially" and "particularly" only serve to emphasise that unlike the Catholic church, the Salvation Army holds that the "common priesthood" and the "ministerial priesthood" differ only in degree and not in essence.

---

25 *Servants Together*, pp.78-9.
26 Robert Street, *Called to be God's People* (London: SA, 1999) p. 89.
27 *Servants Together*, p. 79.

The final section of Chapter Eight refers to "spiritual leadership" and "servant leadership". Maintaining their even-handed approach to the roles of officers and soldiers, the writers note that "When someone is ordained to such spiritual leadership, he or she is ordained to a ministry of servanthood to God and his world. This applies equally to leadership exercised by officers and soldiers."[28] Having referred to "ordained servant leadership" as descriptive of officers at the end of Chapter Seven, the writers now by implication extend the word "ordained" to soldiers as well.

Chapter Nine is about "Team Ministry", which is held up as a model appropriate to the times as well as Biblically and theologically sound. It is noted that theologies of vocation, gifting and the priesthood of all believers have led in places to a startling growth in lay leadership, within both para-church organisations and denominations. Referring to the Army in particular, it mentions that in many places soldiers are increasingly taking responsibility for mission initiatives... "In the Army, we may well retain our military form of government... but we must be careful that the structure does not get in the way of the Army's mission in our present cultural situation."[29]

The writers are aware of concern about the changing relationship of officers and soldiers in this milieu – "Officers should not feel threatened when soldiers and employees take leadership responsibility. Nor should they contrast short-term service unfavourably with their own life-long commitment... Soldiers and employees should take care that they are not overly critical of what they perceive to be unfair advantages associated with being officers."[30]

The final Section of the book deals with the "Character of the Leadership of God's People". Attention is drawn to the tension throughout the ages between "prophetic" and "priestly" modes of leadership and the necessity for both. The requirements of sense of call, spiritual depth, courage, personal discipline, relationship-building, empowerment of others, creativity, passion for mission and personal and vocational growth are discussed.

As throughout the text, it is evident that the writers have to safeguard the principle that all soldiers are equal, including the officers, and that all can do anything required of anyone else, while at the same time having to secure some distinct role for officers. The latter is not unequivocally established. The final chapter, on the Future of Leadership, maintains this even-handed approach, asking, "What shape will officership and all forms of spiritual leadership in The Salvation Army take?"

---

28 *Servants Together*, p. 81.
29 *Servants Together*, p. 89.
30 *Servants Together*, p. 90.

Servants Together offers a range of comments and suggestions for future directions, reflecting the groundswell of officer opinion, particularly in the West. For example:

> • We know that opportunities for full-time spiritual leadership will expand both within officership and alongside it…
> • We know that for some the call to full-time Christian leadership will be less tied to life-long officership in The Salvation Army, but instead may include periods of short-term service.
> • We also know that, in some countries, we will see the traditional model of officers married only to officers altered for those married couples where spouses have separate callings that are incompatible within that model…
> • It observes that alternative forms of officership will need to be explored where traditional officership is declining.
> • It warns against "the temptation to gain acceptance in the wider ecclesiastical world by uncritically adopting practices, rituals and terminologies that devalue our own creative history."[31]

Is it possible that this last point was an oblique reference to the Army's adoption of "ordination"? Or perhaps the writers were thinking rather of the tendency for Corps to become "churches" and Corps officers to style themselves "pastors", and the reintroduction of ersatz sacramental practices unofficially at a local level as an accommodation to the ascendant pentecostal/charismatic religious sub-culture in some western or "first world" countries.

The conclusion refers back to the Council's mandate from the 1995 International Conference of Leaders, which requested, "That the roles of officers and soldiers be defined and a theology of the 'priesthood of all believers' be developed to encourage greater involvement in ministry…" Was that intention realised?

Servants Together does:

- Explore the roles of officers and soldiers.
- Explain what is meant by the "priesthood of all believers".
- Provide, however briefly, the historical and theological context for Salvationist practices in relation to ministry, in a way not hitherto attempted in a Salvation Army publication.
- Point up a number of contemporary issues about officership and ministry in The Salvation Army.
- Exhibit the extent of the Salvationist *glasnost*, being open about problems and disagreements in a way almost unprecedented in official publications.

31 *Servants Together*, pp. 114, 118, 123.

- Establish clearly the principle that there is no distinction in status between officers and soldiers, and that there is nothing done by one which cannot be done by the other. It is notably even-handed in many references – phrases like, "Salvation Army officers, and other leaders…" abound.

In their conclusion, the writers encourage Salvationists to greater involvement as "whether officers or soldiers, they are commissioned by God for ministry in his world and in his Church and that, whatever ordination they may claim, it is essentially an ordination by God to be servants of their Servant Lord."

Having established that principle, *Servants* then struggles a little in clarifying what is unique about the role of the officer. It tries to do this in two ways:

The first simply describes the way the Salvation Army is organised, that officers are paid to run the organisation.[32] It is not mentioned that some non-officers are also paid to run the organisation in most of the ways described, except in availability for appointment. However, this is a pragmatic exposition, uncomplicated by theological special pleading or comparisons.

The other way officership is described is in terms and categories borrowed from the clerical models of other denominations. It is inevitable that similar functions should be described in similar ways, and the book is in part a response to the greater ecumenical awareness of contemporary Salvationists. However, it could imply that the Army is still concerned to show that it is "like the other churches". This illustrates that the ambiguity we have traced through the course of discussion on Salvation Army ministry is still to be found: the adoption of the language of ordination has simply reinforced the tension. We are left with the fact that all soldiers are equal but some are more equal than others. It is sometimes argued that the difference between officers and soldiers is to be found in the officer's "Covenant". However, this document does not commit officers to any more than the soldier's covenant does. Both describe the individual's relationship with God rather than with the Salvation Army. It is the "Undertakings", containing the conditions of service undertaken by an officer, which make the difference.

To sum up the progression to be found through the sequence beginning with the introduction of ordination in 1978 and culminating in the publication of *Servants Together* in 2002, we might suggest that in the 1970s the pendulum had swung as far as it could in the direction of a status for officers, and that the subsequent works show a move to correct an

32 *Servants Together*, p. 78.

imbalance and restore a functional point of view – while retaining the movement's traditional ambiguity about the question.

Part Four: Officers Who May Not Be Officers

This Part considers the situation of Auxiliary Officers, Soldiers and Women in the Salvation Army, in consequence of the movement's claim to *de facto* clerical status for its commissioned officers.

Chapter Fourteen

An Officer by Any Other Name

> What's in a name? That which we call a rose,
> By any other name would smell as sweet;
> So Romeo would, were he not Romeo call'd
> Retain the dear perfection which he owes
> Without that title...
>
> William Shakespeare,
> *Romeo and Juliet,* Act II, Scene II.

The ambiguity about the status of officers – the question of whether they are clerical or lay – brings us to consider the role of those who have clerical functions but are not accorded the status of clergy. This is tackled under two heads; firstly the matter of auxiliary officers, whose status is ambiguous even within the Army's own terms of reference, and secondly the role of the soldiers *vis-à-vis* that of officers.

Geoffrey Rowell notes that amongst the factors bringing "powerful pressures to bear upon older understandings of order and ministry in the Church" are "declining vocations to the ordained ministry and the need to sustain the ministry of the church to the whole nation... financial pressures and burgeoning lay ministries...".[1] The Salvation Army shares these pressures. Comparison of *Year Book* figures show declining officer statistics in some Western territories and rising employee statistics. (Non-western countries' patterns differ.)

	Year	Active Officers	Retired Officers	Employees
New Zealand	1984	403	168	569
	2006	346	195	2552
Norway	1984	387	266	451
	2004	199	247	1357

1 Geoffrey Rowell, in Christine Hall and Robert Hannaford (ed.), *Order and Ministry* (Leominster: Gracewing, 1996) pp. 161-162.

compare with

	Year	Active Officers	Retired Officers	Employees
Zimbabwe	1984	242	71	355
	2006	467	111	1430
Korea	1984	317	45	236
	2006	541	134	415

It is useful to explore the way in which these changes have contributed to the development of auxiliary officership. If the theme of this work is the way in which Salvation Army officers are clergy who are not clergy, the counterpoint is the phenomenon of officers who are not officers.

NCOs

In every army in the world, it is the non-commissioned officers, the NCOs, who train the troops and hold them together and see themselves as the real leaders of the army. The purpose of this chapter is to trace the process by which elements of an unpaid, volunteer group evolved to become a paid, full-time parallel structure to officership, a quasi-diaconate to a quasi-priesthood, and to examine the implications of this development.

At first the volunteer officials of the Mission, the Elders, Secretaries and the Treasurers, became the "local officers",[2] or "petty officers" as the 1878 Orders and Regulations called them. "N.C.O., Non-Commissioned, or Petty Officer, or simply 'officer', one not wholly employed in the service".[3] The Salvation Army had a nautical flavour. The term "Articles of War" was naval, and not really appropriate as a name for a signed covenant, except insofar as it referred to conditions of service. Elijah Cadman's honorific of "captain" at the port of Whitby partly arose from fishermen's usage and older Salvationists still today refer to the Commanding Officer as "skipper". Likewise the 1878 O's and R's refer to assistant officers as "Mates or Lieutenants". The NCOs were the backbone of the corps, as distinct from those commissioned officers who were posted in and quite soon posted away again. The non-commissioned officers have usually been "commissioned" to their tasks – just as Presbyterians ordain Elders, while holding that their ordination differs from that of Ministers.

Catherine Booth, in an address given at Cannon Street Hotel, March 20 1883, having described their forces of voluntary speakers and evangelists (officers), said that, "God is showing us by circumstances the want of other

2 W. Bramwell Booth, *Echoes*, p. 177.

3 *Orders and Regulations for The Salvation Army* (1878) p. iv.

kinds of officers. We have a new order of officers called 'Sergeants', who come between the corps and the paid officers, and we hope soon to have a force of those who will systematically visit every public house in the country..."[4] *The Doctrines and Disciplines* of 1881 already referred to the Colour-Sergeant and the Paymaster-Sergeant, amongst others.[5] The idea must have been taken up enthusiastically, for the 1886 *Orders and Regulations for Field Officers* lists seventeen varieties of sergeants in its index.[6]

It is curious therefore to find *The Officer* remarking in 1893 that "The General feels very strongly that the missing link in our system is between the F.O. and the private soldier. We have perfected the F.O. and perfected the soldier, but what is needed is to hitch the one to the other. This he is confident can be done by means of the Company Sergeant."[7] He may be describing the role of the Corps Sergeant Major, but that worthy had long since been gazetted.[8] Alas, the proposal was not elaborated upon.

Envoys

The next development recorded was the introduction of "Envoy" – a rank seemingly more diplomatic than military. From 1893, in an endeavour to establish and maintain Salvation Army work in country villages too small to support officered corps, the Army began to set up "Circle Corps" to link together a number of village "societies" (a term inherited from Methodism). Meetings in these centres were led by "Local Specials" sent out from other Corps – hence eventually the term "envoy". An 1896 *War Cry* introduced the first of this rank, an ex-officer, Dick Moses, asked by his Divisional Officer to oversight the struggling outpost of Flushing.[9]

In June 1896 *The War Cry* announced that "The new Circle Envoys are being made the most of and put on a proper footing. A commission and a bond are being drawn up for them. The bond will be signed by the British Commissioner, and for the Home Office by the Circle Secretary, and endorsed by the D.O. and the P.O. The Commission will also be signed by the Commissioner, so they will be commissioned direct from the Home

---

4 Catherine Booth, *Church and State*, p. 37. Clarence Wiseman (General, 1974-77) quoted this passage "to show that in the early days, there was no distinction of spiritual status between 'paid' officers and 'unpaid' voluntary speakers, soldiers and sergeants." *Officer* (September 1969) p. 587.

5 *Doctrines and Discipline of The Salvation Army*, pp. 110-11.

6 *Orders and Regulations for Field Officers* (1886) pp. 635-6.

7 *Officer* (July 1893) p. 201.

8 *Orders and Regulations for Field Officers* (1886) pp. 177-8.

9 *WC* (29 February 1896) p. 6, col. 1.

Office like Secretaries and Treasurers."[10] A "General Order" published in the same organ prescribed a regulation badge to be worn on the right arm.[11] In a supplementary book of regulations issued in 1896, Envoys appeared in Chapter XXXV, on "The Circle". "Local Officers, who shall be known as Envoys, will assist in conducting the meetings at the different Societies composing the Circle. They may be men or women, and shall, as far as possible, be appointed two by two. A plan of meetings and appointments of Officers will be necessary, and shall be issued every quarter."[12]

The Local Officer, describing "Envoys: Their Duties and Qualifications" explained that, "It is, in short, the old local-preacher system militarized and adapted to Army warfare."[13] This was a rare instance of a direct comparison being made between a "church" and an "Army" office, and an interesting assumption of the readers' familiarity with a Methodist model. It may also reveal the assumption that officers were thought of as equivalent to ministers.

Envoys would work under the direction of the D.O. and would fulfil at least three appointments per quarter.[14] Shortly afterwards the same periodical noted that "One feature of the British Winter Campaign is the raising of 500 Envoys, in order that the thousands of English villages might hear the glad tidings... Up to the present only between four and five hundred men and women in all have been commissioned Envoys."[15] Week by week from 1896 *The War Cry* named new appointees, such as the 23 announced in the number of 13 November 1897. The impetus must have slackened, however, since a glossary in the 1906 *Year Book* stated that "There are at present 302 Envoys in Great Britain."[16] Or perhaps their numbers had indeed proved a recruiting ground for Officers, as the General had hoped in the four pages he devoted to Envoys in *The Local Officer* of January 1899, at which time he stated that the office of Envoy "was some six months ago created". (Either the editor had been sitting on the article for a couple of years or the General was still not up with the play.) An important consideration for the cash-strapped Army was that "The Envoy will not require monetary support of any kind, seeing that like other Local Officers he either earns his own livelihood by the labour of his hands, or is

10 *WC* (27 June 1896) p. 7, col. 4.

11 *WC* (21 November 1896) p. 8, col.1.

12 *The Why and Wherefore of The Salvation Army Regulations* (London: SA, [1886]) p. 93.

13 *Local Officer* (November 1897) p. 106.

14 *Local Officer* (November 1897) p. 106.

15 *Local Officer* (January 1898) p. 169.

16 *SA Year Book* (1906) p. 49.

possessed of some other means of subsistence… occasionally arrangements will be made by his Captain for the payment of Travelling Expenses."[17]

The next step in the evolution of this subsidiary order of officers was proposed by Bramwell Booth twenty-five years later with "The establishment of a new order of officers – to be known as "Auxiliary Officers" – to be enlisted for a term of years rather than for life; a thousand such for the U.K. and a thousand for other European countries."[18] It would be interesting to know what lay behind this proposal, and why it did not bear fruit for more than thirty more years.

Instead, it took another six years for an arguably further step in the deployment of Envoys to be made. The *War Cry* headed the announcement with "Envoys in Charge – First Commissions Issued". The article went on, "Under the British Commissioner's scheme for appointing Envoys in charge of The Army's work in rural communities and other places where a full-time Officer cannot be stationed", three Envoys were placed in charge of Societies. Envoys would wear Sergeant's stripes with the word "Envoy" in wreath above. It was not spelt out how this differed from what had been happening for forty years because it was still the case that "The Envoy will receive no monetary consideration for his services." Perhaps the heading to the article gave a clue: the novelty may have lain in the fact that these Envoys were permanently attached to a particular Society, in charge there, rather than peripatetic, based elsewhere. Indeed Envoy Mrs Davis of Penrhynduedraeth, Wales, was described as "a stalwart who for a number of years has carried on The Army's activities in her neighbourhood". Mrs Davis in fact ran the Corps without commission or remuneration for 40 years.[19] In such a case, "Envoy" became a less apt description. Possibly another novel feature lay in the proposal of training; Envoys "will be expected to take up 'The Envoy's Efficiency Course', which consists of twelve months' lessons".[20]

Two varieties of Envoys evolved. The first were the unpaid, part-time, volunteer variety, who were engaged in evangelical work, either in charge of smaller corps or outposts, or available for "supply" in the Methodist lay-preacher tradition. The second variety of Envoy were those in whole-time, paid employment in some branch of the Army's work, sometimes in a "ministry" role of spiritual leadership and sometimes in some ancillary support role in clerical or social work. The analogy with Wesleyan "lay preachers" holds good here; American Methodism also distinguished between "lay speakers" or "exhorters" (part-time volunteers) and "lay preachers" (full-time, employed).

---

17 *Local Officer* (January 1899) pp. 161-4.
18 *SA Year Book* (1927) p. 41.
19 *Officer* (December 1964) p. 861.
20 *WC* (7 January 1933) p. 15, col. 1.

In the case of the volunteers, the title of Envoy often appeared to be awarded as a token of esteem for a senior local officer rather than for any specific envoy-like errand. Envoy Olive Lord of Linwood, New Zealand, a long-serving youth worker, would be an example. In New Zealand, Stephen Buick was another outstanding example of Envoy in New Zealand, an ex-officer who from 1887 until his death at the age of 93 sixty-five years later, collected funds from and provided pastoral care for the farmers of north Taranaki.[21] In Rhodesia in the 1960s and 70s Envoy Chasi was a successful builder who moved to a new satellite African township near Harare and found there were no churches. By the time regular officers were appointed, Chasi had a recruited a Corps of two hundred uniformed soldiers, with a brass band, which met in a Hall of his own construction.

Some Envoys (of either volunteer or paid variety) were ex-officers who still felt a call to ministry. Some were younger people testing their vocation before becoming officers. Some were would-be officers who had not been accepted for training, for whom this ministry was a consolation prize (which meant they were loosed upon the world without training to do work for which they had been adjudged unsuitable to be trained.) Others again were people with a "late vocation", or who were not interested in becoming commissioned officers. Commissioner Stanley Walter, outlining "various distinctions" of service, described Envoys as people who did "not qualify for commissioning as officers because their training or abilities may be suitable for only one particular type of appointment, they may not be willing to be moved to a different location, their commitment may have limitations such as the need for part-time secular employment, and of course, their length of service is uncertain."[22]

The other variety of Envoy, those in full-time paid service within the Army structure, were perhaps what Bramwell Booth had intended by "Auxiliary Officers" in 1927; it would have been less confusing had they retained that distinctive title instead of sharing the designation of Envoy. At least in New Zealand their advent appears to have been related to the wartime shortage of personnel for appointments. The first Envoy of this kind to be mentioned in the *Disposition of Forces* (a clerical directory, listing officers under the heading of their appointments) was Envoy Farland, manager of the Wellington Men's Shelter and Labour Yard in 1939-40. The 1940 *Disposition of Forces* showed Envoys stationed at four Corps. In 1944, four were listed as being in "War Work", which meant running canteens for the troops in military camps and at railway stations, and one in Public Relations, which meant raising donations. In 1948, four were leading Corps, two were in social appointments, two worked in "Trade" (the Army's supply company) and one in the property department at THQ. In 1960, there were

21 Cyril Bradwell, *Fight the Good Fight* (Wellington: Reed, 1983) pp. 73-4, 91.
22 *Officer* (September 1988) p. 402.

nine Envoys of this kind serving in New Zealand: three working in Corps, four in Social Services and two on THQ.[23] From being a stopgap measure, Envoys had become part of the regular forces.

In New Zealand at least (and such regulations appeared to be at territorial discretion) by the 1970s these two varieties of Envoy, part-time volunteer and full-time employee, were distinguished as "Divisional" and "Territorial" Envoys. The former were appointed by Divisional Commanders and the latter from Territorial Headquarters. By 1985 the picture was complicated further by a distinction between full-time paid Divisional Envoys and volunteer unpaid Divisional Envoys.[24] In New Zealand, the rank of Envoy as a designation for full-time, paid employees was finally phased out by the end of the century, with the people either retiring or becoming "Auxiliary-Captains". Existing volunteer Envoys and retired employee Envoys retain the rank, although in the case of employed Envoys by the 1990s the rank seemed to be associated with a particular appointment and lapsed when the person left it.

From time to time over the years a few full-time employees, usually in Social Institutions, were ranked as "sergeant". International statistics for January 2002 still gave the number of "envoys/sergeants full time" as 1,130.[25]

As was the case with the later Auxiliary-Captains, the ambiguous character of the Envoy's role sometimes led to uncertainty over the extent of their responsibilities, status and powers. A "name and address supplied" letter to *The Salvationist* from a volunteer, "Divisional Envoy" running a U.K. Corps in his spare-time noted that "In my corps I am not quite a soldier and neither am I an officer... There seems to be an obvious and definite split between officers and soldiers, or even soldier-leaders like myself... At divisional meetings, if I am able to attend, I feel that I am not treated entirely as a colleague."[26] A letter posted on the Salvation Army website by an American Envoy as late as 2000 drew attention to the fact that although acting in a full-time pastoral role as a Corps Officer, he was not empowered to solemnize marriages. "The biggest unanswered question is ordination. Commissioning ties into benefits (eventually), but ordination impacts ministry immediately. Many Envoys (myself included) who serve as Corps Officers are recognized by governmental authorities as having authority to marry and sign marriage certificates. But Policy prevents us from doing so

23 *New Zealand Disposition of Forces* (1960).
24 New Zealand Minute ACE 0585, 9 May 1985.
25 *Army Scene* (April 2003) p. 16.
26 *Salvationist* (30 January 1988) p. 10.

unless we have a prior license from another ordaining body." He went on to enlarge on the pastoral handicap this entailed.[27]

Auxiliary Captains

In the late 1950s Bramwell Booth's plan for the employment of a class of auxiliary officers resurfaced. It seems that at first British military nomenclature was intended, as a 1958 letter from Commissioner Edgar Grinstead (British Commissioner) to Lt.-Commissioner Reginald Woods (Literary Secretary at IHQ) expresses pleasure that "the proposal to appoint Warrant Officers will be proceeded with soon." He also encouraged "the full designation being used in conversation and certainly in public (not 'warrant' or 'WO' as in the forces)".[28] Interestingly, an anonymous feature-writer long after in 1992 explained that "Salvation Army Auxiliary Captains would be better described as Warrant Officers – those who hold their office by warrant and are intermediate between commissioned and non-commissioned officers."[29] However, the Minute from Chief of the Staff, when it appeared, concerned "Auxiliary-Captains".

> The General has decided that Salvationists unable for valid and acceptable reasons to enter a training college but desirous of giving full-time service to The Salvation Army, may, while undertaking responsibility of a Corps, or serving in a similar capacity in Social or comparable work, receive the designation of Auxiliary Captain, provided they have been soldiers for at least two years and are over thirty five years of age. The designation of Auxiliary Captain must not be introduced into any territory, nor exceptions made to the foregoing conditions without the approval of the Chief of the Staff, who will also give directions as to the conditions of acceptance and service…[30]

The draft of the "Employment Statement" was adapted from that for Envoys and included: "I understand that although I may be required to perform duties of a religious nature, an Auxiliary Captain is not a Salvation Army Officer or a Minister of the Gospel of that branch of the Christian Church known as The Salvation Army, and that my appointment as an Auxiliary Captain does not entitle me to the rights and privileges of a Salvation Army officer." This interesting document implies that officers are ministers like those of other churches, but protects the clerical closed shop.[31]

---

27 Garry M. Sapper, USA Central Territory, on www.salvationarmy.org, 30 August 2000.

28 Edgar Grinstead, letter dated 22 December 1958.

29 *Salvationist* (1 February 1992) p. 9.

30 Minute signed by William J. Dray, Chief of the Staff, 23 May 1959.

31 Draft "Employment Statement" in London SA Archives.

In similar vein, a later but undated set of terms of reference includes the clause: "Although an Auxiliary-Captain is not a commissioned officer of The Salvation Army, I understand that, as an Auxiliary-Captain, I may be required to perform duties and accept responsibilities which are usually performed by a commissioned officer to the extent that they may be performed by a lay person."[32] The use of "lay" in this context also reveals an assumption about the clerical status of officers. A later writer asked, "What rights and privileges" are enjoyed by commissioned but not by warranted officers? "Research shows that question to be an unanswerable enigma. Possibly the sentence is intended to cover minor, localised limitations which may arise. In Scotland, for example, Auxiliary Captains may not conduct weddings."[33]

The "Memorandum of an Auxiliary Captain's Engagement with The Salvation Army" (1 January 1960), set out the conditions to be signed by applicants for Auxiliary Captaincy. Amongst significant points made in this document was the insistence that Auxiliary Captain, "it should be understood, is an appointment, not a rank." It also described such persons as, "undertaking as VOLUNTARY WORKERS [*sic*] full-time responsibility for the oversight of a Corps, or serving in a similar capacity in social or comparable work... They will receive a Warrant of Appointment, signed by the Territorial Leader... subject to Orders and Regulations for Officers where applicable [attention was drawn to the 'Undertakings' at this point]... will be regarded as self-employed... will be required to give full-time service to The Salvation Army and engage in no other occupation... both husband and wife will be required to sign the form of application." Although they would "receive a commencing subsistence allowance equivalent to that received by a commissioned officer of 3 years' service", they "will not be employed by the Army under a contract of service, and will have no legal rights to wages, their status as voluntary workers being in this respect the same as that of Officers." Men who had served 25 years before retirement and women who had served 20 years, would be permitted to retain the designation "Auxiliary Captain" in retirement. Applicants had to be at least 35 years of age; if after four years service they had at least 15 years to serve before the retirement ages of 65 for men and 60 for women, they could apply for commissioning to substantive rank as Captains, provided they had completed certain in-service training requirements.

While the details of these conditions varied in time, the essentials remained unchanged for more than forty years; Auxiliary Captains were to

---

32 "Agreement Between Applicant for Auxiliary-Captain and The Salvation Army", undated but including reference to Orders and Regulations Governing the Retirement of Auxiliary-Captains, 1963.

33 *Salvationist* (1 February 1992) p. 10.

enjoy all the disciplines, but were less certain of the "rights and privileges" (undefined) of Salvation Army Officers.

A Minute issued in 1972 provided the opportunity for "carefully selected" Auxiliary Captains and their wives to attain full status as officers. The conditions stated were that they should have done a minimum of four years service, been through the usual processes for the acceptance of officer-candidates, completed a correspondence course, undergone intensive residential training of at least three months and not be above 50 years of age nor within the usual age-span for training. Their commissioning was not to be included with that of cadets but recognised separately as the Territorial Commander may think appropriate.[34] The rank was not intended for short-term service as Envoyship could have been. The distinctive thing about Auxiliary Captains is that they wanted to be officers but were above the age for acceptance into training. Ideally then, their equivalent training was in-service over five years, after which they could apply for commissioning. In practice the quality of training offered varied widely from place to place and from time to time.

Without these late-vocation candidates, the officer shortage would have been much more severe. In 1990, 55 cadets entered the UK Officer Training College; 45 Auxiliary Captains, aged 40 to 55, also began in-service training.[35] The age for acceptance to training college gradually crept upwards. In 1936 permission had to be sought from London for a 30-year-old to enter training in New Zealand; by the end of the century the cut-off age was 50. Flexible training for older candidates serving as "Cadet-Lieutenants" began to be introduced, with a combination of practical appointments with correspondence courses and residential block courses.

Auxiliary Captains appeared on the New Zealand scene in 1961, according to the annual *Disposition of Forces*. Up until 1974 this publication included a summary of the numbers of officers of each rank in the Territory. (This summary did not include the "officer wives". Where the officers were married, wives were enumerated separately.) The statistics shown for Auxiliary Captains in 1961 therefore presented as, "Auxiliary Captains, 1; Auxiliary Captain wives, 1". In 1962 the figures were 5, and 3 wives; in 1963, 9 and 6 wives. The figures levelled off, then declined for some years, but by the late 1990s there were 22 Auxiliary Captains (including wives) in New Zealand, out of a total of 370 active officers. They served in a wide range of appointments; in pastoral, social and administrative work. With the revision of the rank system in 2002, all remaining Auxiliary Captains in New Zealand were commissioned with the substantive rank of Captain. Some Territories intend to phase the rank out over ten years.

---

34 Minute 1972/IA/3, 1 May 1972.

35 *Salvationist* (1 February 1992) p. 8.

McKinley examines the conditions of Auxiliary Captaincy from an American perspective, the rank that was an "appointment" rather than a rank having been introduced in the United States as late as 1975. He notes that the innovation was "partly in response to the need for ethnic and other kinds of qualified leadership and partly to provide for converts who wanted to join the leadership team but were unable… to accept all the requirements for full officership. In the first case the Army broadened the use of a category of employee that was legally empowered to function like an officer. The rank… was first used in 1975 to describe employees recognised as licensed ministers, but several important questions regarding the status of such persons for tax and other legal purposes were not finally resolved until the Army's legal counsel prepared a detailed clarifying document in 1981." It defined an Auxiliary Captain as "an individual who is unable, for valid and acceptable reasons, to become a candidate for commissioned officership in the Salvation Army [such as being over 35 years of age], but who is otherwise qualified."[36] In 1980 there were 137 persons in the two categories of Envoy and Auxiliary Captain in the American field, making up 4% of total full-time leadership personnel; by 1990 there were 204 persons, or 6% of the total.[37]

A down side of this rank that was not a rank, for officers who were not officers, is that they, along with Envoys, were sometimes made to feel second-class by their soldiers, or even worse, by comrade officers. Occasionally this surfaced in print. *The Salvationist* article already cited mentioned that, "One of the group … had met a soldier who said, 'Oh, but you're not really an officer, are you?' The unthinking remark touched a sore spot."[38] Again, in a letter to the editor of *The Officer*, Mrs Captain Eva Phillips of Australia recalled that on the occasion of her commissioning (having been an Auxiliary Captain), she overheard another officer say in the foyer, "Anyone would think it was a proper commissioning! I'm off as soon as it starts…"[39]

Not surprisingly in view of the international variety of interpretation of these appointments, discussion about their character continued. At the 1988 International Leaders' Conference there was some discussion about the difference between "warranting" and "commissioning". In some parts of the world auxiliary captains were apparently commissioned and it was asked why that should not be the case when local officers were said to be commissioned. In the USA auxiliary captains were not warranted but given

---

36 Ed McKinley, *Marching to Glory* (Grand Rapids: Eerdmans, 2nd edn 1995) p. 329.

37 Statistical Report to USA National Headquarters for the years ending 31 December 1980 and 31 December 1990.

38 *Salvationist* (1 February 1992) p. 9.

39 *Officer* (July 1994) p. 336.

a memorandum of appointment and licensed. Other inconsistencies were noted, such as that "auxiliary" implies "assistant" whereas auxiliary captains were often commanding officers. If the title were an appointment rather than a rank, how was it retained in retirement when the appointment was no longer held?

Commissioner Walter mentioned that, "There has been a strong plea from one Territorial Commander to dispense with various grades of officers, as he says a person is either worthy of an officer role or not."[40] However, a proposal from the floor to do away with the distinction between captains and auxiliary captains "was not greeted with any enthusiasm".[41] The question began to be asked more frequently, however. An *Officer* article by Lieutenant Gregory Van Brunt of USA argued strongly that "there is no difference, nor should any be made, between the two... Why can't they sign the officers' covenant and receive an officer's commission, if they are doing the work of an officer?"[42]

Short-term Commissions

At the same time, the idea of short-term commissions – for "real" officers rather than second-class officers – began to be mentioned. One of the earlier protagonists was Major (later General) John Gowans. In an early 1970s article he pointed out that many young people were willing to give service without tying themselves down to a lifetime commitment. He argued that shortage of candidates, the rate of resignation and the increasing dearth of officer-leadership in the United Kingdom all called for desperate measures. Further, given that two thirds of British officers eventually resigned rather than retired from service, short-term commissions were already a reality.[43]

Reaction was not encouraging. Captain O.W. Akpan from Nigeria did "not see the need to make officership an easy 'merry-go-round' contract ... When God calls I believe He gives no limit, it is for all of life's span." He did admit, however, "our service conditions contribute in some measure to officers deserting the ranks and many youths frowning at officership."[44] The economic conditions for officership made it difficult for people with extended-family responsibilities to commit themselves. For Major Stanley Richardson of the British Territory, although he supported such short-term opportunities being made available, the proposal raised fundamental questions about our understanding of officership. These included, "(1) Is the

40 Stanley Walter, *Officer* (September 1988) p. 401.

41 Minutes of the 1988 International Leaders' Conference, Session 1, pp. 1-2.

42 *Officer* (January 1993) pp. 29-30.

43 *Officer* (March 1971) pp. 189-190, 193; *Impact* 3:1 (1973).

44 *Officer* (December 1971) p. 655.

officer a 'minister' who, having received a specific calling, has made a total commitment? (2) Do we accept the fact of 'ministry' and 'laity'? – terms which have no clear meaning in the Army. (3) Are the terms 'the call' and 'covenant', used regarding officership, now redundant? (4) Do we base our practice on expediency or on the basis of scriptural teaching?"[45] Mrs Colonel Rose Fleming of Ceylon wrote that "something in me trembles at the thought of young people entering training to become officers for a few stated years", and asked, "Is there no way in which officers can be convinced that theirs is not a job but a sacred calling?" She also believed that Auxiliary Captaincy already provided for short-term officership.[46]

However, twenty-five years later the question was still live. Lieutenant John Norton, a Canadian serving in the Republic of Georgia, suggested a "new complementary expression of officership..." which would enable people to "minister full-time under a different set of remuneration and commitment standards. These alternate officers would commit to the same spiritual and moral obligations as other officers but would not make the same life-time commitment and/or meet the same requirements as regular officership. These officers could be viewed as like military reserve officers." He felt this would "also answer the inherent paradox already in existence among the many soldier-employees who work for the Army".[47] The question remained sufficiently live to be placed on the agenda of the International Commission on Officership in 1999, although General John Gowans evidently felt unable then to implement his earlier proposal.

It is interesting to compare the ambiguity of auxiliary officers' role with that of the permanent diaconate in the Roman Catholic Church. Frank DeRego and James Davidson draw attention to the tensions arising for the latter from the fact that their role is not adequately defined. "The problem is traceable to the definition of the office of deacon, which is stated in terms of a status, not in terms of a job to be done... Role conflict and ambiguity ... adversely affect the actual relationships among deacons, priests and lay people. Priests are frustrated that deacons... do not provide the relief that the priests are looking for. Lay people tend to view deacons as 'underqualified priests or overqualified laity'."[48] For deacons, a key problem is their inability to perform sacramental functions; for auxiliary officers, the problems relate to status and working conditions. The ambiguity about their

---

45 *Officer* (December 1971) pp. 655-6.

46 *Officer* (January 1972) pp. 37-8.

47 *Officer* (September 1997) pp. 46-7.

48 Frank R. DeRego Jnr. and James D. Davidson, "Catholic Deacons: A Lesson in Role Conflict and Ambiguity", in Madeleine Cousineau (ed.), *Religion in a Changing World: Comparative Studies in Sociology* (Westport CT: Praeger, 1998) p. 96.

respective roles is however similar, suggesting again that the problem is as much sociological as theological.

This survey of auxiliary officership therefore raises questions about the connection between officer status and officer function. People enjoying a variety of status, as Envoys, Auxiliary Captains, Corps Leaders or soldiers without any conferment of rank, have discharged what appear to be the essential functions of officership. They have pastored, preached, taught, managed, led and acted as the focal bearers of the Salvation Army message, tradition and authority, either without rank or with a rank expressly designated as less than "clerical". At the same time, many commissioned officers have over the years served in roles that did not include any of these activities. Their sole officer-distinction has been covenanted appointability. Though the Salvation Army rubric, in distinction from the Church's clerical orders, is that "captain is as captain does,"[49] the exceptions seem to be too numerous to prove the rule.

---

49 John Coutts in *Salvationist* (27 May 2000) p. 7.

Chapter Fifteen

Cannon Fodder?

Every profession is a conspiracy against the laity.

George Bernard Shaw,
The Doctor's Dilemma, Act 1.

An outline of the history of auxiliary officership, in which people who were soldiers rather than "real" officers, functioned as officers, leads us naturally to consider what the Salvation Army has said about its soldiers per se. How are they different from officers?

While we have approached this question as derivative from an investigation of "ordained", officer ministry within the Salvation Army, it is helpful to remember that the last fifty years have seen a general reaction against this approach to the study of Church order within the ecumenical context. The World Council of Churches' establishment of a Department of the Laity in the late 1940s and Vatican II's grounding all Church office in the whole People of God were key markers.[1] The Salvation Army's pragmatic ecclesiology had always been premised on this understanding – officers were soldiers before they were officers. The Territorial Commander or General is still a soldier at some Corps.

Thirty years ago a former editor of *The Officer* noted the decline in candidates for officership and the increase in Salvationist graduates taking up careers in service professions. At that time he felt that "the role of the corps officer as 'minister' is still clearly defined, except, possibly, as between full-time Envoys and part-time Envoys in charge of corps." But, he asked, "Is not the distinction between officer and non-officer in the wider conception of ministry becoming more difficult to make? Are they not all 'on the field'? Maybe the Lord is calling us to analyse our distinctions a little more carefully."[2]

We have seen that in the early Salvation Army, before growing institutionalisation stratified the ranks and roles, there was a clearer recognition that all ranks were "laity"; all were the people of God, all were soldiers called equally to the battlefront. While the Army's military structure enabled rapid deployment, it would be interesting to know how much of its

1 *Lumen Gentium* Chapter II, in Austin Flannery (ed.) *Vatican Council II*, p. 359.
2 *Officer* (December 1973) p. 550.

rapid early spread was independently soldier-led, as in modern Africa. Gordon Moyles says of Newfoundland that

> If one examines only the official records one sees what looks like an orderly, planned progression even in the invasion of the outports. But when one looks deeper, one sees that the spread of Salvationism throughout much of Newfoundland was a spontaneous, catalytic kind of phenomenon. [The growth of small corps, over 40 of which were opened in 1892-1902, were] after-the-fact affairs – the Army being forced to respond to impromptu, unplanned "glory-meetings" conducted by local fishermen who had been converted in the Army elsewhere.[3]

Bernard Watson observed that

> the Army was certainly not created by an officer marching before and a mass of highly docile soldiery coming on behind. Sometimes the picture emerging from a study of Army history is of the soldiery advancing enthusiastically and the officer behind having a bit of a job to keep within shouting distance![4]

John Macquarrie had recognised much the same thing;

> One thing that seems clearly demanded by the secularized situation of today is a fuller recognition and a higher valuation of the lay apostolate… We shall have to be prepared to recognize the Spirit's working outside of the usual ecclesiastical channels, and that we shall also need to be willing to give to the laity more initiative and responsibility than they have usually enjoyed. Both of these points can be illustrated by … the Salvation Army.[5]

We have traced the gradual status-isation of the officers. What, during this process, was happening to the soldiers?

Soldier Attitudes

O'Dea writes that "the development of mixed motivation," while most significant in leadership roles, "is to be seen in the rank and file as well. As 'born members' replaced people who had been converted, a different kind of motivation and identification began to prevail in the church. As laity became a more passive element… lay people began to develop a different kind of identification, and their motives for participation changed as well."[6]

---

3 R. G. Moyles, *The Salvation Army in Newfoundland: Its History and Essence* (Toronto: SA, 1997) pp. 21, 26.
4 *Officer* (April 1970) p. 265.
5 John Macquarrie, *Principles of Christian Theology* (London: SCM, 1966) p. 376.
6 O'Dea, *Sociology of Religion*, p. 92.

Firstly, they came to think of themselves as "laity", and they came to expect of the officers the same kind of pastoral ministry they understood to be incumbent upon the clergy of the churches. David Stirling, writing to *The Salvationist*, perhaps encapsulated this attitude with the remark that he expected his officer to be the professional ministerial person, "my God-appointed priest".[7]

Secondly, they increasingly viewed the officers as the professionals who were paid to evangelise the unconverted. Bernard Watson believed that the "imaginative, more independent freedom of action among our 'laity' declined in the days when the Army had to be organised more precisely and also, perhaps, because there were years when the Army in some countries had a full quota of candidates entering training."[8] From the Headquarters vantage point, officers were easier to control and had more time than the soldiers.

Social evolution, what Donald McGavran called "redemption and lift",[9] already mentioned in Chapter Nine, reinforced this tendency. Evangelism could be left to the officer. Unfortunately, for many officers their time also tended to become wholly absorbed in looking after the soldiers and administering the machinery. It became less clear that anyone was actually attending to the core business of evangelism.

One of the things that happened towards the end of the nineteenth century was the strong development of the Army's musical subculture – bands and songster brigades. Watson argued that "the allocation of large groups of men and women into the musical sections within the Army tended to diminish independent, imaginative, versatile action by non-officer Salvationists."[10] In the early Salvation Army meeting places, the Salvationists sat on the tiered platform, while the unsaved filled up the body of the hall. Those unsaved who came out to the Mercy Seat in due course took their places on the platform. In the course of evolution, however, the musical sections came to occupy the platform, and the remaining soldiers filled the seats left vacant below by the receding tide of popular interest. The ascendancy of these musical combinations in Britain and the "old Dominions" – Australia, New Zealand and Canada in particular – tended to relegate the congregation to an audience role, like the faithful at the Tridentine mass. As, with advancing years and a changing society, that audience too diminished, the band could be left playing to the songsters and the songsters singing to the band. For many Salvationists, "evangelism" came to mean the band playing hymn-

---

7 *Salvationist* (12 September 1998) p. 19.

8 *Officer* (April 1970) p. 264.

9 Donald McGavran, *Understanding Church Growth* (Grand Rapids MICH: Eerdmans, 1970) pp. 262-75. See Bryan Wilson's *Religion in Secular Society*, pp. 107-11 for a succinct account of the process.

10 *Officer* (April 1970) p. 264.

tunes in the street, in a tight circle facing inwards towards the bandmaster, with backs to the audience.

What was true of the "field" (that is, the evangelical, church-oriented work of the Army) was also the case in social work. Amongst the pioneers of Salvation Army social work had been ordinary Salvationists who saw a need and did something. In Britain a Mrs Cottrill of Whitechapel, London, started taking straying girls into her home in the early 1880s.[11] In New Zealand Mrs Rudman and Mrs Hawker in Wellington and the Brownlie sisters in Dunedin undertook the same work.[12] Inevitably such work grew too large to be undertaken by private individuals and was taken over by the organisation, growing into an official and comprehensive social programme, staffed mainly by officers, who became the professionals, paid to care for the needy. It did not take many years for the Social wing to take on an existence almost independent of the Field (church) activities of the Army, particularly after the launching of the "Darkest England" scheme in 1890 and the requirement that social funds be kept separate from those of the field. Social officers were at first trained separately from those intended for the Field, and officers tended to spend their careers in one or the other branch of the service.

The tradition of lay-initiative has never been entirely lost, as exemplified by Envoy David Ndoda of Bulawayo, Zimbabwe, who at his own volition and expense founded a home for orphans.[13] Some non-officer staff have always been employed in social work over the years. However it is only within the past twenty years that serious efforts have been made to reintegrate the differing expressions of the Army's ministry. Soldiers generally have only recently, in some places, begun to reassume interest in and ownership of social work in a voluntary capacity, or, increasingly, as paid employees.

Officer Attitudes

These developments, contributing to a widening gulf between the concerns and preoccupations of officers on the one hand and soldiers on the other, also had consequences in the attitude of officers, perhaps especially corps officers, towards soldiers. A broad divide may be discerned between

- Seeing soldiers as "cannon-fodder", whose role is to be occupied so far as possible in Army activities, building the Salvation Army institution.

---

11 Sandall, *History*, III, p. 15.

12 Bradwell, *Fight the Good Fight*, p. 50.

13 *SA Year Book* (1999) p. 22.

- Viewing soldiers as the front line of evangelism, outside the organisation's official structure and programme, to be resourced and supported as well as led, in building the Kingdom of God.

These points of view represent a divide between the tendency to "clericalise" the "laity" and the recognition of a distinct "lay apostolate". Both have been strongly represented over the years.

The view that the soldiers should be fully engaged in the work of the Salvation Army grew out of two things. Firstly, converts from the kind of social milieu common to many early Salvationists lost their friends and interests with conversion, and had to replace them. The Corps became their new way of life. The dynamic is similar to that in Alcoholics Anonymous, where neophytes are urged to attend, if possible, "ninety meetings in ninety days". A new circle of friends and activities has to be substituted for one now perceived as unsafe. In the same way, in the Army, both the converts and their leaders were so filled with enthusiasm that attending Salvation Army activities every night of the week seemed the most desirable thing possible. Inevitably, as they lost touch with the "world", they were absorbed into what became in time a semi-autonomous religious sub-culture.

Secondly, the expanding Army needed the manpower. Bramwell Booth wrote,

> Every soldier is expected to do something of the collecting, the cleaning, the visiting, the band playing, the caring for the children, the seeking after our lost sheep, and the score of other duties demanding attention. Tens of thousands of our soldiers devote every moment snatched from their daily labour to the work of their Corps. They delight that it should be so. Many of them owe to the Army everything they possess of happiness in this life, and all they can look forward to, of peace in the life to come. In no unimportant sense, it is their mother. It is their home. It is their friend. It is their recreation. It is the embodiment of all that ennobles and elevates their lives.[14]

Colonel Alex Nicol apparently suggested to the Founder that the Army should have an internal, spiritual "Labour Bureau" (it had pioneered the idea of a Labour Exchange for unemployed people in 1890 as part of the "Darkest England" scheme) "for soldiers who were willing to work but had nothing to do. However, it has now been decided that the census meeting of each corps should, for the present, undertake the additional duties of a Labour Bureau."[15]

A paradox may be seen at work, in that on the one hand the soldiers were to be set to work in ministry, while some also came to regard ministry as the exclusive responsibility of the officers. All of these are generalisations of course; both voices continued to be heard, and in recent years there has been

---

14 W. Bramwell Booth, *Servants*, p. 23.

15 *Officer* (June 1893) p. 176.

a renewal of the understanding that pastoral care is a joint responsibility. For example 1991 *Salvationist* correspondent, I.W. Kennedy, asked for the principle of the priesthood of all believers to be explained in some publication as "this biblical principle is surrounded by confusion in our movement with its military terminology and distinction between officers and soldiers". It was suggested that "lay personnel beyond the realm of local officership and envoyship could play an increased role in pastoral care. It might be one answer to the reduced intake at the Training College."[16] In New Zealand at any rate the recent proliferation of lay pastoral teams within Corps has been accompanied by complaints that the officer never visits – a complaint not restricted to Salvation Army congregations.

Quotes like those from Bramwell Booth and Nicol, above, might give the impression that secular work was simply a means to the end of being able to devote the rest of one's time to the War, or at most provided further opportunities for witness to fellow-workers, rather than being a God-given vocation in its own right. Roy Terry, writing in *Magazine* in 1963, lamented that "Even our active laymen are mostly, to use Hendrik Kraemer's phrase, 'clericalised laity'. Most lay Salvationist activity is specifically 'religious' activity – keeping the organisational works going, and while there are Salvationists active in the world at large (whose lives do not revolve solely around the S.A. hall) they don't seem to receive much encouragement from officialdom, still less any constructive help."[17]

Admittedly William Booth wrote a series of letters about "work" in the *War Cry* and the *Social Gazette*, later collected in a volume on "Religion for Every Day". In these he encouraged Salvationists to think of work as of value in itself, "good and honest work, honourable in the sight of God, and serviceable to your fellow-men".[18] However it is true that the main focus on the workplace in Salvation Army writing has been related to the soldiers' witnessing. At least this acknowledged that soldiers' lives were not simply coextensive with the organised Corps programme.

Appreciation of the fact that non-officers are the people nearest the front line tends to be mentioned more often in recent material than in the earlier records. The reason may be that in the early Army it was taken for granted; only with the institutionalising of the officer/soldier roles, and the focus on that of the officer, has it been necessary to re-emphasise the theory to redress an imbalance.

Wilfred Kitching referred to Salvationists in industry as "the 'paratroops for the Kingdom', the behind-the-lines fighters".[19] He also recounted the story of how "in the early days of the second world war negotiations were

---

16 *Salvationist* (28 September 1991) p. 11.

17 *Magazine* (October 1963) p. 13.

18 William Booth, *Letters to Salvationists*, p. 29.

19 Kitching, *Soldier of Salvation*, p. 55.

being conducted with a high ranking military officer on the issue of appointing a number of Salvation Army officers as chaplains in the British Army. The negotiations were not entirely successful but what pregnant truth there was in the observation of the military officer when he said, 'Should you be unduly troubled if none of your officers are appointed as chaplains; for surely if every Salvation Army soldier in our ranks lives up to what I imagine are his convictions, he will always as need arises be an unofficial chaplain?'"[20]

Philip Needham, in a 1965 article, made an impassioned protest against clericalism in the Salvation Army and the systematic officer-recruitment of all the most promising soldiers. He felt it reflected an over-riding concern for the continuation of the institution rather than a commitment to its mission. "There is a sacred aura about officership, that is, the complete identification with the sacred institution. It is as though the Army were God's right hand. That we refer to officership as 'full-time service' is a gross perversion of the Christian faith. If there is any full-time Christian service, it is in the life of the laymen in the world. The particular and inherent weakness of a professional clergy – and this is particularly true of the Army – is that it is not full-time Christian service."[21]

Correspondence in *The Salvationist* has occasionally focussed on the "them and us" aspect of officer-soldier relationships. A letter from J. R. Anderson complained that obituaries of officers were illustrated with photographs while those of soldiers were not: "You should know how the rank and file of the Army feel about it."[22] G. W. Lesworthy of Florida, drawing on 50 years' experience of soldiership in Britain and the USA, complained of the "shunting aside of the soldiers... You stress 'officership' so much that soldiers have no choice but to feel 'put down'".[23] Editorial comment regretted any polarisation, especially "since the Salvation Army advocates the priesthood of all believers and is essentially a lay movement seeking the evangelisation of the people by the people."[24] A decade later Graham Millar, having been an officer for 23 years, then a soldier, and then writing from the perspective of a soldier leading a Corps, had come to the conclusion that the Army existed for the Officers, was "officer-centred". Colonel Glen Shepherd, writing in the same number of *The Officer* expressed a similar point of view. He reported a local officer friend as saying, "...It's an officer's Army. What are you going to do about it?"[25]

---

20 *Officer* (January- February 1959) p. 4.
21 *New Soldiers* (Spring 1965) p. 43.
22 *Salvationist* (3 January 1987) p. 10.
23 *Salvationist* (5 December 1987) p. 12.
24 *Salvationist* (6 February 1988) p. 2.
25 *Officer* (October 1999) pp. 22-3.

Unintended slights can be built into the system, such as in the "Bulletins" issued from Headquarters when for example some Salvationist dies – the names of next-of-kin who are officers may be mentioned while their non-officer siblings are not. Or the statement in the 1987 version of the *Orders and Regulations for Soldiers* giving less than generous recognition to vocations other than clerical with, "No call can be more important than that to officership."[26] Or when a *War Cry* article appealing for candidates for officership, suggested that people who have achieved secular goals might now "move from success to significance", the writer quite unconscious of the slight implied on those fulfilling a different calling.[27]

Commissioner Edward Carey, speaking on the significance of "Layman's Councils", quoted Harvey Cox: "The clergy serve as 'ministers to the ministers', as kitchen troops in the divine army. And kitchen troops should be court-martialed if they confuse the fighting men either by adjuring them to spend more and more time in the mess hall, or by implying repetitiously that the only true job in the army is that of the kitchen officer while the rest are not really full time." Carey asked, "Wouldn't it be the supreme irony if we, in the Army that brought the layman to a new sense of involvement in the supreme task of making the Gospel of Jesus Christ relevant to ordinary people in the ordinary pursuits of life, should now back away from the challenge of a greater sphere, a greater usefulness for talented, dedicated Christian soldiers at the very moment in time when other churches are responding?"[28]

A Voice in Council

As well as the question of how far the soldiers should be involved in the fighting, the question has also arisen as to whether they should have a part in the direction of the War. Norman Murdoch observes that Booth's assumption of total control ran counter to the democratisation of western society. Hattersley suggests the reason was to do with class – middle-class Methodism was becoming democratic while working-class Salvationism was still autocratic.[29] David Bebbington concludes that "a democratic temper was almost as prominent among the Baptists of Britain as it was among the Christians of America."[30] Baptists, like Methodists, ranked

26 *Chosen To Be a Soldier* (London: SA, 1987) Chap. IX, Section 6, p. 79.

27 *WC* (New Zealand) (11 August 2001) p. 14.

28 Minutes of the 1969 Commissioners' Conference, p. 28.

29 Hattersley, *Blood & Fire*, p. 225.

30 David Bebbington, "The Democratization of British Christianity: The Baptist Case, 1770-1870" in Anthony R. Cross (ed.), *Ecumenism and History* (Carlisle: Paternoster, 2002) p. 280.

higher than Salvationists in the English class structure, however. The Army's polity has not been able to respond so easily to subsequent social change, partly because of the absence of any formal representative mechanisms. Soldiers simply did not have any voice in council. Cyril Bradwell, writing of the deposition of Bramwell Booth, describes how "In June 1928 thirty-one leading officers in New Zealand despatched letters to General Booth urging him to agree to some modification of his powers. The rank and file Salvationists in this country were never consulted and never informed, even after the deposition, of this step."[31]

An admission allegedly by the retired General Albert Orsborn in 1963 encapsulated the hierarchy's clericalist mindset. Roy Terry wrote, "That the Salvationist layman has always been passive and receptive was shown recently at a London Regional meeting [of the Students' Fellowship], reported in *Vanguard*, where General Orsborn is said to have deplored the tendency among the present-day youth of the Army to ask questions, and to have affirmed his belief that the motto of the Salvationist layman has always been, and should remain so in the future, 'Ours not to reason why'."[32] (However, the words attributed to Orsborn by Terry are not found in the *Vanguard* report of this meeting, suggesting that either Terry had been misinformed or that *Vanguard* had exercised editorial discretion. In fact, *Vanguard* quoted Orsborn as saying that "questions are a healthy sign."[33])

Philip Needham, in the article already quoted, stated that, "if the Army's soldiery were to become once more a truly Christian lay movement, the Army's official power structure would change accordingly... There is a danger, of course, that the Army's official leaders will have identified themselves so closely with the Army's power structures that reform would meet with misunderstanding and even active opposition."[34]

Nevertheless, in the "Western world" Army, the second half of the twentieth century saw some attempt to accommodate to the more democratic temper of the times with some consultative machinery on both local and territorial level. Perhaps the innovation of Advisory Boards – bodies of well-disposed and preferably wealthy and influential non-salvationists who were invited to support with expertise and fund-raising the activities of the Army[35] – led to questions about why soldiers could not have similar input into the affairs of their own organisation. Corps Councils were the outcome,

---

31 Cyril Bradwell, "Outline History of The Salvation Army in New Zealand" (MA thesis, Canterbury University College, 1950) pp. 91-2. (From interview with Brigadier Samuel Hayes.)

32 *Magazine* (February 1963) uncensored supplement p.(iv).

33 *Vanguard* (March 1962) pp. 13-16 (May 1962) pp. 20-24.

34 Needham, *New Soldiers* (Spring 1965) p. 44.

35 The earliest known was set up in Nanking, China, by Major Yin Hung Shun in the 1930s (Check Hung Yee, *Good Morning China* (Alexandria Va.: Crest, 2005) p.174.

in the late 1950s.[36] A Commission on Corps Councils had reported and General Kitching was able to tell the 1958 International Conference of Commissioners that a Minute would be issued on the subject. The resulting bodies consisted of the senior local officers of a Corps, plus a few other soldiers or adherents or supporters, chaired by the Corps Officer. Personnel are not elected, but appointed by the Corps Officer, the names needing to be approved by the Divisional Commander. A Council's role is advisory only; decision-making is the prerogative of the officer.[37] Decisions, or recommendations, are by consensus, not by voting. The system at least provides a forum where matters concerning the Corps can be discussed. Of course, Salvation Army faith communities, like any other, have their power-brokers – an officer will work with them if he wants to get anything done.

In New Zealand in the 1960s Commissioner A.J. Gilliard convened a successful series of Local Officers' residential Councils – as Cyril Bradwell says, Gilliard was rare in believing that it might be important to discover what the rank and file were thinking.[38] However, his successors did not attempt to institutionalise this development, and the leading "laity" were left feeling that they could keep on saying the same things but that no one would do anything about them. In an article on "Laos – the Whole People of God", New Zealander Max Cresswell appealed against the attitude "which says, 'If you want to influence Army affairs, then you should become an officer.'" He urged that "soldiers should be enabled to make their views known on any subject or plan of action, and that existing boards and councils should be enlarged to include suitable lay Salvationists, including those bodies responsible for officer appointments."[39]

A Canadian initiative in 1966 was the Advisory Council of Salvation Army Laymen, or ACSAL, which operated on both regional and national levels. The Territorial Commander, Commissioner Clarence Wiseman, characterised this development in an *Officer* article as "Coming of Age – A study of Salvation Army Soldiership in the latter twentieth century."[40] Wiseman attributed ACSAL itself to "lay" initiative. It "grew out of the concern of a few soldiers who felt that some method should be developed so that the Army could benefit from the knowledge and experience of

36 *Orders and Regulations for Governing a Corps Council* were issued by IHQ, 21 January 1959.

37 C.f. Roman Catholic Canon 536, stipulating a consultative role only for parish councils.

38 Bradwell, *Touched with Splendour*, p. 149.

39 *Magazine* (June, 1962) pp. 3-7.

40 *Officer* (September 1969) pp. 586-90.

Salvationists holding positions of responsibility in the secular world."[41] This example was followed in a number of other territories.

It did not endure, however. Even in its fourth year, ACSAL evidently had an uncertain tenure in Melbourne.[42] In the words of sometime member of the New Zealand ACSAL, Cyril Bradwell, "the abolition of the Council in the late 1990s appeared regrettable and somewhat arbitrary, with no clear rationale promulgated."[43] Even in the land of its birth ACSAL was dispensed with after thirty years,[44] although new consultative processes are being developed now. Such losses illustrate how vulnerable innovations might be when lacking any constitutional base. Peter Price refers to the same vulnerability in the Catholic Church: "The consultative structures of the Church are still only 'recommended' and 'advisory'. They do not necessarily facilitate Lay participation in real decision-making. Such participation as well as its authority are dependent on the individual Bishop or Parish Priest, and may be dismantled at will."[45]

In 1969, Commissioner Carey, USA National Commander, mentioned that the National Layman's Commission was being disbanded and Territorial and maybe Divisional Commissions were being established instead to allow for broader representation and more frequent meetings. He noted that any recommendations of national import could be referred to the national Commissioners' Conference, "so that the lay voice will still be heard in the top policy body of the Salvation Army in the USA."[46] (Perhaps an echo rather than a voice?) In the non-western world, more conservative attitudes prevailed. At the 1971 International Conference of Leaders, Commissioner Chun of Korea expressed himself anxious that the proceedings relating to Advisory Councils should not be publicised – the Minutes record that "he felt the repercussions might be greater than he could hold."[47]

By this time Wiseman, now General, had had further thoughts on ACSAL, and concluded that the separation of officers from non-officers "was in violation of a very important theological principle… To have segregated groupings is really in violation of the concept of the priesthood of all believers." He had met with ACSAL groups in Canada and persuaded

---

41 Clarence Wiseman, *A Burning in My Bones* (Toronto: McGraw-Hill Ryerson, 1979) p. 166.

42 Doug Smith, "Lay Advisory Council Axed?" *Impact* 4:1 (1974).

43 Bradwell, *Touched with Splendour*, p. 319.

44 Kenneth Pedlar, *Horizons* (May/June 2005) p. 11.

45 Peter Price, "Vatican II: End of a Clerical Church (1)" in *Australian Ejournal of Theology* (http://dlibrary.acu.edu.au/research/theology/ejournal/aet_1Price.htm) Downloaded 23 February 2004.

46 Minutes of 1969 Commissioners' Conference, p. 27.

47 Minutes of the 1971 International Council of Leaders, p. 53.

them that this was the case and "thereafter Officers came officially on to the ACSAL."[48] Not all those with existing lay consultative Councils were persuaded on that occasion, however, and some hoped there would be time allowed for integration.

In 1978 the USA Western Territory initiated a Territorial Laymen and Officers' Council. In 1989 a significant USA National Forum was held, with both officers and soldiers involved.[49] The British *Salvationist* reported in 1990 that an Advisory Council had been set up for the territory, mainly made up from soldiery chosen from each of the territory's 21 Divisions. It described this as the "latest move in the territory's consultative process, which includes Corps Councils and Divisional Advisory Councils".[50] In recent times the Canadian territory has been introducing wider consultative structures.

Another body involving both officer and non-officer representation in New Zealand was the Public Questions Board, established in the mid-1950s.[51] This body, now known as the Moral and Social Issues Council, conforming to nomenclature in other territories, was able to make representations to the Territorial Commander on social issues and proposed legislative changes by Government. It has had a rather chequered history as successive Territorial Commanders have valued it to differing degrees.

Background study material circulated before the 1991 International Conference of Leaders included a section on "Making the Best Use of Soldiery". Recommendations were requested on, amongst other things, "The need for soldiers and local officers to have greater involvement in the decision-making processes of the Army". The paper also suggested that "the danger we are in today is that we are rapidly becoming an Army of, by, and for officers. We are in imminent danger of toppling from the disease of 'executivitis'." The comment was made that "in some parts of the world dialogue between officers and soldiery does not take place because of lack of knowledge of the consultative process – they only know autocratic leadership... Soldiers should be included in the consultative process at corps, divisional and territorial levels."[52]

Shortly after his election as General in 1994, Paul Rader also expressed his support for consultative leadership. He expressed his intention to "encourage the active participation of lay Salvationists in the whole area of the Army's policy development and implementation of our mission".[53]

---

48 Minutes of the 1971 International Council of Leaders, p. 54.

49 Gariepy, *History*, VIII, p. 184.

50 *Salvationist* (20 January 1990) pp. 1,4.

51 Minutes in New Zealand Salvation Army Archives.

52 1991 International Conference of Leaders, Background papers, pp. 54-5.

53 *WC* (USA) (21 January 1995) p. 7.

Some moves were forced upon the organisation by outside pressures. Following a fraud case in 1992 when some funds of the UK Army were invested offshore and disappeared from sight (fortunately to be wholly retrieved some years later after painstaking detective work), the Charity Commissioners insisted on significant reforms in the Territory's financial systems.[54] A working party of Salvation Army and Charity Commission representatives ushered in a new era when qualified non-officer Salvationists and even non-Salvationists were appointed along with officers as Directors of the Army's Trustee Company.[55] For all that, the default, officer-centred position into which the organisation so readily lapses, attributing omnicompetence to commissioned rank, means that too often business decisions are made by officers who are commercial amateurs, entailing a commensurate loss of credibility with Salvation Army soldiers.

Soldiers in Officer Roles

The moves towards soldiers being involved in consultation and decision-making described so far assume the scenario of soldiers giving of their spare time on a voluntary basis to these ends. It is necessary to look also at soldiers in Salvation Army employment. Soldiers had been employed by the Army from the earliest days. Some spent a lifetime in the Army's service, filling very responsible roles, especially financial ones. The difference was that soldiers (not just in the guise of Envoys or auxiliary officers) were now being employed in ministry and administrative roles, hitherto reserved for commissioned officers, or at least for auxiliary officers. By the 1990s this was indeed a growing phenomenon – though not a particularly new one. At the 1971 International Commissioner's Conference, Frederick Adlam had commented that, "In Rhodesia we do not have the rank of Auxiliary Captain but have fifty married Salvationists who are Corps Leaders. They are headmasters of schools where they work and run the Corps. Some are better run than Corps where there are officers."[56]

The "first world" Army was slower in adopting such expedients, although people had begun to call for them. Ron Woodcock, writing in *The Salvationist* in 1987, wrote, "Many times I have suggested that an officer should have the oversight of two or three small corps which would be run by soldiers. Laymen run churches in the Methodist and Congregational Churches. Sure we have nothing to lose and much to gain."[57] Robert Docter in *New Frontier* in 1988 wrote of the need "to use the professional skills of

---

54 Gariepy, *History*, VIII, pp. 278-9.

55 *Salvationist* (2 November, 1996) pp. 8-9.

56 Minutes of 1971 International Commissioners' Conference.

57 *Salvationist* (26 December 1987) p. 10.

non-officer laymen who want to serve God with their skills in the Army."[58] In answer to a letter from Frank Boorman on the need to make better use of Officer Training College facilities by training "lay" Salvationists, the Principal of the International Training College, Colonel John Larsson, explained how Auxiliary Captains made use of the College. He added that the letter raised "matters that would need resolution for more to be done... The Army does not at present work with team ministries of full-time non-officer personnel."[59]

That statement was increasingly less likely to be accurate towards the end of the century. In New Zealand the trend probably began with the appointment of Youth Workers, attached to Divisions or Corps from the mid 1980s on, Graham Goodisson for example spending fourteen years in this role. Over the same period an increasing number of larger Corps employed full-time non-officer pastoral workers or "Corps Assistants", usually second career, late-vocation people recruited from within the congregation. Bruce Vyle, at Hamilton City Corps, was the first to be employed in such a role in New Zealand, in 1989.[60] The shortage of commissioned officers has also meant that responsibility for the leadership of some smaller Corps has devolved upon full-time, employed soldier "Corps Leaders".

Not being subject to the appointability of officers, such non-officer pastoral ministers have tended to serve longer in the same appointments than officers do. Their pastoral relationship with people has also led to questions about how far they can exercise traditionally officer or clerical roles, such as the solemnisation of marriages. Some denominations provide for the appointment of non-clergy, denominational-list marriage celebrants but not yet the Salvation Army. Some non-officers have resorted to the expedient of officiating at weddings while having an authorised celebrant sign the register. This practice has attracted the attention of the Registrar-General, who issued a circular suggesting that while he was "not aware of any New Zealand case law on this point... it is possible that a court will hold that the word 'solemnised' in the Marriage Act and the word 'officiate' in the marriage registration form require the authorised celebrant's active participation in the legal aspects of the ceremony."[61] Unranked soldiers therefore face in this respect the same problem we have met with in the case of Envoys.

The same period has seen the appointment of more and more non-officer Salvationists to senior executive roles in the organisation, especially in the sphere of social work. Gordon Bingham was appointed Social Services

58 *New Frontier* (11 May 1988) p. 7.

59 *Salvationist* (4 October 1986) p. 2.

60 *WC* (New Zealand) (9 April 2005) p. 8.

61 Brian Clarke, Registrar-General of Births, Deaths and Marriages in New Zealand: Circular to Marriage Celebrants, 28 February 2003.

Secretary for the USA Western Territory in 1985 after years in various social work roles in the USA Central Territory. In New Zealand George Borthwick has headed Employment Programmes as National Manager since 1992, directing some two hundred staff. Previously only officers would have held such appointments.

In the USA the utilisation of soldiers in administration had been urged particularly by Commissioner Kenneth Hodder, as Territorial Commander for the Southern Territory and subsequently as National Commander. In the USA Southern Territory the role of Territorial Sergeant Major was instituted around 1990, providing a full-time lay advisor to the Territorial Commander, and also serving as chairman of the Territorial Commission on Planning and Goals. In a farewell message to the Southern Territory, Hodder commented that if he had his time over again, he would "have given greater significance to the place of the lay salvationists, our soldiery, on decision-making bodies". He wanted "to stimulate a recovery of the biblical teaching concerning the status of soldiers and officers as equal partners... and looked forward to the day when non-officer soldiers will serve on territorial boards of trustees, finance councils, property councils and other decision-making bodies."[62]

Hodder returned to his theme when addressing the 1995 International Conference of Leaders. He lamented that

> the Army has yet to appreciate fully the need for the application of these principles to the governance, as well as the ministry, of our movement. ... beyond the scriptural, historical and philosophical dimensions of this issue, there is an additional reason for pursuing it...
>
> The expansion of the work and the small size of the officer corps demands that we take advantage of those Salvationists who, based on their giftedness, training and experience, are prepared and willing to undertake administrative responsibilities. Furthermore... that task of administration necessarily translates into decision-making, meaning that the incorporation of soldiery into our decision-making structure may simply be forced upon us by growth... I suggest that we should now place ourselves in a proactive, rather than a reactive, stance.

Hodder went on to posit four criteria, "four dimensions of effective lay participation in governance": communication, vision, reform and ownership. Hitherto the Army had tentatively tried some models for lay participation, such as the laymen's councils, but Hodder saw these as interim measures, in which the laity would soon lose interest.

---

62 *Officer* (October 1993) pp. 435-6.

> The failure of representative bodies to bring about effective lay participation in the governance of the Army is... traceable to the nature of our polity. As a hierarchical organization it simply is not possible to graft on a representative body of laypersons and expect that it will long endure.

Hodder therefore proposed a three-part action plan. Firstly, forums where soldiers and officers can express their views directly to each other. Secondly, selection of qualified soldiers for service on boards of trustees, finance and property councils and similar decision-making bodies. Thirdly, "The Salvation Army must support organizational change initiatives that take place on a decentralized, localized basis." Hodder felt that these steps would be a start towards formulating and implementing a new theology of the laity. He concluded by quoting Pius X, who

> in his 1906 Encyclical entitled *Vehementer Nos*, said: "As for the masses, they have no other right than that of letting themselves be led, and of following their pastors as a docile flock." Despite many protestations to the contrary, this has sometimes been our functional view. In this we have simply been wrong.[63]

Anxiety about such developments has been expressed, particularly by officers. One concern was that officers with professional qualifications were being squeezed out of roles that enabled them to use that training. Major Gilbert Ellis of Norway felt that, "In the long term, if present developments continue, the officer-role will be reduced. Service in the Army will become increasingly a profession, and officership will be limited to the 'spiritual' sphere. The total dedication that officership has demanded will thereby be limited."[64] Major David Pickard was concerned that "elimination of officer-personnel from many administrative posts will lessen the scope of officership and leave many officers unable to use their principal gifts within the framework of their calling. To deny officers such opportunities on the grounds that they are trained for spiritual ministry, yet at the same time encourage an ever-growing number of lay people into full-time spiritual ministry would seem contradictory."[65]

The view that officers per se bring an added dimension to administrative tasks is also expressed. Major Margaret Castley wrote that "As financial secretary in two territories it was a privilege to bring to territorial leaders not only financial figures and advice but also an added spiritual dimension to very practical situations. Often, I believe, only an officer could offer that dimension."[66] Such concerns may be reflected in Recommendation 7 of the

---

63 Kenneth Hodder (paper given at the 1995 International Conference of Leaders).

64 *Officer* (September 1994) pp. 418-20.

65 *Officer* (March 1995) p. 143.

66 *Officer* (September-October 2005) p. 10.

"Vocation Path Project for The Salvation Army, United Kingdom Territory" (Second Draft, December 2002): "That the emerging practice of officer appointment opportunities being taken by lay professionals be re-evaluated."[67]

Another concern was that the availability of non-officer work within Army service would adversely affect officer recruiting. Jean Seymour thought that the "the massive input from lay personnel is having an adverse effect on young peoples' willingness to consider officership. Being a layperson means that you choose a job that is suited to you, and you are given consideration, security of tenure and financial stability. You are a part of the Army and you have the kudos of a place in that organisation. That is not so for officers. They are subject to the authoritarianism of senior officers ... officers need to be treated no worse than lay persons."[68] Major Graham Mizon of UK had a like concern for the recruiting implications. The "many opportunities that now exist for non-officers to engage in full-time service, coupled with flexible approaches to officer-training and service... poses the question: what is distinctive about a commissioned officer?" He was worried "that officership could lose out for two fundamental reasons. First, a lack of clarity about what an officer is (or is not)... Secondly... if messages are sent out ... which seem to devalue this position."[69]

Yet another implication of the trend was spelt out by Commissioner Earle Maxwell, Chief of the Staff, in an address to the 1998 International Conference of Leaders. While the majority of governments still accepted the officer's relationship with the Army as being entirely "spiritual" and therefore not subject to employer/employee legislation, it was a different matter when the Army engaged an employee to do the same work as an officer. "Then it becomes very difficult – almost impossible – for the Army to claim that the officer performing this parallel function to that of the employee, should not be regarded as an employee! This relates particularly to administrative, financial, social service and public relations appointments."[70]

This situation – that the Army (in some Territories) has a dwindling pool of candidates but many able people wanting to serve in officer-roles although not under officer-conditions admits of a different solution; that leadership should be the sole criteria for holding officer rank rather than appointability or certain financial arrangements. My own suggestion was that "Salvationist leaders in full-time ministry, whatever the formula for

67 Report and Recommendations of the UK Gender Issues Commission, 2004, p. 20.

68 *Salvationist* (13 July 1996) pp. 18-9.

69 *Salvationist* (8 June 2002) p. 11.

70 *Officer* (August 1998) p. 5.

their relationship with the Army structure, should be called 'officers'."[71] This at least has the virtue of consistency, though it depends upon the view that all Salvationists are lay, and that officership is simply functional. The question arising then would be what functions can properly be described as leadership or ministry, and the corollary could be that all officers performing other than those functions should be reduced to the ranks. The proposal arises firstly from a sense that the existing two-tier system is inherently unjust. Secondly, from anxiety that with a diminishing pool of commissioned officers from which future leadership might be chosen, an increasing proportion of such leaders, willing to operate within the status quo, might tend to be conformists, excluding many entrepreneurial types upon whose initiative the movement's survival might depend.

Soldiership

The tacit assumption in much of this material, that soldiers are lay, with its implication that officers are clergy, has not gone unchallenged. Gordon Taylor asked in 1990, "Am I alone in disliking the increasing use of such terms as 'lay evangelists' or 'lay-personnel' when referring to non-officers? Is it appropriate to use such terminology when we do not have salvationist clergy or priests? Surely we are all salvationists with a divine commission."[72] Letters from Andrew Trim and Mavis Cavell supported him in subsequent issues.[73] The Army's theology of the laity, that all are laity, was not going to go away.

A recent contribution to this debate has been that of John Cleary, an Australian Salvation Army soldier, journalist and broadcaster. Cleary is concerned that in the "western" Army, the very institution of soldiership is withering away, with increasing numbers of both the "children of the regiment" and of new attenders at Army worship preferring some ambiguous membership status rather than making the lifestyle commitments incumbent on soldiers. For example, in the year-ending June 2003, an old-established New Zealand Corps, Auckland Congress Hall, had an average Sunday morning attendance of 228 with a Soldiers' Roll of 340; whereas a new (9 years old) Corps, Johnsonville, had an average attendance of 164 but only 43 enrolled soldiers.

Cleary sees the crisis as resulting in part from the Army's inadequate ecclesiology, with its lack of clarity over the years about the connection between soldiership in the Army and membership of the Church. His remedy for this trend is a revitalisation of soldiership as special class of

---

71 *Officer* (October 1999) pp. 24-5.

72 *Salvationist* (12 May 1990).

73 *Salvationist* (9 June 1990, 23 June 1990).

membership, a kind of elite shock troop or cadre, with a higher commitment to the War than that of ordinary members. By analogy Cleary suggests soldiership might be the equivalent of the diaconate in the traditional three-fold order of the Church.[74] He believes that this would attract the commitment of a new generation looking for "something to live for, something to die for". Certainly the decline of interest in soldiership in some western territories could, extrapolating present trends, eventually lead to it being merely a staging post on the way to officership, much as the "transitional" diaconate has been in the Catholic and Anglican churches until comparatively recently. Cleary's proposal does resemble more closely the recovered Catholic institution of the "permanent diaconate".

Another analogy for soldiership apart from the diaconate might be the Third Orders of the Franciscans, Dominicans and Carmelites. These Secular Tertiaries are bound by promises to a distinctive life-style and have a special interest in the particular focus and charism of their order but pursue ordinary secular vocations and may marry. For Salvationists, evangelism and social service could be postulated as the particular callings of their "order" – although that would in fact be true now of only a minority of Soldiers.

Analogies between traditional church categories and Salvation Army terms are at best only approximate, despite the similarities. While these analogies may or may not be entirely appropriate, and whether or not Cleary's proposal implicitly accepts the existence of "orders" of "status" or simply delineates roles within the movement; it looks as though his solution is predicated upon the validity and appropriateness of a traditional church model incompatible with one aspect of the Army's genius. It certainly assumes that officers are the equivalent of presbyters/priests.

Although this study is not concerned with soldiership as such, except in so far as it relates to leadership, the confusion between role and status also affects soldiers. The Salvation Army having inherited from Methodism the sectarian concept of membership, protected by commitments and covenants, there is always a tension between soldiership and simply being a Christian, which in a traditional church setting would derive from infant baptism. In societies where people are increasingly reluctant to be tied down, such a concept is being widely questioned. From an American perspective, Tony Campolo comments, "I think church 'membership' is a false definition of reality. In our society two-thirds of the people who claim church membership never go… Maybe the time has come to do away with 'church membership' and just say whosoever will may come into the congregation and be a part of the growing ministry and fellowship."[75]

---

74 John Cleary, "Chosen to be a Soldier" (Unpublished paper presented March 2002 at the Salvation Army College of Further Education, Sydney).

75 *Leadership* (Summer 2004) 25:3, p. 54.

Within membership of the Salvation Army there are degrees of association – Adherent Member, Recruit, Soldier, Local Officer – about which questions of status arise, quite apart from the officer-role. "Adherency" was a concept first mooted in 1886.[76] It provided for people to identify with the Salvation Army as their "church" without making any profession of faith, although there too there was local variation – in India profession of faith and abstinence from alcohol were required. Recently, after international consultation, it was decided that in future people wishing to join the Salvation Army but not wanting to become soldiers could, upon profession of faith, be enrolled as "Adherent Members".[77]

The Salvation Army in the "West" would now appear to be facing more acutely than hitherto the situation outlined by a Wesleyan preacher in 1907: "All the Christian Churches of England today have to deal with the question of their relation to numbers of people who join them in public worship, subscribe to their funds, live honourable lives, but decline to take the definite responsibilities of Church membership."[78] A crisis is faced when external recruitment tails off and endogenous growth is not providing replacement recruits. In the light of the tendency for sects to make less rigorous demands upon their members as they denominationalise, this change in the requirements for "Adherents" could be interpreted in more than one way. It raises the bar for Adherents by requiring a profession of faith, but it lowers the bar for Salvationists who wish to belong without embracing the sectarian lifestyle of soldiership, leading some to question the future of Soldiership: "Does it lower our standards? Will soldiership survive? Why become a soldier?"[79]

Major David Taylor proposed in 2004 a solution somewhat akin to Cleary's.

> Presently many types of ministry and leadership are only for soldiers [that is, excluding Adherents], deeply threatening the integrity of the "priesthood of all believers" which *Servants Together* seeks to uphold. The Army faces the spectacle of two tiers of membership, in which to be an adherent – a Christian and a member of God's church – is to be a second class member of The Salvation Army, with restricted access to ministry. If we want to work out the consequences of transitioning towards "a Church", it will be more authentic biblically to embrace adherents (with a more helpful name) as full members and to acknowledge soldiership as an order within this branch of the Church,

76 Paper prepared by Gordon Taylor for leaders at the request of General Larsson in 2003.

77 John Larsson, Letter to Territorial Commanders, Officers Commanding, National Commander, International Secretaries and all other members of the General's Consultative Council, 12 September 2003; Minute 2004/IA/05.

78 Gilbert, *Religion and Society*, pp. 198-9.

79 *Horizons* (May/June 2005) p. 11.

> in some ways akin to the Nazarites, with whom Paul identifies on several occasions. The only alternative would be to scrap Adherency and keep to being an Order within the Church, a decision that is no longer realistic for us at this stage of our development.[80]

Can a case still be made for seeing the Salvation Army as an "order" within the Church as a whole, as an alternative to the present acquiescence to "denominational" type-casting? It would be no more counter-cultural than the Army's sacramental position. However, David Martin draws attention to the fact that orders in the Catholic church have provided a domain for Christian *virtuosi,* those with an exceptional vocation. Because Protestantism in theory rejected this dual standard for Christians, "in Protestant cultures all men are called to be tertiaries".[81] By "denominationalising", the process whereby a sect loses its zeal and its members accept for themselves an "ordinary" rather than an "exceptional" spirituality, the sect becomes like the Catholic church from which it sought to distance itself, and a new elite has to emerge within it. Both Taylor's and Cleary's proposals acknowledge that this is what has happened to the Salvation Army.

The pastoral implications of these "tiers of membership" have been alluded to in connection with uniform-wearing (see p. 60). The setting of such boundaries of association is particularly appropriate to what James Fowler would characterise as a "Level Three" kind of faith, comfortable for people requiring firm direction, black and white morality and official answers to all questions, and which have therefore served the Salvation Army well.[82] The model is what Paul Hiebert describes as a "bounded set", where high thresholds protect the doctrine and mores of the ecclesial body, as against a "centred set", where attention is on message rather than the rules, and all-comers are equally valued.[83] The "bounded set" culture now contributes, at least in the "West", to declining membership rolls as many who grow in another direction no longer feel comfortable in such a milieu.

An alternative view on this is provided by Rodney Stark's "religious economy" model, whereby sects which maintain a moderate to high tension with society, making greater demands upon their members but offering higher rewards (in terms of status in this life and felicity in the next), are

---

80 David Taylor, "Army, Order or Church? An attempt to locate The Salvation Army within the wider family of churches and to consider the implications of this position." (Paper read to the United Kingdom Territory Theological Symposium, July 2004) p. 15.

81 David Martin, *Pacifism* (London, Routledge and Kegan Paul, 1965) p. 163, quoted by Michael Hill, *The Religious Order* (London, Heinemann, 1973) p. 15.

82 James Fowler, *Stages of Faith* (New York: Harper Collins, 1981) pp. 151-73.

83 Paul Hiebert, *Mission and Renewal of the Church* (Pasadena CA: Fuller, 1983).

likely to grow, while denominations which have relaxed that tension and no longer insist that their members "come out from among them" tend to lose market share.[84] The growing churches – tending to be right-wing, fundamentalist, charismatic – mop up those people still attracted by the "bounded set" culture. Wilson notes that "some sects show a capacity for growth and endurance, even when major religious organizations are suffering decline if not decay."[85] The comparison with newer conservative bodies suggests further that the growing preference for membership rather than soldiership, with less stringent personal commitments to the organisation, can also be seen as indicative of a continuing denominationalising tendency in the Salvation Army. Perhaps all this may argue that the Salvation Army is losing members in both directions or failing to gain recruits from either – some preferring a more liberal approach and others gravitating to more conservative bodies.

Comparisons between the Salvation Army and the Church do however lead to one further observation. In both the Salvation Army and the Catholic Church in particular a shortage of vocations to officership or priesthood has, as we have seen, been met by an increase in the number soldiers or laity involved in roles hitherto reserved for commissioned or ordained people. Yves Congar, so radical as to warrant silencing by the Vatican in the 1950s, now sounds positively reactionary on this. Allowing that the laity could be involved in the temporal but not the spiritual or ecclesiastical aspects of the church's life, he was at pains to caution that even such temporal involvement "is not properly power, authority, participation in the ruling function of the church as power… It is chimerical to consider handing over the care of the Church's temporalities to the laity… This task of the Church should be for its essential part, in the hands of Churchmen."[86]

The more recent expansion of ministries in the life of the Church has been deplored as a distraction from the laity's real task of witness and service to the world. Pope John Paul II in *Christifideles Laici* n. 13, 1987, has warned of the laity "being so strongly interested in Church services and tasks that some fail to become actively engaged in their responsibilities in the professional, social, cultural and political world."[87] This has become a theme, repeated in, for example, the Vatican's *Instruction on Certain Questions Regarding the Collaboration of the Non-Ordained Faithful in the Sacred Ministry of Priests* (15 August 1997), which aroused strong

---

84 Stark and Fink, *Acts of Faith*, pp. 193-217.

85 Wilson, "The Persistence of Sects", *DISKUS,* 1:2 (1993) p. 1.

86 Congar, *Lay People in the Church*, pp. 244-6, 254.

87 Neil Ormerod "Mission and Ministry in the Wake of Vatican II" in *Australian Ejournal of Theology*. Downloaded 23 February 2004 from (http//://dlibrary.acu.edu.au/research/theology/ejournal/aet_Ormerod.htm).

reactions.[88] Mary Ann Glendon, Harvard law professor and member of the Pontifical Council for the Laity, has regretted that "many Catholics came to believe that the principal way to be active as Catholics is to participate in the internal life of the Church."[89] A similar critique from a Lutheran source claims that

> American Evangelicalism has spawned what may be referred to as "neo-monasticism". Like its medieval counterpart, neo-monasticism gives the impression that religious work is more God-pleasing than other tasks and duties associated with life in the world... Similar to neo-monasticism is the neo-clericalism which lurks behind the slogan, "Everyone a minister". This phrase implies that work is worthwhile only insofar as it resembles the work done by pastors.[90]

Similar anxieties have been expressed about the "clericalisation of the laity" in the Salvation Army debate reviewed in these pages. The difference between the Church and the Salvation Army lies in the fact that the Army does not in theory reserve spiritual ministry and leadership roles for a sacerdotal class. The similarity lies in the fact that in practice, because of its hierarchical structure, the Army has tended to behave in the same way as the Church, and change in this area therefore occasions similar tensions.

---

88 See Helen Hitchcock, "Vatican Instruction on Lay Ministry...", *Voices*, XIII, 1-2, Online Edition. Downloaded 1 November 2004 from (http://www.wf-f.org/priest(win-spr98).html).

89 Mary Ann Glendon, "The Hour of the Laity", *First Things*, 127 (November 2002) pp. 23-9. Downloaded 25 May 2004 from (http://print.firstthings.com/ftissues/ft0211/articles/glendon.html).

90 John T. Pless, "Vocation: Where Liturgy and Ethics Meet", *Journal of Lutheran Ethics* 2:5 (13 May 2002). Downloaded 29 December 2005 from (www.elca.org/jle/articles/vocation/article.pless_john.html).

Chapter Sixteen

A Monstrous Regiment of Women[1]

Some of my best men are women.

Attributed to William Booth

> Like many sayings attributed to public figures, this remark may be apocryphal, or part of the Army's oral tradition. According to Gordon Taylor, it first appeared in print in Albert Orsborn's 1958 autobiography, *The House of My Pilgrimage*. Given that Orsborn's parents were early day officers and that he himself was commissioned in 1905, it may have been part of his family tradition. Richard Collier accepted it as genuine in his 1964 *The General Next to God* and Flora Larsson used it as the title of her book about Salvation Army women officers in 1974. Jenty Fairbank found a similar quote from Booth in *The War Cry* of 4 January 1887. When Booth was speaking in New York on the 7 December 1886, "a gentleman enquired, 'Why do you have women leaders?' To this the General replied with a bland smile, 'Because they often lead better than men.'"[2]

If a question at the heart of this study is whether Salvation Army officers are, or are not, clergy, the question may have even more point in the case of women Salvation Army officers, given that ordination of women was not generally accepted in the nineteenth century. While the Army has usually explained its stand on gender equality in theological terms, sociologists have seen its championing of women's rights as yet another aspect of sectarian protest of the disinherited. Werner Stark sees the suffragette movement and Mary Baker Eddy's Christian Science sect, contemporary with the Booths, in the same light.[3] James A. Beckford, relating "the question of gender relations in religious communities" to "the dynamic between individuals and collectives", observes that "religious movements permit and encourage some dramatically extreme forms of gendered social relations and innovative approaches to sexuality among their members. [Some] seem to favour a heightened form of subordination of women to men. At the other

---

1 I cannot claim this seriously inappropriate pun on John Knox as my own; Lt. Colonel Bernard Watson has anticipated me in *A Hundred Years War* (London: Hodder & Stoughton 1964) p. 28.

2 *Salvationist* (19 February 1994) p. 12.

3 Werner Stark, *Sectarian Religion*, p. 41.

extreme there are religious movements... that have aspired towards... unusually high degrees of equality between male and female followers in some respects."[4]

The Boast

While the Army was not the first to accept the ministry of women on equal terms with that of men (the Quakers recognised women preachers as equal with men), equality of the sexes has always been one of the Army's boasts. "In the Army," wrote Florence Booth, "we know no distinction, because of sex, which is calculated to limit either a woman's influence or her authority, or her opportunity to serve, by sacrifice, the Kingdom of God."[5]

Over many years, Salvationists regarded the struggles of other denominations over this question with a certain smugness. Bramwell Booth said, "Few things the Army stands for have been more bitterly assailed than this – that woman is on an equality with man. Even yet many of the civil laws in the West make differences against her, although many have been altered. Many of the churches still refuse to allow her to witness for Christ in their 'sacred' buildings and their privileged conventicles. But, in general, the western world has changed its views, and very soon the religious section of it will have to follow or be hopelessly left behind."[6] Of the furore following the ordination of eleven women by the American Protestant Episcopal Church in 1974, the editor of *The Officer* wrote, "Salvationists may be forgiven for asking, in response to such an item of news... What is all the fuss about? We settled the issue long ago."[7]

In fact such smugness was not always justified, and on two grounds. The first was theological, in that Salvation Army commentators did not always understand that the debate had moved on; by the twentieth century the point at issue was not whether women could exercise public ministry, but whether they could be priests. The Army's tendency to overlook the distinction probably arose from the sketchy nature of its own theology of ministry. A later editor acknowledged this point, noting that "in one sense it might seems that we are not concerned with such an argument. The Salvationist stands outside all controversies between sacramental Christians..."[8] (Although he did go on to make the point that any officer, of whatever sex, is competent to administer whatever means of grace Salvationists do

4 James A. Beckford, *Social Theory and Religion* (Cambridge: Cambridge University Press, 2003) p. 181.
5 *Officer* (August 1914) pp. 509-10.
6 W. Bramwell Booth, *Talks with Officers*, p. 16.
7 *Officer* (November 1974) p. 527.
8 *Officer* (January 1979) pp. 1-2.

practise.) Commenting on the 1992 decision of the Church of England General Synod to ordain women, *The Salvationist* editor noted that "We ought not to use the moment to boast … There are too many differences between Army officership and Anglican priesthood to make the comparison very useful."[9]

The second reason for some modesty on the question is that the Army's practice has not always matched its precepts. In fact, over much of its history the Army appeared to retreat from its early promise of gender equality, certainly relative to the general movement of Western society, and even by its own standards. Certainly this view was held by Mrs General Marie Wahlström, who referred to the equality of sexes in the Army's early days when speaking at the 1984 International Conference of Leaders. She went on to ask, "Would it not be correct to say that today this is rather the exception than the rule. If so, when and how was the development reversed? Has the development of the Army begun to move in the opposite direction to the general trend in society, where women are increasingly active in every field…?"[10] Or Mrs Commissioner Marjorie Gauntlett, wife of the Chief of the Staff, claimed in an interview in the same year that "The role of women in The Salvation Army seems to be going backwards – it's less now than when we started!"[11] Or Mrs Commissioner Marjorie Hodder, on her installation as National President of Women's Organisations in the United States in 1993, observed that "among the twenty-two officers holding the principal positions of leadership in the USA today, not one is a woman."[12]

Such concern was not new: Mrs General Bramwell Booth wrote in 1913 that

> Sometimes I am almost tempted to feel that the progress of woman's position in the SA might be described in the words of the Irishman who wrote to a friend from one of the battlefields of the American Civil War, "We are advancing backwards and the enemy is retreating on to us!"[13]

In 1930 Staff-Captain Mary MacFarlane of Australia had claimed that

> to many of the younger thinking women-Officers of The Army, this question of equality of treatment and opportunity for men and women in the Army is a burning one. Many of them work on Headquarters where they see and hear much that makes them ask – "ARE EQUAL STANDARDS MAINTAINED

---

9 *Salvationist* (28 November 1992) p. 2.

10 Mrs General Marie Wahlström, "The Place and Position of the Woman Officer in The Salvation Army" (Paper read at the 1984 International Conference of Leaders, Berlin.)

11 *New Frontier* (30 June 1984) p. 1.

12 *WC* (USA) (23 October 1993) p. 19.

13 *Field Officer* (March 1913) p. 84.

> FOR MEN AND WOMEN OFFICERS ACCORDING TO THE ARMY'S CONSTITUTION?" And with no uncertain voice they are answering "No!"[14]

In some ways the experience of women officers parallels that of soldiers in the dynamic of Salvation Army history – beginning with a claim to equality, then experiencing a steady eclipse in role and respect, and then a slow and as yet tentative reassertion of significance. Another parallel might be found in the internationalism of the Army, always claimed as a leading principle but also perhaps honoured in the breach. Despite its rapid international advance and the pioneering appointments to high rank of a very few Asian leaders, the high command of the Army remained largely European, if not British, in character until late in the twentieth century. Like Hobbes' papacy, the Army resembled the ghost of the deceased British Empire lingering, crowned, and seated upon its grave. Only at the first High Council of the twenty-first century did non-Europeans comprise as many as a third of its members, although by now 80% of Salvationists could be found in Africa, India, Asia and Central/South America. (824,533 soldiers out of 1,025,173 world-wide in the 2004 *Yearbook*.) Lack of third world leadership has arisen from colonialist attitudes and inadequate personnel strategies and training. It is difficult to avoid the conclusion that change has been forced upon the Army by political considerations and the non-availability of visas as much as by progressively enlightened attitudes. Commissioner Paul du Plessis notes that "Both Methodism and The Salvation Army have been committed to the deployment of national full-time workers and leadership. But the extent to which the Army has retained central control militates against this ideal."[15] The comparison with female ministry is not so far-fetched: in both cases the cultural conditioning is about power and control – which is the shadow side of orders in the church.

These three chapters trace the rise and fall and rise again of gender equality in the Salvation Army.

Catherine Booth

Catherine Booth was of course the moving spirit and exemplar of the role of women in the Army, having been a freelance preacher of some reputation from the early 1860s. Although she never held a rank or an independent command in her own right, Catherine Booth was in the centre of the Army's counsels as long as she lived and was known then and later as the "Mother of the Salvation Army". The movement's ethos reflects not only the force of her influence but also her husband's support for her position. Catherine's

14 *Staff Review* (October 1930) p. 339.

15 *Word and Deed* (November 2004) p. 9.

first essay on the rights of women, written at the age of 21, was a rebuttal of rather patronising and derogatory words about woman as a moral being, in a sermon she heard in a Congregational Church.[16] The following year a connexional magazine article signed "C.M." (Catherine Mumford, her maiden name) claimed, "It is a significant fact that in the most cold, formal and worldly churches of the day we find the least female agency."[17]

Shortly before her marriage she addressed one of her long, instructional letters to her intended, about teetotalism (which he had adopted at her persuasion), and the equality of women with men in ministry. He responded briefly, "I would not stop a woman preaching on any account. I would not encourage one to begin. You should preach if you felt moved thereto; felt equal to the task. I would not stay you if I had the power to do so. Altho' I should not like it..."[18]

Catherine Booth was strong-minded, but far from a virago; none of this meant that she saw herself in this preaching role. As a young married woman when she was invited to address a Church leaders' meeting in the Circuit, "Of course I declined... I don't know what they can be thinking of."[19] Her next step was more public however. In 1859, Sunderland minister Arthur Rees attacked the preaching of Mrs Phoebe Palmer, then touring England, later publishing his sermon as a pamphlet. Catherine sprang to the lady's defence with a pamphlet of her own, the vigorous and erudite *Female Preaching*.[20] It was not until the following year, however, that she herself told her husband, "I want to say a word," and preached at Gateshead's Bethesda Chapel on Whitsunday 1860. She continued to fill churches for the following twenty-eight years, and William *did* like it. Not infrequently in the early years of their freelance ministry, the family survived on Catherine's earnings from platform and pulpit.

Within weeks of Catherine's first sermon, William fell ill and for the following nine weeks Catherine filled his preaching engagements in the Circuit. In a letter to William, who was away recuperating at a health spa, she wrote, "Don't forget to pray for me. I have borne the weight of circuit matters to an extent I could not have believed possible and have been literally the 'Superintendent'."[21] After the founding of the Christian Mission similar situations arose – according to Sandall, in 1872 Catherine ran the

---

16 Letter to Rev. David Thomas, in 1850; Catherine Bramwell Booth, *Catherine Booth*, pp. 49-52.

17 F.L. Coutts, *In Good Company* (London: SA, 1980) p. 64.

18 Catherine Bramwell Booth, *Catherine Booth*, p. 143.

19 Catherine Booth, letter to her mother in 1858, quoted in Catherine Bramwell Booth, *Catherine Booth*, pp. 180-1.

20 Reprinted in various forms, including as a chapter in Catherine Booth's *Practical Religion* (London: SA, 4th edn 1891) pp. 131-67. Later titled *Female Ministry*.

21 Catherine Bramwell Booth, *Catherine Booth*, p. 190.

Mission for six months while William was having a nervous breakdown from over-work.[22] That the Booths were seen by others as equal in ministry is suggested by the foundation stone of Methodist Church at Ninfield East, Sussex, laid in July 1871 "...by Mrs Booth, assisted by the Rev. Wm. Booth, Founders of the Christian Mission".[23]

Encouraged by Catherine's example others joined forces. In 1870 Mrs Collingridge, who in 1868 was the first person employed by the Mission, was Superintendent of the Shoreditch Circuit and presided at meetings, becoming the first woman to hold office in the Mission as well. She was the usual preacher at the Peoples' Mission Hall, Whitechapel Road, and when her health broke down, was replaced by Mrs Reynolds. In 1873 Miss Billups and Miss Funnell were supply evangelists while Miss Walker and Miss Sutton assisted at Whitechapel and Poplar respectively.[24] From 1874 however, evangelists were not merely on "supply", but stationed in charge of their local mission stations. Of the 27 evangelists early in 1875, 8 were women, but none of these were "in command".[25] However, there was a shortage of Evangelists for the expanding work and, encouraged by Railton, Booth considered appointing more women, and in charge.

The 1875 Conference, over the reservations of some Evangelists and even of Mrs Booth,[26] appointed Annie Davis in charge of the Barking Station – in what Railton described as a "daring experiment". Evangelist Abram Lamb resigned over this development.[27] Her success led to women evangelists being in the forefront of the great expansion by the end of the decade. Sisters Rachel and Louise Agar opened fire on Felling on Tyne in March 1878, the printer dubbing them "Hallelujah Lasses" on their posters. Booth or Railton wrote, "We have commenced operations on the Tyne at Felling, where a Mr Sharp... importuned us to send a sister. We sent two, and such has already been their success that we are sending two more, with whose help they will be able immediately to seize another town."[28] Within twelve months there were 22 Stations, 47 officers and more than 3,000 members in the Tyne district.[29]

In Coventry Mrs Caroline Reynolds and Mrs Honor Burrell led the charge. While Mrs Burrell was a widow, Mrs Reynolds was accompanied by her husband, who was not employed by the Mission. At Salisbury, Mrs

22 Sandall, *History*, I, pp. 144-5.
23 Wesley Harris, *Salvationist* (20 May 2000) p. 24.
24 *Christian Mission Magazine* (September 1873) p. 136.
25 *Officer* (November 1972) p. 517.
26 W. Bramwell Booth, *Echoes and Memories*, pp. 178-9.
27 Catherine Bramwell Booth, *Catherine Booth*, p. 263.
28 *Christian Mission Magazine* (May 1878) p. 122.
29 Sandall, *History*, II, p. 7.

Sarah Sayers was assisted by 16-year old Henry Edmonds.[30] Of 91 officers in the field in 1878, 41 were women.[31] By 1880, women were in charge of 46 out of 118 Corps.[32]

Mrs Reynolds, her husband deceased, went on to open fire in Ireland in 1880, and in this appointment became first woman Divisional Officer.[33] Mrs Major Harriet Lawley served briefly as Divisional Officer for the Channel Islands in 1887 as a married woman (baby in arms) but had to give it up for family reasons – her husband, John Lawley, worked in the Candidates Department but then became ADC to William Booth.[34] Captain Polly Ashton, with an encouraging letter from the dying Catherine Booth, was appointed "England's first woman Divisional Officer" only in 1890.[35] Bramwell Booth paid tribute to the examples of his sister Catherine as pioneer and leader of the Army in France and Switzerland from 1881 and of Hannah Ouchterlony as pioneer and leader in Sweden from 1883, as showing "that there was no adequate reason for withholding the higher Commands from women".[36]

The role of women was enshrined in the Constitution of the Christian Mission, Section XII of which stated,

> Female Preachers – As it is manifest from the Scripture of the Old and especially the New Testament that God has sanctioned the labours of Godly women in His Church; Godly women possessing the necessary gifts and qualifications, shall be employed as preachers itinerant or otherwise and class leaders and as such shall have appointments given to them on the preacher's plan; and they shall be eligible for any office, and to speak and vote at all official meetings.[37]

The Orders and Regulations for Salvation Army Staff Officers followed this up with,

> One of the leading principles upon which the Army is based is the right of women to have the right to an equal share with men in the great work of publishing Salvation to the world... She may hold any position of authority or power in the Army from that of a Local Officer to that of the General. Let it

30 Sandall, *History*, I, pp. 177, 214-5.

31 Flora Larsson, *My Best Men Are Women* (London: Hodder and Stoughton, 1974) p. 17.

32 P.J. Walker, "Proclaiming Women's Right to Preach", *Harvard Divinity Bulletin* (1994) p. 22.

33 Sandall, *History*, II, pp. 18-9.

34 Minnie Lindsay Carpenter, *Commissioner Lawley* (London: SA, 1924) p. 96.

35 Jenty Fairbank, *Salvationist* (14 October 1995) p. 10.

36 W. Bramwell Booth, *Echoes and Memories*, p. 181.

37 *Christian Mission Magazine* (July 1877) pp. 182-3.

therefore be understood that women are eligible for the highest commands – indeed, no woman is to be kept back from any position of power or influence merely on account of her sex... Woman must be treated as equal with men in all the intellectual and social relationships of life.[38]

Although the reiterated gender-exclusive language of the Orders and Regulations strikes a discord in this age, for the nineteenth century the Army's stance was radical. An introductory note to the Orders and Regulations for Field Officers of 1886 and subsequently also safeguarded this commitment:

> In the Army men and women are alike eligible for all ranks authorities and duties, all positions being open to both alike. In these Orders, therefore, the words "man," "he," or "his" must be understood to refer to persons of either sex, unless otherwise indicated or evidently impossible.[39]

At intervals William Booth promoted the principle of equality. For example, in 1901 he wrote a "Letter to the Soldiers of the Salvation Army" on "Salvation Women", about the Position and Opportunities possessed by Woman in the Army.

> Shall we tell them (young girls in the Army) that they are to grow up and settle down to the idea that the back-door drudgery of the Corps is all that lies before them? – that they can Give and Collect and do Tea Meetings and Harvest Festivals? That they can have Husbands and Children, and keep their Homes in order with a little singing, and a prayer, and a testimony or two thrown in now and then? Or shall we say to them, "Come along and take your stand by our side on the Salvation Army platform?..."

Quoting from *The Orders and Regulations for Staff Officers* he reiterated

> Let it therefore be understood that no Woman is to be kept back from any position of power or influence merely on account of her sex.[40]

Booth returned to the subject in November with another letter, "More about Women's Rights", in which he urged women to take the initiative and claim their place.[41] In another letter on the subject, in 1908, to be read out in

---

38 *Orders and Regulations for Staff Officers of The Salvation Army in the United Kingdom* (London: SA, 1895) pp. 16-7.
39 *The Orders and Regulations for Field Officers* (1886) [p. iv].
40 *Field Officer* (September 1901) pp. 422-4.
41 *Field Officer* (November 1901) pp. 513-4.

every Corps on the 23rd of August that year, he stated that "woman is equal to man."[42]

Women went on to provide more than half of the officer strength of the Army, since over the years there have usually been more single women officers than single men, and in the case of married couples, both partners have been officers. In the earlier years the Army's ranks offered a greater opportunity for independence than most available for women. Horridge notes that "by the 1890s, more women Methodists and Anglicans were becoming officers, for the Army still offered a greater degree of equality than available elsewhere in religious societies."[43] In every part of the world women became the shock troops of salvation.

Some achieved some celebrity beyond the ranks. Thousands of others have worked unsung for many years in hard and lonely places. Of single women officers Bramwell Booth wrote that, "Those women are worthy successors of the Apostles. Their devotion to the interests of others, their kindness, their patient toil, their enduring zeal, their humble following in the footsteps of their Master have done much to make The Salvation Army what it is." Booth, while not claiming any special virtue for the single life, noted with approbation that many single women officers chose to remain single rather than to "marry out of the work".[44] Reportedly pressure was sometimes put on women not to marry: William Booth forbade Evangeline to marry, saying to her suitor, "You and Eva are both too important to The Salvation Army as individual leaders to be tied up together."[45]

The Glass Ceiling

There was another side to all this of course, and because it bears on our theme it must be explored as well. Whatever the Army's aspirations to equality, women were not treated equally with their brethren in many respects. The phenomenon of the glass ceiling was painfully apparent to women officers long before Ann Morrison identified the problem in the American corporate world. Mary MacFarlane, already quoted, gave examples from Australia of women being given less significant appointments than men and deprived of opportunities, their relegation to tea-making and sandwich-serving while men junior to themselves were given

42 Quoted by Mary Morris, "Female Ministry, Equality and the Salvation Army" (Dissertation, Oak Hill Theological College, London. Undated but accessed by the Heritage Centre Archives on 6 April 1998).

43 Horridge, *Origins*, p. 225.

44 W. Bramwell Booth, *Servants*, p. 109.

45 Margaret Troutt, *The General Was a Lady* (Nashville: A.J. Holman, 1980) p. 78.

recognition and authority, and the dearth of women in executive roles and on Boards.

Lt.-Commissioner Mrs Povlsen, commenting on MacFarlane's article, quoted "a lady doctor who ... declared her opinion that a woman officer would have to be practically abnormally gifted in order to get the same place in the ranks as an average man." [46] A similar comment was made in a 1948 radio lecture on "The woman officer of the Salvation Army" by Dr Laura Petrie of Sweden.[47] (Was she the same doctor?) Major Jenty Fairbank held the same view forty years later: "For a woman to be recognised as equal to a man she must show exceptional qualities – far surpassing his."[48]

Internationally, there has always been a tiny minority of senior women leaders – and this was true even in the days when there were far more women officers than at present. The 1908 *Year Book* listed only two women as Territorial Commanders, while Mrs Bramwell Booth was the executive head of Women's Social Work, assisted by Commissioner Adelaide Cox. In 1920 there were three women Territorial Commanders – all of them Booths – and two other women Commissioners. Soundings in the *Year Book* at ten year intervals between 1910 and 2000 reveal that the highest number of women Commissioners, Territorial Commanders or Officers Commanding was six, in 1990; numbers mostly fluctuated between two and four. An analysis of High Council membership provides the following figures:

Year	Number attending	Number of women included
1929	63	7 (5 of them Booths)
1934	47	4 (3 of them Booths)
1939	55	2
1946	50	3
1954	48	3
1963	49	3
1969	45	2
1974	40	3
1977	41	3
1981	44	2
1986	46	5
1993	50	3
1994	44	2

Sources:[49] (After 1994 the criteria for attendance were altered.)

46 *Staff Review* (October, 1930) p. 348.
47 Flora Larsson, *My Best Men*, p. 83.
48 *Officer* (October 1988) p. 408.
49 Frederick Coutts, *History* VI, pp. 85-8, 123-6, 155-8, 283-6; Frederick Coutts, *The Weapons of Goodwill: History of The Salvation Army* VII (London: Hodder &

Only two out of the eighteen Generals to date have been women; Evangeline Booth 1934-39 and Eva Burrows 1986-93. In the history of The Salvation Army in New Zealand there have been only three women Divisional Commanders – Brigadier Florence Birks in the 1940s (being also Training Principal at the same time), Lt.-Colonel Edna Grice in the 1950s and Lt.-Colonel Raeline Savage, a married woman, in the 1990s.[50] There have been no women Territorial Commanders or Chief Secretaries in New Zealand – nor in the majority of Territories.

In most countries the number of single woman officers, once the backbone of both Field (Corps) and Social work, has steadily diminished. This has been partly because of the "officers marry officers" policy – and partly because of a decline in the number of unmarried candidates. In New Zealand, for example, analysis of appointments given in the annual *Disposition of Forces* shows that in 1918 there were 142 single women officers out of a total of 408 – 34.8% of the total. 80 out of 142 social officers were single women (25 were men 25 were their wives, and 12 were single men.) Single women provided 54 out of 146 field officers (45 of these were men, with 45 wives, and there were 2 single men.) This means that about a third of all Corps were led by single women, usually appointed in pairs, at that time. While single women have usually been appointed to smaller Corps, especially in recent decades, a minority have held large field commands. Two women were leading the largest Auckland Corps in 1918. By contrast, in 1998 there were 16 single women amongst a total of 380 officers – 4.2%. Of these, there were 9 single women in social work out of a total of 95 officers, and 7 out of a total of 191 field officers, leading about 6% of Corps. In 2006, just four New Zealand Corps were led by three single women, working on their own (one being responsible for two centres).

Richard Pears gives the figure of 168 single women out of 1,184 field officers in the United Kingdom Territory in 1996, with no women Divisional Commanders amongst the eighteen officers in that position.[51] The decline in the number of women officers in top leadership positions reflects the decline in the number of single women officers, as well as the Army's reluctance to give independent senior commands to married women. Single officers are always more "appointable" and the majority of single officers are women. Insecurity of tenure is a disincentive to retention or recruitment.

The fact is that gender equality has probably always been resisted to some extent within the Army. Bramwell Booth recalled that this had been

---

Stoughton, 1986) pp. 70-2, 154-6, 241-3, 294-6, 324-6; Henry Gariepy, *History*, VIII, pp. 70-1, 134-5, 285-6, 300-2.

50 Information from New Zealand *Disposition of Forces*.

51 Richard Pears, "Towards a Theology of Salvation Army Officership; An Examination of Officer Ministry in the United Kingdom" (MTh thesis, Oxford, 1996) p. 60.

the case from the beginning. "Some of the men who had been converted in the Mission … as soon as they found themselves in office and with a certain influence in their own societies, demurred when women were placed beside them in similar positions… To place a woman in charge of one of these Societies… involved a new departure… Some of the leading Evangelists… were opposed to anything of this kind."[52] Catherine Bramwell Booth believed that "many Salvation Army officers have accepted the Booths' ruling as to the position of women in the movement rather because it was their ruling than because the principle had been either understood or approved." She also suggested that Bramwell Booth was in the end deposed because his subordinates feared that he had nominated a woman to succeed him.[53] Alas, it was probably not because they feared women in general, but a *particular* woman – Bramwell's daughter, Catherine herself, whose name was believed to be in the sealed envelope. They did, after all, elect Evangeline Booth five years later. On the other hand, Evangeline was then 69 years of age, and they knew they would not have her forever, whereas Catherine was only 46 at the time. Had they known she would live to be 104, no doubt that would have strengthened their resolve.

Colonel Julius Nielsen of Czechoslovakia / Hungary, invited by the editor to comment on MacFarlane's article, questioned

> the wisdom of women-Officers being made Divisional Commanders, or being given similar positions… Take the highest positions in the Army – those of the General, and the Chief of the Staff: surely every one of us wishes to see only a strong man in those positions… Let me speak quite frankly. We all know… that there are times when a woman needs to be alone in quietness and certainly not on the public platform. Her whole mental outlook and ability are influenced by the condition in to which women come at such times.[54]

One can only imagine the reaction of the soon-to-be General, Evangeline Booth, on reading this delicate allusion.

At grass roots level, male chauvinism has continued to be alive and well. When Captain Minnie Rowell was appointed to Fremantle, Australia, in the 1890s "the soldiers let her know; we don't want women officers. You can't manage our corps."[55] In his memoirs Cyril Bradwell records the diffidence of Adjutant Edna Grice when appointed as Commanding Officer of the Linwood Corps in 1938, "in that male dominant decade", when "lassie officers had not commanded the corps since before the beginning of the

---

52 W. Bramwell Booth, *Echoes*, pp. 177- 8.

53 Catherine Bramwell Booth, *Bramwell Booth*, p. 198.

54 *Staff Officer* (October 1930) pp. 346-7.

55 Stella Carpenter, *A Man of Peace in a World of War* (Montville, Qld: Privately published, 1993) p. 63.

century."[56] Richard Pears in his 1996 thesis says that "anecdotal evidence gathered from dialogue with soldiers over recent years coupled to the comments of the interview group (of officers) clearly suggests that Corps in fact do not really want single women officers as their leaders… it is not unreasonable to suggest that the autocratic structure of the Army, which enables the officer appointment system to function, has also been instrumental in maintaining women officers in ministry. Had there been a membership-based selection system it may well have been a different story."[57] Colonel Brindley Boon wrote a column on "Feminism" on reading of a married couple described as the "Commanding Officers" of a corps, and quoted with apparent approval "a heading in my morning paper which stated, 'It is still the men who wear the trousers and the women who iron them.'"[58] He was duly castigated by other correspondents.

One American woman sued the Army in 1970 for discriminating against her in appointments on the basis of her sex. The Army won the case on the grounds that relations between a church and its Ministers were exempt from the relevant provisions of the Civil Rights Act.[59]

The overlooking of the possibility of women's contributions is not confined to matters of appointment and promotion. A 1991 *Officer* editorial asked, "Where are the women?", and drew attention to the fact that at the 1989 International Strategy for Growth Conference, 80 out of 96 delegates were men.[60] A Commission on Wellington appointed in July 2002 to propose rationalisation of Salvation Army services in the City, consisted of one woman and eight men (all of whom were officers). To be fair, it transpired that it had been intended all the officers responsible for Wellington city appointments, both husbands and wives, would attend the meetings. That the wives all chose not to attend, or had perhaps not been specifically invited, also reflected the culture. Again, when two delegates were nominated by leadership from each of the three Australasian Territories to form a Tri-Territorial Theological Forum in 2003, members of the new body discovered that only men had been chosen. (Three women were appointed upon this being made known.)

In Western countries the retirement age for single women officers has until recently been set lower than that of men; 60 as compared with 65. When men Commissioners retired at 70, women Commissioners retired at 65, until 1986, when a graduated lowering of the retirement age to 65 was

56 Bradwell, *Touched With Splendour*, p. 250.

57 Pears, Thesis, "Towards a theology", p. 64.

58 *Salvationist* (10 March 1990) p. 3.

59 Ed. McKinley, *Marching to Glory*, p. 203. (McClure v. Salvation Army, 323 F.Supp. II00 (1971) aff'd at 460 F.2d 553 (Sth Cir. 1972), cert. denied, 409 U.S. 896, 93 S.Ct. 132 (1972).)

60 *Officer* (September 1991) p. 385.

instituted. In the 1970s Major Roy Lovatt of Great Britain suggested that this was one reason for the lack of women in the higher levels of leadership and proposed that "equal length of service is more likely to produce a more equal balance of leadership than any other single factor."[61] This was vigorously denied by Lt.-Colonel Ruth Brewer of USA who believed such a change would only make "necessary a longer time for them to live with existing inequities!"[62]

Some of those inequities have been material. Financial differentials and discriminatory housing practices have in part derived from the English class system (inevitably echoed in the international but long British-centred Salvation Army hierarchy) and the application, until the last quarter of the twentieth century, of benefits for those higher up the pecking order. Such factors have perhaps impacted more on single women officers simply because few of them have risen high in the hierarchy.

For many years the rates of allowances (officers are not guaranteed wages or salary) discriminated against women. For example, when *The Officer* of February 1897 announced new allowances, single men Captains were to receive15/5 per week and Lieutenants 12/-; single women Captains were to receive 12/- and Lieutenants 9/-. A Minute of 1948 set the allowances of male and female Probationary-Lieutenants at £1.17.0d and £1.14.0d respectively.[63] Complaints about this sort of thing were not aired in print in the early days, whatever the private thoughts of the officers. While Staff-Captain Mary MacFarlane, in the October 1930 *Staff Officer* article already cited, denied that equal standards were maintained "in the matter of salary and quarters", she did not allude so much to the discriminatory pay rates as to the living conditions. Field and Social officers had quarters provided free, as did married staff officers, while single staff officers had to find their own accommodation and were allowed a mere 5/- extra for rent. She was supported in this complaint by Commissioner Johanna Van den Werken, to whom also the editor had referred the article for comment.[64] In fact it was the normal expectation of society that women could live more cheaply than men. Equality in Salvation Army single officer allowances was achieved after the Second World War, still putting the Army well in advance of secular salary structures. Finding a just balance between single officer and married couple allowances remains a vexed question, however.

A continuing sense of grievance is however evidenced by a letter from Major Fay Lewis (British Territory) who joined in a 1988 exchange on the plight of officer wives. "As I look at the role of female officers in our movement, I feel that in spite of the fact that our General is unmarried, the

---

61 *Officer* (January 1976) p. 37.
62 *Officer* (June 1976) p. 279.
63 *Salvationist* (12 July 2003).
64 *Staff Review* (October 1930) pp. 340, 353.

people who have suffered most are the single officers. I am becoming increasingly convinced that there will gradually be no place for us, unless it is to fulfil the 'demeaning roles'." (An earlier correspondent had so characterised the work of "typist and filing clerk.")[65]

With concern mounting that the single woman leader was an endangered species, targeting or positive discrimination was floated by some as a solution. An *Officer* editorial in July 1984 suggested that "a positive bias towards female ministry is needed among those who make appointments and policy at every level, if the opposite tendency, which has to some extent developed, is to be addressed. And they need to make an honest assessment across the whole range of useful characteristics, and not just concentrate on those male-oriented qualities which have been traditionally regarded as essential to leadership and more or less exclusive to men."[66]

Eva Burrows, whose election as General some hoped would signal a move in this direction, actually opposed the appointment of any "statutory woman" on Boards and Councils. Rather than tokenism she said that women "have to take their place by reason of their gifts and abilities".[67] Burrows was criticised by some for being insufficiently pro-active on behalf of women. *A propos* Burrows' role, Captain Christine Clement noted that "Mrs Thatcher has been Britain's Prime Minister for 10 years, but is there a woman in the cabinet?"[68] Questioned on the subject, Burrows is reported as asking, "Where are the women?" Bishop Penny Jamieson's comment is apt, however: "The fundamental question for women in positions of power is whether the culture of these institutions is so intractable and seductive that they become themselves taken over and remade in an old likeness, taking on the characteristics of those who held that power before them..."[69]

Nevertheless, Burrows directed Territories to promote women to leadership and laid it down that each Territory should have at least one single woman Lieutenant Colonel. Pears says that "Territories, however, rarely complied, or in some cases responded with token appointments or promotions."[70] Despite this, Captain Donna Ames, in a 1996 series of articles on "Changing Women's Roles", felt that Minutes issued in the previous year were beginning make a difference.[71] Her articles drew a mixed response, with Captain Allister du Plessis cautioning that cultural factors in

65 *Officer* (October 1998) p. 422.

66 *Officer* (July 1984) p. 291.

67 Henry Gariepy, *General of God's Army* (Wheaton Ill.: Victor Books, 1993) p. 204.

68 *Officer* (January, 1990) p. 32.

69 Penny Jamieson, *Living at the Edge: Sacrament and Solidarity in Leadership* (London: Mowbray, 1997) p. 32

70 Pears, Thesis, "Towards a Theology", p. 63.

71 Donna Ames, in *The Officer* (December 1996) pp. 549-50.

some territories made the application of such policies difficult and Major Cecil Waters drawing attention to legal repercussions and counterproductive consequences of affirmative action for minorities in the USA.[72]

In recent times Commissioner Kay Rader challenged the prejudices of assembled Salvationist leaders:

> Perhaps even within this company of international leaders there are those who oppose this definite view held by The Salvation Army regarding its policy of equality between the sexes, married and single, in ministry and leadership.

She also stated that

> Although women in the Army enjoy the privilege of rank and, in most cases, an avenue of service, we must admit that they are working within a system which is for all intents and purposes, predominantly patriarchal. If women officers are to become equal partners in the business of running the Army, we may be called upon to remove what one author refers to as "patriarchal shackles".[73]

To balance these examples, it should be recognised that the Salvation Army's precept and practice of gender equality, however flawed, has been a significant factor in improving the respect accorded to women officers in patriarchal, third world countries. Sociologist Lorraine V. Aragon writes of Sulawesi in Indonesia,

> European Protestant missionaries partly succeeded in their attempts to alter marriage patterns, household relations, and naming practices according to an idealized European model. While these transformations by the mission and colonial state might be said to generally undermine aspects of the indigenous status of women, the Salvation Army subsequently created a novel set of career opportunities that specifically favored women. Young girls no longer were destined exclusively to become dry rice farmers and mothers but some could aspire to be educated and trained as hospital aides, nurses, teachers, or even ministers — that is, Salvation Army officer wives.[74]

---

72 *Officer* (January 1997) pp. 46-7; (February 1997) p. 93.

73 Kay Rader, "Women in Ministry" (Address to the International Council of Leaders, Melbourne, 12-20 March 1998) pp. 5, 6.

74 Lorraine V. Aragon, abstract of paper, "Making a Male God and Female Careers: The Salvation Army and Gender in Central Sulawesi, Indonesia", paper given at American Association of Sociologists Annual Meeting, March 1999. (http://www.aasianst.org/absts/1999abst/SE/se-115.htm) Downloaded 29 November 2005.

Chapter Seventeen

Being Equally Yoked

> By marriage, the husband and wife are one person in law: that is, the very being or legal existence of the woman is suspended during the marriage, or at least is incorporated and consolidated into that of the husband; under whose wing, protection, and cover, she performs every thing...
>
> William Blackstone
> *Commentaries on the Laws of England.* 1, (1765).

It is necessary to note at this point that quite soon officers were permitted to marry only other officers. (In this, the Army had been anticipated by the Bible Christians, a West Country Methodist splinter group founded by William O'Bryan in 1815, whose female preachers could marry only other preachers.[1]) With the decline in the number of single women officers in the course of the twentieth century, the role and situation of married women officers has become the focus of attention so far as gender equality in the Army is concerned. We need to step back and trace the history of this practice before going further.

Officers' Wives

In the early days of the Christian Mission, although we have seen that some married women took a leadership role, it was not expected that wives of Evangelists would automatically join their husbands up front. "Mrs Garner, 'a sweet though mouse-like nature, was totally incapable of commanding anyone,' Mrs Beadle 'was little more than a domestic servant to her husband,' Mrs Clare was 'a good woman but entirely taken up with the affairs of her home'."[2]

Later, in the transition period from Mission to Army, before the training system for married people or the commissioning procedure became formalised, it seems to have been the case that women married by men officers automatically became officers. (Or rather, "officers' wives".) When Sergeant Marianne Parkyn of Torquay married George Scott Railton in

1 John Coutts, *Salvationist* (27 May 2000) p. 7.

2 Quoted by Hubert Boardman in *Officer* (November 1972) pp. 517-8.

1884, she became Mrs Commissioner Railton.[3] Until the mid-1880s, wives of married entrants were given the choice of coming into training or remaining at home during the training period. Married men Candidates were asked if they could, while away being trained, support their wife if she chose not to be trained.[4]

The 1886 *Orders and Regulations*, under the general heading of "The Social Relationships of the F.O.", included the following:

> Before being received as an Officer the following engagement is made by every F.O.:-
> (a) Not to marry anyone who is not a Soldier in The Army. (b) To abstain from courting for at least twelve months.
> (c) Not to do any courting with any Soldier in the Corps in which he may be stationed. (d) Not to make any engagement without first giving information to Headquarters.[5]

The argument then follows that since an officer's life is wholly given over to the work of the Army:

> It must be indispensable that he shall select a wife having the same convictions... especially in a path requiring so much self-sacrifice and toil... Further, to marry one outside The Army would probably mean leaving it... This must be seen to be most unfair and dishonourable. The Army cannot afford to pay the expenses and expend the labour and time of its Staff Officers in training men and women unless they agree to every arrangement which seems likely to secure them for its future service.[6]

The Orders and Regulations warned Female Officers particularly,

> to be very careful in this matter, seeing that to marry other than an Officer removes them from a position of great usefulness and honour, such as they will probably never have the opportunity of attaining again... lest...she should enter into relationships which would drag her down from this honourable and Christ like career to spend the remainder of her life in looking back on what she has sacrificed, with bitter regret, if not with absolute despair.[7]

The paternalistic role of the organisation is explicitly defended: "Many Officers are so young and inexperienced that they require some older person to give them counsel in such matters."[8] Salvation Army marriage practices,

---

3 Watson, *Soldier Saint*, p. 76.

4 Redstone, *Ex-Captain's Experience*, pp. 8-9.

5 *Orders and Regulations for Field Officers* (1886) p. 52.

6 *Orders and Regulations for Field Officers* (1886) p. 53.

7 *Orders and Regulations for Field Officers* (1886) p. 55.

8 *Orders and Regulations for Field Officers* (1886) p. 54.

like everything else about the organisation, were the subject of much speculation and rumour. Catherine Booth felt obliged to respond to

> the slanderous assertion that we are opposed to marriages amongst our officers!... In judging our instructions, however, on this point, please bear in mind that we have, I should think, 200 women officers not more than twenty, and perhaps as many men of the same age, and you will see the absolute necessity, for their own sakes, for some oversight with respect to engagements. I believe the Wesleyans refuse to accept a candidate for the ministry if he is engaged, and do not allow their young ministers to marry until their four years probation has expired. How awful this must be in the eyes of our critics![9]

A revision to the Regulations, 2 August 1887, restricted both men and women to engagement either to other officers or to soldiers suitable for officership and willing to enter training.[10] In the words of Colonel Laurence Hay, "It seems likely that the reasons were administrative: changes of appointment could more easily be made if married officers had officer spouses. This administrative factor is still one of the major justifications given, yet, in the hierarchy of Christian values, administrative convenience must surely rank very near the bottom!"[11] The burden of this work is that the whole polity and history of the Salvation Army illustrates that practical measures soon become sacralised and fairly resistant to further adaptation.

A correspondent to *The Officer* in 1915 asked why officers had to marry officers. Why not let the men officers marry soldiers? (He was obviously indifferent to the plight of single women officers wanting husbands.) Colonel James Whiller, Assistant Field Secretary, equally indifferent, gave the standard answer that the officer's partner was not only his wife but also his fellow leader.[12]

The *Appointments of Officers* 1883 list gives the names of 723 men and 746 women officers. As Horridge points out, there were many more women officers than acknowledged in this way, because a fifth of the men were married and although their wives were expected to work as officers in their corps, they were not listed separately.[13] Until 1970 the New Zealand *Disposition of Forces*, the annual publication listing appointments and officers, gave only the husband's name. If he were married, this would be followed by an x, and a number denoting how many children "on strength" – that is, still living at home with their parents, who therefore received an

---

9 Catherine Booth, *Church and State*, p. 91.

10 *Orders and Regulations for Field Officers* (London: SA, 1888) Supplement, p. 122.

11 *Officer* (October 1999) p. 26.

12 *Officer* (July 1915) p. 445.

13 Horridge, *Origins*, p. 80.

additional allowance for their maintenance. In fact wives of THQ married men officers remained x's until 1976. When statistical summaries of officers were given in the *Disposition of Forces* (until 1974) by rank, wives were not included but enumerated at the end as "staff officers' wives" and "officers' wives". Advice of promotion, Farewell Orders and Marching Orders (to leave an appointment and proceed to another) were issued to the husband only.

Clearly the Army was not totally emancipated from the usual expectations of society; normally the husband's calling was presumed to have priority, and a woman officer, in marrying, lost her independent officer-status. In Horridge's words, "The loss of women officers' rights when marrying contradicts the constant statement regarding equality."[14] Commissioner Kay Rader, in an essay on the role of women in the Army, quotes Rebecca Merrill Groothuis as sourcing this practice in English common law as described by William Blackstone. In his 1765 commentary Blackstone upheld the "civil death" of women who married.

The Founder himself had expressed concern at this mindset, evident in his lifetime. In 1888, addressing a meeting in Exeter Hall, William Booth said, "We have a problem. When two officers marry, by some strange mistake in our organisation, the woman doesn't count."[15] However Booth did nothing to ensure that it did not happen beyond exhorting his senior officers to value the work of married women officers. In his 1900 letter to senior leaders he urged,

> Let us maintain it with a jealous regard for the sacred rights of every woman, whether married or single, to the free and full exercise of all her gifts in the glorious work of the Salvation Army. To this end – Let women have the fullest opportunity to work. Let them be promoted in harmony with their ability and worthiness. Let women be treated as equal with men in all the social relations of life. Let consideration be shown to the Mothers of young children. Bear in mind that after a few years, the circumstances of such women will allow them to come to the front with almost as much freedom as before marriage, and that they will likely take their places in the fight with greatly increased love and wisdom, and, consequently, with greatly enlarged influence and power.[16]

No structural provision was made to ensure this happened, however. Bramwell Booth in his turn struggled apparently in vain against the cultural norm. A letter to a Territorial Commander in 1924 instructs him,

---

14 Horridge, *Origins*, p. 81.

15 *WC* (12 May 1888). Cited in *Salvationist* (22 November 2003) p. 15.

16 William Booth, *Letter to Commissioners and Territorial Commanders*, pp. 25-6.

> Do not fail me with the women. I look anxiously for the War Cry reports about their work... it is not only a principle with us, but it is a very strong personal desire on my own part that the women of the Army should be kept to the front; and that the married women should be made to feel that their responsibilities are not all dissolved in those of their husbands when they marry.[17]

Some notable exceptions still only tended to prove the rule. In the case of Captain Rachel Agar's betrothal to William Ebdon, and their joint appointment to open a Corps at Northampton in 1879, William Booth agreed to the marriage only on the condition that Rachel should be first in the partnership so far as Salvation Army officership was concerned.[18] When Major and Mrs Simmonds "opened fire" in South Africa in 1883, it would appear that Mrs Simmonds, a talented evangelist, spearheaded the work, while her husband operated in a less prominent role.[19] Another example was that of Brigadier Hedwig Haartmann, a Finnish officer serving as Provincial Commander for German-speaking Switzerland when she married her ADC, Staff Captain Franz von Tavel. They hyphenated their names but retained their ranks and roles. Alas the lady died soon afterwards, in 1892.[20] Booth's own married daughters, of course all retained or received their own Ruritanian ranks and shared joint commands when they hyphenated their names with those of their husbands.[21]

The resolution of the tension between the assumptions behind the framework of officer marriage and the movement of societal expectations occupied the whole of the twentieth century, and the process is not by any means complete. Florence Booth claimed that "the work and influence of women in The Salvation Army is not confined to unmarried women... The work of married women, though often more indirect and unseen, has been of as great, and even of greater importance."[22] It had to be indirect because

---

17 Catherine Bramwell-Booth, *Bramwell Booth*, p. 197.

18 Sandall, *History*, II, p. 37.

19 Escott, Thesis, "Church Growth Theories", p. 53.

20 Mildred Duff, *Hedwig Von Haartman* (London: SA, 1904).

21 Catherine (Mrs Booth-Clibborn) was the "Maréchale"; Emma (Mrs Booth-Tucker), the "Consul"; Evangeline styled herself the "Commander" for over thirty years until her election as General in 1934. (The 1908 *Year Book* entry for the USA has "Territorial Commander, Miss Eva Booth.") Of the sons, Herbert was the "Commandant" and Ballington the "Marshall". Only the youngest, Lucy (Mrs Booth-Hellberg), was ranked a mere Commissioner. Bramwell, the eldest, never held a rank until he became General in 1912, being simply "Mr Bramwell" as in a Victorian family firm, or, "The Chief". His wife Florence was "Mrs Booth" until she became "Mrs General Booth", although William Booth had made her a Commissioner in 1888. *SA Year Book* (1958) p. 7.

22 *Field Officer* (March 1913) p. 122.

after marriage the actual appointment would be their husband's. Commissioner Karl Larsson cautioned women officers from running into marriage too soon because "Some of our best and most promising women, who have a good head and a good heart, and who as single officers would go far and occupy important positions, enter into marriages which hinder their development and circumscribe their sphere of work."[23]

Officers' wives' officership was merged with that of their husbands. The husband received the appointments and the promotions; the wife just tagged along. A Memorandum from the Territorial Commander in New Zealand as late as December 1963, on "Officer Commission and Promotion Certificate", reiterated the position (perhaps it was beginning to be questioned). "Husband to receive promotion certificate for each promotion up to and including the rank of Brigadier. Wife to receive no promotion certificate: she takes her husband's rank."[24] The Regulations provided that when widowed, an officer-wife "if, or when, she has served the required number of years as an officer... will receive rank in her own right, except where the husband held the rank of Lt.-Colonel or above, when the case will be reviewed by the Chief of the Staff."[25] The husband also received the allowance, augmented appropriately if he had a wife and family to support.

The system worked well for many people. Frederick Coutts described it in his memoirs as

> this unique form of service in which husband and wife work as one. Brigadier A. may be appointed divisional commander for the Cumbrian division, and Commissioner B. to be the territorial commander for Westralia, but Captain <u>and</u> Mrs C. will be sent to take charge of the corps at Middletown. This turns out to be not only for the good of the work but for the good of their marriage as well, insofar as they share not merely their leisure – which is all many husbands and wives can do – but their vocation also. Both have accepted the same calling. Both are trained for that calling. All that Captain does Mrs. Captain can do as well. She does not sit in the congregation but shares with her husband the Salvation Army equivalent of the pulpit – the platform. Captain will rejoice that Mrs. Captain is no cipher. Mrs. Captain will rejoice that she is no dumb piece of platform decoration...[26]

Voices of Dissent

By the 1970s the relationship between officer husbands and wives was being described as a "joint covenant", although the actual term was not used in

---

23 *Officer's Review* (Sept-Oct 1939) p. 479.

24 Memorandum in New Zealand Salvation Army Archives.

25 Minute by The Chief of the Staff, 1977/IA/4.

26 Frederick Coutts, *No Continuing City* (London: SA, 1976) pp. 34-35.

regulations. The *Orders and Regulations* were amended to this effect in 1981: "In marriage an officer's consecration is joined with that of the chosen partner and the united consecrations become one just as do husband and wife become 'one flesh' (Mark 10:8)."[27] Mrs Commissioner Hilda Cox, wife of the Chief of the Staff, in a 1990 article on "Married Women's Officer-role Within The Salvation Army", found the concept of a "joint covenant" "puzzling and unhelpful", and "only useful if we were able to envisage a complete and secure possibility of role-sharing or equality".

Mrs Cox, in the article referred to, admitted that "the equality policy within our midst has been... implemented with a mixture of success and failure," and that she had been "bewildered, perplexed and not a little frustrated by its interpretation." She noted the danger of spiritual abuse: "The emphasis placed on a 'spiritual commitment' must never be used to force anyone into simply conforming to any situation, especially to one only partly understood, or to push anyone 'aside' into a non-existent channel." However, she also believed that women had to come to terms with the Army's administrative structure as a cultural given, and learn to work for equality within it.[28]

Mrs Major Margaret Hay (New Zealand) rejoined with the affirmation that "principles are sacred; structures and roles are not." She drew attention to the way in which the principle of equality had been eroded in successive editions of the *Orders and Regulations for Officers*. The 1900 edition had named gender equality as "one of the leading principles upon which the Army is based". The 1925 edition dropped the word "leading". The 1974 edition omitted the whole section on the position of women, "stressing instead the supportive role of the 'officer-wife'". Hay also took up Cox's cue on "the exploitation of spiritual commitment to reinforce a reactionary social climate and bar women from the exercise of real authority." She believed that "given the will, structures can be transformed."[29]

The official assumption of male control continued to be reflected in *The Orders and Regulations for Officers* as late as the 1987 edition which, in the section devoted to "The officer and his wife" included the words, "In most appointments... an officer-wife should assist her husband. He is of course, responsible, but she should interest herself and, as opportunity permits, take her full share in every phase of the work under his direction..."[30] Major John Coutts commented on the 1974 edition,

27 Minute by The Chief of the Staff, 1981/IA/7.

28 *Officer* (September 1990) pp. 408-12, 415.

29 *Officer* (February 1991) pp. 70-1.

30 *Orders and Regulations for Officers of The Salvation Army* (London: SA, 1974) Part 5, Section 3, para. 4, p. 77.

> In seventh-century England, the blood-money for killing a churl was, of course, only half that payable for killing an earl. For a Welshman, of course, it was lower still. In seventeenth century Scotland, the children of miners were, of course, placed in life-long bondage to the pits at their baptism. In nineteenth-century America, Booker T. Washington was, of course, refused admission to College because he was black, while in Britain Catherine Booth came under fire for preaching. Of course – she was a woman.[31]

Alas, the offending phrase persisted until the 1997 edition. From 1987 comes an apparently unembarrassed admission in an Australian ecumenical publication: "In the case of married couples, it is the man who receives the appointment. In some situations (mainly headquarters) the wife may receive a separate appointment but it is subordinate to that of her husband."[32]

The matter of the role and status of married women officers (including those widowed or divorced) generated a great deal of discussion in the final third of the twentieth century. Mrs General Marie Wahlström noted in 1984 that "there is a good deal of uncertainty and dissatisfaction among women officers, both married and single, with regard to their place and position in the Army."[33] Looking for letters and articles on this subject, I found 50 in *The Officer* between 1972 and 1996 and 15 in *The Salvationist* between 1990 and 1996. It seemed that the pressure on the traditional structure was steadily increasing and this no doubt contributed to the progressive modifications and reforms that have been instituted over the past few years.

Correspondents addressed a variety of themes. Some were concerned with the officer as a wife and mother, and juggling those responsibilities with ministry.[34] Some dealt with the nature of the officer husband-wife partnership.[35]

Some correspondents revisited the scriptural basis of Salvation Army practice. Major Howard Davies (Australia), for example, responded to Mrs Major Margaret Hay's argument from Salvation Army tradition and "sacrosanct principles"[36] by expressing unease and suggesting that many officer-wives held back from exercising their ministry out of "scripturally-based reservations." He was supported by some correspondents and denounced by others.[37]

---

31 *Officer* (December 1974) p. 562.

32 Captain David Perry, in William Tabbernee (ed.) *Ministry in Australian Churches* (Melbourne: Joint Board of Christian Education, 1987) p. 107.

33 Address to the International Conference of Leaders, Berlin 1984.

34 Mrs Major Franklyn Thomas (West Indies), *Officer* (December 1981) pp. 560-562, 555.

35 Captain and Mrs Martin and Linda Howe (UK) *Officer* (April 1993) pp. 170-2.

36 *Officer* (February 1991) pp. 70-1.

37 *Officer* (July 1991) p. 325; (November 1991) pp. 491-4; (November 1996) pp. 515-7.

Other reactionary concerns were also referred to. Major Miriam Vinti (IHQ) asked how practical could a regulation be that allowed complete independence of career to man and wife? "How would a man accept the promotion of his wife to a Commissioner and Territorial Commander, while he remained a Major in his wife's Headquarters?"[38] Lt.-Colonel Arthur Thompson believed that "if some husbands would find it intolerable to be in a lesser role than their wives, then lessons may have to be learned from the world, where this painful adjustment is taking place."[39]

For some, a serious problem in the existing structure was the waste of human resources, desperately needed by an Army stretched for personnel. Brigadier Lawrence Weggery (New Zealand) discovered from the Orders and Regulations that a wife "can in fact 'in certain circumstances' be entrusted by headquarters with some definite responsibility distinct from that of her husband," and urged that "ways will be found to encourage the officer-wife... to move out of her supernumerary position and undertake leadership in her own right."[40]

Lt.-Colonel Arthur Thompson regretted that "whilst the autocratic command structure was designed to produce quicker decision-making our leaders at almost every level seemed to be locked in a kind of paralysis because of ... prejudice and tradition... Without doubt, if we are not to be guilty of poor stewardship of our leadership resources, the time must soon come for the Army to move purposefully towards using our best talent most wisely, whether it be male or female, single or married."[41] Captain Geoffrey Parkin similarly condemned "the possible waste of a valuable resource, the loss of personal fulfilment and the potential strain between husband and wife."[42]

Against this, Major Patricia Yon discovered in the 1990s that 60% of married women officers surveyed in the UK "were to some degree satisfied to be appointed with their spouse... Some women would be vehemently opposed to the prospect of sacrificing this privilege."[43]

Others again expressed strong feelings about the situation of widowed and particularly separated or divorced officers. *The Orders and Regulations* confirmed that the "Officer's wife is herself an Officer... Should she become a widow, she is still an Officer... The widow of an officer may be appointed directly to another department or section of service and thereby be

---

38 *Officer* (February 1975) p. 78.

39 *Officer* (October 1984) p. 460.

40 *Officer* (January 1972) pp. 36-7.

41 *Officer* (October 1984) pp. 459-61.

42 *Officer* (June 1988) pp. 268-9.

43 Patricia Yon, "Areas of Stress and Conflict in the Lives of Married Women in Ministry Within The Salvation Army" (MA thesis, University of Keele, 1991-93) p. 36.

considered a widow on Active Service...She may be appointed as an employee..."[44] However this was all a matter of discretion and it had not been uncommon for widowed women officers to be given no option other than premature retirement. Mrs Major Harry Parkinson, whose husband died in his forties in 1942 while in command of Wellington City Corps in New Zealand, brought up her family on a small pension and spent over fifty years in retirement. Some however stuck it out and a few reached or maintained executive roles. Mrs Colonel Violet Stobart, widowed in 1960, took over her late husband's role as Territorial Commander in Ceylon (perhaps inspired by Mrs Bandaranaike?) and retired from the command of Switzerland as a Lt.-Commissioner.

The situation of officers who suffered the breakdown of their marriage was perhaps worse, as both parties had to resign their officership regardless of where the "fault", if any, lay. Those who chose could reapply for acceptance as officers at a later date. Captain Mrs Miriam Fredericksen (IHQ) described the dynamics of such service[45], as did "Eunice", who wrote, "I know what it feels like to be made to feel 'second-class' because of something on which you had no influence... I know what it means to experience personal rejection and public humiliation."[46]

The administrative structure whereby the wives of Corps, Divisional and Territorial leaders automatically assumed responsibility for the "women's work" and women's organisations, also came under fire. Mrs Lt.-Colonel Emily Fritz (USA) believed that "the whole concept of the women's service department has outlived its usefulness... Salvation Army women may be better served if the women's service departments were absorbed into mainline administration. In the USA this would free a lot of officer-wives now stationed on divisional and territorial headquarters to be reassigned to appointments matching their special gifts."[47] Lt.-Colonel Mary Elvin (Caribbean) also denounced this "Army within an Army". "To concentrate so much time, effort and personnel upon one aspect of the ministry will inevitably produce substantial results in that one aspect... but it often leads to a serious imbalance in both church attendance and in membership."[48]

To anticipate, the on-going reforms have left this women's "ghetto", to use Captain Danielle Strickland's term for it, untouched as yet. She explains,

> By women's ghetto I mean that part of the system of the Salvation Army that allows men to exercise leadership within the formal system while deploying

---

44 *Orders and Regulations for Officers* (1930) Part ix, Chap. VIII, Sect. 2, p. 486.
45 *Officer* (September 1981) pp. 418-20, 426.
46 *Officer* (December 1991) pp. 546-9.
47 *Officer* (December 1988) pp. 496-7.
48 *Officer* (November 1996) pp. 518-20.

> their wives into corresponding positions over other women in a weird parallel universe. The end goal in this corporate structure is to be married to a Commissioner – and ultimately to be the wife of the General. It has no bearing on the election of a General whether or not his wife is even good at her job – as the position is not functional but positional... it is not a merited position and is not considered an appointment providing leadership experience to become a General... all the women's ghetto positions in the world cannot offer a reasonable opportunity for women to learn, cultivate or prove leadership qualities enough to get out of the ghetto... and any single woman General can add the job description of World President of Women's Organizations to her responsibility as international leader of the Salvation Army. Nice.[49]

The majority of correspondents however dealt with some aspect of the way in which married women officers felt that their ministry had been diminished or held in less regard once they married. The extent to which married women officers were able to maintain their ministry depended to some extent on the kind of work in which their husbands were engaged. In the case of married women Corps Officers, there was a pastoral role in which they could be fully absorbed along with their husbands. Responsibility for the pastoral care of women and children, often along with the leadership of particular women's groups, usually devolved upon officer-wives. The degree to which they shared public work, such as meeting leadership and preaching, depended on their individual capabilities, the dynamics of the marriage, family responsibilities and sometimes the expectations of the Corps. "In one Corps she is kept from the hall kitchen, it being unthinkable that she should leave the word of God and serve tables; in another... everyone goes home and leaves her with the dishes."[50]

The organisation sometimes failed to recognise their work. A correspondent in 1919 took issue with the

> boast of The Salvation Army that women in its ranks are on an equality with men. I do not think that is wholly true... There are more women than men in our ranks, and many of them possess brains, education and godliness which qualifies them to occupy responsible positions. The married women officers might receive more recognition than they do. At the last Congress I attended not one married woman was asked to speak or pray. I know of one DC who sent out Christmas gifts to officers in his Division, and in the case of a married couple who had a young Lieutenant as an assistant, there was a remembrance to the Lieutenant and to the Officer in Charge, but the letter conveying Christmas greetings was addressed to "Adjutant Blank and Lieutenant So-and-so". The poor wife was not even wished a happy Christmas. It was not the gift

---

49 Danielle Strickland, "Married Women's Ghetto Rant", *Journal of Aggressive Christianity Online* 41 (February-March 2006) www.armbybarmy.com.
50 *Officer* (September-October 1960) p. 358.

> that mattered but the utter ignoring of a woman who did an equal part of the platform work, a fair share of the visitation and all of the clerical work, so as to free her husband for the demands of outside Corps work. I do not think an officer's wife should be treated as though she were a sort of upper servant...[51]

Such voices were not heard very often until much later in the century. When the debate then flared up, some expressed surprise. Retired officer, Mrs Major Ruth Saunders (UK) recalled that on her marriage "everyone... naturally expected that I would really share the platform ministry[52], the visitation, the census board meetings, etc, with total equality, and I, and the officer-wives of the previous generation as well as my own, did do that."[53] Some put the blame for loss of status on the wives themselves. Mrs Captain Katrina Thomas (British territory) wrote that "... a great many female married officers have allowed their spouses to be the commanding officer... I regard myself as a commanding officer and I expect to be treated as such." She allowed that there were moments of frustration – "e.g. letters for my attention addressed to my husband, a divisional commander refusing to discuss corps business with 'Mrs Captain'..."[54]

On the other hand, some were happy to take a back seat. Mrs Captain Arvilla Hostetler (USA Eastern) explained, "He is the Captain, the pastor, of the Corps. A church has one pastor but there may be many ministers. Our people are not likely to introduce me as their Captain. I am the Captain's wife... My role is not secondary but complementary. My husband and I are a team... My pastoral duties may be different from my husband's but they are no less important."[55] Mrs Colonel May Holland (Retired, UK) admitted, "most of us accepted that when it came to marriage that our husbands were responsible for the decision making. There cannot be two Commanding Officers in one battalion. Personally that is how I wished it, and I was never brought into corps, Divisional Headquarters or Territorial Headquarters decision-making regarding any aspect of administration."[56] Mrs Captain Ruth Hampton (Australia) felt that "women in our Corps need an example of true motherhood, the joy of being a wife and the responsibility of being a home-keeper, as well as being a servant of God."[57] Lt.-Colonel John Gowans expressed regret that "some women officers have sold their birthright and retreated from any kind of public service altogether."[58]

---

51 *Officer* (April 1919) p. 357.

52 "Platform ministry": Leading services and preaching.

53 *Officer* (June 1993) pp. 287-8.

54 *Officer* (July 1989) pp. 320-1.

55 *Officer* (December 1981) pp. 457-8.

56 *Officer* (February 1975) p. 81.

57 *Officer* (December 1989) pp. 567-8.

58 *Officer* (October 1984) p. 449.

In the case of social officers the wives' roles perhaps depended more on the nature of the appointment. In some cases there was more than enough to do – unremitting toil at laundry, cooking, sewing, cleaning and supervision as occasion required, and responsibility as matron for large numbers of people. On the other hand, Mrs Major Gladys Ford of New Zealand wrote of arriving at an appointment where her husband was to be manager, only to be greeted by the non-Salvationist Assistant Manager with the comment, "There is no work here for you to do."[59] She found plenty to do however.

It was the problem of unemployed staff wives, whose husbands had positions on Headquarters, which first attracted official notice however. Mrs Bramwell Booth, at the suggestion of Mrs Carpenter, decided in 1912 to set up what she called "The Bond of Service and Fellowship". This was partly to provide pastoral care for the wives of staff officers, and also to find work for wives of Staff Officers on IHQ. This labour-exchange directed such wives to the needs in corps, social institutions and hospital visitation.[60]

Perhaps this kind of thing was not to everyone's liking because from time to time chiding articles urged greater participation, noting "the danger of being the wife of a mandarin."[61] Another writer, having referred to the "humble and unobtrusive opportunities for work with Home Leagues, the YP Corps, League of mercy, prison, hospital, common lodging house or saloon visitation," suggested that perhaps "such unobtrusive work does not attract them...", they "want to preserve the freedom from official responsibilities of a soldier while retaining the position, the honour, and the prerogatives of a staff officer!"[62]

Such official responses missed the point, that married women officers were increasingly feeling devalued by the lack of respect shown for their calling as officers. Even in the early years this must have been felt: in 1899 Captain Minnie Rowell wrote to her intended husband, George Lyndon Carpenter, of her fear of being reduced to being a housewife upon marriage. "I am practically marrying out of the work. What am I to do? Keep my house nice and once a week visit a hospital?"[63] While this frustration was contained or had little opportunity for expression in earlier years, the comparative freedom of the official publications towards the end of the twentieth century permitted a clear picture to emerge. Mrs Captain Joan Hutson (New Zealand) wrote of the "prolonged period of soul-shock – a type of grief and mourning for their identity that must be felt to be believed" when "the husband receives a 'husband-only' appointment either at

59 *Officer* (February 1985) p. 81.
60 *Officer* (July 1917) pp. 395-8; Carpenter, *Man of Peace*, p. 198.
61 *Officer* (June 1916) pp. 419-22.
62 *Staff Review* (January 1922) pp. 110-11.
63 Carpenter, *Man of Peace*, p. 102.

Headquarters or in social work."[64] Mrs Major Gwenyth Redhead (UK) described how, twenty-five years earlier, upon her husband's appointment to the staff of the Officer Training College, she sat through an interview in which the Principal explained at length her husband's duties. "Finally... I plucked up courage to ask, 'And my responsibilities?' Then came the sword-thrust deep into my heart, reducing my sense of self-worth to nil. 'It is not training college policy to provide officer-wives with official appointments.' I felt as if the word 'rejected' had been branded into my forehead for all the world to see."[65] Mrs Major Joy Emmons of South America West put it like this: "When we were brought to headquarters and I was not listed in the dispo I was crushed. I did what I was asked to do... but felt like excess baggage."[66] Another writer said she "felt as though I had been sacked... I felt hopeless, powerless and worthless... I felt as though I had been thrown on the scrapheap."[67]

The *Manual of Guidance for Staff Officers* included a short passage on "The Staff Officer's Wife".

> It is not given to the wife of every Staff Officer to have specific or separate responsibilities. When such is the case, however, the husband will give encouragement to see that her duties are carried out without let or hindrance... Throughout the world, many Staff Officers' wives are a tower of strength to their husbands in a "behind the scenes" ministry, as well as exercising an independent influence in the districts where they live or in the Corps where they are soldiers.[68]

The wives of officers below staff rank serving on Headquarters presumably knew their place without being expressly instructed. The *Orders and Regulations for Divisional Commanders* still advise that "A DC's wife needs to be especially careful not to intrude upon her husband's prerogatives of administration. She may not assume any of her husband's powers of authority."[69]

The Officer editorialised in 1984: "The crunch comes in specialist or headquarters appointments where the husband has a specific appointment which does not... include the wife, and where very often no effort is made

---

64 *Officer* (June 1975) p. 273.

65 *Officer* (December 1991) p. 561.

66 *Officer* (October 1989) pp. 436-7.

67 *Officer* (July 1984) pp. 295-6.

68 *Manual of Guidance for Staff Officers* (London: SA, Undated, but copies in the New Zealand THQ Archives were issued, over the signature of the General, in 1969 and 1971) pp. 16-7.

69 *Orders and Regulations for Divisional Commanders*, Chapter 1 Section 3 Para 5. Quoted in "Report and Recommendations of Gender Issues Commission, 2004," UK Territory, p. 16.

to find her suitable and fulfilling work. She is often left to languish in a limbo of frustration and rejection in which she may (a) lose her sense of vocation... (b) Become satisfied with Martha tasks [by which the writer probably included the kind of work offered by the 'Bond of Service and Fellowship']. (c) Find some second-best fulfilment in agencies outside the Army, if such is available. None of these is a substitute for her officer vocation, and the organisation has an obligation to find really fulfilling service for every officer."[70]

Personal experience of this situation led at least one senior officer to begin attending to the problem. Colonel Gordon Swansbury, appointed Staff Secretary at IHQ, found that his own wife had no designated assignment "and there was no peace in our house until her importuning secured an opening in another department in which she has found complete job satisfaction." Swansbury discovered that a study group had been commissioned to investigate the position of officer-wives and had made recommendations. Accordingly he initiated individual letters of appointment for all officer-wives serving on IHQ and also for officer-wives who had found roles elsewhere though their husbands worked on IHQ. He made it standard practice for wives of all in-coming officers to be interviewed as to their preferred service. As he stated, this did not mean that the ideal had been reached – the wives' appointments were still secondary to their husbands' – but it was a start.[71]

Major Patricia Yon, surveying married women officers in the UK in the early 1990s, learned that 23% of respondents to her questionnaire reported that "they have their own named appointment, which is separate from and independent of their spouse." She suggested that "this possibly reflects the fact that recently policy changes have occurred which support the provision of enhanced professional opportunities for married women. However, being appointed independently is no guarantee of being given a job in any authentic sense."[72] John Coutts had warned some years earlier that, "No improvement will come by tinkering with the system or by 'finding little jobs for the ladies'. We need here, as in other matters, real openness about such sensitive matters as jobs and job satisfaction, rank and status and, lastly, money and allowances."[73]

So why was the general trend throughout most of the twentieth century towards a curtailment of woman's role in the Salvation Army?

Firstly, there could be unacknowledged but influential theological reasons. It could be that the alternative Salvation Army tradition, that of theological reservations about gender equality, has remained a significant

70 *Officer* (July 1984) p. 291.
71 *Officer* (September 1984) pp. 414-5.
72 Patricia Yon, Thesis, "Areas of Stress", p. 35.
73 *Officer* (July 1975) p. 322.

factor for some people despite the official line. We have seen this for example in Major Howard Davies' letter cited above on page 253. Again, Major Karen Shakespeare drew attention to the influence of the Genesis 2 account of creation, which presents woman as being essentially and intrinsically different in nature because of her gender, in contrast to Genesis 1 which describes male and female as created in the image of God.[74] Danielle Strickland notes that "a subtle yet increasing theological and systemic shift... has managed to render a huge section of the Army's leaders unusable...Now there are officers who believe that 'headship' is a scriptural principle and as a direct result keep married women in submissive positions as leaders. Married women officers themselves often have been taught and continue to believe this lie... Not only does the Army perpetuate it by its current system but has probably even established it by its current practice."[75]

Secondly, it could be argued that the situation did not actually deteriorate, but that women became more vocal in their objection to the status quo, and that this was made possible by more liberal opportunities for public debate. And it could also be pointed out that the gradual decline in the number of women in senior leadership was a consequence of the decline in the number of single women officers in general – the potential pool was smaller. That, however, does not explain why the organisation was so reluctant to give married women independent commands as it sometimes had in the early days of the movement. And was the pool smaller because women were less willing to accept an inferior status?

Unfortunately the gradual changes noted by Margaret Hay in the *Orders and Regulations* suggest that the real reason was simply male chauvinism and the increasing conservatism of a movement institutionalising and tending to be on the defensive. This touches on our clericalising theme as well. Whatever the Army's rhetoric, the men thought of themselves as clergy, and in the world to which the Army was accommodating it was not yet trendy to think of the women as clergy as well. Salvationist men increasingly sought to represent themselves as clergy while in practice denying this status to most women officers. Inevitably, however, attempts to redress this inequity would further clericalise the women.

---

74 Report and Recommendations of the Gender Issues Commission 2004, UK Territory, p. 5.

75 Strickland, "Married Womens' Ghetto Rant."

Chapter Eighteen

Steps to reform

Make haste slowly.

Aldus Manutius

Conferences and Commissions

The steps were somewhat leaden. The subject of gender equality was aired at successive Conferences of Commissioners and Territorial Leaders but action was tardy. The 1971 Conference "recommended women being given a fuller representation in the top echelons of world leadership."[1] 1975 being International Woman's Year, wives of Commissioners were invited for the first time to be present at the International Conference. However they were not included in every session but held their own parallel sessions, bringing their report to the final plenary session. Commissioner Kathleen Kendrick (a single woman) hoped "that it might be but the beginning of wider participation of women in the central councils of the Army", and quoted a senior woman delegate as saying, "The idea that a woman's place is in the home and that there she must stay – I resent it!"[2]

In 1979 a similar arrangement obtained. Debating the Equality of Men and Women Officers, Mrs Commissioner Harry Williams (IHQ) asked why the longstanding passage on the principle of equality had been omitted from the 1974 *Orders and Regulations*. However Commissioner Ernest Holz (USA) "pointed out the difficulties in connection with the over-emphasis of equality, specific appointments and designation". The Minutes did not record what difficulties he meant, but "it was pointed out that what a woman officer seeks is the satisfaction of using her best in the Master's Service."[3] It was also mentioned that women officers' names were now included in the *Disposition of Forces* and in the *Official Gazette*.[4] Previously only their husbands had been named.

---

1 *Officer* (January 1972) p. 36.

2 *Officer* (March 1976) pp. 123-5.

3 Minutes of the International Conference of Leaders, 1979, p. 90.

4 The *Official Gazette* is the publishing of appointments, promotions etc., usually in *The War Cry* or other periodicals.

At the 1984 Conference in Berlin, wives were for the first time invited to participate as full delegates, and the Conference produced three recommendations affecting women in particular. (1) All gazetting should be for the couple and not for the husband alone – the 1979 statement must have been premature, (2) all correspondence concerning an officer couple should always be addressed to both, and (3) whenever possible the officer wife should be given her own appointment.[5] Such Conferences could not enact decisions but only recommend to the General. However, under Burrows a further step was taken in that for the first time the wives of territorial commanders and chief secretaries were invited to participate in zonal conferences – a step which had been urged in 1984 by Mrs General Wahlström.

The background study material for the 1991 Conference, which asked if it "was time to speed up implementation of earlier recommendations", suggested that the recommendations had not got much further. The 1991 appointment of a married woman as Training Principal in New Zealand (Mrs Major Margaret Hay), with her husband as a part-time member of her staff, was stated to have given impetus to the question. It was also asked whether the concept of a joint-covenant for married officers was still a live issue – apparently the 1988 Conference had recommended that it remain in the expectation. The 1991 Conference decided to propose an International Commission to consider: (a) a review of the Orders and Regulations; (b) review of the position of Territorial President of Women's Organisations; (c) separate appointments for married women; (d) the concept of joint-covenant; and (e) loss of officership in the event of marriage breakdown.[6] Such a Commission was in due course appointed by General Burrows, shortly before her retirement in 1993.

The 15-member commission chaired by Mrs Commissioner Rosemarie Fullarton presented its report in May 1994, with recommendations "based on the belief that men and women are equal in the sight of God, and that there is no theological conflict in the ministry of women in all spheres of service." The ten recommendations covered the following areas:

> (1) official encouragement for the enrichment of officer family life; (2) revisions of sections of Orders and Regulations for Officers; (3) recognizing all officers by rank, Christian name and surname regardless of marital status; (4) upgrading the role and duties of the territorial president of women's organizations; (5) equality of consideration to be given to the vocation of all officers at all levels of service, and in making appointments; (6) every woman officer, married/single, to be seen as a resource and developed to her full potential; (7) attention given to the full use of skills and gifts of women officers at all levels of service, including boards and councils; (8) a new

5 Minutes of the International Conference of Leaders, 1984.

6 Background study papers and Minutes of 1991 Conference of Leaders.

system for calculating allowances replacing the tenure of married men officers as the basis; (9) single women officers to have appointments of opportunity according to their gifts and abilities; (10) child care and domestic support to be available where family duties may affect the ministry of married and single officers.[7]

New Champion, New Minutes

General-elect Bramwell Tillsley, interviewed by *New Frontier*, admitted, "We haven't done very well in giving married women officers the opportunity to develop fully the gifts God has given them... Too often the assignments of wives have been dictated by the assignment of their husbands."[8] However Tillsley's term of office was cut short by ill-health in less than a year, and it was left to his successor, Paul Rader, to implement some changes recommended by the Commission. The new General's wife, Kay Rader, was a forceful personality and a vigorous campaigner on women's issues so her husband's election heralded major steps forward. Pears refers to her in his thesis as "a new champion".[9] Kay Rader's passion for reform arose from her own experience of injustice under a patriarchal system.[10]

New Minutes affecting women's service took effect in mid-1995. Most of the Commission's proposals were actioned, although recommendations 8 and 10 were a matter for territorial discretion, according to local conditions, and some were expressions of principle rather than specific changes to practice. The most obvious and major change, able to be implemented at once, was the recognition that "in the case of active officers, up to and including the rank of Commissioner, each spouse holds their joint rank in his or her own right."[11] Mrs Captain Jones became Captain Mary Jones, or, if she preferred, Captain (Mrs) Mary Jones. Curiously, this does not seem to have been made much of in the Army's press, with no reference to the change in the British *Salvationist* or in the New Zealand or Australian editions of the *War Cry*. Perhaps it was thought unwise to call attention to the fact that it was only just happening in 1995 – or perhaps it was not thought significant by those who determined editorial policy.

One of the downstream and apparently unanticipated implications of this change was that all Commissioners' wives, now Commissioners in their own right, would become eligible for summons to the High Council and

---

7 Gariepy, *History*, VIII, pp. 318-9.

8 *New Frontier* (30 April 1993) p. 6.

9 Pears, Thesis, "Towards a Theology", p. 66.

10 Carroll Ferguson Hunt, *If Two Shall Agree* (Kansas City MSS: Beacon Hill Press, 2001) p. 84.

11 Minute of the Chief of the Staff, 1995/IA/20, dated 7 July, 1995.

given a vote in the election of the next General. This increased female representation on that body at its next meeting from 10% to 37% - the male majority was maintained because the non-Commissioner Territorial Commanders were nearly all men, whose wives were not eligible to attend. Another even-handed change was that whereas previously a woman officer marrying a man holding a rank lower than her own assumed the husband's rank, now whichever spouse had the lower rank would take the same rank as his or her new partner.

Other elements in this reform package included individual appointments, equality of consideration being given to both spouses' vocations in the making of appointments, appointments of both spouses being announced simultaneously (instead of the wife's being tacked on as a later afterthought), individual personnel reviews and service record cards, and appropriate assessment, orientation and on-going training for women whose family responsibilities or husband's appointments had restricted their own development. It was also provided that "a married woman officer may be given the leadership role in a joint appointment where this is appropriate and the stability of the marriage and family is not placed at risk."[12] Some cautious moves in this direction have been made in a few territories. In the Philippines Major Noveminda Tanedo became Divisional Commander for Mindanao in 2000, with her husband as Divisional Secretary. In New Zealand Major Lynette Hutson became National Manager for Addictions Services in 2003, and thus line manager for her husband, Director of the Auckland Bridge Centre.

In 1997 Paul Rader took the further step of ruling that his wife would be ranked as a Commissioner. Hitherto the General's wife had been known as, for example, Mrs General Rader. While not binding on his successors in office, this more than brought international leadership into line with the new provision for all wives to hold their rank in their own right; it also fuelled "speculation that the time may come when other married officers will hold different ranks from their spouses."[13] And such in fact proved to be the case. Within a few years some corps were intrigued by the fact that their married officer couples now wore different insignia, dependent upon their individual length of service. In some countries cultural norms made this impracticable, and in territories embracing more than one country and culture the application of the new rule could cause embarrassment. Tonga for example is part of the New Zealand Territory and subject to New Zealand regulation, but Tongan Salvationists found it difficult to fathom why their Regional Commander should be a Captain while his wife was a Major. (Ranks under the level of Lt.-Colonel are based on years of service.)

---

12 Minute by the Chief of the Staff, 1995/IA/15.

13 *Salvationist* (30 August 1997) p. 3.

A marker of the changes over these years was the way in which the official form of address for married women officers changed from, for example, "Mrs Lieutenant Murray Flagg", to "Mrs Lieutenant Murray (Deborah) Flagg", to "Mrs Captain Deborah Flagg", to "Major Deborah Flagg".[14] The official designation changed from "officer-wife" (considered a great advance on "officer's wife")[15] to "married woman-officer" – although Captain Violet Smart wanted to know if men were now to be "married men-officers" as well. "No more labels, please!" she requested.[16]

Other anomalies remained in the new ranking system. Commissioned ranks of Lt.-Colonel and above are described as "conferred ranks" (once described as "staff ranks"), and go with certain senior administrative roles. The practice of individual ranks has not yet been extended to this level, except in the case of the General's spouse. Major Vinti's 1975 vision of a woman Commissioner with her spouse a major serving in her headquarters has not yet been realised. Dr John Coutts, still campaigning for the principle of equality, rained on the Army's parade in 1998 by pointing out: "Now the wives of officers have gained their rank in their own right. This will certainly improve the gender balance at the High Council. But will the wives really be there in their own right? The new women Commissioners have in fact been appointed by virtue of being married to their husbands. A 'Mrs Major' – no matter how well qualified – will not progress until her other half is promoted."[17] Despite their new rank and status the women leaders may still be at a disadvantage in conference and council, without the necessary opportunities for real leadership over the years and experience that would give greater credibility to their views. That may take a generation of "real" appointments to establish.

A piece of window-dressing in the *Yearbook* from 2003 is that the entry for each Territory is now headed with the names of the Territorial Commander and spouse as "Territorial Leaders", but so that there should be no mistake this is immediately followed by the name of the "Territorial Commander". At this time, the latter name is always that of the male partner.

The developments described above were taken further by the International Commission on Officership and subsequent changes in regulations. However at this point it is appropriate to pause and take stock. The story of women's ministry within the Army really provides a sub-plot or counterpoint to the theme of this book – the question of whether Salvation Army officers are really "clergy". The issue for women, and

---

14 Major Deborah Flagg in "Softly Eclipsed", in *New Frontier* (30 April 1997) pp. 6-7, and in *Officer* (October 1997) pp. 12-7.

15 *Officer* (September-October 1960) p. 358.

16 *Officer* (June 1992) pp. 287-8.

17 *Salvationist* (28 March 1998) p. 7.

particularly for married women, has been whether they were really "officers". While the stand taken by the Booths was ground-breaking in the nineteenth century, they found it difficult to apply the principle of gender equality across the board, quite naturally because they were prisoners of their own times and assumptions. Theological principles are not easily imposed on resistant cultural norms. Andrew Mark Eason's *Women in God's Army* explores and analyses

> the cultural and theological foundations upon which the organisation was established. Reflecting views that were similar to those of their male counterparts, most Army women espoused beliefs and accepted roles that were incompatible with a principle of sexual equality. A female officer's moral and spiritual functions in the home, combined with her other domestic tasks, either called into question or placed constraints upon her public ministry... Within the public realm, a married or single female officer was usually confined to responsibilities consistent with the notion of sexual difference. She was encouraged to possess a femininity defined in terms of self-sacrifice, weakness, dependency and emotion. This construction of womanhood allowed women to challenge sinners publicly from the platform or engage in social work, but their overall ministry remained a modest one... Her ideal role was one of service and submission rather than leadership and authority.[18]

Lt. Colonel Barbara Robinson (Canada), reviewing Eason's book for *Word and Deed*, concluded, "The most disturbing aspect of this book... is that while Andrew Eason is a historian and *Women in God's Army* is a historical monograph, his book comes far too close to describing the contemporary Army practice for comfort. So read it – and shudder!"[19]

Major Karen Shakespeare also addressed the cultural factor in a theological reflection in the 2004 Report of the Gender Issues Commission in the United Kingdom.

> Historically the culture of British society has supported a patriarchal model for the theology of gender. The assumptions of modernity encouraged a gender separation in which men were seen to be logical, unemotional and suited to public life and leadership and women found their role in relational activities, most often in the home or in a 'caring' profession. The Salvation Army, whilst affirming the equality of all in doctrinal and policy statements, has in practice demonstrated a theology which privileges men and assumes an essentially different role for women, especially those who are married. In the post-modern world, which no longer accepts the assumptions of modern

18 Andrew Mark Eason, *Women in God's Army: Gender and Equality in the Early Salvation Army* (Waterloo, Ontario: Wilfred Laurier University Press, 2003) p. 152.
19 *Word and Deed* (November 2003) pp. 90-3.

> culture, there is a need to re-assess and possibly re-think our theological understanding of gender.[20]

The principle of genuinely shared married leadership is however also enjoying a new lease of life. Major Richard Munn (USA), writing on "Married Officer Leadership", while noting that the Army is positioned "to speak with some authority on the subject of dual clergy couples" and so "effectively poised to engage a culture that is increasingly faced with the familial and marital ramifications of two employed parents", goes on to say that,

> While purporting egalitarian leadership... and advocating shared formal authority for men and women, the married officer leadership model often functions along quite traditional gender roles. Externally this is expressed through denominational polity with men consistently holding the dominant leadership positions. Internally it is expressed with the majority of officer couples indicating that the man is the "spiritual head of the family". Thus, while demonstrating much strength, the unique contribution of the married officer leadership model may not be fully maximised. The matter might be deficient theology.[21]

Munn takes Priscilla and Aquila as "the quintessential dual clergy couple" and explores the principles found in the six Bible references to them as appropriate for officer couples' ministry.[22] He suggests that the married officer leadership model is a unique strength of the Army and that "we seem unusually primed 'for such a time as this'."

It took a long time for the Christian ethic to bring about the cessation of gladiatorial contests and longer for it to achieve the abolition of slavery. It was only towards the end of the twentieth century that the mainstream Protestant Western Church began to bring its understanding of ordained ministry into line with its belief that in Christ there is neither male nor female.[23] The Salvation Army, having in some senses pioneered this direction, evidently lost its momentum fairly early in its history, while continuing to believe its own rhetoric, and has only recently begun to address the issues again.

---

20 Quoted by Major Chick Yuill in "Nettles and Wineskins" (Frederick Coutts Memorial Lecture for 2004 at the College for Further Education, Sydney) and published in *Practical Theologian*, 2:2 (September 2004) pp. 1-22.

21 *Officer* (July/August 2004) pp. 10-11.

22 Acts 18:2, 18, 26; Rom. 16:3; 2 Tim. 4:19; 1 Cor. 16:19.

23 Galatians 3:28.

Part Five: Things that are Shaken, Things that Remain

The final Part reflects on how the Salvation Army has attempted to adjust to various pressures on the officer-role towards the end of the twentieth century, and suggests some further ways forward.

Chapter Nineteen

The International Commission on Officership

> We cannot revive old factions
> We cannot restore old policies
> Or follow an antique drum.
>
> T.S. Eliot,
> *Little Gidding, Four Quartets.*

General Paul Rader set up an International Commission on Officership, on the recommendation of the 1998 International Conference of Leaders held in Melbourne. Its purpose was "to review all aspects of the concept of officership in the light of the contemporary situation and its challenges, with a view to introducing a greater measure of flexibility" into officer service.[1] Twenty-three people were appointed to serve on the commission, representing a wide range of cultures, experience and age groups. Nearly a third were unmarried; eleven were women; three were non-officers.

The terms of reference reflected both the concerns of the Army's leadership and the areas of debate within the ranks of officers in particular. These were in the main about essentially practical matters but inevitably carried ecclesiological implications. They were:

- The strengthening and promoting of the ideal of lifetime service as an officer.
- The possibility of short-term officer service, and, if such is considered viable, the practical and legal implications, including training, contract/covenant, ordinations, benefits and pensions.
- Separate vocations for husbands and wives as an option from the time of entering officer training.
- The continuation of the service of a married officer in cases where the spouse ceases to be an officer for such reason as misconduct, marital breakdown or illness, and possibly even ineffectiveness or lack of commitment.
- The introduction of separate ranks for spouses.
- Separate allowances for married officers.
- Portable pensions for officers.

1 Norman Howe, "The International Commission on Officership, A Report", *Officer* (August 1999) p. 19.

- Administrative policies and regulations related to officers' conditions of service, including those to do with marriage.
- The possibility of the "tent-maker" concept, i.e. part-time secular employment by officers being considered in certain circumstances, in order to assist with the funding of the appointment.

Commissioner Norman Howe, the Commission's chairman, noted that the real issues ran deeper, and concerned such questions as, "How is the Army best to engage in mission in the contemporary world?" and "What kind of leadership can best enable that mission endeavour?" Howe also admitted that there was "an inherent tension within the terms of reference", particularly between the first two points, but regarded this as a positive tension.[2]

The Commission met in October 1998 and February 1999, and submitted to the General an Interim Report containing 28 draft recommendations. Rader, who was nearing retirement, had copies of the Report distributed to all territories and commands, asking for responses to be made and received at International Headquarters by September 1999. 41 out of the Army's 54 territories and commands responded, as did a number of individuals. A working party of six members of the Commission then prepared a final draft, which the full Commission reviewed and presented to the new General, John Gowans, in January 2000.

Introducing the Final Report, the Commission referred to the Biblical principles on which their work was based, and in particular to the mission of proclaiming the Gospel (Mark 1:14-15) and the prophetic role of those called to ministry (Matthew 10:7-8). It referred to the Spirit-led adaptability of the early Church as the basis of "a functional view of officership". It also identified four factors foundational to its work. These were:

- That "officership is part of a wider resource of spiritual leadership..." and "ministry opportunity must be open to both officers and soldiers...". Nevertheless officers have a particular function "to provide direction and spiritual, theological and practical resources to mobilize Salvationists for mission," and "the effectiveness of the mission would be seriously disadvantaged" without "dedicated, motivated and qualified officers who are willing to give sacrificial service."
- That "Officership is the outworking of a covenant relationship between an individual and God". The individual's calling is tested by the Salvation Army, which "trains for spiritual leadership, acknowledges the ordination of the Holy Spirit and commissions to service."
- That "Officership implies obligation by The Salvation Army as well as the officer..." and "this is much more about attitude than provision, and

2 Norman Howe, *Officer* (August 1999) p. 19.

requires a shift from paternalism to partnership and from command to facilitation."

- That "The mission context changes significantly from generation to generation and from place to place. These changes demand renewal and refocus in mission... a major challenge to a movement originally structured as a quasi-military and hierarchical system with international regulations."[3]

Gowans then took a step unprecedented in Salvation Army history, and in February 2000 circulated the Final Report to all 17,362 active and 8,113 retired officers in the world, asking for an expression of opinion (Agree, Somewhat agree, Somewhat disagree and Disagree) on each of the 28 recommendations.

In his covering letter, Gowans reserved his prerogative as General – "This is not a voting process by which the majority opinion absolves me from taking the hard decisions. It is a consultative process..." He wanted that process to be complete in time for the International Conference of Leaders scheduled for Atlanta in June, and therefore asked that responses be returned to the London-based MORI organisation (Market and Opinion Research International Ltd) by late May for computer processing. In the event a 50% return was received on time. A month later a summary and statistical analysis of the response was also made available to all officers in a letter from the Chief of the Staff.

All of the Commission's 28 recommendations were endorsed globally, most by a substantial margin. Six were supported by 90% of respondents, twelve by 80%, six by 70% and two by 50%. Of these last two, the one concerning "tent-maker ministry" was supported by all zones except North America. The proposal that officers might be married to non-officers received a bare 50% support of respondents but Africa, North America and South Asia (comprising the Indian subcontinent) disagreed.[4]

By August 2000 Gowans had published his responses to the recommendations, along with his action plan for each. These ranged from immediate implementation to "acceptance in principle", sometimes with numerous qualifications and recognition that the extent or timing of implementation would depend on the circumstances and cultural milieux of particular territories. Many issues were left to territorial discretion and in some cases the objective was to be sought by means other than those suggested, but none was rejected out of hand.[5]

---

3 *Officer* (August 1999) pp. 2-3.

4 John Larsson, "Findings of the General's consultation with officers regarding the Recommendations of the International Commission on Officership", 24 June 2000.

5 John Gowans, "The Recommendations of the International Commission on Officership: The General's Response and Action Plan", 24 August 2000.

By November a series of revisions to *Orders and Regulations for Officers*, giving effect to changes, had begun to appear. At the same time territories responded to Recommendation 28 by appointing their own task forces to work out how the international changes might be effected locally, and responses from these were due back at IHQ by December 2001. (By that time some of their deliberations had been pre-empted by the new regulations being promulgated from London, such as those concerning the ranks of auxiliary captain and lieutenant.)

To what extent do these findings and changes bear upon the matters at the heart of this book – the character of officership, and the question of whether officership is perceived as a functional role or a clerical status? Most of the recommendations deal with "officer conditions", the distinctive circumstances discussed in the chapter, "What manner of men – and women". These included such areas as poverty, obedience, the role of women and spouse-relationships. To that extent the commission was a response to the ways in which the original expectations of both the officers and the Army as a whole have drifted out of synch with the changing times and world-view of newer generations. Regulations framed for Victorian times could not be expected to fit the needs of the twenty-first century; they had been stretched as far as possible but the time had come for structural adjustments. In so far as the character of officership is bound up with and even determined by such features, it is inevitably changing.

As far as the matters whose history has been traced in this work are concerned, we need to look at what happened to the recommendations affecting two areas in particular. Firstly, we consider the recommendations having to do with the role of women and the equality of their status with that of men officers. Recommendations 13, on allowances, 15, on women's appointments, and 16, on the need for gender balance on Boards and Councils, are relevant here. Secondly, we look at those recommendations bearing directly on the status-function dichotomy we have observed through the Army's (and the Church's) history. Under this heading we could place numbers 8 and 9, to do with Covenant and Undertakings; number 18, on open-ended or short-term commissions; 22 on models of spiritual leadership; and 24 on tent-making ministry.

Concerning Women

Gowans agreed in principle to recommendation 13, that equal and separate allowances should be paid to both officer spouses, "on condition that they are not financially disadvantaged by the change, that it is culturally appropriate, and that the interests of single officers are safeguarded."[6] This would be a matter for individual territories to address. The United Kingdom had already begun doing this. New Zealand had long since worked out an arrangement with the Inland Revenue Department whereby 3/5 of the combined officer allowance was credited to the husband and 2/5 to the wife as this seemed to offer the best tax advantages. A New Zealand task force reporting in mid-2001 recommended a change as "we felt the separate payments would help to recognise the important concept of the individual officer, especially in relation to the ministry opportunity for women within the movement." However it also wanted research to ensure the best possible tax advantage.[7] A change to a 50/50 payment to spouses was made in New Zealand mid-2003. In the United States at time of writing, the whole of the pay cheque for the couple is still made out to the husband and the wife is classed as a "volunteer" worker under an agreement made with the IRS in 1957.

Recommendation 15 reiterated the need to affirm women officers, whether married or single, by appointing them to positions commensurate with their gifts and experience. All Gowans could do about this was to accept the recommendation and encourage territories to keep the matter to the fore: territorial task forces should consider the findings of the 1993 Commission on the Ministry of Women Officers, territorial reviews by zonal international secretaries should address performance in this area, and Orders and Regulations for Territorial Commanders would give increased emphasis – and IHQ should set an example. Such exhortations had been made often enough before and soon forgotten; abstract objectives are difficult to quantify and therefore hard to monitor and enforce. The New Zealand task force suggested various areas in which the leadership could be proactive in implementing this recommendation.

Number 16, concerning gender balance on planning and decision-making bodies, was also accepted and territories asked to implement it quickly. Tokenism was to be avoided. Perhaps such an objective could be quantified – but was not. Gowans contented himself with reiterating that it was now acceptable for spouses to serve on the same Boards and Councils – once not permitted – and with pointing out that the best way of achieving the aim was to ensure a gender balance amongst office holders. (Most such bodies had membership drawn from people holding specific related responsibilities.) The New Zealand task force supported, without offering suggestions for specific measures.

---

6 John Gowans, "The Recommendations of the International Commission on Officership; the General's Response and Action Plan", 24 August 2000, p. 14.

7 "Commission on Officership, NZ Task Force Findings", Wellington, May 2001, pp. 17-18.

It could be said that as far as women's ministry is concerned, the Commission's proposals really followed on from the Rader reforms of the mid-1990s without adding very much that would specifically advance practical gender equality. In some territories the implications of the changes are still being explored. In the United Kingdom for example a commission was set up in 2003 to examine gender issues relating to the appointment, ministry and personal fulfilment of officers. Key points being considered are Gender issues relating to territorial structures, Cultural factors and Work/Life balance. Only by such serious exploration of practical problems will further progress be made.[8]

Concerning Status

The "inherent tension" Norman Howe had noted between the first and second of the commission's terms of reference reflected again the ambiguity of the Army's position regarding "status" and "function". If officership were seen in terms of (indelible?) priestly or clerical character, its concomitant would be the "ideal of lifetime service". On the other hand, if officership were simply functional, there would be no theological impediment to short-term officer service. In John Gowans' words, "The traditional understanding within the Army is that officership is a lifelong commitment. Those who set out on the path of officership do so with the intention of it being for life – though it is also informally understood and accepted that it may not work out that way for everyone."[9]

As might be expected, the wording of the Covenant has usually expressed this ambiguity, implying a commitment to lifetime officership without explicitly stating it. Although the 1922 rubric used the expression "Life Covenant", this was always represented as between the officer and God ("to love and serve Him supremely all my days") rather than with the Army. Being "true to The Salvation Army and the principles represented by its flag" was a promise that could be fulfilled in service as a soldier, not necessarily as an officer only. The preamble to the version I signed in 1972 began, "Called by God to proclaim the Gospel of our Lord and Saviour Jesus Christ as an officer of The Salvation Army...", which could imply more strongly though still not necessarily insist that the lifelong covenant which followed would operate exclusively within the calling of officership.

The commission's rewording in Recommendation 8 perhaps slightly tempered that assumption with the words, "Called by God to preach the Gospel of Jesus Christ and to meet human need in his name, I dedicate myself to service as an officer of The Salvation Army." (The decision to

---

8 *Salvationist* (12 April 2003) p. 5.

9 Gowans, "Recommendations", p. 16.

work out that calling within officership has become the officer's decision rather than God's imperative.) And where the seventies version concluded, "and, by God's grace, to prove myself a worthy officer," the commission favoured the more generic and ambiguous "and, by God's grace, to be all that he has called me to be."

It cannot be said therefore that the commission decisively fulfilled its mandate to "strengthen and promote the ideal of lifetime service as an officer". Gowans accepted the proposed wording in principle but saw it as a draft capable of further amendment.

Recommendation 9, on the Undertakings, was notable in suggesting for the first time that officer and Army might have reciprocal obligations, while cautiously preserving the legal basis for clerical status. No signature is appended on behalf of the organisation, however, lest the whole be construed as a contract. Gowans accepted the recommendation and said that a reviewing group would be appointed.

Recommendations 18, 19 and 20 dealt with aspects of "open-ended" service by which the commission evidently meant service other than lifelong. While 19 and 20 referred to the pastoral and financial aftermath of resignation, 18 addressed the issue of intentionally short-term service. We have seen that Gowans himself had been a proponent of this idea for many years. (See Chapter 14.)

In his response to Recommendation 18, Gowans summarised the commission's choice as between, "(a) the concept of officership can be made more open-ended so that it formally allows for both short term and lifelong service, or, (b) whether we must think in terms of a parallel structure that exists alongside, but outside, of officership". The commission preferred the experimental testing of (a), which would have tipped the theological seesaw away from officership as a status and towards a simply functional definition. However, contrary to their recommendation and with no further consultation preceding its inauguration, Gowans opted for (b). He claimed that it had "the great advantage of leaving untouched the basic concept and structure of officership as it has been traditionally understood, and not seeking to merge two contrasting approaches – short-term and lifelong – within the one concept of officership".

Noting that the existing warrant officer auxiliary-captain and envoy systems already constituted "two parallel structures alongside commissioned officership", Gowans decided to supersede these with one new parallel structure, a new kind of lieutenancy.[10] By maintaining the two-tier system, the non-commissioned second tier being for functional, short-term service, he preserved the possibility that the commissioned first tier enjoyed a different ministerial character or status from the second. In fact he might be said to have strengthened this assumption, in that the hybrid auxiliary-

10 Gowans, "Recommendations", pp. 16-7.

captain status was discontinued and the new lieutenancy was more explicitly a non-officer rank. Gowans therefore drew back from tipping the balance decisively in the direction of functional officership, and the time-honoured ambiguity was maintained. The essential features of the new system were:

- The rank of lieutenant would become a non-commissioned rank, while officers would in future be commissioned as captains.
- Lieutenants would provide spiritual leadership and service, and could be accepted at any age. Gowans intended the system to be available both for those who wished to commit to a finite number of years and those who set no specific time limit. However the regulations eventually settled on three-year terms, renewable if both the lieutenant and the Army agreed.[11]
- Lieutenants would serve under "officer conditions", but, like the existing auxiliary captains, not be commissioned as officers.
- Lieutenants could move into commissioned officership once they had completed training requirements, which might be satisfied by flexible training rather than by the usual residential course, and would sign the officers' undertakings and covenant when commissioned as captains.

Like officers, lieutenants "must be prepared to forgo all other occupations and accept total involvement in the branch of Army service to which they may be appointed". The Minute also stipulates that "lieutenants' service will be a non-contractual relationship so far as legally possible in each territory... [they] will be asked to sign undertakings similar to, but different from, officers' undertakings... [which] will reflect the spiritual non-contractual relationship with The Salvation Army."[12]

While subject to the Orders and Regulations for Salvation Army Officers, lieutenants under the new system do not serve entirely under "officer conditions", at least not in New Zealand. They receive salary supplements in lieu of the usual officer fringe benefits such as medical insurance and funded extra training. Furthermore, like envoys but unlike auxiliary captains, should they later become officers their time as lieutenants will not be credited towards their officer service – a significant disadvantage in terms of retirement allowances or financial settlements which are calculated according to years of service. (Pension arrangements are a matter for territorial policy.) Unlike Envoys or Auxiliary Captains, they would revert to soldier status when leaving the service; there would be no retired Lieutenants.[13]

---

11 John Larsson, Minute 2000/1A/13 from the Chief of the Staff: *Orders and Regulations for the Lieutenants System*, 1 May 2001, p. 2.

12 John Larsson, Minute 2000/1A/13, p. 3.

13 *Salvationist* (19 May 2001) p. 9.

The upshot is that with this hybrid rank, the Army continues to have a two-tier system of ranked leadership, performing identical ministry roles but with some regarded as officers and others not. This is not a priesthood/diaconate distinction.

The New Zealand task force supported Gowans in maintaining officership as a "vocational" service, and agreed that the new Lieutenancy model adequately provided for "open-ended" service where the individuals wished to maintain more lifestyle choice.

Recommendation 22 urged the development of other models of spiritual leadership – that is, other than officership. This responded to the reality that with fewer officers available in some territories (especially in Europe) and the expansion of work beyond available officer-leadership in others (especially in Africa), "positions traditionally held by officers can be occupied by soldiers with an equal sense of vocation."[14]

Gowans, while endorsing this and urging comprehensive review by territorial task forces, concentrated his observations particularly on how local volunteer ("lay" – though he did not use that word) spiritual leadership might be strengthened. He did not refer to the increasing phenomenon of full-time, employed soldier-ministry, except by the provision of the lieutenant system already described. The paradoxical situation, that some people can do the ministry work of officers (such as being pastors) and be officers in everything but name, while other people can actually be officers in name while not engaged in any distinctively "ministry" role (being, for example accountants within the Army administrative structure), was not addressed. Such a situation clearly implies that officership is a status rather than a function dependent on a particular role.

The New Zealand task force, like the General, saw this recommendation in terms of spiritual leadership by the soldiery in a voluntary capacity, although they also posed the question "as to whether opportunity to demonstrate spiritual leadership within a Salvation Army community of faith should be restricted to those who were formally committed to soldiership". This was not explored further, but did acknowledge the fact that an increasing number of New Zealand Salvationists and people willing to belong to a Salvationist community, including many who would and did provide significant local leadership, did not want to commit to soldiership. They saw their association in terms of the local congregation rather than the national, let alone international, body. This reference did acknowledge the fact that not just officership but also soldiership in the Army is in the midst of a crisis of identity and direction, at least in countries like New Zealand. The task force affirmed that they did "not see the officer as having priestly status or function above the soldier".[15]

---

14 International Commission on Officership, "Final Report", 2000, p. 16.

15 "Commission on Officership, New Zealand Task Force Findings" pp. 25-6.

Recommendation 24, on "tent-making ministry", approached a similar problem from another direction and with a different outcome. "Tent-making" ministry, named from St. Paul's occupation, resembles the "worker-priest" solution attempted in France after the Second World War, where clerical persons supported their ministerial vocation by secular employment (abandoned in part because it was less amenable to hierarchical control), or the non-stipendiary priesthood increasingly common in the Anglican communion. Equally relevant to the theme of this thesis is the theological question of what a worker-priest had to offer in the workplace that a layman did not. The concept of the worker-priest could be seen as essentially clericalist, dependent on the view that clergy have some special and necessary character, or task such as celebration of the Eucharist; clergy doing the laity's work is the counterpoint to laity doing the clergy's work.

Gowans realised that the "concept in relation to officership bristles with difficulties". He led an organisation in which in some countries officers received full allowances in addition to state welfare support, while in others officers enjoyed neither – in some cases had to farm land to feed their children and sell the produce to pay for their education. Colonel David Edwards (Caribbean) in a paper given to the 1991 International Conference of Leaders, had recommended the worker-priest concept because it was impossible economically in some countries to sustain full-time officership, which he described as a "ridiculous luxury".[16] At the same time, the official *Orders and Regulations* still define officers as "those who have relinquished secular employment ... so as to devote all their time and energies to the service of God and the people".

Gowans therefore decided to leave the matter to territorial discretion, but to "hedge that acceptance with a number of qualifications and restrictions".[17] Here Gowans, while conceding that there were powerful and practical arguments in favour of "tent-making", apparently attempted by these restrictions to hold a line opposite that logically required by his retention of the two-tier structure, so that commissioned officers ideally need to be engaged in full-time ministry, ensuring that officership can actually be seen as a matter of role or function (full-time ministry) rather than a matter of status.

The New Zealand task force also felt that the tent-maker concept "compromises the basis of officership in that an officer is set aside by the Church for ministry and removed from the need for secular employment". They therefore recommended the concept "as particularly appropriate for non-officer soldiers".[18] (But are not *all* Soldiers actually "worker-priests"?)

---

16 Minutes of the 1991 International Conference of Leaders.

17 Gowans, "Recommendations", pp. 20-1.

18 "Commission on Officership, New Zealand Task Force Findings", pp. 26-7.

By the most recent "official word", therefore, ambiguity about the nature of officership has been perpetuated. John Gowans, the General regarded as most able to think outside the square, was nevertheless unable or unwilling to take the decisive step needed to commit the Army to an entirely functional concept of ministry. The organisation has not been able to escape trying to have it both ways.

Geoff Ryan, a Canadian officer, summed up the situation as follows:

> When General Gowans, in response to the cry of the grassroots and through the International Commission on Officership, created new policies governing officership, he further muddied the waters. By giving freedom for local definition while retaining centralised control to a large degree, the General created a "push-me-pull-you" hybrid compromise. Individual territories have been allowed to progress with the redefinition of officership as they see fit and so the traditional homogeneity of officership has given way to a patchwork of localised definitions. It is somewhat akin to the effect that pluralism has had on religion – 50 years ago if you referred to "God" everyone more or less knew who you were talking about. That is not the case now. An officer in Canada or Bermuda means something different to an officer in the U.K. for starters...[19]

Against that conclusion, one could say that Gowans had little choice, and for two reasons. The first is that the international diversity of the Army is now such that one size no longer fits all. This was admitted by Commissioner Earle Maxwell, Chief of the Staff, at the 1998 International Conference of Leaders, when he said that "it is becoming increasingly difficult, from an IHQ point of view, to formulate international decisions, with their implied global relevance, that can then be comfortably implemented in every territory or command."[20] It interesting to read this alongside Avery Dulles' prediction concerning the post-Vatican II Catholic Church. "The internal pluralism in the church itself will be such that directives from on high will be variously applied in different regions, so that the top officers will not be able to control in detail what goes on at the local level."[21]

The second reason is that there has not for a long time been a consensus on the issue of the status of officers – any more than there was in fact any consensus fifty years ago on the meaning of "God". This history has shown that the movement has been uncertain about this from comparatively early in its history. Perhaps this diversity of viewpoint has not been consciously geographically distributed, although it should also be remembered that a

---

19 *Horizons* (July/August 2003) p. 20.

20 *Officer* (August 1998) p. 5.

21 Avery Dulles, *Models of the Church* (New York: Image/Doubleday, 1978) p. 208.

majority of contributions to *The Officer* originate from Europe, the U.K., the "Old Dominions" and the U.S.A. and so no longer necessarily represent majority opinion in the Army. Indeed the distribution of responses to the General's questionnaire suggests that the Army in the developing world tends to be as conservative as other denominations in those areas.

One other matter touching the matter of status of officers might be mentioned – the vexed subject of ranks. Officers were invited to express a preference either for retaining the present system with minor amendments or having only the ranks of Captain and General. The majority of British and Australasian officer-respondents voted for the latter course but were in a minority internationally. Gowans did manage to greatly restrict the incidence of Colonels. The ranks of Lt.-Colonel and Colonel are now to be reserved for those serving as Chief Secretary, Officer Commanding, Territorial Commander or as senior IHQ administrators. Gowans had also wanted to abolish both Commissioner and Lt.-Colonel. "'They' told me that it would need an Act of Parliament which would take forever... I allowed myself to be persuaded and I regret it!" he later wrote.[22]

In sum, the International Commission's Report, in for example its support for both the aim of life-long service and its tentative (and abortive) exploration of short-term service, exhibits the same ambivalence about officer status as we have seen in the contemporary work, *Servants Together*. The Commission was not set up to address the issue of clericalisation, so it is not surprising that it did not resolve the tensions between the Salvation Army's theology and its ecclesiology apparent throughout its history. It was intended to suggest solutions to practical, organisational problems arising from the tensions between an institutional structure, its evolving constituents and its ever changing milieu. In particular, it sought to modify those service conditions which were bringing pressure to bear on officers and making it harder to recruit and retain officers in some territories. However, those conditions and tensions are to some extent the result of and inseparable from the process we have described as clericalisation. Pragmatic re-jigging of regulations without recognising and adequately taking into account the underlying sociological and ecclesiological processes involved, is dealing with symptoms without addressing causes. Such measures may meet the need of the hour, or of a decade or two, but do not go far enough to help regroup the Army for the battles of the coming century. On the other hand, the four "fundamental factors" identified by the Commission (see pp. 272-3, above) do offer scope and hope for continuing development.

22 In Denis Hunter, *While the Light Lingers*, p. 56.

Chapter Twenty

Knowing the Place

We shall not cease from exploration
And the end of all our exploring
Will be to arrive where we started
And know the place for the first time.

T.S. Eliot
Little Gidding, Four Quartets

This historical analysis of Salvation Army ministry has been in terms of the tension between function and status; between the view that members of the church differ only in that they have distinct roles, and the tradition that some enjoy a particular status by virtue of their ordination to one of those roles in particular.

Options

The Salvation Army had three options regarding the question of ordination and clerical status.

1. There *are* priests/clerics/people in orders in the Church, with a status distinct from that of the laity, but we *do not* have them in the Salvation Army.

This would mean the Salvation Army's acceptance of an "all lay" status for its soldiers and officers, and acknowledging itself to be something like an order or an *ecclesiola in ecclesia* rather than a "church" or "denomination". While William Booth sometimes implied that this option was his intention, at least in the early days, especially when he did not wish to offend churchmen, or hoped for something from them, it is clear that he did not believe this to be the case. We have seen that negotiations with the Church of England in 1882 foundered on this point amongst others. For Booth it was not enough that his officers should be regarded as Deacons and Deaconesses, members of an "inferior" order.

2. There *are* priests/clerics/people in orders in the Church, and we *do* have them as officers in the Salvation Army.

The adoption of "ordination" by Arnold Brown, and the claim that the Army's commissioning had always been equivalent to ordination, amounted to this position. This seemed to be an attempt to endorse officially what Salvationists had come to accept in practice over many years, without being very clear about what was meant by it. The confusion that has grown up on this issue within the Salvation Army is, as has been suggested, partly a result of ambiguity about church order inherited from Methodism, and partly from a desire to be accepted by other Christian denominations as one of them.

There was no question of the Army wanting or being able to claim that its ministry was in the Apostolic Succession, or that officers enjoyed some *sacra potestas*, in a way that would satisfy the criteria of the Catholic, Orthodox or Anglican churches, so Brown's ordination must have been conceived of in the sense that the churches of the Reformation and the free churches or dissenting groups have used it. Those bodies did not all see the matter in the same light either, and the Army's dressing up in clerical vestments, so to speak, has not conveyed the intended message to everyone. Anthony Cross writes of the Baptists as having "an ecclesiology which other 'Churches' struggle to understand. Other traditions for whom this is problematic are the Society of Friends and Salvation Army, neither of whom practise the sacraments of baptism and communion. What is more, neither they nor the Brethren have a ministry as understood by others..."[1]

The history outlined in the introductory chapters suggests that this no man's ground between having a priesthood and not having a priesthood is difficult to hold. This was not only the case for those churches which perpetuated the Christendom model but for those which rejected it. Mascall quotes Paul Tillich as struggling with coherence on this point. Tillich claimed that, "Protestantism demands a radical laicism. There are in Protestantism only laymen; the minister is a layman with a special function within the congregation; and, in addition to possessing certain personal qualities, he is qualified for the fulfilment of this function by a carefully regulated professional training. He is a non-layman solely by virtue of this training."[2]

An analogy, in Brueggemann's schema, is that of the Davidic monarchy as an intermediate stage between the Israelite Amphictyony and the Solomonic Empire, between the Mosaic vision of an alternative community of free Israelites and regression to the power structures of oppression and exploitation. Brueggemann says that "...David, genius that he was, managed to have it both ways."[3] Booth also tried to have it both ways, but whatever his intentions, officership came to be identified with an ambivalent form of

---

1 Anthony Cross, in Anthony Cross (ed.), *Ecumenism and History* (Carlisle: Paternoster, 2002) p. 24.

2 Paul Tillich, *The Protestant Era* (London: Nisbet, 1951) cited by E.L. Mascall, *Recovery of Unity*, p. 7.

3 Brueggemann, *Prophetic Imagination*, p. 25.

clericalism. The point is that any kind of function gravitates towards status. The trick is to find a way of preventing that happening.

The way in which the Army has sought recognition for its ministry by attempting to graft on a soi-disant ordination might be analogous to the elders of Israel appealing to Samuel for a King, so that they "might be like the nations round about".[4] Such a request rather loses its point when monarchies elsewhere are going out of fashion. It is ironical that the Army's attempts to be more church-like have come at a time when the mainline denominations of the West have been entering a period of rapid decline. Steve Bruce says that "Recently gathered data on Church membership and Church attendance show that unless trends are reversed, major British denominations will cease to exist by 2030."[5] This is masked by the rise of more conservative, evangelical and pentecostal groupings as some passengers on the Titanic scramble for those parts of the ship still above water. Research in such countries as New Zealand, Australia, Canada, Great Britain and USA shows that where evangelical, pentecostal and charismatic churches were growing, around 90% of growth came from other conservative churches or from children of church members. "What has happened is merely a reconfiguration of existing church goers."[6]

In this connection I repeat that I write from a vantage point situated in New Zealand, one of the more secularised countries of the Western world. Rodney Stark and Roger Finke produce persuasive evidence that particularly in the United States church culture is alive and well. They show that churches asking sacrifices of their members continue to grow; it is those which have reduced the cost of belonging which are in decline.[7] The intriguing thing is that while the Salvation Army *has* lowered its sectarian expectations of its members over the twentieth century, it retains a significantly high threshold to full participation as far as both belief and lifestyle are concerned. Despite this, the Western Army's statistics belong with those of the declining old, mainline denominations rather than with the growing newer, conservative groups.

3. There are *no* priests/clerics/orders in the Church, and the Salvation Army does *not* aspire to any. All Christians are "lay", in the sense that all belong to the people of God, without distinction of status.

---

4 1 Samuel 8:5.

5 Steve Bruce, in "Christianity in Britain RIP", *Sociology of Religion* 62:2 (2001) p. 191. David Hay in *The Biology of the Human Spirit* (London: Darton, Longman and Todd, 2006) is more optimistic, suggesting 2050 as the date by which "there will be virtually no Christian institutional presence in Britain." Cited by Elena Curti, "Once a Catholic…", in *The Tablet* of 18 March 2006.

6 Kevin Ward, "Christendom, Clericalism, Church and Context" (http://www.presbyterian.org.nz/441.98.html) accessed 1 December 2005.

7 Stark and Finke document these propositions in *Acts of Faith*.

Booth in fact made it clear on more than one occasion that this was his theoretical position; his theology required it and a significant body of opinion within the Salvation Army still adheres to it. However, we have seen that the line was impossible to hold. The Army's ecclesiology was shaped instead by Booth's autocratic temperament, the need for organisation, the twin demons of militarism and bureaucracy, the susceptibility of human nature to pride and ambition, along with historically conditioned expectations. All these meant that the leadership function, as always, appropriated to itself a dominant role and assumed a regular status. The difficulty lies in the tension between the Salvation Army's hierarchical institutional structure and the "all lay" ethos inherited from its radical Protestant antecedents.

Is this then simply a matter of semantics, without practical implications? Not if praxis is rooted in theology… and even such pragmatic steps as led to the present situation have depended on theological assumptions, albeit sometimes unconscious, and sometimes contradictory. This exploration of historical ecclesiology has been intended to help clarify the present situation and suggest that future developments ought to be premised on theological understanding. Against that, I concede that the history of the church shows that theology almost invariably *follows* practice – what works becomes orthodoxy, and theology is then adjusted to fit it. Once established, both doctrine and praxis become highly resistant to change. Change may eventually become possible, not because the theology has been shown to be inadequate but because it is no longer working successfully. The addictive disposition to denial may prevent this being conceded until the organisational journey has gone beyond the point of no return. Schaef and Fussell have drawn attention to the way in which the addictive behaviours of individuals tends to be projected on to and acted out by the whole organisation of which they are members. They specifically note the weakness of churches in this respect.[8]

This history illustrates that the Salvation Army has not been immune from the normal process whereby practical measures become set in concrete and functional roles sacralised, especially if reinforced by religious sanctions. The founders had hoped it might be otherwise. Railton exulted that

> The Army has only escaped from the old ruts in which it would have stuck fast and been incapable of accomplishing its great work by desperate fighting against itself… [It had succeeded] because the General has had, from the first, a single eye, and that single eye will enable us, if necessary, to emancipate ourselves further still, will make it as easy to abandon Army customs, as the

8 Anne Wilson Schaef and Diane Fussell, *The Addictive Organisation* (New York: Harper Collins, 1988).

> custom which prevailed before The Army, whenever it may be proved to our satisfaction that, by so doing, we should more rapidly or completely attain the one great end in view.[9]

Were Railton's hopes not realised? If not, why not?

Firstly, as the initial, reforming, evangelical zeal fades and becomes institutionalised, more and more effort has to be expended on ensuring the survival of the institution. Generations derive from it their identity and sense of security, so that it becomes increasingly resistant to change. The "children of the regiment" tend to be maintainers rather than entrepreneurs like their forebears. At the local level the trauma associated with changing anything may be illustrated by a South African officer's anecdote of a soldier rising in a meeting (that is, church service) to correct the new Commanding Officer, informing him that, "Here we always have the announcements *after* the collection." Course corrections on the global scale are commensurately ponderous and slow – the Titanic's rudder was too small to permit seriously agile manoeuvres. A bureaucracy created to facilitate action ends up by impeding it.

We are accustomed to seeing how the bright, progressive young corps officer can become the conservative Territorial Commander – Lord Acton lamented the same phenomenon in the history of Pius IX, bright hope of European liberalism in the 1840s and darling of the reactionaries in the 1870s. The more senior the responsibility, the more likely the officer is to become a prisoner of the machine, more regulated and with less freedom of action. The institution is protected by the status of its functionaries. The bond of self-interest between them will always ensure that function assumes a status.

Secondly, at a more fundamental level, all these things are about the exercise of power and control – the subject of the temptations in the wilderness, and the default position of humanity – which always finds institutional expression. The Church, whether at the local or the international level, is not exempt from the political processes of human nature. While institutionalising power, the Army has been unable to institutionalise appropriate boundaries – only that informal boundary described by Lenin in 1917: "The soldiers vote with their feet."

The tendency to clericalisation has had two related adverse effects on the Church, and, the material collected here demonstrates, on the Salvation Army.

Firstly, clericalism fosters a spirit incompatible with the "servanthood" Jesus taught and modelled. As the opinions collected under the heading "The Dark Side of the Force", below, illustrate, it is inimical to the kind of community Jesus appeared to call together.

---

9 George Scott Railton, *Twenty-one Years*, p. 93.

Secondly, clericalisation can diminish the Church's effectiveness in its mission of evangelising and serving the world. By concentrating power and influence in the hands of a minority it disempowers the great majority of members of the Church, obscuring and distorting the essential nature of the Church. It might be possible in fact to argue that the effectiveness of function is in inverse proportion to status claimed.

The following two sections argue and illustrate these assertions in more detail.

The Dark Side of the Force

The military metaphor, for all its Biblical allusions and practical advantages, carried with it dangers from which the Army has not entirely escaped. Adolf Harnack warned that,

> If the forms of the military estate are transferred to the higher religions, it appears that what is warlike is turned around and changed into its strict opposite or transformed into a mere symbol. But the form has its own logic and necessary consequences. At first unnoticeably, but soon ever more clearly, the warlike element which is accepted as a symbol ushers in the reality itself, and the "spiritual weapons of knighthood" become carnal.[10]

Dennis Garland notes that "just as William and Catherine Booth reworked the discourses of their time, they were influenced in turn by these discourses and the organization they created, namely, The Salvation Army, was transformed through the use of discourse."[11] While the Salvation Army has not gone all the way with the Knights Templar, the hierarchy of ranks has in the view of many Salvationists given permission for attitudes incompatible with the gospel. Robertson observes that, "Roman Catholicism, and some sects such as the Salvation Army, have developed elaborate bureaucratic apparatuses which appear to be particularly productive of status motivations per se... doctrine has been invoked to infuse the structure itself with religious significance."[12]

---

10 Adolf Harnack, *Militia Christi* (Philadelphia: Fortress Press, [1905] 1981) p. 32, cited in Walter Wink, *Engaging the Powers* (Minneapolis: Fortress Press) 1992, p. 291.

11 Dennis Garland, "The Salvation Army and the state of welfare: an analysis of text and narrative: an analysis of the discourses influencing the development of Salvation Army policy" (MA thesis, University of Western Sydney, 2004) downloaded from (http://library.uws.edu.au/adt-NUWS/public/adt-NUWS20040723.130012/) 1 November 2005.

12 Roland Robertson, *The Sociological Interpretation of Religion* (Oxford: Blackwell, 1970) p. 139.

The founders early became aware of the danger of creating a monster. Railton wrote in 1881 of the creation of Divisions under "District Generals" (ordinarily taking the rank of major) the previous year, "I well remember our doubts and fears as to the effect of creating a superior rank in the system of district divisions..." though he concluded that "officers and people evidently love and delight in their Majors..."[13] Perhaps twelve months were not long enough to see the longer view. By 1892 Bramwell was asking, "Are we not overdone with Staff... which in turn makes more Staff?"[14] In 1894 he was complaining that there were too many staff on Headquarters, and that "the D.O.'s [Divisional Officers] are often much more separate from their F.O.'s than they ought to be. Class and caste grows with the growth of the military idea. Needs watching."[15] Thirty years later he was still anxious about Divisional and Territorial leaders in that "they are open to special dangers in that they rise and grow powerful and sink into a kind of opulence..."[16]

It must be admitted that regulations like that making staff officers more distinguishable from those of lower rank by ordering subordinates not to wear shoulder straps, accompanied by an admonition that disregard for rank "must be discontinued", perhaps reinforced the very attitudes Bramwell did not want to encourage.[17] The elaboration of hierarchy and bureaucracy inevitably created a culture of caste.

William Booth was anxious about motivation rather than bureaucracy, but thought the toughness of the battle would be sufficient safeguard.

> It is difficult to imagine how there could be in the labour of a Army officer any sufficient earthly inducement to lead anyone to desire it for its own sake. Still, the publicity, rank and power may be attractive to some. But, if these are all, the charm will of necessity soon wear out, and the devotion inspired by it will soon pass away...[18]

But by 1900 he was warning senior leaders,

> Beware of flattery. Shut it out. Writers for our papers will sometimes seek to curry favour with their superiors by praising the natural ability displayed in their public performances and leading officers are occasionally influenced by the temptation to think that it is necessary for them to be praised... I do not

---

13 Quoted by Victor Doughty in *Officer* (August, 1974) pp. 345-6.

14 *Officer* (August, 1974) pp. 346 .

15 W. Bramwell Booth, letter of October 1894, in Catherine Bramwell Booth, *Bramwell Booth*, p. 218.

16 W. Bramwell Booth, letter to his wife, 27 April 1924, in Catherine Bramwell Booth, *Bramwell Booth*, p. 437.

17 Minute 44, October 3 1888, cited by Norman Murdoch, *Origins*, p. 132.

18 *Orders and Regulations for Field Officers*, 1886, p. 2.

> believe a word of it... I am sure, also, that it injures the younger officers, by leading them to ask and expect for themselves the same adulation which, in too many cases, they will be unable to bear.[19]

Again, addressing staff officers in Conference in 1907, he spoke of the difficulties some officers had with promotion – "because their promotion is not as rapid as they think it should be, or as they think the promotion of other officers is... That is sometimes baldly styled ambition, and when that ambition is based on selfishness it is a very ruinous quality."[20]

A "below stairs" opinion, so to speak, suggests that others shared Booth's fears. Staff-Captain E. Kirk (surely *ex*-Staff-Captain) wrote,

> It is a moot point as to whether the creation of so many distinctions in rank has not proved a greater curse than a blessing among us, and whether the course of things would not be infinitely smoother if ranks were abolished altogether, or at least, nearly so.

He also had a tilt at sycophancy:

> Many (War Cry) reports of meetings, of the General's and Mrs Booth's in particular, are sometimes positively nauseating in the plenitude of their laudatory adjectives, and in the evident desire... to please the Army's chiefs.[21]

Later writers continued to sound similar warnings. Commissioner Charles Jeffries expressed concern at officers' "tendency to make the desire for promotion the 'first thing' in their career".[22] The editor of the *Staff Review* in 1930 quoted letters sent by Field Officers to Commissioners Samuel Logan Brengle and Samuel Hurren, in USA and Great Britain respectively, both expressing dismay at the effect of the division of officers into Field and Staff streams. They referred to "inequities, nepotism, discrimination, favouritism and unfairness". Hurren commented that "No amount of religion or counsel or talk is going to damp down a sense of inequality which is founded on fact."[23] A Commission on Staff promotions was established by the General in 1929; possibly one outcome of this was the ending of the greatly resented dual system of ranks – the dead-end Field track and the Staff escalator – in 1931.

---

19 William Booth, *Letter to Commissioners and Territorial Commanders*, pp. 28-9.
20 William Booth, *Addresses to Staff Officers* (London: SA, 1907) pp. 24-5.
21 E. Kirk, *Unveiled: A Study of The Salvation Army from Within* (London: Dharma Press, undated but from internal evidence about 1914-15) pp. 57, 83.
22 *Staff Review* (July 1929) p. 255.
23 *Staff Review* (April 1930) pp. 109-115.

Commissioner Brengle also wrote against the "diotrephesian spirit".[24] "Every Diotrephesian," he wrote, "'loveth to have the pre-eminence' – not pre-eminence in goodness, Christlikeness, brotherly love, humility, meekness, or holiness, but pre-eminence in name, in fame, popular acclaim, in wealth, in place, or authority. These it is that the members of the tribe lust after, scheme, plot and plan, whisper and fawn and flatter and backbite to obtain."[25] Obviously the 1929-30 Commission didn't solve all problems as General Carpenter set up another Commission on Ranks and Promotions, identifying it as

> a question sadly disturbing in its influence... Ranks are to serve the purposes of organisation... It was not in the Founder's mind that they would ever come to be regarded as rewards for service to Christ, or as honours such as are sought in a secular organisation.[26]

General Albert Orsborn acknowledged to the 1949 Commissioners' Conference that

> dissatisfaction and decline... is blamed on our system of ranks, promotions, positions and differing salaries and retirements... that it has created envy and kindred evils and developed sycophancy, ingratiation, "wire-pulling", favouritism, etc... It is a sad reflection that we are in character, in spirituality, unable to meet the strain of our own system.[27]

The attraction of power and prestige is of course only part of the danger of a militaristic bureaucracy. Other consequences are less likely to be aired in public by senior administrators. They include the loss of institutional memory with too rapid changes of leadership. The average duration of appointment for Territorial Commanders in New Zealand since 1912 is four years and four months. Hodder (1914-1923) was exceptional. Over the past 33 years, the average has been 33 months. There is also the effect of promotion system which allows senior officers to promote in their own image, although the Salvation Army has not gone so far down the track of "professionalism" as to achieve the institutional isomorphism DiMaggio and Powell have observed: "Many professional career tracks are so closely guarded, both at the entry level and throughout the career progression, that

---

24 *Staff Review* (October 1930) pp. 317-24. The reference is to 3 John 9.
25 *Officer* (March 1931) pp. 222-3.
26 *Officers Review* (July-September 1944) pp. 129-34.
27 General Eric Wickberg, "Movements for Reform" (Address at the 1971 International Conference of Leaders, Minutes) p. 9.

individuals who make it to the top are virtually indistinguishable."[28] Perhaps more to the point is the predominance of STJ personality types (in Myers Briggs categories).[29]

Brengle did reflect in private on his concerns, in a 1912 letter to his wife:

> I think probably most of our difficulty at present in this country arises from this multiplicity of details and the infinite red tape with which we are tied up which sap the strength and frustrate the piety of our people. If our officers had the spirit of the General when he refused to be tied up to a pastorate and broke away from the church, I am not sure that there are many of them who would remain with the present concern. To my mind it is one of the paradoxes of history how the General, with his free, large spirit which refuses to be bound by the mild rules of a Methodist conference, could have developed a system which binds men hand and foot with red tape, which is to Methodist rules what... calculus is to the multiplication table.[30]

None of this is to say that the Salvation Army has been particularly worse than any other organisation or church in that human nature will find the means to exploit any structure for personal ends, but as Colonel Harry Williams reminded officers, "If all power corrupts, religious power corrupts most diabolically."[31] It does demonstrate that by adopting a military hierarchical system the founders exposed their followers to a heightened danger in this respect, and opened the farm gate a little wider for what Lear called "the great image of authority – a dog's obeyed in office".[32] Having said that, there is no system above which it is impossible to rise, and a host of men and women have shone like lights in a naughty world.

Power and Disempowerment

The introductory chapters described the way in which a clerical caste has always established or re-established a dominant role. For all intents and purposes it *is* the Church, with the rest of the *laos* serving either as passive audience for the clerical performers, or as supporting cast and extras. As

---

28 Paul DiMaggio and Walter Powell, "The Iron Cage Revisited: Institutional Isomorphism and Collective Rationality in Organisational Fields", *American Sociological Review*, 48 (1991) pp. 152-153.

29 An analysis of New Zealand Salvation Army officers in the 1990s found 80% SJs (strong on obedience, duty, service, a type common amongst police and accountants) compared with about 40% of the general population.

30 S.L. Brengle, in letter to his wife 22 July 1912, in William Clark (ed.), *Dearest Lily: a selection of the Brengle correspondence* (London: SA, 1985) p. 112.

31 *Officer* (August 1970) p. 550.

32 William Shakespeare, *King Lear*, Act IV Scene vi.

Hendrik Kraemer concluded, "in raising today the lay issue in the Church, one raises at the same time the demand for a new ecclesiology..."[33] The shallowness of the Salvation Army's ecclesiology afforded it no defence against the clericalising process which rapidly vitiated its original lay genius. (Although one has to say that the richer theological heritage of many older Church bodies has proved equally ineffectual in this respect; ecclesiology has only served to extend and codify that process.)

Can it be argued that clericalisation has been accompanied by a decline in the Church's effectiveness? Perhaps it depends on the measure used for "effectiveness". Clearly the centuries in which the Church clericalised were also years in which it grew to become a significant world religion. The Salvation Army's greatest growth areas today are in the developing world where rank and status seem more important and its clericalist tendencies seem more marked. (Although this growth is often the result of "lay" initiative, like that of Envoy Chasi, described on page 198.)

On the other hand, Brunner drew attention to a contrary tendency in considering the early history of the Church: "The emergence of ecclesiastical rule and jurisdiction is coincided with the loss or weakening of the community's messianic consciousness."[34] Yves Congar wrote of the end result of clericalism being that "the faithful got into the habit of receiving without activity, leaving to the clergy the charge of building up the Church – like citizens who leave the making of their country to the civil servants and officials, and the defence of it to the military."[35] The Indian Jesuit Kurien Kunnumpuram claims that "the clergy-laity divide and the consequent lack of power-sharing in the Church are largely responsible for the apathy and inertia that one notices in the bulk of the laity today."[36] The American Nazarene sociologist Kenneth E. Crow sums up: "Loyalty declines when ability to influence decision and policies declines. When institutionalization results in top-down management, one of the consequences is member apathy and withdrawal."[37]

Evidence of the results of this tendency can be found. Finke and Stark link the decline in the growth of Methodism in the USA in the nineteenth century with growing clericalism. "We think it instructive that Methodists began to slump at precisely the same time that their amateur clergy were

---

33 Kraemer, *Theology of the Laity*, pp. 48-9.

34 Brunner, *Misunderstanding*, p. 59.

35 Congar, *Lay People in the Church*, p. 47.

36 Kurien Kunnumpurum, "Beyond the Clergy-Laity Divide" (http://www.sedos.org/english/kunnumpuram.html) May 2000, downloaded 22 December 2000.

37 Kenneth E. Crow, "The Church of the Nazarene and O'Dea's Dilemma of Mixed Motivation" (www.nazarene.org/ansr/articles/crow_93.html) downloaded 30 March 2005.

replaced by professionals who claimed episcopal authority over their congregations."[38] A. D. Gilbert produces statistics showing how the decennial increase of membership per minister in the Wesleyan Church in Great Britain declined steadily from 93.7% in 1801 when there were 334 ministers, to 12.6% in 1911 when there were 2,478 ministers. The reasons were of course various, but Gilbert does suggest that it was partly that "maintaining themselves, their families, and their homes, tended to divert preachers from the business of itinerant evangelism still expected of them by many laymen". To that had to be added "the increasingly complex task of running a massive national association... The preachers more or less consistently displayed a willingness to accept reduced recruitment and even schism as a price for organisational consolidation under ministerial leadership."[39]

The Salvation Army stopped publishing its soldiership statistics as its growth in the United Kingdom faltered in the 1890s and did not reveal them again until late in the following century. Figures for soldiers' rolls reappeared in the *Yearbook* of 1995. Murdoch suggests that "Booth's unpublished statistics were significant. In the 1890 May meeting (voluntary societies published annual reports in May) at Exeter Hall Booth listed the number of officers and corps abroad but not the British totals, which had declined by fifty Corps since May 1889."[40]

The number of British Corps declined from 1412 to 1211 between 1888 and 1894.[41] In Escott's words, growth in the British Isles "tailed off around 1890... Though some growth continued until the mid-1930s it was slow. Since that point there has been almost constant decline."[42] Inglis comments that "the Army's golden age had been those few years after 1880 when the excitement and energy of the people already enlisted were fanned by accounts of fresh successes won by shock tactics up and down England and abroad."[43] By the early twentieth century Salvation Army meeting places were attracting less spectacular attendances than in the 1880s; greater London Corps attendances were 53,591 on one Sunday in 1887, down to 38,896, with 22,402 in inner London, in 1903.[44] British *War Cry* sales, from

38 Roger Finke and Rodney Stark, "How the Upstart Sects Won America: 1776-1850", *Journal for the Scientific Study of Religion* (1989) 28 (1) p. 42.

39 A. D. Gilbert, *Religion and Society*, pp. 152,3,4.

40 Murdoch, *Origins*, p. 133.

41 Murdoch, *Origins*, p. 122.

42 Escott, Thesis, "Church Growth Theories", p. 335.

43 Inglis, *Churches and Working Classes*, p. 212.

44 Wilson in *Patterns of Sectarianism*, p. 101, cites Inglis, *Churches and Working Classes*, pp. 196-197; Richard Mudie-Smith (ed.), *The Religious Life of London* (London: Hodder and Stoughton, 1904) pp. 288-90. See also John Kent, *Holding the Fort: Studies in Victorian Revivalism* (London: Epworth, 1978) p. 300.

a peak of 350,000 copies weekly in 1883, fell to under 290,000 in 1890.[45] Official Census figures showed fewer Salvationists in the Southern (Australian) Command in 1901 than in 1891 and the Army's share of total church attendance there declined between 1891 and 1896.[46] In New Zealand the proportion of Salvationists reached a peak of 1.5% of the population in 1895 and declined slowly but steadily thereafter.[47] By 1926 it was 0.91% and by 1956, 0.65%. In the 2001 census, it was 0.33%.[48] One interpretation of these figures is to say that as the movement institutionalised, and officership clericalised, it lost momentum.

This is not to argue that this was the only process going on, or that there was a direct cause and effect. Firstly, it would be difficult to establish whether clericalisation had led to a loss of zeal, or loss of zeal had been compensated for by a growing preoccupation with status, or whether each process fed the other. There is a paradox here: the military system, quite apart from the fact that it fitted Booth's autocratic temperament, was designed for rapid response, and is still officially justified in those terms: "We are the 'special forces unit' of his Church on earth," claims Commissioner Israel Gaither.[49] The Army's first period of rapid growth followed its introduction. It caught the imagination for a time. However the concomitant burgeoning of hierarchical and bureaucratic attitudes – which Brengle has been cited above as deploring – came to exert a counter-influence. The reason for success contained the seeds of failure. The longer-term effects of autocracy and "sectarian totalitarianism" were to lose the loyalty of many of those hitherto enthusiastic, and to deter subsequent generations, more habituated to free thought and democracy, from joining.

On the other hand, Dean Kelly's 1972 book, *Why Conservative Churches are Growing*, drew attention to the long-term decline of the American mainstream, liberal churches, contrasted with the growth of bodies like the Southern Baptists.[50] Rodney Stark argues that "strong" sects or churches, with firm doctrines, distinctive practices and clear boundaries, tend to thrive and grow. Conversely, "weak" bodies, less clear about their beliefs, becoming more generic, mainstream and Church-like, and accommodating to the society around them, inevitably decline.[51]

---

45 Inglis, *Churches and Working Classes*, p. 197, cites *WC* (17 May 1890).

46 H.R. Jackson, *Churches and People in Australia and New Zealand* (Wellington: Allen & Unwin/Port Nicholson Press, 1987) p. 62.

47 New Zealand *WC* (26 June 1965) p. 9.

48 New Zealand census figures.

49 *SA Year Book* (2004) p. 3.

50 Dean M. Kelly, *Why Conservative Churches are Growing* (New York: Harper and Row, 1972.)

51 Stark and Bainbridge, *The Future of Religion: Secularization, Revival and Cult Formation* (1985); Finke and Stark, *The Churching of America, 1776-1990* (1992); Stark and Finke, *Acts of Faith* (2000); See also Laurence Iannoccone, "A Formal

In general terms we could say that the period of the Army's stagnation and decline in some areas has coincided broadly with its increasing accommodation to the "world", its becoming more like a mainstream denomination in the attitudes of both soldiers and officers and its experiencing some erosion in its distinctive identity. The chapter on "Transitions" has described how this began to happen – and the process accelerated towards the end of the twentieth century. However, the Army's growth peaked well before these tendencies became marked, so the Stark thesis does not provide a total explanation. (Stark is also writing from an American perspective, and the religiosity of the United States has followed a different trajectory from that of Europe and the "Anglo-Saxon" Commonwealth.)

Two mutually contradictory explanations may therefore be advanced for the Army's decline in the West: firstly that its strictness ran counter to the temper of the times and alienated those preferring a lighter discipline, and secondly that its liberalising, denominationalising tendencies weakened its aggressive spirit and failed to satisfy those wanting a more earnest evangelicalism, or a more spectacular, charismatic profile. Perhaps there is something to both arguments.

The Developing World

The foregoing observations apply particularly to the "West"; the Army in the "developing world" is a different matter. Internationally the Salvation Army is larger than ever before. One hundred years ago the Army's franchise was marketed around the globe. While it adapted effectively to indigenous culture in some places – Booth-Tucker's red shoulder cloth, dhoti and bare feet ensured its success in India[52] – the momentum of Empire and the dedication of its officers secured a foothold even when the results were less happy. What worked in England in the 1880s worked in many places. The irony is that while the formula is no longer working in Europe, England, or in the "Old Dominions", it is now working better than ever in the developing world. More than three quarters of the Army's strength is now found in Africa and Asia. The Army of the nineteenth century is alive and well in such places. I have listened to a 25-piece "brass" band fashioned entirely of bamboo playing early Salvation Army melodies in an Indonesian village accessible only on foot or by bullock cart.

Model of Sect and Church", *American Journal of Sociology* 94 Supplement (1988) pp. S241-S268; and "Why Strict Churches are Strong", *American Journal of Sociology* 99:5 (March 1994) pp. 1180-1211.

52 Frederick Booth-Tucker, *Muktifauj: Forty Years with The Salvation Army in India and Ceylon* (London: Marshall Brothers, [1923]) p. 78.

The dynamics of an international organisation are complex; a host of historical, sociological and cultural, even political, factors are involved. Possibly the Salvation Army's current growth in the third world is because those societies, less individualistic, with a stronger culture of "belonging" and traditional respect for authority, have elements in common with Victorian British working class, rendering them susceptible in turn to the attractions of firm and decisive leadership.

Officers in Southern Africa for example all take for granted that they are *umfundisi* (ministers) as much as their Episcopal or *vaPostori*[53] colleagues and their soldiers recognise them as such. M. L. Daneel refers to Zimbabwean independent churches' "well-differentiated and flexible hierarchies which allow for the majority of capable and adult members to hold office... With it goes a certain status in the in-group which often compensates for the lack of prestige or influence elsewhere."[54] There is a waiting list for officer training in such Territories.[55] It is interesting to compare this with Roland Robertson's comment concerning the early Salvation Army, that "many Salvationists... were drawn from socially disadvantaged lower-middle-class, working class and destitute strata, and this in itself presented a strong incentive to achieve status *qua* status within the Army itself."[56]

Minna Karlström, corps officer from Finland and member of the International Commission on Officership, acknowledged that "unease with the authoritarian system is not universal. Different nations are at different stages on the modernisation-postmodernisation continuum and this becomes evident in the range of attitudes towards changing our system."[57] Of course the Salvation Army is not alone in experiencing this third-world conservatism. Opposition to having women priests or homosexual bishops in the Anglican Communion is strongest in Africa and Asia (and Sydney...). Gerald Arbuckle, referring to the "Pre-Vatican II tribe" (writing as an anthropologist), notes that, "I rarely meet 'pure type' representatives of this tribal model in the Western World today, but they remain relatively common in parts of the Third World."[58]

---

53 Members of the African Apostolic Church of Zimbabwe.

54 "The Growth and Significance of Shona Independent Churches" by M.L. Daneel, in M.F.C. Bourdillon (ed.) *Christianity South of the Zambezi* (Gwelo: Mambo Press, 1977) Vol. 2, pp. 178, 184.

55 *SA Year Book* (2004) p. 190 records that in 2003 in Pakistan, 154 applications for officer training were received. 40 were accepted, the maximum that could be accommodated.

56 Wilson, *Patterns of Sectarianism*, p. 88.

57 *Officer* (October 1999) p. 17.

58 Gerald Arbuckle, *From Chaos to Mission* (Collegeville MN: Liturgical Press, 1996) p. 75.

Having said that, it is possible that the processes that have led to the present situation in the West will also become operative to some degree elsewhere in the future. Arbuckle observes that, "Today's candidates for the religious life are confronted not by the characteristics of one of the preceding culture models (he has described Pre-modern, Modern, Post-Modern and Para-modern), but by all the models at the same time, even in the Third World, as a consequence of globalisation of the information media."[59] In another twenty or thirty years the march of the Third World Army may encounter obstacles similar to those with which we are familiar in Europe or Australasia. However, such an outcome cannot be predicted with any certainty so my concluding chapter, and any suggestions for changes, are therefore applicable only to the Armies of the West at this juncture. And it was for the West that Lesslie Newbigin urged the need for "the energetic fostering of a declericalized, lay theology."[60]

Perhaps a formula taking into account the cultural factors could be designed. Certainly serious research needs to be done to see how far hard data supports the general theory advanced in this section. However the general argument stands, at least as societies become more individualistic in ethos, that the more power is concentrated in a minority of hands, the less enthusiastic and effective participation in the task can be expected from the majority. Expectation grows that the professionals will do everything. The tendency towards clericalism is thus reinforced.

---

59 Arbuckle, *Chaos to Mission*, pp. 5, 7.

60 Lesslie Newbigin, *Foolishness to the Greeks: The Gospel and Western Culture* (Grand Rapids MICH: Eerdmans, 1986) p. 142.

Chapter Twenty-One

The Trick of Standing Upright

> Not I, some child, born in a marvellous year,
> Will learn the trick of standing upright here.
>
> Allen Curnow,
> *Attitudes for a New Zealand Poet (iii).*

If officership is inevitably enmeshed in these forces of sociology and psychology, or in thrall to such demons, depending on one's theological preference, what future for the officer role? How might the effect of clericalisation be mitigated? This can be considered under three headings, concerning firstly the vocation of the officer as an individual, secondly the role of the officer, and thirdly the relationship of the officer to the organisation.

The Officer Vocation

While a hall-mark of the Protestant reformation was the acknowledgement that all vocations are equally God-given and God-glorifying, it is another indication of clerical reaction that in evangelical circles "the call" has been increasingly assumed to be pre-eminently to "the Ministry". The chapter "What manner of men…" showed that the Army encouraged its members to respond to a call to officership, and "Putney Debates" that some officers represented their experience of the call as the reason they became, and remained, Salvation Army officers. While only one person of my acquaintance has described their call as an auditory experience, the majority of officers would still regard their commitment to the Army as a response to some sense of calling.

This has been less emphasised in recent times in this country – there has been some reticence about putting the hard word on young Salvationists. John Townsend wrote, "The *ecclesiastical call* was once a high priority in Army services especially on special occasions such as Candidate's Sunday and Youth Councils. However in recent years this style has lapsed because some salvationists considered that the appeal for leaders was too emotive and created undue guilt."[1] Young people have also become less responsive to such appeals. It has to be asked to what extent the earlier response level was conditioned by the expectations of the Salvation Army community of faith, and how far the decline in officer-vocations is indicative both of the post-modern mindset and of the wider choices now available. With so many ministry roles now open even within the Army, many prefer to respond to their sense of vocation in ways that leave them more in control of their lives and without any expectation of life-long service. Whereas the traditional acceptance of officer-conditions, obedience and appointability was seen as a sign of spirituality, more recent generations tend to believe that taking responsibility for discerning God's will for one's own life is a greater mark of Christian maturity.

Some attribute a decline in officer-morale to the employment of non-officers in roles formerly reserved to officers. Again, the phenomenon is not confined to the Salvation Army. Fr Timothy Radcliffe, Master General of the Dominicans 1992-2001, asking "Why is morale among priests so low?" included this same development amongst the reasons he offered. "In the USA 80% of people who are ministers in the Church are lay, and 80% of these lay people are women… The priest feels less special."[2] Susanne Monahan, researching clergy morale, had expected to find less role ambiguity among clergy in hierarchical churches under these circumstances and expressed surprise at finding more. Her research did not include Catholic clergy or Salvation Army officers, but both work at the more hierarchical end of the spectrum.[3] The ensuing identity crisis and evident low morale amongst the clergy again deters other people from taking up that vocation.

Given these developments, there would appear to be a choice of ways forward for vocation in the Salvation Army. One is the equivalent of what in the Catholic Church is described as the "restorationist" agenda, where it is seriously attempted to set the clock back to pre-Vatican II ways. This would involve renewed efforts to convince a new generation of Salvationists that they ought to commit themselves to life-long obedience to the organisation. In some territories – UK for example – in recent years the numbers of

1 John Townsend, "Where have all the Leaders Gone? Officer Recruitment in The Salvation Army of Aotearoa New Zealand" (MMin thesis, Melbourne College of Divinity, 1999) p. 13.

2 Timothy Radcliffe, "Why is morale among priests so low?" (Address to National Conference of Priests at Digby Stuart College, Roehampton, London, on 3 September 2002). Downloaded 8 April 2003 from (www.onlineopinion.com.au/2002/Nov02/Radcliffe.htm).

3 Susanne C. Monahan, in "Role Ambiguity Amongst Protestant Clergy: Consequences of the Activated Laity", *Review of Religious Research* 41 (1999) pp. 79-94.

people offering for officer-training have been roughly equalled by the numbers offering for auxiliary officership. Until the introduction of the new Lieutenancy system, these latter were usually second career, late-vocation people. Of these one might observe that, firstly, they were by definition not offering for life-long service, and secondly, that they belonged to a generation more willing to accept such conditions as "appointability". The new Lieutenancy appears to be attracting, as well as these older candidates, equal numbers of younger people for whom the short-term nature of the commitment (three years at a time) apparently compensates for the absence of longer-term benefits such as retirement packages. It is not yet clear that beating the antique drum will muster the same numbers of this generation for traditional officership.

An alternative way forward is the solution proposed by John Townsend in his thesis on the causes and extent of the dearth of ecclesial leadership in the Salvation Army: to increase the variety of options available to those who believe themselves called to serve God within the Salvation Army. "There are many models of ecclesial leadership both biblical and extra-biblical, that could challenge the Salvation Army to expand its base for leadership, rather than seeing the role primarily as the domain of a commanding officer."[4] However this would run counter to a deep lode of clericalist thinking in the officer corps.

Stark and Finke, in their analysis of the impact of Vatican II on vocations, to which reference has already been made, believe that

> To generate and sustain religious virtuosi requires constant reinforcement from an equally committed community of peers, firm belief in divine appreciation of the relevant sacrifices, and special levels of worldly recognition of virtue.[5]

The problem is how to combine that precept with an equal commitment to equality. If there is any validity to the argument that status is ultimately inhibitive of function, there needs to be found a way of giving full value to the vocation of officership as one ministry option without by implication devaluing other vocations – either those which might be defined as "ministry", within the ecclesial structure, or those we choose, within the framework of an inappropriate dualism, to describe as "secular".

4 Townsend, Thesis, "Where have all the leaders gone?", p. 116.

5 Stark and Finke, *Acts of Faith*, p. 190. See also the same authors' "Catholic Religious Vocations: Decline and Revival", *Review of Religious Research* 42:2 (Dec. 2000) pp. 125-145.

The Officer Role

The chapters on "Putney Debates" collect a variety of attempts to describe, define or clarify the role of the Officer within the organisation. Some assumed one of the conventional clergy roles in the modern church – that of leader, teacher, pastor, preacher, evangelist, and representative figure (like the keystone of the arch) or a mix of all of these. Some saw all these as aspects of an equipping task, enabling other members of the Army to be Christ in the world.

Unfortunately, from the time charismatic leadership – where each person contributed their particular gifts and skills to the group as a whole – was superseded in the early church by the three-fold orders and monarchical episcopate (that is, from the time function began giving way to status as the guiding principle) the Church has tended to expect its leaders individually to demonstrate all of the gifts, and has been correspondingly disappointed in them when they have not been able to deliver. Meanwhile the gifts of other members of the church have tended to atrophy.

The majority of contributors to the debate seemed to see officership pre-eminently in terms of "field" or Corps work (that is, to do with what might be described as parish, congregational or evangelical activities), closest to those tasks occupying the time of other clergy. That such an assumption has a long history is suggested by the fact that the *Officer* magazine, for all branches of the service, was known as *The Field Officer* between 1900 and 1913. However only about half of Salvation Army officers are found in such roles. An almost equal number are engaged in social or welfare activities and in administration, as well as in a great variety of specialist roles. The Army has a much more extensive bureaucracy than the majority of denominations. In New Zealand, the 2003 *Disposition of Forces* gave 186 officers (or 54% of the total) engaged in Corps work compared with 95 (27%) in administration, including training, and 66 (19%) in social work and other roles. (The majority of social workers are now non-officers.) While some clergy of other denominations are also found in other than the traditional parish roles, such involvement is more commonly *outside* the ecclesiastical structure; Salvation Army officers on the other hand are absorbed *within* the structure. The tendency to ignore this reality illustrates how thoroughly the Army's thinking has accommodated to a conventional denominational ethos.

The chapter "Putney Debates" and the book *Servants Together* show that a variety of attempts to define the officer role over against that of soldiers all came to grief over the basic presupposition, derived from the rejection of any hint of sacerdotalism, that there was nothing done by an officer that could not be done by a soldier. It is necessary to admit that officership is simply the way in which we choose to organise the Army; it has no sacred dimension in itself.

The organisation of the Army on the basis of the military metaphor would suggest that leadership is the chief function of officership. However, the Salvation Army, like any military support structure, includes numbers of people who hold ranks but whose function is to support and follow rather than to lead. Parkinson's Law would suggest that their numbers rise in inverse proportion to the actual fighting engaged in.[6] We could say that all officers are leaders, and that all leaders must be officers. This would be logical but it would require a revolution. In practice it would involve great numbers of officers being divested of their ranks, and the conferring of commissioned rank on the increasing number of people who are not presently officers but who serve in leadership roles.

Whether or not such a course were followed, it is still necessary to ask how we might have leadership unattended by the abuse of power which all leadership risks, and which is especially hard to prevent in a hierarchical system. There has been increasing emphasis on the concept of "servant leadership" in Salvation Army writing. Major Phil Garnham writes

> In a postmodern world where the Church is seen as just another instrument of power, control and oppression, there is a great need to demonstrate that the character of the Church at both leadership and congregational levels is that of compassionate servanthood. If Salvation Army leadership at all levels [were to] take this model as a serious alternative to the autocratic, hierarchical control model, whether we are engaged in pastoral, managerial, mundane or public ministry, then we would represent a genuinely alternative value system, that at the same time would be shocking and attractive to a postmodern generation.[7]

As Timothy Radcliffe observes, "the words ['servant' and 'leadership'] tend to pull in opposite directions"[8] but given that truth is often characterised by paradox this is no argument against trying. Certainly this would cohere with the concept of equipping as the central role of the officer-leader. It would also be consistent with the Trinitarian concept of ministry, where the relationship of the persons of the Trinity, undivided in essence and co-equal in power and glory, is seen as a model for dynamic relationship within the church, as an alternative to the hierarchical model. Jurgen Moltman urges that the logical implication of a perichoretic understanding of the Trinity is that "the ecclesiastical structures that flow from a notion of Divine hierarchy, must give way to the horizontal

6 C. Northcote Parkinson, *Parkinson's Law* (London: John Murray, 1958) p. 11.
7 Phil Garnham, "Postmodernity and Faith education in The Salvation Army", e*Journal of Aggressive Christianity* (April 2005) www.armybarmy.com.
8 Radcliffe, "Clergy Morale".

structures of fellowship, equality and interdependence."[9] However, that is a concept difficult to implement when the structures do not support it.

Despite this recent emphasis noted on servant leadership in Army publications, such words can so easily be used to legitimate a reality of another kind. The cynic would note that the ancient Papal title, Servant of the Servants of God, could long co-exist with ultramontanism. Power is the shadow side of servant leadership, and must be recognised, faced up to and incorporated knowingly and with boundaries if it is not to usurp total control. Without structural safeguards, all talk of servanthood too easily becomes an instrument of spiritual abuse. Hans-Ruedi Weber's neat aphorism, that "Jesus transforms the love of power into the power of love," is reversed by clericalisation.[10]

What kind of structures could ensure the successful practice of servant leadership? Political systems often incorporate checks and balances to prevent abuse of power. In recent years there have been serious attempts to build more accountability into the structure of the Salvation Army with enhanced officer review processes, but it would be helpful if ways could be found of making this flow both ways, so that those in the hierarchy owed a duty of transparency and accountability to those below them as well as to those above. The most recent changes to the Officer Undertakings have attempted to make explicit the organisation's obligations to its officers as well as the officers' duties to the organisation (without however a signature on behalf of the organisation as that would amount to a contract), but this does not address structural issues within the hierarchy. Sadly, the situation still obtains that occasionally people widely known to abuse power, having set foot on the escalator, continue to rise in influence and authority. Of money, sex and power, clerical misdemeanours relating to the first two are usually attended by rapid retribution, whereas abuse of power rarely attracts rebuke. The abusers can be judges in their own cases.

Over the years the structural measure most often urged has been "clearly defined consultative processes"[11] or some "forum for discussion"[12] – the lack of which leads to frustration and anger or loss of interest. A rare early

---

9 Quoted by Colin Hunter in *Supervised Theological Field Education: A Resource Manual* (Melbourne: Evangelical Theological Association.) (http://mc2.vicnet.net.au/home/chunter/web/resource.html) downloaded 21 December 2005.

10 Hans-Ruedi Weber, *Power, Focus for a Biblical Theology* (Geneva: World Council of Churches, 1989) p. 167.

11 Major Aubrey Barfoot (Canada) in *Officer* (August 1987) pp. 347-8.

12 For example, Editorial in *Battlepoint* 1:1 (September 1963); Cedric Jackson in *Crossfire* 1 (March 1971) [p.5]; Colonel George Carpenter (Australia) in *Impact* 4:1 (1974) pp.8-14; Richard Smith, "An Open letter to Commissioner John Larsson and other leaders of The Salvation Army", Wellington, New Zealand, 28 June 1994.

voice was that of John Hollins, salvationist and journalist, who wrote in *The Contemporary Review* in 1898 that

> Under the domination of the military idea and in the name of loyalty we appear to have all agreed to keep silence concerning the disquieting symptoms and weak places existing in this... The Salvation Army is sound enough and strong enough to profit by an honest exchange of opinion among its members in their councils and publications.[13]

While boards and councils have long since filled the vacuum left by the founder's abolition of committees, and ad hoc consultations, commissions, quality improvement working parties and special forums have proliferated in recent years, no consistent attempt has been made to initiate structural reform along the lines suggested by Hodder in Chapter Fifteen. "Lay" advisory councils have been ephemeral. There does not seem to have been any strong demand expressed for elected offices or institutions. The High Council reformers of the 1920s never envisaged their own commands being touted for election. Because "representative" institutions have never been allowed to take root, the next stage of constitutional evolution, to "responsible" bodies, has not taken place. That would be incompatible with the military model.

Some other suggestions have been made over the years. For example, Captain John Wordsworth, speaking at a "Cutting Edge Conference" in Christchurch, New Zealand, in 2001, proposed:

> Firstly, all systemic privilege and power must be removed. If one officer gets a free TV licence and Koru club card, all officers should get equal opportunity. And further the class system between officers and, just as committed, lay staff must be removed. Secondly, the thorny issue of who reviews the reviewers must be courageously addressed. Thirdly, the systemic barriers to constructive communication must be carefully dismantled.[14]

It is true, however, that servant-leader behaviour flows only from servant-leader attitudes, and attitudes are notoriously unamenable to legislation. They have to be caught as well as taught, by the example of what Paul called "working together", by way of contrast with "ruling over".[15] Just as early officer training sought to inculcate the Salvationist spirit, perhaps

---

13 John Hollins, "The Salvation Army: A Note of Warning", *The Contemporary Review* (London: Isbister & Coy, 1898) p. 437. Cited by Barbara Robinson in her Coutts Memorial Lecture, 21 July 2005, printed in *Practical Theologian* 3:2 (September 2005) p. 8.

14 Captain John Wordsworth, in papers from the Cutting Edge Conference, Christchurch, New Zealand, 20 August 2001, p. 36.

15 2 Corinthians 1:24.

servant leadership modelling and conditioning should be more of a priority in officer-formation today. Such a priority would help tilt the balance towards the functional end of the continuum and away from that of status. Ken Booth's words are relevant here:

> Ordination is about apostolic leadership, and you cannot have apostolic leadership in the church without the risk of clericalisation; and the key to overcoming the risk lies in the recovery of the servant (the diaconal) nature of all ministry in the church, including the ministry of apostolic leadership.[16]

Both structural and attitudinal change is required for this to happen.

The Officer Covenant and Undertakings

The Undertakings signed by the officer, as we have seen, commit the individual to a number of conditions intended to ensure his or her full availability to the service. Amongst these the commitment to appointability has long been identified as defining the officer's relationship with the organisation.

A useful analogy might be found in the Catholic Church's insistence on celibacy for clergy. Nearly forty years ago Ivan Illich pointed out that celibacy, protected by "two devices to control an evangelical charisma" – "the social and juridical organization of religious communities and the ritual celebration of vows" – served to maintain a "captive personnel force." Noting the Pope's insistence on retaining the institution in the face of growing discontent, Illich suggests, "I believe that the emergence of a new pastoral Church depends largely on compliance with his directive during our generation. His position helps assure the speedy death of the clergy."[17] Those who see the decline in the numbers of candidates for officership in some Territories as arising from the reluctance of young Salvationists to serve under the conditions of officership, especially that of appointability, though keen to serve God in some capacity within the Army, might identify with Illich's view. In New Zealand training intakes have ranged from 5 to 13 (not including Fiji and Tonga) in recent years, against a replacement need of about 22-25 to maintain existing personnel levels. The 2004 intake of cadets for training in the United Kingdom was 30. Thirty years ago it was about 100. Fifty years ago it was 200. In 1930, it was 350.

The conditions of officer service have helped create status, in so far as they have set officers apart from other Salvationists, and this was

16 Ken Booth, "Something about Ordination", p. 2.

17 Ivan Illich, "The Vanishing Clergyman" (1967) reprinted in *Celebration of Awareness* (Harmondsworth: Penguin, 1976) pp. 75-6.

deliberately fostered, along with all the other devices used to create morale and *esprit de corps*. Perhaps they have now become counterproductive, in that these conditions no longer serve that purpose for people who are already officers and make more difficult the recruitment of their replacements.

Lt. Colonel Wilfred Arnold, the New Zealand Territory's Secretary for Personnel addressed this in a paper on "The Officer Rank Structure". Referring to candidates for ministry, he wrote that

> those who were offering may meet all the criteria except...no distinct call to ministry (other than the call to evangelise, teach...) a life serving the church, shown in an unwillingness to be portable (I determine where I will serve) and maintaining a certain lifestyle (I agree the period and the financial return)... When I discuss this with those involved with potential leaders, they challenge that there is any less of a call to ministry. What appears to be significant is the difficulty of submitting to a life serving within the Church. Debate ensues as to whether this is an element of post-modernism (I am arbiter of my calling) or an expression of Christian maturity in an individual taking responsibility under God. The result is an unwillingness to trust their lives in submitting to the authority of the Body of Christ as represented in the movement The Salvation Army. It is expressed in terms of a distrust of "Leadership" or "the movement" to safely handle the life that is being entrusted to it.[18]

Just as celibacy – required of the western priesthood for only the second half of Christian history after all – was in part a practical measure intended to meet a particular temporary and local need, and not of the essence of clerical life, so "adaptation of measures" (Catherine Booth's phrase) could require the Salvation Army to abandon appointability today. It is of course reluctant to do so, just as the Pope is determined to retain celibacy even although it is widely seen as a serious impediment to vocations to the priesthood. Responding to the looming fulfilment of Illich's prediction, *The Tablet* editorialised in 2005, "The question is whether the Holy Spirit is calling forth new responses to the challenges of the times, requiring not one pattern of ordained ministry by a full-time professional resident celibate, but various models of which the traditional is but one..."[19] Salvationists might echo the *Tablet*'s words. While this clinging to past policies is partly for logistical and management convenience, in both cases it is probable, as Illich suggests, that it is also to do with control. Anyone working in the addictions field will recognise that we always prefer the pain we have to the perceived pain of changing, and will go to any lengths to maintain our habit. The Catholic Church deals with the problem partly by making fewer priests

---

18 Wilfred Arnold, "The Officer Rank Structure" (Paper circulated to officers in New Zealand, dated 27 March 2001) p. 4.
19 *The Tablet* (15 October 2005).

go further; the Salvation Army by employing more employees. Both are temporizing measures, entailing adverse consequences in the longer term.

The other main feature of the Undertakings is that with the officer's explicit renunciation of any legal claim to remuneration or other benefits of employed status, they are the cornerstone of the Army's sharing the "employed by God" status enjoyed by the clergy of most churches.[20] Until now this has served to safeguard the Army against legal action by its officers. A vigorous rearguard action against any change is to be expected. In the paper quoted above Lt. Colonel Arnold claimed that

> this non-contractual "religious" relationship is vital to the protection of the ability of the Church (The Salvation Army) to invoke moral and religious beliefs as the code of conduct for its ministers. If this was not so then the "church" would be subject to other generic "human rights" that would not allow it to hold to its specific beliefs and behavioural standards. It is therefore imperative that... the engagement of people in pastoral ministry be on officer terms and conditions and not be allowed to erode over time or proliferate into wage or salary employment contracts.[21]

It is likely that the non-contractual basis of clerical engagement will come under increasing pressure in modern secular societies – falling into the same category as tax-exemption for churches. A recent Australian High Court decision concluded, at the end of a series of appeals, that it can no longer be assumed, or presumed, that a minister is not an employee when exercising "spiritual duties" for a church group – rather, each case will have to be judged upon its own facts to determine whether it was the intention of the parties that there will be a legally binding (and thus enforceable) relationship between them, or whether the relationship was not one of that character.[22]

The Army's Undertakings are still sufficiently explicit in that respect to maintain the status quo in common law jurisdictions, but the trend is clear. In the United Kingdom the process was advanced by a protracted dispute between an Anglican priest and his diocese, and its referral to the European Parliament on the grounds that UK law discriminated against clergy.[23] The Interim Report of the Archbishops' Council's Review of Clergy Terms of Service in July 2003 recommended, amongst other things, that "the rights conferred by section 23 of the Employment Relations Act 1999 are seen as

---

20 A recent test case in New Zealand was Mabon v The Conference of the Methodist Church of New Zealand, CA 250/97.

21 Wilfred Arnold, "Officer Rank Structure", p. 6.

22 Archbishop Spyridon Ermogenous versus the Greek Orthodox Community of South Australia Inc [2002] HCA8; 7 March 2002.

23 Council for World Mission webpage, 28 November 2002 (www.cwmission.org.uk/features/default.cfm?FeatureID=981).

good practice and should be granted to clergy..."; that "clergy should have the rights conferred by section 23 not just in practice but in law"; and that "clergy should have access to Employment Tribunals...." It was recognised that giving clergy these rights "does not necessarily require them to have contracts of employment... Other possible models also need to be considered."[24] While this referred only to clergy of the established church, the Clergy and Church Workers Section of Amicus Union came out strongly for a system "applicable across denominations and faiths".[25] A non-officer Salvationist employed in a ministry role in the United Kingdom expressed the expectation that, "...employment law in the UK will demand major changes in the nature of officers' contracts with the organisation...Officers will become closer to employees in their length of tenure, nature of payment and relationship to the organisation."[26] It has already been noted that the employment of non-officers in roles hitherto reserved for officers has raised the question of legal implications – an officer also performing those roles might also now be regarded as an employee. Relinquishing the "employed by God" status would negate any defence against such a claim.

Commissioner Israel Gaither, Chief of the Staff, told the 2004 International Conference of Leaders that "some nations see leaders as contracted employees while others acknowledge and respect the covenanted relationship that embraces our calling."[27] However, the "employed by God" status, secured by this "covenanted relationship", is really an anachronism left over from Theodosian polity. In the case of clerical orders, to which the Army aspires, the special status has somehow been allowed to remain, attenuated in relevance and serving mainly to buttress the power of the ecclesiastical institution over against its functionaries and negate their civil rights.

The relationship between covenant and employment might now be compared with that of religious and civil marriage. These are viewed as identical by some and as distinct by others, but the state recognises only the latter. In practice people relinquish clerical roles as readily as they forsake the married state. We need to distinguish between civil contract, which relates to law, and covenant, which is of grace. All Christians, clergy or not, participate in covenant – and Salvation Army soldiers, whether officers or not, specifically sign a covenant with God. The law cannot prescribe for such a relationship.

If it were possible, without sacrificing the integrity of the Army's beliefs and life-style, for officers to be employees, so that there were uniform terms

---

24 Archbishops' Council, Ministry Division; GS1518, Review of Clergy Terms of Service: Interim Report, July 2003.

25 The Union's Response to GS1518, 28 October 2003.

26 Russell Rook, letter, 21 November 2003.

27 *Officer* (September–October 2004) p. 8.

of engagement for all the organisation's personnel, this would help chip away at one of the foundations of "status" of officers. (The other – the very obvious hierarchical ranking structure – would probably have to be lived with as an inevitable concomitant of the military metaphor, and means sought to keep it in check – a "harm minimisation" strategy.) Putting this together with the suggestion that officership and leadership might be more closely identified, we would have the following scenario.

1. Anyone in leadership would be an officer, regardless of his or her terms of engagement.

2. Officers would be employees like anyone else, with no covenant other than that of a soldier.

That would put an end to the two-tier structure in which some officers are more equal than others, and also to the anomaly whereby a soldier can be the leader and focal representative of the Army in a whole community, while an officer of senior rank may be a book-keeper. It would mean that both the institution and its functionaries would have to sacrifice something presently perceived as of value. The institution might have to give up some control, like appointability and the remaining apparatus of paternalism. The functionaries would have to abandon any pretensions to any kind of priesthood and any attempt to conform to the shibboleths of the churches. Such a solution would also mean inequalities between officers under different terms of employment, which could be politically unacceptable, though it is already the case internationally anyway, but at least the inequities would not be identified with rank and status, with a pseudo-theological rationale.

If officership continues to be the most practical way to organise an Army, the question has to be whether the conditions under which leadership has been exercised remain appropriate to current and future circumstances. Most of the issues debated by the International Commission on Officership were of this kind, and we saw that given the Army's international diversity, General Gowans was unable to cut any Gordian knots – many were left to local discretion. Solutions too often give the impression of being rearguard actions in defence of as much of the status quo as can be salvaged; stages in a long retreat. Institutions find it difficult to be bold, and often face sabotage from within when they are. The experience of the Catholic Church over the past forty years, has felt to some like a sustained attempt to reverse the boldness of the Second Vatican Council. Cathy Molloy claimed that "efforts to encourage the role and vocation of the laity are frequently impeded, either by fear of particular clerics in the face of change they cannot cope with, or by instructions from Rome."[28] Re-founding happens from below, but in a

28 Cathy Molloy, "Church and Laity" in *The Way Supplement* 101 (2001) pp. 111-2 (http:/dlibrary.acu.edu.au/research/theology/ejournal/aet_1/Price.htm) downloaded 23 February 2004.

hierarchical structure institutional permission has to come from above. Perhaps the Salvation Army can still do this.

Of the two questions posed by Ken Booth, mentioned at the conclusion of the first chapter, the second was about how, in giving structure to apostolic leadership, the tendency towards clericalisation might be resisted. There is ample evidence that leadership is indispensable to the effectiveness of a movement. It is not suggested that structure be abolished; the nature of human affairs is that structures will happen anyway, and their having some continuity, accountability and legitimacy is necessary to help mitigate the effect of unrestrained personal power. As O'Dea says, "charismatic authority is inherently unstable and... its transformation into institutionalised leadership is necessary for the survival of the group."[29] O'Dea also refers to "the perennial tension between stability and creativity characteristic of institutional life. The two pitfalls with respect to them should be avoided. The first is to see institutions as simply constraints and as extrinsic interferences with the life of the spirit. The second is to fail to realize the seriousness of the tensions that exist between the spirit and the institutional pathways it has created in the past."[30]

If institutionalisation is inevitable, the prophetic critique, the Reformation's *ecclesia semper reformanda*, is equally necessary. Werner Stark quotes Bramwell Booth writing to Railton, "I am convinced that we must stick to our concern, and that we must also keep up its so-called extravagances. They, and they only will save it from drooping down into a sectarian nothing." Stark comments, "What Booth wanted was precisely what Trotsky wanted: a permanent revolution."[31] If the picture of Church movements described in this work is accurate, a counter, perhaps more egalitarian, movement is inevitable. The Salvation Army has a choice between either going with that or standing against it. It will happen anyway, but that wave may leave the hierarchical, bureaucratic Salvation Army diminished and stranded on the beach.

This section of the Conclusion has attempted to propose some small changes in how the vocation of officership is viewed, in how the role of officership is expressed and in the conditions of officer-service, all with a view to moderating the clericalist tendency. Such comparatively minor modifications to Salvationist culture, some structural, some attitudinal, might at least contribute to the process of re-founding, necessary to the future of the Salvation Army.

---

29 O'Dea, *The Sociology of Religion*, p. 49.

30 O'Dea, "Pathology and Renewal of Religious Institutions", *Concilium* (1974) 1, p. 119.

31 W. Bramwell Booth, Letter of 6 October 1874, quoted from Th.F.G. Coates, *Prophet of the Poor*, p. 98, in Werner Stark, *Sectarian Religion*, pp. 284-5.

However, these suggested changes do not amount to any more than "tinkering", while it may be that the challenges facing the Church today are of the same order as are the implications of global warming and environmental degradation for the biosphere. The Salvation Army, with a history of *ad hoc* reactions and pragmatic measures, does not yet have a strong theological and ecclesiological base on which to begin framing its response. Perhaps Hans Küng's words from forty years ago need to be revisited today:

> There have been times in the history of the Church when it was theology's task to establish the structures of the Church. The task was a necessary one. Today the task of theology should be to lay bare the original structures that have been covered over in the changes wrought by time. This too is a necessary task.... It can be more satisfying to settle problems. But it is more fruitful to raise them, though admittedly it is more difficult. For whoever does not want simply to be helpless in face of antinomies may not content himself with routine movements. On occasion he must take it upon himself to execute an unusual and bold stroke in order to arrive at a good solution... the exigencies of the Church in the critical situation of this time...demand that this service... be performed soberly and with a sense of responsibility.[32]

---

32 Küng, *Structures of the Church*, p. 352.

Postlogue

The range of ways in which the Salvation Army in the West is attempting to come to terms with post-modern society could be compared with various contemporary trends in motor car design. At one end of the spectrum there are those manufacturers fashionably "retro" in style, deliberately evoking the design cues of long-past glory days as a market ploy for the present but technologically thoroughly advanced – the recent S-type Jaguar, harking back to the classic Mark II of the 1960s would be a prime example. At the other end of the spectrum is the handful of curious "green" hybrid petrol-electric or hydrogen-powered vehicles, not usually able to demonstrate the grace, space or pace of the Jaguars, but showing that manufacturers are trying to plan ahead for the day the oil runs out. And in between, the majority of the industry continues to make incremental model changes from year to year as fashion dictates in the hope of improving their market share.

Likewise, in the Salvation Army, there are the "retros" who seek to reawaken the radical passion of the 1880s – witness an "Armybarmy" website, a "War College" in Vancouver (where trainees live, work and study in an inner-city slum ghetto), an on-line *Journal of Aggressive Christianity* (the title taken from a book by Catherine Booth), and a fashion for "Roots" conventions, designed to motivate Salvationists to recover the original charism of the early Salvation Army. An Australian observer notes that

> Evidence of the web like networking of emerging missional church within The Salvation Army can be found in the 614 [Isaiah 61:4] phenomena; a series of church communities which began in inner city Toronto (Canada) in the late 1990s and now finds expression also in inner city Vancouver (Canada), Melbourne (Australia) and Manchester (United Kingdom). Melbourne 614 engages in meaningful ministry to the most underprivileged of the inner city whilst developing a relevant expression of church that is a mix of young people and the marginalised. Currently they are seeking to establish a special "Order:614" for young people who are "a group of passionate Christians who, for one year, will live and work together and be abandoned to the cause of winning the City of Melbourne for God...[1]

Such activists have been described as "neo-primitive salvationists"[2] and are likely to be increasingly influential in the Army of the future. They

1 Gregory Morgan, "What are the impacts and implications of postmodernism and the emerging missional church for The Salvation Army?" (http://www.salvationarmy.org.au/Melbourne614/) downloaded 12 October 2004. See also http://www.armybarmy.com/614.html.

2 Shaw Clifton, "What on Earth is Neo-Primitive Salvationism?" (Coutts Memorial Lecture given at the Salvation Army College of Further Education, Sydney NSW, July 2003).

possibly demonstrate what Gerald Arbuckle calls "refounding" ("the process of returning to the founding experience of an organisation or group in order to rediscover and re-own the vision and driving energy of the pioneers.") as distinct from "renewal" ("a process of improving existing responses to problems").[3] They are, in Weber's terms, the Army's *virtuosi.*[4]

The Salvation Army's hierarchy in the United Kingdom is experimenting with permission for its youthful enthusiasts to virtually start again, to rebrand the Army and do whatever it takes to refound it, creating possibly a parallel Army alongside the existing structure.[5] The leader of this enterprise, Russell Rook, writes that,

> People often ask whether the new brand of the Salvation Army is led by lay people, lieutenants or officers? The answer is simply "yes"... I guess we are moving to the point where previous delineations of rank and file are becoming redundant, aside from within our administrative purposes. I think the challenge for the priestly code in this, as oft repeated in history, is the vast cultural shift taking place in society means that many of our ordained brothers and sisters have been shaped, trained and programmed to work in a world that no longer exists and in forms of ministry that are no longer viable. The laity often avoid this problem because their status means that the real world is a more present reality, or at least a more recent memory...[6]

Whatever this will mean in practice, for the theme of this book it is significant that this is to some extent a non-officer movement, led by a non-officer (albeit still an employee) – in church terms, a "lay" revival.

Is this a reversion to a "sectarian" ethos? Is it a very long-delayed example of the "splitting of sects" into left and right wings described by sociologists as one of the signs of the denominationalising process? Despite their "retro" language, the post-modern, neo-primitive Salvationists are another kind of animal from Booth's ragged, essentially modern, street-fighters. A re-birthed Salvation Army, a post-modern generation in a post-Christian world, cannot be time-travellers, and cannot undo the intervening century. Future researchers might profitably compare and contrast the highly literate, highly educated ranks of these new forces with their forebears of the 1880s. Nevertheless, in an examination of "church to sect" movements, Stark and Finke produce statistics showing how in the United States the tide

---

3 Arbuckle, *Chaos to Mission*, p. 3. Cf. Michael Hill, *The Religious Order* p. 3: "Tradition is the basis on which virtuosi claim legitimacy."

4 Max Weber, *The Sociology of Religion* (Boston, Beacon, 1964) pp. 162-5.

5 *Salvationist* (2 March 2004) pp. 3-5; (3 April 2004) pp. 5, 7; Mark Gadsden, "A New Model Army: New Expressions of Salvationism Within Youth Culture" (London: undated). (www.salvationarmy.org.uk/alove) Downloaded 21 December 2005.

6 Rook, letter, 21 November 2003.

is being turned in several declining liberal denominations by younger clergy committed to an evangelical ethos.[7] While the Salvation Army has not liberalised significantly in doctrine, the neo-primitive Salvationists do fit Stark and Finke's template in that they call for a revival of sectarian tension with the prevailing culture. It is also no accident that their activity tends to be located in the slums rather than in the leafy suburbs.

At the other end of the spectrum there is the secret, underground army of those who have gone Absent Without Leave, of those who would prefer to disavow the whole military metaphor, for whom every convention is up for grabs and every received truth open to re-negotiation; who believe that the "oil is running out" for the institutional church. They are not likely to be reported in the *War Cry* or listed in the *Disposition of Forces*. They are of that great company from every denomination who have taken their faith with them when they have left the church.[8] Many are "church-burnt" and are unlikely to return to the ranks under existing conditions. They nevertheless represent enormous potential for some future form of the Church, because they are attempting to work out in practice what it means to be Christian in a secular society without any of the traditional supports or conventions, or are in some cases involved in new, experimental forms of Christian community or "emergent church". Behind the lines is always a dangerous place to do the fighting, and casualties are likely to be high. Stark and Bainbridge warn that "...culture can be sustained and transmitted only through social relationships and organizations. When people are not linked organizationally to a religious meaning system, their belief in, and conceptions of, that system tends to drift."[9]

And in between the "retros" and those gone AWOL, the majority of Salvation Army units try to maintain market share, sometimes by soldiering on and trying to hold the line against change, and sometimes by borrowing

---

7 Stark and Finke, *Acts of Faith*. p. 262.

8 See Grace Davie, *Believing Without Belonging* (Cambridge: Blackwell, 1994); Alan Jamieson, *A Churchless Faith* (Wellington: Garside, 2000); Alan Jamieson, *Called Again: In and Beyond the Deserts of Faith*, (Wellington: Garside, 2004). James A. Beckford, in *Social Theory and Religion* (Cambridge: Cambridge University Press, 2003) p. 58, notes: "Terms such as 'customary religion' ("Common Religion and Customary Religion: A Critique and Proposal", Michael Hornsby-Smith, Raymond Lee & Peter Reilly in *Review of Religious Research* 263 pp. 244-251, 1985), 'implicit religion' (Edward Bailey, *Implicit Religion in Contemporary Society*, Kampen Neth.: Kok Pharos, 1997) have captured aspects of this subterranean religiosity. What they have in common is the capacity to lend religious meaning to everyday life without necessarily being closely associated with the patterns of believing and belonging advocated by religious organisations."

9 Rodney Stark and William Bainbridge, *The Future of Religion: Secularization, Revival and Cult Formation* (Berkeley: University of California Press, 1985) p. 392.

whatever seems to be working somewhere else – usually from some fashionable US megachurch like Willow Creek or Saddleback, or trying to implement the current gospel of "church growth" or "natural church growth" – or attempting to become a generic "community church".[10] Despite huge effort and some outstanding successes, they tend in the main to be either just holding their ground or are retreating. The casualties are high here too. They are the denominational Army.

The kind of leadership or officership required by each of these models is likely to differ markedly. For the third of these models the present conception of officership could continue to do duty, still with its tension and ambiguity on the question of status and function. However, retaining such a theological hybrid may continue to give rise to the same kinds of inconsistency and inequity observable in the past, and limit the ability of the Army to harness fully the resources of its non-officer personnel. The neo-primitive Salvationists, on the other hand, might just possibly stake out the original conception of a "lay" Salvation Army and, for the time being at least, resist the process of clericalisation. Status is of less significance in the trenches than on the parade ground.[11] The "Underground Army" is unlikely to have officers of any kind, and be less interested in questions of accountability or apostolicity.

In these days of exponential change, when a cultural generation in the West is reckoned at less than seven years, it would be foolish to assume that the present fragmentation and individualism experienced in western life, including religious life, will not swing back towards a desperate search for certainty and authority, for which a restorationist theology, or perhaps neo-primitive Salvationism, might be tailor-made. But there is also the possibility that only the underground church will survive the coming storm.

This history has shown that the Salvation Army, like most renewal movements, has gradually institutionalised and its leadership has become clericalised. At the same time it has retained some of its sectarian character and some of its soldiers have to some degree retained, or attempted to recover, its earlier revivalist ethos. The institution has of course moved inexorably in the direction of accommodation to the world and assimilation into the generic church, both in representing its officers as "clergy" and more recently by describing itself as a "church". In this "watershed in its self-understanding", as General Larsson has called it (see the Preface), the Army's leaders have a choice as to what traits in its DNA they will promote as dominant and what aspects will be relegated to the status of recessive

10 See for example, John Larsson, *How Your Corps Can Grow* (London: SA, 1988) or Tim Beadle and Joel Matthews, *Let the Son Shine Out: Let God's Church Find its Place in Your Community* (Toronto ONT.: SA, 2000).
11 Recognising the paradox that the *virtuosi*, while eschewing the baubles of institutional status, tend to claim an informal, spiritual status!

genes. The "neo-primitive" ideals call for an emphatic rejection of clerical status and a turning away from the trap of denominational identity. Those directions offer a chimerical security, whereas the Army's true vocation is as an egalitarian, counter-cultural movement.

Admittedly, things have "gone far enough already for the good and safety of our Movement" as old Oliver Clarke put it forty-five years ago (p. 134). Doctrine follows praxis; those characteristics which are exercised become dominant. As its second century passes, the Movement inevitably comprises a wide range of viewpoints and modes of expression. The Army is becoming as diverse as its Anglican ancestor or its Methodist parent. There may be no turning back for a major part of its constituency. At the same time, the doors through which revival may come must not be closed, and retaining the language and categories of mission can contribute to that refounding. The Army's ecclesiology must not be shaped only by its military language and hierarchical structure; but also by its egalitarian, evangelical theology.

If we recall that almost every revival of Christian religion in the past has involved a reaction against priestly presumption and a renewal of lay power and activity, it may be that the Salvation Army's best hope is to rediscover this aspect of its original genius. This is the age of irregulars, not of parade grounds or set piece battles. Like William Booth, one hundred and forty years ago, the Salvation Army might admit that it did not know where it was going, but that would not matter. The institutional Church always seems to be bound by the answers to the previous age's questions. It might be better, David Pawson's words, to "find out what the Holy Spirit is doing and join in".[12]

12 David Pawson, freelance British house-church leader, speaking in Queenstown, New Zealand, 9 January 1986.

Bibliography

Sources by or about the Salvation Army

Salvation Army Periodicals

Battlepoint (New Zealand, independent quarterly, 1963-1988).
Full Salvation (Australia, weekly, 1880s-1890s).
Horizons (Canada, bi-monthly, from 1980s).
Impact (Australia, independent quarterly, 1970s).
Journal of Aggressive Christianity (Canada, independent, on-line, from 1999).
Magazine (British SA Students' Fellowship quarterly, 1955-1970s).
New Frontier (USA Western, weekly, from 1984).
New Soldiers (USA, independent quarterly, 1965-67).
The Army Scene (Hong Kong, quarterly from 2003).
The Christian Mission Magazine (London, monthly, 1870-1878).
The Local Officer (London, 1890s-1900s).
The Field Officer (London, monthly, 1900-1913).
The Officer (London, monthly, 1893-1899, 1913-1931, 1950-2003, bi-monthly since February 1998).
The Officer's Review (London, monthly, sometimes bi-monthly or quarterly during and after World War II, 1932-1949).
The Practical Theologian (Sydney, bi-annual, from 2003).
The Salvationist (London, monthly, 1879).
The Salvationist (London, weekly, from 1984).
The Staff Review (London bi-monthly, 1921-1931).
The War Cry (London, weekly, from 1880). National editions published in other countries. References are to the London, or "International", *War Cry* unless otherwise indicated.
Word and Deed (USA, bi-annual, from 1998).

Salvation Army Official Statements

Minutes, Orders and Regulations

Chosen to be a Soldier: Orders and Regulations for Soldiers (London, 1987).
Manual of Guidance for Staff Officers (London, undated).
Minute 44, 3 October 1888.
Minute by the Chief of the Staff, 1972/IA/3.
Minute by the Chief of the Staff, 1977/IA/4.
Minute by the Chief of the Staff, 1981/IA/7.
Minutes of the Chief of the Staff, 1995/IA/15, 20.
Minute by the Chief of the Staff, 2000/1A/13.

Minute by the Chief of the Staff, 2001/1A/09.
NZ Minute PAO 1202.
NZ Minute ACE 0585.
Orders and Regulations of The Salvation Army (London: SA, 1878).
Orders and Regulations for Field Officers (London: SA, 1886.
Orders and Regulations for Field Officers (London: SA, 1888).
Orders and Regulations for Staff Officers of The Salvation Army in the United Kingdom (London: SA, 1895).
Orders and Regulations for Corps Councils (London: SA, 1959).
Orders and Regulations for Officers (London: SA, 1930).
Orders and Regulations for Officers of The Salvation Army (London: SA, 1974).
Orders and Regulations for Corps Officers (London: SA, 1976).
Orders and Regulations for Officers of The Salvation Army (London: SA, 1997).
The Why and Wherefore of The Salvation Army Regulations (London: SA, [1896]).

Doctrinal Statements

Doctrines and Discipline of The Salvation Army (London: SA, 1881).
Handbook of Doctrine (London: SA, 1923).
Handbook of Doctrine (London: SA, 1940).
Handbook of Doctrine (London: SA, 1969).
One Faith One Church: The Salvation Army's Response to Baptism, Eucharist and Ministry (London: SA, 1990).
Salvation Story (London: SA, 1998).
Salvation Story, Study Guide (London: SA, 1999).
Servants Together (London: SA, 2002).
The Doctrine We Adorn (London: SA, 1982).
The Salvation Army Directory, No II (London: SA, 1900).

Other Official Salvation Army Publications, Statements, Circulars, Reports

Background Papers to the 2006 International Theology and Ethics Symposium.
Background Papers, 1991 International Conference of Leaders.
Booth, William: *Letter to Commissioners and Territorial Commanders*. London: 1900.
Commission on Officership, New Zealand Task Force Findings. Wellington: 2001.
Gowans, John: *The Recommendations of the International Commission on Officership: The General's Response and Action Plan*. London: 2000.
Findings of the Commission Appointed to Review the Relationship with the World Council of Churches, January 1980.
Larsson, John: *Findings of the General's consultation with officers regarding the recommendations of the International Commission on Officership*. London: 2000.
Minutes of The Christian Mission Conference, 1870.
Minutes of the 1969 Commissioners' Conference; Report on the 1969 Commissioner's Conference.
Minutes of the 1971 International Council of Leaders.
Minutes of the 1979 International Conference of Leaders.

Minutes of the 1984 International Conference of Leaders.

Minutes of the 1988 International Leaders' Conference; Conference Implementation Committee, Minute 1, 1988 ICL.

Reports and Recommendations of the 1958 International Conference of Commissioners.

The Disposition of Forces. A directory of Salvation Army appointments and personnel, published annually for internal circulation in each Salvation Army Territory.

The International Commission on Officership: *Final Report*. London: 2000.

The Role of the Corps Officer in the United States of America: Guidelines for COs in the USA. Approved by the Commissioners' Conference, USA. October, 1972.

The Salvation Army Year Book. Since 1906 an annual report on the Salvation Army internationally, published by International Headquarters, London.

The Salvation War. An annual publication giving narrative accounts of Salvation Army activities, along with a balance sheet and statistical summary, 1881-1885.

Books, Papers, Articles by, for or about The Salvation Army

Anon. (ed.), *Another Harvest of the Years* (London: SA, 1975).

Anon. (ed.), *The Life of General Booth* (London: Nelson, [1912?]).

Anon., *The Training of Salvation Army Officers* (London: SA, 1927).

Arnold, W., "The Officer Rank Structure" (Paper dated 27 March 2001, circulated to officers in New Zealand by Personnel Section, THQ).

Bell, F., *The Fight for the Flag* (Sydney: Privately Circulated, 1948).

Begbie, H., *Life of William Booth, Founder of The Salvation Army* (London: Macmillan, 1920).

Booth, Bramwell, *Echoes and Memories* (London: Hodder & Stoughton, [1925] 3rd edn 1977).

- *General Booth's Journal 1921-22* (London: SA, 1925).
- *Servants of All* (London: SA, 1899).
- *Talks With Officers* (London: SA, 1921).
- *These Fifty Years* (London: Cassell, 1929).

Booth, Catherine, *Aggressive Christianity* (London, SA, 1880).

- *Popular Christianity* (London: SA, 1887).
- *Practical Religion* (London: SA, 4th edn 1891).
- *The Salvation Army in Relation to the Church and State* (London: SA, 1889).

Booth, Catherine Bramwell, *Bramwell Booth* (London: Rich & Cowan, 1932).

- *Catherine Booth* (London: Hodder & Stoughton, 1970).

Booth, Emma, and Booth, Herbert, *Called Out, and What Comes of It* (London: SA, [1887?]).

Booth, Florence, *Powers of Salvation Army Officers* (London: SA, [1928]).

- *Wanted – An Elite* (London: SA, [1928]).

Booth, Maud, *Beneath Two Flags* (New York: Funk & Wagnall, 1889).

Booth, William, *Addresses to Staff Officers* (London: SA, 1907).

- *In Darkest England, And the Way Out* (London: SA, 1890).
- *International Congress Addresses* (London: SA, 1904).
- *Letters to Salvationists on Religion for Everyday* [London: 1902] (Atlanta: SA, 1987).
- *Salvation Soldiery* (London: SA, 1889).

Booth-Tucker, F., *The Life of Catherine Booth* (London: SA, 1892).

- *Muktifauj: Forty Years With The Salvation Army in India and Ceylon* (London: Marshall Brothers, [1923]).
Bradwell, C. *Fight the Good Fight* (Wellington: Reed, 1983).
- *Touched With Splendour* (Wellington: Flag, 2003).
Brown, A., *The Gate and the Light* (Toronto: Bookwright, 1984).
Brown, F., *Secular Evangelism* (London: SCM, 1970).
"Caractacus", *The Question of Questions* (London: SW Partridge, 1882).
Carpenter, M.L., *Commissioner Lawley* (London: SA, 1924).
- *William Booth* (London: SA, 1942).
Carpenter, S., *A Man of Peace in a World of War* (Montville, Qld: Privately published, 1993).
Clark, W., *Samuel Logan Brengle* (London: Hodder, 1980).
- (ed.): *Dearest Lily: A selection of the Brengle correspondence* (London: SA, 1985).
Cleary, J., "Chosen to be a Soldier" (Paper presented at College of Further Education, Sydney, 2002).
Clifton, S., "What on Earth is Neo-Primitive Salvationism?" (Frederick Coutts Memorial Lecture 2003, Sydney Officer Training College, 31 July 2003).
- *Who Are These Salvationists?* (Alexandria, VA: Crest, 1999).
Coates, Th.F.G., *The Prophet of the Poor: The Life Story of General William Booth* (London: Hodder and Stoughton, 1905).
Collier, R., *The General Next to God* (London: Collins, 1965).
Cooper, I., "A Theology of Salvation Army Officership" (Unpublished paper, 198?).
Coutts, F. L., *In Good Company* (London: SA, 1980).
- *No Continuing City* (London: SA, 1976).
- *No Discharge in This War* (London: Hodder [1975] 1981).
- *The Call to Holiness* (London: SA, 1957).
- *The Better Fight: The History of The Salvation Army, Vol. VI* (London: Hodder, 1973).
- *The Weapons of Goodwill: The History of The Salvation Army, Vol. VII* (London: Hodder, 1986).
[Dean, H.], *The Sacraments: the Salvationist's Viewpoint* (London: SA, 1960).
Duff, M., *Hedwig Von Hartman* (London: SA, 1904).
Eason, A. M., *Women in God's Army: Gender and Equality in the Early Salvation Army* (Waterloo, Ont.: Wilfred Laurier University Press, 2003).
Ervine St J., *God's Soldier, General William Booth* (London: Heinemann,1934).
Friederichs, H., *The Romance of The Salvation Army* (London: Cassell, 1907).
Gadsden, M., *A New Model Army: New Expressions of Salvationism Within Youth Culture* (London, undated. www.salvationarmy.org.uk/alove).
Gariepy, H., *The History of The Salvation Army, Vol. VIII* (Atlanta, Ga.: SA, 2000).
- *General of God's Army* (Wheaton, Ill.: Victor, 1993).
Garnham, P., "Postmodernity and Faith Education in The Salvation Army", e*Journal of Aggressive Christianity* (April 2000) www.armybarmy.com.
de Gasparin, A., *Read and Judge The (So-Called) Salvation Army* (London: Griffiths and Farran, 1883).
Gowans, J., *There's a Boy Here* (London: SA, 2002).
Haggard, H. R., *Regeneration* (London: Longmans Green, 1910).
Hattersley, R., *Blood and Fire: William and Catherine Booth and Their Salvation Army* (London: Little, Brown & Co., 1999).

Hazzard, J. W., "Marching on the Margins: An Analysis of The Salvation Army in the United States", *Review of Religious Research* 40:2 (December 1998).

Higgins, E.J., *Stewards of God* (London: SA, Undated but early 1930s).

Hodder, K., "The Development and Use of Lay Leaders Within the Decision-Making Processes of The Salvation Army" (Paper given at the 1995 International Conference of Leaders).

Horridge, G. K., *The Salvation Army, Origins and Early Days, 1865-1900* (Godalming: Ammonite Books, 1993).

Hunt, C. F., *If Two Shall Agree: The story of Paul A. Rader and Kay F. Rader of The Salvation Army* (Kansas City, Miss.: Beacon Hill Press, 2001).

Hunter, D., *While the Light Lingers* (Privately published, 2005).

Hutson, J., *As for Me and My House: A salute to early Salvation Army families of Gisborne, 1886 to 1952* (Wellington: Flag, 2004).

Jamieson, C.J., "Status of Officers" (Opinion provided for The Salvation Army in New Zealand by Bell Gully Buddle Weir, October 1992).

Kew, C., *Closer Communion: The Sacraments in Scripture and Tradition* (London: SA, 1980).

Kirk, E., *Unveiled: A Study of The Salvation Army from Within* (London: Dharma, Undated).

Kitching, W., *Soldier of Salvation* (London: SA, 1963).

Kunz, V., "The Salvation Army – Its Origin, Spirit and Work" (Unpublished paper, 1947).

Larson, F., *My Best Men are Women* (London: Hodder & Stoughton, 1974).

Lunn, B., *Salvation Dynasty* (London, W. Hodge, 1936).

Mckenzie, F.A., *The Clash of the Cymbals* (New York: Bretano's, 1929).

McKinley, E. H., *Marching to Glory: The History of The Salvation Army in the United States of America, 1880-1980* (San Francisco: Harper & Row, 1980).

- *Marching to Glory* (2nd edn expanded, 1995).

Mason, R., "The Salvation Army and the Sacraments" (Submission to the International Spiritual Life Commission, 1997).

Metcalf, W., *The Salvationist and the Sacraments* (London: SA, 1965).

Moyles, R.G., *Blood and Fire in Canada: A History of The Salvation Army in the Dominion, 1882-1976* (Toronto: Peter Martin Associates, 1977).

- *The Salvation Army in Newfoundland: Its History and Essence* (Toronto: SA, 1997).

Murdoch, N.S., "Evangelical Sources of Salvation Army Doctrine", *The Evangelical Quarterly* (July 1987).

- *Frank Smith: Salvation Socialist* (Alexandria, VA: SA, 2003).

- "In Darkest Africa: Martyrdom and Resistance to Colonialism in Rhodesia", *Journal of Third World Studies* (Spring 2005).

- *Soldiers of the Cross*, (Alexandria, VA: Crest Books, 2006).

- "Suzie Forest Swift (1862-1916)" (Unpublished paper).

- *The Origins of The Salvation Army* (Knoxville: University of Tennessee Press, 1994).

- "The Salvation Army and the Church of England 1882-83", *Historical Magazine of the Protestant Episcopal Church* (March 1986).

- "The Salvation Army's U.S. Arrival", *Ohio Academy of History Newsletter* (May, 1987).

- "Wesleyan Influence on William and Catherine Booth", *Wesleyan Theological Journal*, 20:2 (Fall 1985).

Needham, P., *Community in Mission: A Salvationist Ecclesiology* (London: SA, 1987).
Nichol, A.M., *General Booth and The Salvation Army* (London: Herbert & Daniel, 1910).
"Norah Marks", *Facts About The Salvation Army* (Chicago: Rand McNally, 1889).
"One of the Scholars", *A School of the Prophets* (London: SA, 1901).
Pitt, D., *Pilgrim's Progress: 20th Century: The Story of Salvation Army Officership* (New York: SA, 1950).
Prescott, P., *The Salvation Army, The Secret of Its Success: A Message to the Churches* (London: Commonwealth Publishing Company, 1891).
Rader, K., "Keeping the Dream Alive", in *Terms of Empowerment: Salvation Army Women in Ministry* (West Nyack NY: 2001).
- "Women in Ministry" (Address to the 1998 International Conference of Leaders).
Railton, G. S., *General Booth* (London: Hodder & Stoughton, 1912).
- *Heathen England* (London: S.W. Partridge, 2nd edn 1878).
- *Twenty-One Years Salvation Army* (London: SA, 1886).
Redstone, J.J.R., *An Ex-Captain's Experience of The Salvation Army* (London: Christian Commonwealth Publishing Coy., 2nd edn 1888).
Rhemick, J., *A New People of God: A Study in Salvationism* (Des Plaines, Ill.: SA, 1993).
Rightmire, R. D. *Sacraments and The Salvation Army: Pneumatological Foundations* (Metuchen, NJ: Scarecrow Press, 1990).
Sandall, R., *The History of The Salvation Army Vol. I* (London: Nelson, 1947).
- *The History of The Salvation Army Vol. II* (London: Nelson, 1950).
- *The History of The Salvation Army Vol. III* (London: Nelson, 1955).
Satterlee, Allen, *Turning Points* (Alexandria Va.: Crest, 2004).
Scott-Howman, A., "Status of Officers in The Salvation Army" (Memorandum provided for The Salvation Army in New Zealand by Bell Gully, October 2003).
Smith, F., *All About The Salvation Army* (New York, SA, 1885).
Smith, P., "Current and Future Legal Issues" (Paper for 1998 International Conference of Leaders).
Street, R., *Called to be God's People* (London: SA, 1999).
Strickland, D., "Married Women's Ghetto Rant", e*Journal of Aggressive Christianity* 41 (February-March 2006) www.armybarmy.com.
[Sumner, Abner] "An Ex-Staff Officer, A.S.", *The New Papacy: Behind the Scenes in the Salvation Army* (Toronto: Albert Britnell, 1889).
Taylor, D., "Army, Order or Church? An attempt to locate the Salvation Army within the wider family of churches and to consider the implications of this position" (Paper read at United Kingdom Theological Symposium, July 2004).
Trout, M., *The General Was a Lady* (Nashville: A.J. Holman, 1980).
Wahlström, M., "The Place and Position of the Woman Officer in The Salvation Army" (Paper read at the 1984 International Conference of Leaders).
Waldron, J. (Comp.), *The Salvation Army and the Churches* (New York: SA, 1986).
Walker, P.J., "Proclaiming Women's Right to Preach", *Harvard Divinity Bulletin* (1994).
Wallis, H., *Commissioner Cadman* (London: SA, 1928).
Watson, B., *Soldier Saint. George Scott Railton: William Booth's First Lieutenant.* (London: Hodder, 1970).

- *A Hundred Years' War: The Salvation Army 1865-1965* (London: Hodder, 1964).
Wickberg, E., "Movements for Reform" (Address to the 1971 International Conference of Leaders).
Wiggins, A., *The History of The Salvation Army, Vol. IV* (London: Nelson, 1964).
- *The History of The Salvation Army, Vol. V* (London: Nelson, 1968).
Williams, H., *Booth-Tucker – William Booth's First Gentleman* (London: Hodder, 1980).
Winston, D., *Red Hot and Righteous: The Urban Religion of The Salvation Army.* (Cambridge, Mass: Harvard University Press, 1999).
Wisbey, H. A. Jnr., *History of the Volunteers of America* (Chicago: VOA, 1954).
- *Soldiers Without Swords: A History of The Salvation Army in the United States* (New York: Macmillan, 1955).
Wiseman, C., *A Burning in My Bones* (Toronto: McGraw-Hill Ryerson, 1979).
Yee, Check Hung, *Good Morning, China* (Alexandria Va.: Crest, 2005).
Yuill, C., "Nettles and Wineskins" (Frederick Coutts Memorial Lecture for 2004 at the College for Further Education, Sydney, and printed in the *Practical Theologian*, 2:2, September 2004).

Theses

Aitken, T. G., "Aspects of the History of The Salvation Army in New Zealand 1929-1963: A Study in Adjustment" (MA thesis, Victoria University of Wellington, 1964).
Bradwell, C. R., "An Outline History of The Salvation Army in New Zealand" (MA thesis, Canterbury College, University of New Zealand, 1950).
Clifton, S., "The Salvation Army's Actions and Attitudes in War Time 1889-1945" (PhD thesis, King's College, London, 1989).
Escott, P., "Church Growth Theories and The Salvation Army in The United Kingdom" (PhD thesis, University of Stirling, 1996).
Garland, D., "The Salvation Army and the State of Welfare…: an analysis of the discourses influencing the development of Salvation Army policy. (MA thesis, University of Western Sydney, 2004).
Morris, M., "Female Ministry, Equality and the Salvation Army" (Dissertation for Oak Hill Theological College, London. Undated).
Munn, R. J., "Salvation Army Married Officer Leadership: For Such a Time as This." (DMin thesis, Gordon-Conwell Theological Seminary, N.C., 2004).
Pears, R., "Towards a Theology of Salvation Army Officership; An Examination of Officer Ministry in the United Kingdom" (MTh thesis, Oxford, 1996).
Townsend, J., "Where Have all the Leaders Gone? Officer Recruitment in The Salvation Army of Aotearoa New Zealand" (MMin thesis, Melbourne College of Divinity, 2000).
Yon, P., "Areas of Stress and Conflict in the Lives of Married Women in Ministry within The Salvation Army" (MA thesis, University of Keele, 1993).

General Background Material

Archbishops' Council, Ministry Division. – GS1518 Review of Clergy Terms of Service, England. Interim Report (July 2003).

Abbott, A., *The System of Professions: An Essay on the Division of Expert Labour* (Chicago: University of Chicago Press, 1988).

Ammerman, N.T., "Organized Religion in a Voluntaristic Society," *Sociology of Religion* 53:3 (1997).

Anon., *A Tent-Making Ministry: Towards a more flexible form of ministry* (London: World Council of Churches, 1962).

Arbuckle, G.A., *From Chaos to Mission: Refounding Religious Life Formation* (Collegeville, Min.: Liturgical Press, 1996).

Bartholemew, J.N., "A Sociological View of Authority in Religious Organizations", *Review of Religious Research* 23:2 (December 1981).

Beckford, J.A., *Social Theory and Religion* (Cambridge: Cambridge University Press, 2003).

Bettenson, H. (Ed.), *Documents of the Christian Church* (Oxford: Oxford University Press, 1956).

Booth, Ken, "Something about Ordination" (Paper read at a seminar arranged by the Ministry and Training Division of the Christchurch Diocese, held at Bishop Julius Hall, 31 July, 1999).

Borg, M. and Wright, N.T., *The Meaning of Jesus: Two Visions* (San Francisco: Harper, 1999).

Bourdillon, M.F.C. (Ed.), *Christianity South of the Zambezi* Vol. 2 (Gwelo: Mambo Press, 1977).

Bruce, S., "Christianity in Britain R.I.P.", *Sociology of Religion* 62:2, (2001).

Brueggemann, W., *The Prophetic Imagination* (Minneapolis, Min.: Fortress Press, 2nd edn 2001).

Brunner, E., *The Christian Doctrine of the Church, Faith and the Consummation Dogmatics Vol. III* (London: Lutterworth, 1962).

- *The Misunderstanding of the Church* (London: Lutterworth, 1953).

Bulley, C., *The Priesthood of Some Believers* (Carlisle: Paternoster, 2000).

Calvin, J., *Institutes of the Christian Religion*, 4:3:1 (http://www.smartlink.net/~douglas/calvin/bk4ch03.html#one.htm).

Clarke, B., Registrar-General of Births, Deaths and Marriages in New Zealand, "Circular to Marriage Celebrants" (28 February, 2003).

Cohn, S.F., "Ministerial Power and the Iron Law of Oligarchy: A Deviant Case Analysis", *Review of Religious Research* 35:2 (December 1993).

Colless, B. and P. Donovan, *Religion in New Zealand Society* (Palmerston North: Dunmore Press, 2nd edn 1985).

Congar, Y., *Lay People in the Church: A Study for a Theology of Laity* (London: Bloomsbury, 1957).

Cousineau, M. (ed.) *Religion in a Changing World: Comparative Studies in Sociology* (Westport, CT.: Praeger, 1998).

Cross, A., (ed.), *Ecumenism and History* (Carlisle: Paternoster, 2002).

Crossan, J.D., *The Historical Jesus: The Life of a Mediterranean Jewish Peasant* (North Blackburn, VIC: Collins Dove, 1991).

Cyprian of Carthage, *Epistle* 55:8 (http://justus.anglican.org/resources/pc/england/jwords/saltum.html).
- *Epistle* 65.1 (http://www.auburn.edu/~allenkc/openhse/money.html).

Department of Trade and Industry, United Kingdom, "Discussion Document on Employment Status in Relation to Statutory Employment Rights", URN 02/1085 (July 2003).

Didascalia Apostolorum 2:25 (http://www.piney.com/DocAposConstitu.html#have).

DiMaggio, P. and W. Powell, "The Iron Cage Revisited: Institutional Isomorphism and Collective Rationality in Organisational Fields", *American Sociological Review* 48 (1991).

Dulles, A., *Models of the Church* (New York: Doubleday, 1974).

Finke, R., "The New Holy Clubs: Testing Church-to-Sect Propositions", *Sociology of Religion* (Summer, 2001).

Finke, R. and K. Dougherty, "The Effects of Professional Training: The Social and Religious Capital Acquired in Seminaries", *Journal for the Scientific Study of Religion* 41:1 (2002).

Finke, R. and R. Stark, "How the Upstart Sects Won America: 1776-1850", *Journal for the Scientific Study of Religion* 28 (1) (1989).

Finke, R. and R. Stark, *The Churching of America 1776-1990: Winners and Losers in Our Religious Economy (*New Brunswick NJ: Rutgers University Press, 1992).

Flannery, A. (ed.), *Vatican II, The Conciliar and Post-Conciliar Documents* (Collegeville, Min: Liturgical Press, 1975).

Gilbert, A.D., *Religion and Society in Industrial England: Church, Chapel and Social Change 1740-1914* (London: Longman, 1976).

Glendon, M., "The Hour of the Laity", *First Things* 127 (November 2002). (http://print.firstthings.com/ftissues/ft0211/articles/glendon.html)

Haag, H., *Clergy and Laity* (London: Burns and Oates, 1998).

Hall, C. and R. Hannaford (Ed.), *Order and Ministry* (Leominster: Gracewing, 1996).

Hanson, R., *Christian Priesthood Examined* (London: Lutterworth, 1979).

Harrison, P.M., *Authority and Power in the Free Church Tradition: A Social Case Study of the American Baptist Convention* (Princeton, NJ.: Princeton University Press, 1959).

Hennessey, P.K. (ed.), *A Concert of Charisms: Ordained Ministry in the Religious Life* (New York: Paulist Press, 1997).

Hill, M., "Methodism as a Religious Order: A Question of Categories", *A Sociological Yearbook of Religion in Britain* 6 (1973).
- *The Religious Order* (London, Heinemann, 1973).

Hornsby-Smith, P., R.M. Lee and P.A. Reilly, "Common Religion and Customary Religion: a Critique and a Proposal", *Review of Religious Research* 26:3 (March 1985).

Horrell, D., "Leadership Patterns and the Development of Ideology in Early Christianity", *Sociology of Religion* 58:4 (Winter 1997).

Iannaccone, L., "A Formal Model of Church and Sect", *American Journal of Sociology* 94, Supplement (1988).
- "Why Strict Churches are Strong", *American Journal of Sociology* 99:5 (March 1994).

Ignatius, *Epistle to Magnesians* IV (www.ccel.org/fathers2/ANF-01/anf0117.htm#P1486_261369).

Illich, I., *Celebration of Awareness* (Harmondsworth: Penguin 1976).

Inglis, K.S., *Churches and Working Classes in Victorian England* (London: Routledge and Kegan Paul, 1963).
Irenaeus, *Against Heresies*, iv.8.3 (www.ccel.org/fathers2/ANF-01/anf01-62.htm#P8629_2440260).
Jackson, H.R., *Churches and People in Australia and New Zealand, 1860-1930* (Wellington: Allen & Unwin/Port Nicholson Press, 1987).
Jamieson, A., *A Churchless Faith* (Wellington: Garside, 2000).
- *Called Again: In and Beyond the Deserts of Faith* (Wellington: Garside, 2004).
Jamieson, P., *Living at the Edge: Sacrament and Solidarity in Leadership* (London: Mowbray, 1997).
Johnson, B., "A Critical Appraisal of the Church-Sect Typology", *American Sociological Review* 22:1 (February 1957).
- "On Church and Sect", *American Sociological Review* 28:4 (August 1963).
- "Church and Sect Revisited", *Journal for the Scientific Study of Religion* 10 (1971).
Kent, J., *Holding the Fort: Studies in Victorian Revivalism* (London: Epworth, 1978).
Knowles, B., *New Life: A History of the New Life Churches of New Zealand 1942-1979* (Dunedin: Third Millennium Publishing, 1999).
- *The History of a New Zealand Pentecostal Movement* (Lewiston: Edwin Mellen, 2000).
Knox, R., *Enthusiasm* (Oxford: Oxford University Press, 1950).
Kraemer, H., *A Theology of the Laity* (London: Lutterworth Press, 1958).
Küng, H., *The Church* (London: Search Press, 1968).
- *Structures of the Church* (London: Burns & Oates, 1965).
Kunnumpuram, K., "Beyond the Clergy-Laity Divide" (www.sedos.org/english/kunnumpuram.html).
Luther, M. "An Open Letter to the Christian Nobility of the German Nation" (1520). *Works of Martin Luther* (Philadelphia: A.J. Holman Coy., 1915) (http://www.iclnet.org/pub/resources/text/wittenberg/luther/web/nblty-04.html).
Macy, G., "Who and How: Debates about Consecration in the Twelfth Century" (http://naal-liturgy.org/Members/papers/Gary_macy.htm).
McCallum, D., "The Waldensian Movement From Waldo to Reformation" (http://www.xenos.org/essays/waldo1f.htm).
McGavran, D., *Understanding Church Growth* (Grand Rapids, MICH.: Eerdmans, 1970).
McGowan, A., "Water in the Desert: Wine, Water and the Eucharist in Tertullian and Cyprian" (http://divinity.library.vanderbilt.edu/burns/chroma/eucharist/euchMcGowan.html).
Macquarrie, J., *Principles of Christian Theology* (London: SCM, 1966).
Marshall, C., "Following Christ in Life: The Anabaptist-Mennonite Tradition", *Reality* 37 (February/March 2000).
Martens, L., "Anabaptist Theology and Congregational Care", *Direction Journal*, 21:1 (Spring 1992).
Martin, D., "The Denomination", *British Journal of Sociology* 13 (1962).
- *A Sociology of English Religion* (London: SCM, 1967).
- *Reflections on Sociology and Theology* (Oxford: Clarendon Press, 1997).
Mascall, E.L., *The Recovery of Unity: A Theological Approach* (London: Longmans, 1958).

Molloy, C., "Church and Laity", *The Way Supplement* 101 (2001). (http:/dlibrary.acu.edu.au/research/theology/ejournal/aet_1/Price.htm)

Moltman, J., *The Trinity and the Kingdom of God* (London: SCM, 1981).

Monahan, S. C., "Role Ambiguity among Protestant Clergy: Consequences of the Activated Laity", *Review of Religious Research* 41 (1999).

Monahan, S. C., W.A. Mirola, and M. O. Emerson (Ed.), *Sociology of Religion: A Reader* (Upper Saddle River NJ: Prentice-Hall, 2001).

Neuner J. and J. Dupuis, *The Christian Faith: The Doctrinal Documents of the Catholic Church* (Bangalore: Theological Publications in India, 3rd edn 1978).

Newbigin, L., *Foolishness to the Greeks: The Gospel and Western Culture* (Grand Rapids, Mich.: Eerdmans, 1986).

New Code of Canon Law, 1983, Canon 207 #1, of the Roman Catholic Church (http://www.justiceforpriests.org/part_1_christs_faithful.htm).

Niebuhr, H. R., *The Social Sources of Denominationalism* (New York: Meridian, [1929] 1957).

O'Dea, T. F., "Five Dilemmas in the Institutionalisation of Religion", *Journal for the Scientific Study of Religion* 1:1 (October 1961).

- "Pathology and Renewal of Religious Institutions", *Concilium*, 1 (1974).

- *Sociology and the Study of Religion* (New York: Basic Books, 1970).

- *The Sociology of Religion* (Englewood Cliffs NJ: Prentice-Hall,1966).

Ormerod, N., "Mission and Ministry in the Wake of Vatican II", *Australian Ejournal of Theology* (http//://dlibrary.acu.edu.au/research/theology/ejournal/aet_Ormerod.htm).

Packer, J.I., "A Stunted Ecclesiology? The Theory and Practice of Evangelical Churchliness", *Touchstone* (December, 2003) (www.latimer.org.nz/morecomment.asp?CoID=13).

Piepkorn, A.C, "Plymouth Brethren", *Concordia Theological Monthly* 41 (1970) (http://www.breuderbewegung.de/pdf/piepkorn.pdf).

Plumb, J.H., *England in the Eighteenth Century* (Harmondsworth: Penguin, 1950).

Price, P., "Vatican II: End of a Clerical Church?(1)" *Australian Ejournal of Theology* (http://dlibrary.acu.edu.au/research/theology/ejournal/aet_1Price.htm).

Rack, H.D., *Reasonable Enthusiast: John Wesley and the Rise of Methodism* (Nashville: Abingdon, 2nd edn 1993).

Radcliffe, T., "Why is Morale Among Priests So Low?" (Paper given at the National Conference of Priests, at Digby Stuart College, London, 3 September 2002) (www.onlineopinion.com.au/2002/Nov02/Radcliffe.htm).

Ricca, P., "Sect or Order? (Waldensians-Franciscans)", *Concilium* (October 1982).

Roberts, J. H., *Thinking Theologically in Aotearoa New Zealand* (Paihia: Colcom Press, 2000.

Robertson, R., *The Sociological Interpretation of Religion* (Oxford: Blackwell, 1970).

Rowdon, H.H. (Ed.), *Servants of God: Papers on the use of full-time workers in Brethren Churches* (Exeter: Paternoster Press, 1986).

Roxborogh, J., "Persistent Presbyterianism? Lay Leadership and the Future of a Reformed Christian tradition in the West" (http://www.roxborogh.com/missiology.htm).

Salmon, J., "Is it Ordained?" (Address at Wesley Dinner, Trinity College, Auckland, 24 May 1999).

Schaeff, A. W. and D. Fassell, *The Addictive Organisation* (San Francisco: Harper, 1991).

Schillebeeckx, E., *Ministry: A Case for Change* (London: SCM, 1981).
- *The Church with a Human Face* (New York: Crossroad, 1985).
Schoenherr, R. A., "Power and Authority in Organised Religion: Disaggregating the Phenomenological Core", *Sociological Analysis* 47:S (March 1987).
Sharot, S., "Beyond Christianity", *Sociology of Religion* 29 (August 2003).
Sherkat D.E. and C.G. Ellison, "Recent Developments and Current Controversies in the Sociology of Religion", *Annual Review of Sociology* 25, 1999.
Southern, R.W., *Western Society and the Church in the Middle Ages* (Harmondsworth: Penguin, 1972).
Stacey, J., *About the Ministry* (London: Epworth, 1964).
Stark, R. and W. S. Bainbridge, *The Future of Religion: Secularization, Revival and Cult Formation* (Berkeley: University of California Press, 1985).
Stark, R. and R. Finke, *Acts of Faith: Explaining the Human Side of Religion* (Berkeley: University of California Press, 2000).
Stark, W., *The Sociology of Religion.* Vol. 2, *Sectarian Religion* (London: Routledge and Kegan Paul, 1967).
Swatos, W. D. Jnr., "Church-Sect and Cult: Bringing Mysticism Back In", *Sociological Analysis* 42:1 (1981).
- "Beyond Denominationalism?: Community and Culture in American Religion", *Journal for the Scientific Study of Religion* 20:3 (September 1981).
Tabbernee, W. (Ed.), *Ministry in Australian Churches* (Melbourne: Joint Board of Christian Education, 1987).
Tertullian, *Baptism* 17 (www.piney.com/Tertullian-Baptism.html#P11686-3287159).
Thornton R. and P.N. Nardi, "The Dynamics of Role Acquisition", *American Journal of Sociology* 80 (1975).
Thurian, M. and G. Wainwright, (Ed.), *Faith and Order Paper 117: Churches Respond to Baptism, Eucharist and Ministry* (Geneva: World Council of Churches, 1986).
Torrance, T.F., *Royal Priesthood: A Theology of Ordained Ministry* (Edinburgh: T&T Clark, [1955] 2nd edn 1993).
Volf, M., *After Our Likeness: The Church in the Image of the Trinity.* Grand Rapids, Mich.: Eerdmans, 1998).
Von Campenhausen, H., *Tradition and Life in the Early Church* (London: Collins, 1968).
Ward, K., "Christendom, Clericalism, Church and Context" (http://www.presbyterian.org.nz/441.98.html).
Weber, H. R., *Power. Focus for a Biblical Theology* (Geneva: World Council of Churches, 1989).
Weber, R. K., "A History and Theology of Sharing Responsibility for the Church" (http://www.spiritualitytoday.org/spir2day/853721weber.html).
Wiles, M., *The Christian Fathers* (London: Hodder and Stoughton, 1966).
Williams, J. R., *Renewal Theology: The Church, the Kingdom and Last Things* (Grand Rapids, Mich.: Zondervan, 1992).
Wilson, B. R. (Ed.), *Patterns of Sectarianism* (London: Heinemann, 1967).
- *Sects and Society: A Sociological Study of Three Religious Groups in Britain* (London: Heinemann, 1961).
- *Religion in Secular Society* (London: C.A. Watts, 1966).
- "An Analysis of Sect Development", *American Sociological Review* 24 (February 1959).

- "The Pentecostalist Minister: Role Conflicts and Status Contradictions", *American Journal of Sociology* 64 (March 1959).
- "The Persistence of Sects", *Diskus* 1:2 (1993).

Wink, W., *Engaging the Powers: Discernment and Resistance in a World of Domination* (Philadelphia: Fortress Press, 1992).

World Council of Churches, Faith and Order Paper 111: Baptism, Eucharist and Ministry (Geneva: WCC, 1982).
- "Towards a Common Understanding of the Theological Concepts of Laity/Laos: The People of God". Consultation Statement, May 7-10, 1997 (http://www.wcccoe.org/wcc/what/education/statemnt.html).
- "Canberra Statement", adopted by the Seventh Assembly of the WCC in 1991 (www.wcc-coe.org/wcc/what/faith/canb.html).

Glossary of Salvation Army Terms

Adherent Member: A person who wishes to regard the Salvation Army as their "church", without taking upon themselves the life-style commitments involved in being a "Soldier".

Advisory Council to the General: Body established in 1947 to advise the General on policy and senior appointments. Made up of selected Commissioners appointed to serve for a set term of three years. Replaced by General's Consultative Council in 2001.

Articles of Faith: The "11 points" of Salvation Army Doctrine, professed by all soldiers.

Articles of War: Now known as the "Soldier's Covenant", signed by soldiers when enrolled, or "sworn in", confessing personal salvation, adherence to Salvation Army beliefs, and committing to a Salvation Army life-style.

Cadet: Person in training for Salvation Army officership.

Candidate: A soldier who has been accepted for training as an officer.

Census Board: The body of senior "local officers" of a Corps, charged with maintaining the rolls. Now known as the "Pastoral Care Council".

Chief of the Staff: Second in command to the General.

Chief Secretary: (CS) Officer second in command of a Territory.

Command: Salvation Army term for a distinct geographical area, usually a country, with fewer than about 40 Corps. There are historically-derived inconsistencies – Tanzania, with 60 Corps and 3,438 soldiers in 2003, is a Command, while France, with 28 Corps and 892 soldiers, is a "Territory", normally denoting a larger operation.

Commanding Officer: (CO) Usually the officer in charge of a Corps.

Commissioner: Senior commissioned rank usually held by Territorial Commander or Head of Department at IHQ.

Corps: Local Salvation Army unit, equivalent to a parish or congregation.

Corps Council: Advisory group of senior Local officers and other people in a Corps, advising the Corps Commanding Officer on local policy and programme.

Corps Sergeant Major: (CSM) Senior local officer, principal "lay" volunteer assistant to the Commanding Officer.

Dedication: Equivalent to infant baptism or Christening, without use of water. Does not denote reception into the church but is regarded as occasion for thanksgiving and opportunity for parents to make commitments regarding the child's upbringing in the faith..

Division: Geographical area comprising a number of Corps. Equivalent of diocese in episcopal church polity. Smaller units, comprising fewer Corps than a Division, are Districts led by a District Officer

Divisional Commander: (DC) Officer in charge of a Division.

Field: Generic term for evangelical operations, including Corps. Sometimes inclusive of the "social work", and sometimes used as exclusive of or distinct from social or welfare operations.

General: International leader of The Salvation Army.

General's Consultative Council: Council advising the General on matters of mission strategy and policy. Operates through an electronic database, with selected members also meeting quarterly at IHQ with the General in the chair.

Hall: Salvation Army meeting place. Often termed a Barracks in early days; later many terms such as Citadel, Fortress.

High Council: Gathering of all Commissioners, along with Territorial Commanders of the rank of Colonel, for the purpose of electing the General. Convened upon the General's retirement, or if a number of Commissioners requisition a High Council to determine the General's fitness for office.

International Headquarters: (IHQ) London-based head office of the Army.

Junior Corps: Sunday School, also known as Young People's Corps, under direction of the Young People's Sergeant Major, or YPSM.

Junior Soldier: Young person, from age of 9 upward, who signs a pledge, affirming faith and making promises regarding life-style.

Local Officer: (LO) Non-commissioned, volunteer "lay" official of a Corps.

Meeting: A religious service. The Army employs no set form of liturgy, and extempore prayer and testimony are valued.

Minute: The Army's legislative instrument. Administrative order issued by Territorial Commander or Chief of the Staff.

Officer: Full-time, commissioned (since 1978, "ordained") worker in the Army. Regarded as equivalent to clergy.

Orders and Regulations: Rules governing Salvation Army operations.

Outpost: Small centre of work, subsidiary to a Corps.

Promoted to Glory: Deceased.

Recruit: A person who has professed conversion and is undergoing instruction to prepare for enrolment as a soldier.

Region: Small administrative grouping, comprising a number of Corps, often pertaining to a national political unit. (Tonga is a Region of the New Zealand, Fiji and Tonga Territory.) Led by a Regional Commander.

Salvationist: A generic term for a member of The Salvation Army

Soldier: A person who has signed the Soldier's Covenant (Articles of War) and been enrolled as a member of The Salvation Army. Must have professed conversion and accepted Salvation Army doctrines, and committed to a distinctive lifestyle involving not only normal Christian ethical standards but also abstention from alcohol, tobacco, gambling and other than medically prescribed use of drugs.

Territorial Commander: (TC) Officer in charge of a Territory.

Territorial Headquarters: (THQ) Administrative office from which a Territory is directed.

Territory: Major geographical unit of command, which may comprise a country (such as Germany), part of a country (such as the USA Western) or several countries (such as New Zealand, Fiji and Tonga).

Appendix One:

Ranks of The Salvation Army 1878-2003

Current ranks shown in **bold.** Arrows show promotion routes at various times.

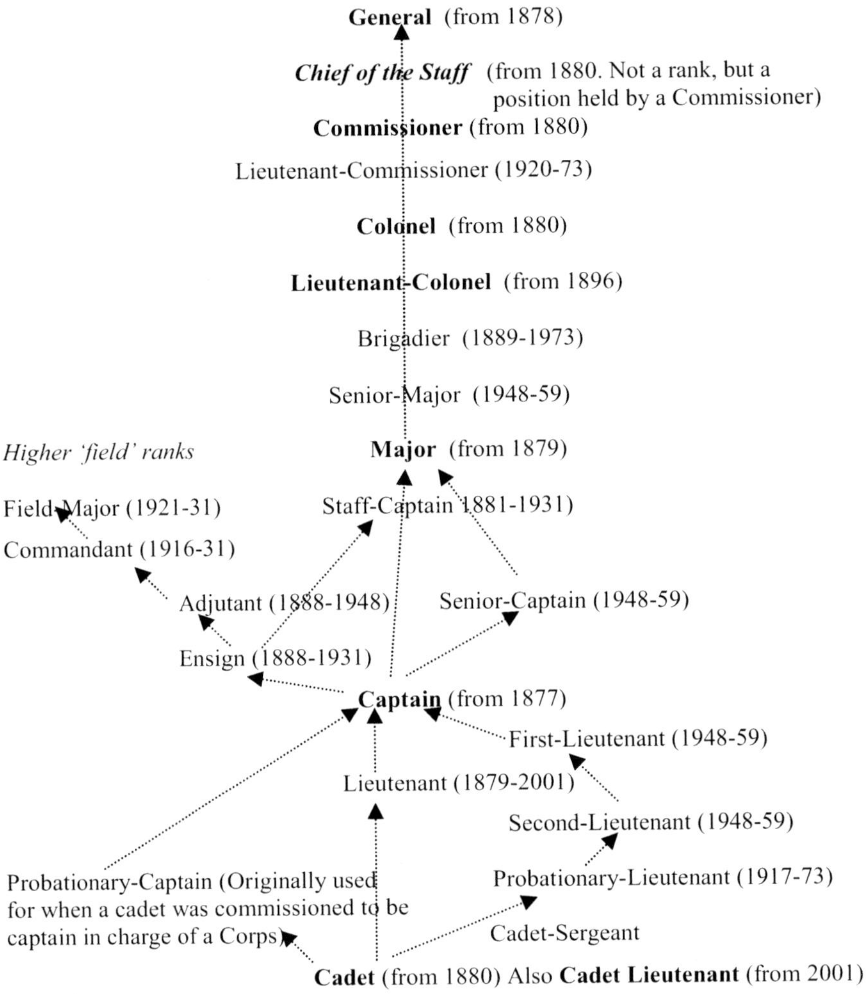

Auxiliary, or warranted officers

Auxiliary-Captain (1959-2002. To be phased out but still in use in some Territories)

Envoy (1896 – still in use in some Territories)

Lieutenant (as non-commissioned rank from 2001)

Sergeant (Still in use as rank for full-time employees in some territories)

Appendix Two:

The Booth Dynasty

(Showing family members who were officers)

William Booth - **Catherine Mumford**
1829-1912 1829-1890
General 1878-1912

William Bramwell Booth - **Florence Soper**
1856 -1929
General 1912-1929

Ballington Booth - **Maud Charlesworth**
1857-1940
The Marshall
resigned 1896

Catherine Booth - **Arthur Clibbon**
1858- 1915
The Marechale
resigned 1902

Emma Booth - **Frederick Tucker**
1860-1903
The Consul

Herbert Booth - **Coraline Schoch**
1862-1925
The Commandant
resigned 1902

Marion Booth
1864 – 1937
*Captain**

Catherine (*Commissioner*)**
Wycliffe (*Commissioner*)
Mary (*Colonel*)
Bernard (*Lt.-Colonel*)
Dora (*Major*)
Olive (*Major*)
Miriam (*Captain*) ***

Evangeline Booth
1865-1950
The Commander
General 1934-39

Lucy Booth - **Emmanuel Hellborg**
1868- 1953
Commissioner

Muriel (*Colonel*)
Catherine Motee – Hugh Sladen (*Commissioner*)

* Marion, an invalid, held the honorary rank of Captain.
** Catherine took her father's name after his death, becoming Catherine Bramwell Booth.
*** Miriam, also an invalid, was commissioned but did not serve in an appointment.

Index

Studies in Christian History and Thought

(All titles uniform with this volume)
Dates in bold are of projected publication

David Bebbington
Holiness in Nineteenth-Century England

David Bebbington stresses the relationship of movements of spirituality to changes in their cultural setting, especially the legacies of the Enlightenment and Romanticism. He shows that these broad shifts in ideological mood had a profound effect on the ways in which piety was conceptualized and practised. Holiness was intimately bound up with the spirit of the age.

2000 / 0-85364-981-2 / viii + 98pp

J. William Black
Reformation Pastors
Richard Baxter and the Ideal of the Reformed Pastor

This work examines Richard Baxter's *Gildas Salvianus, The Reformed Pastor* (1656) and explores each aspect of his pastoral strategy in light of his own concern for 'reformation' and in the broader context of Edwardian, Elizabethan and early Stuart pastoral ideals and practice.

2003 / 1-84227-190-3 / xxii + 308pp

James Bruce
Prophecy, Miracles, Angels, *and* Heavenly Light?
The Eschatology, Pneumatology and Missiology of Adomnán's Life of Columba

This book surveys approaches to the marvellous in hagiography, providing the first critique of Plummer's hypothesis of Irish saga origin. It then analyses the uniquely systematized phenomena in the *Life of Columba* from Adomnán's seventh-century theological perspective, identifying the coming of the eschatological Kingdom as the key to understanding.

2004 / 1-84227-227-6 / xviii + 286pp

Colin J. Bulley
The Priesthood of Some Believers
Developments from the General to the Special Priesthood in the Christian Literature of the First Three Centuries

The first in-depth treatment of early Christian texts on the priesthood of all believers shows that the developing priesthood of the ordained related closely to the division between laity and clergy and had deleterious effects on the practice of the general priesthood.

2000 / 1-84227-034-6 / xii + 336pp

July 2005

Anthony R. Cross (ed.)
Ecumenism and History
Studies in Honour of John H.Y. Briggs

This collection of essays examines the inter-relationships between the two fields in which Professor Briggs has contributed so much: history—particularly Baptist and Nonconformist—and the ecumenical movement. With contributions from colleagues and former research students from Britain, Europe and North America, *Ecumenism and History* provides wide-ranging studies in important aspects of Christian history, theology and ecumenical studies.

2002 / 1-84227-135-0 / xx + 362pp

Maggi Dawn
Confessions of an Inquiring Spirit
Form as Constitutive of Meaning in S.T. Coleridge's Theological Writing

This study of Coleridge's *Confessions* focuses on its confessional, epistolary and fragmentary form, suggesting that attention to these features significantly affects its interpretation. Bringing a close study of these three literary forms, the author suggests ways in which they nuance the text with particular understandings of the Trinity, and of a kenotic christology. Some parallels are drawn between Romantic and postmodern dilemmas concerning the authority of the biblical text.

2006 */ 1-84227-255-1 / approx. 224 pp*

Ruth Gouldbourne
The Flesh and the Feminine
Gender and Theology in the Writings of Caspar Schwenckfeld

Caspar Schwenckfeld and his movement exemplify one of the radical communities of the sixteenth century. Challenging theological and liturgical norms, they also found themselves challenging social and particularly gender assumptions. In this book, the issues of the relationship between radical theology and the understanding of gender are considered.

2005 */ 1-84227-048-6 / approx. 304pp*

Crawford Gribben
Puritan Millennialism
Literature and Theology, 1550–1682

Puritan Millennialism surveys the growth, impact and eventual decline of puritan millennialism throughout England, Scotland and Ireland, arguing that it was much more diverse than has frequently been suggested. This Paternoster edition is revised and extended from the original 2000 text.

2007 */ 1-84227-372-8 / approx. 320pp*

Galen K. Johnson

Prisoner of Conscience

John Bunyan on Self, Community and Christian Faith

This is an interdisciplinary study of John Bunyan's understanding of conscience across his autobiographical, theological and fictional writings, investigating whether conscience always deserves fidelity, and how Bunyan's view of conscience affects his relationship both to modern Western individualism and historic Christianity.

2003 / 1-84227-223-3 / xvi + 236pp

R.T. Kendall

Calvin and English Calvinism to 1649

The author's thesis is that those who formed the Westminster Confession of Faith, which is regarded as Calvinism, in fact departed from John Calvin on two points: (1) the extent of the atonement and (2) the ground of assurance of salvation.

1997 / 0-85364-827-1 / xii + 264pp

Timothy Larsen

Friends of Religious Equality

Nonconformist Politics in Mid-Victorian England

During the middle decades of the nineteenth century the English Nonconformist community developed a coherent political philosophy of its own, of which a central tenet was the principle of religious equality (in contrast to the stereotype of Evangelical Dissenters). The Dissenting community fought for the civil rights of Roman Catholics, non-Christians and even atheists on an issue of principle which had its flowering in the enthusiastic and undivided support which Nonconformity gave to the campaign for Jewish emancipation. This reissued study examines the political efforts and ideas of English Nonconformists during the period, covering the whole range of national issues raised, from state education to the Crimean War. It offers a case study of a theologically conservative group defending religious pluralism in the civic sphere, showing that the concept of religious equality was a grand vision at the centre of the political philosophy of the Dissenters.

***2007** / 1-84227-402-3 / x + 300pp*

Byung-Ho Moon

Christ the Mediator of the Law

Calvin's Christological Understanding of the Law as the Rule of Living and Life-Giving

This book explores the coherence between Christology and soteriology in Calvin's theology of the law, examining its intellectual origins and his position on the concept and extent of Christ's mediation of the law. A comparative study between Calvin and contemporary Reformers—Luther, Bucer, Melancthon and Bullinger—and his opponent Michael Servetus is made for the purpose of pointing out the unique feature of Calvin's Christological understanding of the law.

***2005** / 1-84227-318-3 / approx. 370pp*

John Eifion Morgan-Wynne

Holy Spirit and Religious Experience in Christian Writings, c.AD 90–200

This study examines how far Christians in the third to fifth generations (c.AD 90–200) attributed their sense of encounter with the divine presence, their sense of illumination in the truth or guidance in decision-making, and their sense of ethical empowerment to the activity of the Holy Spirit in their lives.

***2005** / 1-84227-319-1 / approx. 350pp*

James I. Packer

The Redemption and Restoration of Man in the Thought of Richard Baxter

James I. Packer provides a full and sympathetic exposition of Richard Baxter's doctrine of humanity, created and fallen; its redemption by Christ Jesus; and its restoration in the image of God through the obedience of faith by the power of the Holy Spirit.

2002 / 1-84227-147-4 / 432pp

July 2005

Andrew Partington,

Church and State

The Contribution of the Church of England Bishops to the House of Lords during the Thatcher Years

In *Church and State*, Andrew Partington argues that the contribution of the Church of England bishops to the House of Lords during the Thatcher years was overwhelmingly critical of the government; failed to have a significant influence in the public realm; was inefficient, being undertaken by a minority of those eligible to sit on the Bench of Bishops; and was insufficiently moral and spiritual in its content to be distinctive. On the basis of this, and the likely reduction of the number of places available for Church of England bishops in a fully reformed Second Chamber, the author argues for an evolution in the Church of England's approach to the service of its bishops in the House of Lords. He proposes the Church of England works to overcome the genuine obstacles which hinder busy diocesan bishops from contributing to the debates of the House of Lords and to its life more informally.

2005 */ 1-84227-334-5 / approx. 324pp*

Michael Pasquarello III

God's Ploughman

Hugh Latimer: A 'Preaching Life' (1490–1555)

This construction of a 'preaching life' situates Hugh Latimer within the larger religious, political and intellectual world of late medieval England. Neither biography, intellectual history, nor analysis of discrete sermon texts, this book is a work of homiletic history which draws from the details of Latimer's milieu to construct an interpretive framework for the preaching performances that formed the core of his identity as a religious reformer. Its goal is to illumine the practical wisdom embodied in the content, form and style of Latimer's preaching, and to recapture a sense of its overarching purpose, movement, and transforming force during the reform of sixteenth-century England.

2006 */ 1-84227-336-1 / approx. 250pp*

Alan P.F. Sell

Enlightenment, Ecumenism, Evangel

Theological Themes and Thinkers 1550–2000

This book consists of papers in which such interlocking topics as the Enlightenment, the problem of authority, the development of doctrine, spirituality, ecumenism, theological method and the heart of the gospel are discussed. Issues of significance to the church at large are explored with special reference to writers from the Reformed and Dissenting traditions.

2005 / 1-84227-330-2 / xviii + 422pp

Alan P.F. Sell

Hinterland Theology

Some Reformed and Dissenting Adjustments

Many books have been written on theology's 'giants' and significant trends, but what of those lesser-known writers who adjusted to them? In this book some hinterland theologians of the British Reformed and Dissenting traditions, who followed in the wake of toleration, the Evangelical Revival, the rise of modern biblical criticism and Karl Barth, are allowed to have their say. They include Thomas Ridgley, Ralph Wardlaw, T.V. Tymms and N.H.G. Robinson.

2006 */ 1-84227-331-0 / approx. 350pp*

Alan P.F. Sell and Anthony R. Cross (eds)

Protestant Nonconformity in the Twentieth Century

In this collection of essays scholars representative of a number of Nonconformist traditions reflect thematically on Nonconformists' life and witness during the twentieth century. Among the subjects reviewed are biblical studies, theology, worship, evangelism and spirituality, and ecumenism. Over and above its immediate interest, this collection provides a marker to future scholars and others wishing to know how some of their forebears assessed Nonconformity's contribution to a variety of fields during the century leading up to Christianity's third millennium.

2003 / 1-84227-221-7 / x + 398pp

Mark Smith

Religion in Industrial Society

Oldham and Saddleworth 1740–1865

This book analyses the way British churches sought to meet the challenge of industrialization and urbanization during the period 1740–1865. Working from a case-study of Oldham and Saddleworth, Mark Smith challenges the received view that the Anglican Church in the eighteenth century was characterized by complacency and inertia, and reveals Anglicanism's vigorous and creative response to the new conditions. He reassesses the significance of the centrally directed church reforms of the mid-nineteenth century, and emphasizes the importance of local energy and enthusiasm. Charting the growth of denominational pluralism in Oldham and Saddleworth, Dr Smith compares the strengths and weaknesses of the various Anglican and Nonconformist approaches to promoting church growth. He also demonstrates the extent to which all the churches participated in a common culture shaped by the influence of evangelicalism, and shows that active co-operation between the churches rather than denominational conflict dominated. This revised and updated edition of Dr Smith's challenging and original study makes an important contribution both to the social history of religion and to urban studies.

2006 */ 1-84227-335-3 / approx. 300pp*

Martin Sutherland

Peace, Toleration and Decay

The Ecclesiology of Later Stuart Dissent

This fresh analysis brings to light the complexity and fragility of the later Stuart Nonconformist consensus. Recent findings on wider seventeenth-century thought are incorporated into a new picture of the dynamics of Dissent and the roots of evangelicalism.

2003 / 1-84227-152-0 / xxii + 216pp

G. Michael Thomas

The Extent of the Atonement

A Dilemma for Reformed Theology from Calvin to the Consensus

A study of the way Reformed theology addressed the question, 'Did Christ die for all, or for the elect only?', commencing with John Calvin, and including debates with Lutheranism, the Synod of Dort and the teaching of Moïse Amyraut.

1997 / 0-85364-828-X / x + 278pp

David M. Thompson

Baptism, Church and Society in Britain from the Evangelical Revival to *Baptism, Eucharist and Ministry*

The theology and practice of baptism have not received the attention they deserve. How important is faith? What does baptismal regeneration mean? Is baptism a bond of unity between Christians? This book discusses the theology of baptism and popular belief and practice in England and Wales from the Evangelical Revival to the publication of the World Council of Churches' consensus statement on *Baptism, Eucharist and Ministry* (1982).

***2005** / 1-84227-393-0 / approx. 224pp*

Mark D. Thompson

A Sure Ground on Which to Stand

The Relation of Authority and Interpretive Method of Luther's Approach to Scripture

The best interpreter of Luther is Luther himself. Unfortunately many modern studies have superimposed contemporary agendas upon this sixteenth-century Reformer's writings. This fresh study examines Luther's own words to find an explanation for his robust confidence in the Scriptures, a confidence that generated the famous 'stand' at Worms in 1521.

2004 / 1-84227-145-8 / xvi + 322pp

Carl R. Trueman and R.S. Clark (eds)

Protestant Scholasticism

Essays in Reassessment

Traditionally Protestant theology, between Luther's early reforming career and the dawn of the Enlightenment, has been seen in terms of decline and fall into the wastelands of rationalism and scholastic speculation. In this volume a number of scholars question such an interpretation. The editors argue that the development of post-Reformation Protestantism can only be understood when a proper historical model of doctrinal change is adopted. This historical concern underlies the subsequent studies of theologians such as Calvin, Beza, Olevian, Baxter, and the two Turrentini. The result is a significantly different reading of the development of Protestant Orthodoxy, one which both challenges the older scholarly interpretations and clichés about the relationship of Protestantism to, among other things, scholasticism and rationalism, and which demonstrates the fruitfulness of the new, historical approach.

1999 / 0-85364-853-0 / xx + 344pp

Shawn D. Wright

Our Sovereign Refuge

The Pastoral Theology of Theodore Beza

Our Sovereign Refuge is a study of the pastoral theology of the Protestant reformer who inherited the mantle of leadership in the Reformed church from John Calvin. Countering a common view of Beza as supremely a 'scholastic' theologian who deviated from Calvin's biblical focus, Wright uncovers a new portrait. He was not a cold and rigid academic theologian obsessed with probing the eternal decrees of God. Rather, by placing him in his pastoral context and by noting his concerns in his pastoral and biblical treatises, Wright shows that Beza was fundamentally a committed Christian who was troubled by the vicissitudes of life in the second half of the sixteenth century. He believed that the biblical truth of the supreme sovereignty of God alone could support Christians on their earthly pilgrimage to heaven. This pastoral and personal portrait forms the heart of Wright's argument.

2004 / 1-84227-252-7 / xviii + 308pp

Paternoster: thinking faith

Paternoster
9 Holdom Avenue,
Bletchley,
Milton Keynes MK1 1QR,
United Kingdom
Web: www.authenticmedia.co.uk/paternoster

July 2005